# JOBS AND BODIES

JOBS AND ROGUES

# JOBS AND BODIES

## AN ORAL HISTORY OF HEALTH AND SAFETY IN BRITAIN

*Arthur McIvor*

BLOOMSBURY ACADEMIC
LONDON • NEW YORK • OXFORD • NEW DELHI • SYDNEY

BLOOMSBURY ACADEMIC
Bloomsbury Publishing Plc
50 Bedford Square, London, WC1B 3DP, UK
1385 Broadway, New York, NY 10018, USA
29 Earlsfort Terrace, Dublin 2, Ireland

BLOOMSBURY, BLOOMSBURY ACADEMIC and the Diana logo
are trademarks of Bloomsbury Publishing Plc

First published in Great Britain 2024

Copyright © Arthur McIvor, 2024

Arthur McIvor has asserted his right under the Copyright,
Designs and Patents Act, 1988, to be identified as Author of this work.

For legal purposes the Acknowledgements on pp. x–xii constitute
an extension of this copyright page.

Cover image © Bettmann/Getty

All rights reserved. No part of this publication may be reproduced or transmitted in
any form or by any means, electronic or mechanical, including photocopying,
recording, or any information storage or retrieval system, without prior
permission in writing from the publishers.

Bloomsbury Publishing Plc does not have any control over, or responsibility for,
any third-party websites referred to or in this book. All internet addresses given in
this book were correct at the time of going to press. The author and publisher
regret any inconvenience caused if addresses have changed or sites have ceased
to exist, but can accept no responsibility for any such changes.

A catalogue record for this book is available from the British Library.

A catalog record for this book is available from the Library of Congress.

| ISBN: | HB: | 978-1-3502-3622-6 |
| | PB: | 978-1-3502-3621-9 |
| | ePDF: | 978-1-3502-3630-1 |
| | eBook: | 978-1-3502-3624-0 |

Typeset by Integra Software Services Pvt. Ltd.
Printed and bound in Great Britain

To find out more about our authors and books visit www.bloomsbury.com
and sign up for our newsletters.

**For my dear brother Kev ('Mac'), 1953–2022**

*A generous, warm-hearted skilled craftsman who trained me in the art of painting and decorating and whose body was knackered by the work and painfully consumed by the myeloma that he did not deserve.*

# CONTENTS

| | | |
|---|---|---|
| List of illustrations | | viii |
| Acknowledgements | | x |
| List of abbreviations | | xiii |
| **1** | **Memory, context and the working body** | 1 |
| **2** | **Talking dirty: Narrating toxic exposure and danger stories** | 37 |
| **3** | **Industrial legacies; damaged bodies** | 77 |
| **4** | **'Fit for the scrap heap': Remembering losing work and health** | 101 |
| **5** | **Stress and burn-out: Narrating the modern work-health epidemic** | 129 |
| **6** | **Infected bodies: From anthrax to Covid-19 in the workplace** | 157 |
| **7** | **Pushing back: Health and safety activism and environmentalism** | 179 |
| **Conclusion** | | 217 |
| Notes | | 222 |
| Bibliography | | 260 |
| Index | | 280 |

# ILLUSTRATIONS

| | | |
|---|---|---|
| 1.1 | Abdul Ghan, burnt in an explosion at work at the Birmingham Battery and Metal company, April 1977. (Photo by Birmingham Post and Mail Archive/Mirrorpix/Getty Images) | 5 |
| 1.2 | Female workers in the Atlas Glass Works in Lancashire, c.1950. Courtesy of Getty Images | 8 |
| 1.3 | Piper Alpha oil rig disaster (1988) memorial, Aberdeen. Courtesy of WikiCommons | 15 |
| 1.4 | Will Brown, formerly a fit member of the Aberpergwm Football Club and a miner from South Wales (now totally incapacitated by silicosis, 1945). Courtesy of Getty Images | 17 |
| 1.5 | Seamstress sewing together an asbestos mattress, Thomas Ward Asbestos Co, 1961. Note the fibre dust all over the Singer sewing machine and the lack of any PPE. Courtesy of Getty Images | 22 |
| 1.6 | The Flixborough Nypro Gas and Chemical Plant disaster, 1 June 1974 where twenty-eight workers were killed. Courtesy of Getty Images | 28 |
| 2.1 | Machinists working at Steinberg and Sons gown factory at Hawthorn, Pontypridd, 1969, where, unusually for the 1960s, the company provided a works' nursery for the working mothers' children. Courtesy of Getty Images | 41 |
| 2.2 | Pouring a two ton casting, Osborn Hadfields Steel Founders, Sheffield, South Yorkshire, 1968. Courtesy of Getty Images | 44 |
| 2.3 | Foreman being raised from sewer repair workings twenty-five feet underground in London, 1954. Courtesy of Getty Images | 51 |
| 2.4 | Ex-chemical industry worker Richard Fitzpatrick at the time of his oral history interview with David Walker, August 2004. Courtesy of David Walker | 52 |
| 2.5 | Poster issued by the Central Council for Health Education, depicting a waitress. Outside of wartime, this is a relatively rare depiction of a female figure in a health and safety poster. Courtesy of Getty Images | 63 |
| 2.6 | Women workers at an iron and steel company at Park Gate, Rotherham, c.1940. Courtesy of Getty Images | 66 |
| 3.1 | Testing for pneumoconiosis by Charles Fletcher, Director of the Pneumoconiosis Research Unit in South Wales, 1951. Courtesy of Getty Images | 80 |
| 3.2 | Paraplegics arriving by bus at the CISWO Paraplegic Centre, Pontefract, Yorkshire, 1960. Courtesy of Getty Images | 82 |

## Illustrations

3.3 International Asbestos Memorial, Clydebank. (Photo by Arthur McIvor) 90

4.1 Derek Case (age twenty-two), holds a 70/80 lb. piece of coal that has just been dug from the seam behind at the open cast mine at Mitcheson's Gill, near Durham, 1976. Courtesy of Getty Images 108

4.2 Coal miner at Bentley colliery, South Yorkshire, after news of its imminent closure, October 1992, as part of a new mine closure programme with the loss of 31,000 jobs. Courtesy of Getty Images 114

4.3 Some of the 300 Berlei factory workers made redundant in South Wales filling in application forms for new jobs, January 1986. Courtesy of Getty Images 118

6.1 Scottish herring gutters at Great Yarmouth, 1948. Note the protective waterproof boots and oilskins, as well as the finger 'clooties'. Courtesy of Getty Images 159

6.2 Three policemen carefully destroying a cow with anthrax, Gloucestershire, 1954. Courtesy of Getty Images 160

6.3 Sex workers demonstration in Soho, London on International Women's Day, March 2018. Courtesy of Wiktor Szymanowicz/Future Publishing via Getty Images 163

6.4 Flu vaccine being given to Courage Brewery workers, London, January 1968. Courtesy of Getty Images 164

7.1 Protest lobby at the TUC 1976 (Brighton) by workers sacked from the Isle of Grain Power Station site (by contractor Babcock and Wilcox) for refusing to work with asbestos without protective clothing. Courtesy of TUC Library Collections at London Metropolitan University, see www.unionhistory.info 197

7.2 International Workers' Memorial Day Poster, 2020, courtesy of *Hazards* magazine, www.hazards.org 203

7.3 Lilian Bilocca (right of policeman) leading a protest march in Hull, 2 February 1968. Courtesy of Mirrorpix/Getty Images 205

7.4 SPAID poster, late 1980s. Courtesy of University of Strathclyde Archives and Special Collections (where the SPAID/OEDA Archive is located) 207

7.5 Newspaper clipping of Nancy Tait, Director of SPAID. Courtesy of University of Strathclyde Archives and Special Collections 209

7.6 Phyllis Craig, Manager and Senior Welfare Rights Officer, Action on Asbestos (formerly Clydeside Action on Asbestos). Courtesy of Phyllis Craig 210

# ACKNOWLEDGEMENTS

I owe an enormous debt to many people who have assisted with this book. My earnest thanks and appreciation go to all those who have given their time to be interviewed by myself and others, in our Scottish Oral History Centre (SOHC) projects and in other research and community history projects up and down the UK which provide the backbone for this book. I've drawn upon over 150 oral interviews in writing this book and most are cited in the references and bibliography by name (where narrators have agreed for names to be used and not anonymized). This oral history book is based on these personal accounts, and without this generous sharing of stories and outpouring of memories it could not have been written.

Colleagues at the SOHC and the School of Humanities at the University of Strathclyde where I've worked since moving to Scotland in 1984 have been hugely supportive and I want to thank them. The University has provided a really supportive research environment over the almost forty years I've worked there, including major investment in the oral history work of the SOHC. Amongst the colleagues who I'd like to highlight for thanks in this respect are David Murphy, David Goldie, Kirstie Blair, Hamish Fraser, Richard Finlay and Jim Mills. Ronald Johnston, who retired in 2010, worked with me on two formative projects on asbestos and coal mining, and helped shape my development and thinking on the relationship between work and the body. I recall warmly our interviewing journeys together up and down the UK, including our memorable fieldwork trips down to the South Wales coalfield, where we were made so welcome in the coal mining communities we visited. David Walker stands out as someone I have especially benefitted from working with closely over many years. David is one of the UK's most experienced oral history interviewers and shares a deep interest in the history of occupational health and safety. He has been enormously generous in his support and I've appreciated his frank, critical engagement with my work. Many thanks, David! Alison Chand – our senior oral history trainer at the SOHC – likewise, and I'm grateful to Alison for some assistance researching oral history collections beyond Scotland and for making some interviews accessible from her current project on Covid-19. The above are amongst those (which also include Andy Perchard, Hilary Young, Angela Bartie, Susan Morrison, David Bradley, Rory Stride, Marion Henry, James Ferns and our lost but always warmly remembered dear colleague and friend Neil Rafeek) that have conducted, compiled and archived history of work interviews in the SOHC collection in the Archives and Special Collections at the University. And relating to the latter I'd especially like to thank Victoria Peters (University Archivist) and Rachael Jones for their help and support across many years.

I'd also like to thank those in History at the University who have carried the burden of teaching and oral history training when I was awarded research leave to write this book

## Acknowledgements

over 2021–2. They include, especially, Co-Director of the SOHC, Yvonne McFadden, who took over much of my teaching and a number of SOHC duties from 1 January 2022, and we share research participation on a new research project – an oral history of deindustrialization in the mining communities of East Ayrshire. I've also worked closely with disability historian Angela Turner at the University, and thank her for her wonderfully insightful work in the field. I've drawn inspiration from a number of oral historians and oral-labour historians over the years, who I'd like to thank, including Callum Brown, Lynn Abrams, Steven High, Tim Strangleman, Christine Walley, Andy Perchard, Geoff Tweedale, Keith Gildart and many others. I'd like to thank Steven High especially for his inspirational, cutting-edge work in oral history that has shaped my thinking, for his generosity and support, including his feedback on earlier iterations of my work on the health impacts of deindustrialization. Also for drawing me into the wonderful ongoing global-leading transnational research project Deindustrialization and the Politics of our Time (DePOT, 2020–7) that Steven leads. I have benefitted enormously from conversations with DePOT colleagues, including with gender initiative lead Jackie Clarke. I also owe a great debt to all the undergraduate and postgraduate students I have supervised who have explored aspects of oral-labour history, and those who have endured my History of Occupational Health and Safety Masters and History of Work honours classes at the University and my 'Mining Lives' MOOC class.

I also want to thank all the researchers, archivists and curators who have assisted with my search for oral testimonies and personal accounts, undertaken and archived interviews themselves (see bibliography) and provided permission to use material. Some are mentioned above. The British Library Sound Archive houses many wonderful work-history interviews, some of which have been drawn upon here – and I thank all those involved (notably Rob Perks and Mary Stewart). Others I'd like to thank include Nigel Ingham, who conducted a series of wonderful interviews of members of the Greater Manchester Asbestos Victims Support Group; Emily Grabham (whose work is deposited in the 'open access' UK Data Archive); the late great Ian MacDougall, doyen of oral history in Scotland, who sadly succumbed to Covid-19 in 2020; Joanne McKerchar (Diageo Archive); Nicky Wilson (NUM); and Dave Welsh, Stefan Dickers and Chris Coates in relation to the TUC-sponsored Britain at Work: Voices from the Workplace, 1945–95 oral history project. And thanks to Rab Wilson, Tutor at the TUC Education course at City of Glasgow College, who kindly put me in contact with health and safety representatives to interview.

The author and publisher wish to thank the following for making material open access online or for permission to reproduce copyright material: the Archives and Special Collections, University of Strathclyde; Rory O'Neill, editor of Hazards magazine; The Trades Union Congress Library Collections, Metropolitan University, London; The UK Data Archive; the British Library Sound Archive; David Walker; Getty Photo Archives; Wikicommons; Action on Asbestos (formerly Clydeside Action on Asbestos); the Greater Manchester Asbestos Victims Support Group; the Trades Union Congress, Britain at Work Oral History Project; the Scottish Working Class People's History Trust; Warwickshire County Council Working Lives (Memories of Work and Industry

## Acknowledgements

in Nuneaton and Bedworth project); the Imperial War Museum; Diageo Archivist Joanne McKerchar (for the 'Johnnie Walker: Stories from Kilmarnock' project); the Mass Observation Archive, University of Sussex; Motherwell Heritage Centre; Glasgow Museums; the South Wales Coal Collection, University of Swansea; the Health and Safety Executive; BBC People's War Archive; NHS Voices from Covid-19 Project: Manchester University. Every effort has been made to trace rights holders, but if any has been inadvertently overlooked the publishers would be pleased to make the necessary arrangements at the first opportunity.

Most important of all I want to thank my family for all their support and encouragement over the years. My civil partner Margot and my sons Kieran and Tom have provided enduring and unstinting love and support; have made me proud; provided inspiration and distraction; put up with my moods, weaknesses and absences; and lifted me when I've been down. They have been absolutely fundamental to the success of this project. My stepdaughter and stepson, Siobhan and Daniel, have also kept me grounded, as have our beautiful grandchildren, Aila (to Esther and Kieran), Harris (to Emma and Daniel) and Ruairi, Grace and Orlaith (to Siobhan and Aaron). I hope this book will encourage them all to seek, as far as they are able, a healthy work-life balance. And I want to thank my long lost parents (Barbara Joan and Arthur McIvor) and my three brothers (John, Kevin and Jeff) for their support and for reminding me on many occasions, and usually with good humour, of my working-class roots in Coventry, in the Midlands. My book is dedicated to my dear brother Kev (or 'Mac' as he was widely known), a generous, warm-hearted master craftsman who trained me as a youth in the art of painting and decorating (and inculcated a strong work ethic and so much more). His body was knackered by the work and he retired early at fifty-nine with a repetitive strain injury. He didn't deserve the myeloma that so painfully consumed his body as I wrote this book.

# ABBREVIATIONS

| | |
|---|---|
| **AIDS** | Acquired Immune Deficiency Syndrome |
| **ARD** | Asbestos-Related Disease |
| **AUEW** | Amalgamated Union of Engineering Workers |
| **BBC** | British Broadcasting Corporation |
| **BME** | Black and Minority Ethic |
| **BOS** | British Oxygen Steel |
| **CAA** | Clydeside Action on Asbestos (now Action on Asbestos) |
| **DHSS** | Department of Health and Social Security |
| **DVLA** | Driving Vehicle Licencing Agency |
| **EU** | European Union |
| **FBU** | Fire Brigades Union |
| **FE** | Further Education |
| **FI** | Factory Inspectorate |
| **GMB** | General and Municipal Builders' Union |
| **GP** | General Practitioner (doctor) |
| **HMRC** | Her Majesty's Revenue and Customs |
| **HSE** | Health and Safety Executive |
| **HSWA** | Health and Safety at Work Act (1974) |
| **IBAS** | International Ban Asbestos Secretariat |
| **ILO** | International Labour Organisation |
| **IMO** | Industrial Medical Officer |
| **MAG** | Greater *Manchester Asbestos* Victims Support *Group* (GMAVSG) |
| **MFGB** | Miners' Federation of Great Britain |
| **MI** | Mines Inspectors/Inspectorate |

## Abbreviations

| | |
|---|---|
| **MSD** | Musculoskeletal Disorders |
| **NCB** | National Coal Board |
| **NHS** | National Health Service |
| **NUM** | National Union of Miners |
| **NWSN** | National Work Stress Network |
| **OEDA** | Occupational and Environmental Diseases Association |
| **OHS** | Occupational Health and Safety |
| **OILC** | Offshore Industry Liaison Committee |
| **ONS** | Office for National Statistics |
| **PCS** | Public and Commercial Services Union |
| **PPE** | Personal Protective Equipment |
| **PTSD** | Post-Traumatic Stress Disorder |
| **RCN** | Royal College of Nursing |
| **RSI** | Repetitive Strain Injury |
| **SAC** | Scottish Advisory Committee (House of Commons) |
| **SARS** | Severe Acute Respiratory Syndrome |
| **SMR** | Standardized Mortality Rate |
| **SOHC** | Scottish Oral History Centre |
| **SPAID** | Society for the Prevention of Asbestosis and Industrial Diseases |
| **STI** | Sexually Transmitted Infection |
| **STUC** | Scottish Trades Union Congress |
| **SWMF** | South Wales Miners' Federation |
| **TB** | Tuberculosis |
| **TGWU** | Transport and General Workers' Union |
| **T&N** | Turner and Newall Company (asbestos manufacturer) |
| **TNT** | Trinitrotoluene |
| **TUC** | Trades Union Congress |
| **UCU** | University and Colleges Union |
| **WCA** | Workmen's Compensation Act |

# CHAPTER 1
## MEMORY, CONTEXT AND THE WORKING BODY

In an oral history interview conducted in 2004 ex-miner Alan Napier (from North-East England) recalled the carnage in his community:

> The club I drank in, they used to call 'Death Row'. When you were going in there was a row and there was about ten miners used to sit on that ... You saw it go from ten, to nine, to eight, to seven, and they were all, in the main, mining related injuries or diseases that killed them off. And you can see the ones who were lucky to be alive mind, but they can't get the words out, they can't breathe properly ... So you can see the legacy, you can see the legacy of the pit. So you can understand the anger we've got.[1]

This reminiscence reveals something of the material impact industrial work could have on the body – 'they can't breathe properly' – but also the texture of feeling and the emotional and moral dimensions the memory evoked – 'the anger we've got'. It conjures the intimate, embodied legacies of this work and hints at the potential of an oral history approach in deepening our understanding of the ways that work impacts upon the body. This book tries to do just that, exploring work and the body through the personal lens of workers' voices, memories and narratives.[2] It draws upon a wide range of primary sources, notably some 150 or so oral interview testimonies and a series of work-health stories from the Mass Observation (MO) Archive.

This book tells the story of British workers and how their employment affected their bodies in the period from the Second World War to the present; from blue-collar workers in heavy industries to stressed-out office workers and those exposed to infection at work, including Covid-19. Born in 1956, I lived through a large chunk of this. Through much of my career as an academic historian I've been trying to understand what work meant and the impact it had on workers and working-class families like my own. Let me give you a brief personal/family history – as this positions me as author, says something of my subjectivity and identity and enables you as the reader to perceive something of the lens through which I interpret the past. My Mum worked in a grocery shop when she was younger, giving it up, as many women did back then at mid-twentieth century, transitioning to unpaid work as a homemaker, rearing four sons through the 1950s, '60s and '70s. She returned to paid work later in life after we had all grown up. The story we recall is that Dad was reluctant and only 'agreed' after Mum went to the family GP and he appealed directly to my father that this would be good for Mum's mental health.

## Jobs and Bodies

She died young, aged fifty-six, of heart failure. Dad was born in Liverpool, worked on the docks and served in the Navy during the Second World War. He moved to Coventry chasing secure work, getting a job on the assembly-line at the Standard Triumph car factory. The West Midlands were booming in the post-war years, epitomizing, perhaps, the so-called 'Golden Age' of work, from the Second World War to the 1970s. Like most car factory workers Dad joined a union – the National Union of Vehicle Builders – and steady well-paid work enabled my parents to support the family, buy their own home and move (in 1966) from Coventry to the more affluent leafy dormitory town of Kenilworth. It was tough, monotonous work on the track though, and hard on the body, especially working the (better paid) nightshift in Standard Triumph. This relatively stable world collapsed for him, and many other UK car workers from the late 1970s as the car industry contracted sharply, short-time working increased and, eventually, plants closed, including British Leyland (where he then worked) with mass redundancies. Dad then went from job to job, including taxi driving and finally worked as a factory cleaner. These days he found much solace in a bottle of Bells whisky. Unfortunately, coming home from work one day, he was killed in a car crash.

My eldest brother John followed Dad into the 'El Dorado' of the car industry in 1967, expecting a job for life. Without educational qualifications he struggled to find other work after making cars went down and was unemployed and 'economically inactive' for more than thirty years through most of his adult life. My other two brothers fared better on the work front, both doing apprenticeships and becoming self-employed painters and decorators (mostly in house-painting) in rewarding jobs that provided a real sense of pride and identity. They inherited Mum and Dad's strong work ethic. Given the high unemployment and deepening deprivation in the 1980s and 1990s in the deindustrializing West Midlands areas where they lived, however, the work flow in house-painting was sometimes uneven. And, the type of hard, physical manual work they did working long hours (often including weekends) took a toll on their bodies. Jeff is still working; Kev had to retire prematurely at aged fifty-nine with a repetitive strain injury. I was both lucky and unlucky to escape this world – and the constrained opportunities and precarity of working-class life in the Midlands from the mid-1970s. Lucky in the sense of moving (after a year of stultifying boredom in an office job) to University, then to a relatively benign (at least then) and very well-paid and secure unionized University academic job, probably (with a bit more luck) increasing my healthy life span and life expectancy by a decade or more over my brothers. Unlucky, as it moved me (as it did many others) into a state of limbo, casting me adrift from a rich, vibrant working-class culture, based on mutual support, black humour, community and camaraderie. I am reminded of that richness and warmth when I go back home. I miss some aspects of that world and feel pretty disconnected from it now – an outsider. Perhaps this book, as in much of my other work, is a way to try to reconnect.

This first chapter provides context and background, exploring the place of memory in the reconstruction of health and safety at work. Chapter 2 explores the lived experience of dangerous and risky work in British industry in the post-war decades and how this was remembered. The focus here is on ways workers themselves narrated and reconstructed the body in employment. Chapter 3 moves the focal point to the damage wrought by industrial injuries, fatalities and diseases, and how this was recalled, with case studies of disability and death in coal mining and asbestos. Chapter 4 investigates 'scrap heap' stories: how workers like my Dad recalled the long-drawn-out process of deindustrialization in Britain and how they reconstructed the health deficits of losing work as factories, car plants, mines, textile mills, chemical plants, shipyards and steelworks closed. Chapter 5 analyses the modern-day stress epidemic at work and some of the ways that burnt-out workers have narrated their experiences. Chapter 6 evaluates infection at work, tracking the story from anthrax through to Covid-19, and drawing upon some of the testimonies and stories of those affected. The final chapter investigates the occupational health and safety *movement*, focusing on workers' agency, trade unions and community activism, exploring how those affected pushed back in campaigns to improve safety and health. Here the stories of activists are drawn upon to argue the case for the pivotal importance of trade unions, community activism and environmentalism in protecting workers' bodies and improving occupational health and safety standards on the job, as well as the lives of sick and disabled ex-workers and their families.

To be sure, the impact of work can be and frequently was positive as well as negative – and it's important to acknowledge this up front. A wide range of types of work from manual labouring through unpaid domestic work in the home to skilled and creative work gave people a sense of satisfaction and pride and purpose, and could be wonderfully fulfilling and health-enhancing. And some *moderate* degree of stress at work can be good for mental health. Frequently workers express this pleasure in work in stories about pride and identity in the work they do, and did, and the joy they derive from it. But work could also be intensely exploitative, degrading and damaging, destroying bodies in needless 'accidents', causing fatigue, overstrain, excessive stress and burn-out, and exposing workers to a wide range of life-threatening dust, toxins, fumes and chemicals. And work without dignity and respect could be demoralizing and psychologically destabilizing. These apparently contradictory emotions from joy to alienation could and did co-exist across the labour market. Latterly, the post-Fordist neo-Liberal workplace has been associated with an epidemic of stress and burn-out, with government spending cuts in the National Health Service (NHS) and in the Health and Safety Executive (HSE) deepening the Covid-19 crisis as the virus hit different occupational groups harder than others and the depleted NHS and HSE struggled to cope. This was particularly the case with the NHS, social and care workers and those jobs that were publically facing (such as schools and public transport), or involved overcrowded workplaces (as, for example, in meat processing plants).

## Memory and narrating the workplace

The approach adopted is this book is to try as far as possible to draw upon workers own personal accounts and testimonies relating to their encounters with the labour process and the workplace. So, I draw heavily on oral history interviews and an oral history methodology, privileging workers' own voices, drawing upon co-created oral testimonies and other personal accounts to reconstruct the past. This approach is premised on the notion that we can learn much about the complex relationship between work and the body, and work-health cultures by listening closely to those who directly experienced or bore witness to these events. Oral historians Michelle Winslow and Graham Smith have commented: 'It is a mark of the contribution of oral history to the history of medicine that studies located within living memory are open to criticism if they fail to include oral history.'[3] This book draws upon many oral history interviews from several projects that I've been directly involved with as co-investigator or supervisor through the Scottish Oral History Centre. It also benefits from many archived oral interviews conducted by a wide range of oral historians archived in places like the British Library Sound Archive, the UK Data Archive and the British Trades Union Congress Archive, as well as the SOHC. Joanna Bornat has persuasively argued for the benefits of re-using and analysing existing oral history archives (whilst also noting some pitfalls), arguing there is space for reinterpretation, diverse perspectives and new and different ways of reading testimonies.[4] There is certainly a rich seam of archived materials – going back to the origins of oral history interviewing – to draw upon.

This book places personal memoirs, accounts and oral history testimonies at centre stage in exploring occupational health history. Work and the body are examined through these personal lens, approached through the memories, voices and articulations of workers' themselves. This methodology is still relatively unusual in the history of occupational health and safety in the UK. In contrast, North American scholars have been the pioneers of oral-history infused histories of workers, their bodies and their occupational and environmental health movements.[5]

Oral history testimonies are frequently rich and wonderfully informative. Those that were actually there educate us on how it was to be risking their lives on a building site, quarry or in a mine, toiling in a noisy textile factory, working deep underground or amidst the asbestos dust clouds of a 1960s shipyard or locomotive works. Similarly, how it *felt* to be stressed out in a call centre, or the modern-day NHS, or a housewife trying to juggle formal employment with the demands of a family. Oral history testimony evokes the sensory experience of work particularly well. We learn much about how this was felt through workers' bodies, remembered and expressed in their own words – the pain and anguish; shame and embarrassment; frustration and anger; the joys and satisfaction. This gets us closer to the texture of lived experience, to the embodiment of work; privileging (and empowering) workers' own voices and modes of articulation – how workers remember it.

But our interest goes beyond this to consider such stories as subjective accounts where narrators are re-interpreting their past, sieving and ordering their memories to compose a lucid story – an account they are comfortable telling and sharing. We are interested in how and why the particular embodied stories are told, as well as the erasures, or silences in these stories: what is not disclosed. We need to be sensitive to the language being used in the dialogic framework of the interview. Also to how narrators relate to the unequal power dynamic in the interview, how inter-subjectivities (of interviewer and interviewee)

## Memory, Context and the Working Body

shape the story-telling and how, if at all, memories are influenced or framed by cultural norms or 'scripts', such as books, TV or movies – what has been termed 'the cultural circuit'. These areas have all been the subject of recent theorizing around oral history and we need to be cognizant of these insights and conversations.[6] The proliferation of 'memory studies' has shown how complex recall can be, informing us on how popular or collective memory can impinge upon and shape the way people *individually* recall the past. That said, workers' voices certainly suggest that memories can be autonomous, or at the least that workers are capable of framing their memories in ways that critically

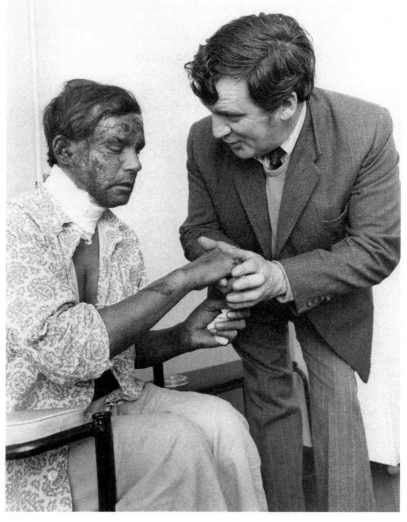

**Figure 1.1** Abdul Ghan, burnt in an explosion at work at the Birmingham Battery and Metal Company, April 1977.
(Photo by Birmingham Post and Mail Archive/Mirrorpix/Getty Images).

5

## Jobs and Bodies

engage with public memory and in the process shed deep insights into how they felt they experienced work and its effects on their bodies.[7] Such reflexive oral-history-based research has the capability to take us beyond the statistical body counts of accidents and industrial disease epidemics such as pneumoconiosis, mesothelioma and stress to a deeper focus on lived experience and meanings for those directly affected; what it *felt* like. It also gets us closer to understanding the damage to bodies, the residues and the legacies of these occupational health disasters, in terms of rehabilitation, adaptation, identity mutations and economic, social and human harms and deficits. Listening helps us to connect better to their worlds – and in many cases with their fast disappearing realms of work, and how employment marked their bodies.

## The oral history of occupational health and safety

Oral interviewing as a research methodology has been applied to the history of work since oral history began, emerging as it did from socialist- and feminist-inspired research – for example in the UK from Paul Thompson and Elizabeth Roberts.[8] Illness and occupational health featured in such early studies, though was not a primary focus. Subsequently, historians deploying an oral history interviewing methodology have drilled down and focused more on health experience and health cultures. One example would be Lucinda McCray Beier's 2008 monograph *For Their Own Good* which explored changing working-class attitudes to health and illness in England from 1880–1970.[9] Based on Elizabeth Roberts classic study involving oral history interviews with 239 people from North-West England undertaken in the 1970s and 1980s, McCray Beier's work shows the potential of oral history and its capacity to inform us about every-day health cultures, behaviour and responses to disease and disability in working-class communities. That is, how people understood and managed their illnesses, and, later, engaged with state services (the NHS).

Other work has shifted the focus to the patient, including those injured and disabled through their work – and here oral testimony is especially vital, providing a counter-narrative to hegemonic medical models.[10] An oral history approach essentially enables a *refocused* history centred on peoples' lives, on emotions, on personal experience and on narrators' voices. In context here, it informs us about how big processes such as industrialization and deindustrialization impacted upon working-class lives and on their bodies. In her work on disability in Alberta, Canada, Claudia Malacrida has argued persuasively that oral history enables people to 'bear witness': 'These narratives provide a politicized reading of relations of power, offering the patient an opportunity to bear witness to harms suffered, and drawing on the perspectives of subordinated individuals to expose the workings of power and domination within the medical encounter.'[11] This potential has been further affirmed in a paper published in 2018 reviewing over 100 recent oral history and digital storytelling publications (from the PubMed database) relating to health where Tsui and Starecheski argue that an oral history methodology can crucially aid understanding and that such research has significant public impact: 'These methods have substantial potential for supplementing public health activities, allowing the field to glean additional lessons from its experiences, to educate its practitioners further, and to better learn from the experiences of communities affected by public health problems.'[12]

And much of the best work is gendered, enriching, for example our understanding of health cultures and the agency, interventions and roles working-class women played as 'guardians' of family health, care and well-being as well as directly as workers, both paid and unpaid.[13] Caring was a core element of unpaid domestic labour and pivotal when it came to looking after those directly injured (and traumatized) by their work, or those burnt out, stressed or made chronically ill because of their work, or damaged psychologically from being made redundant from it. Working-class femininity, gender relations and the body have been a key focus, for example, in the pioneering work of Ann Oakley (1984), Jocelyn Cornwall (1990), Jan Walmsley and Joanna Bornat (1999).[14] These writers have drawn heavily upon oral interviews to critically examine issues around gender, ageing, health, disease, disability and illness in working-class communities. The focus here has often been upon unpaid domestic labour dominated by women, and upon the 'double burden' of paid work combined with domestic 'home work' where women shouldered the burden in a very unequal way compared to men. This inequitable sexual division of labour within the home changed only very slowly in Britain in the later twentieth century, and the gender gap in terms of hours worked in the domestic/family setting continues to persist (as demonstrated, for example, in the unequal distribution of caring duties in lockdown during the Covid-19 pandemic). The workload implications of this unequal burden took its toll upon women in diverse ways, as for example Ali Haggett's oral-history-based research on 'neurotic housewives' has shown.[15] We'll come back to these issues around gendered workloads and stressors, most notably in Chapters 5 and 6. Suffice to note at this point that an oral history methodology is capable of enriching our understanding of encounters between the environment (work; home; family) and the body and how this experience was and is gendered. It enables us to locate those affected by illness within the specific socio-cultural spaces they occupied at that time.

The history of occupational health and safety has been dominated by studies that have focused on the role of the state, policy-making (e.g. on Factory Acts and compensation systems) and corporate irresponsibility and neglect.[16] In some notable cases such research has forensically exposed the prior knowledge of hazards, neglect, and abuse that resulted in disasters – like the chemical leak at Bhopal, India – and epidemics of industrial disease – such as 'black lung' (coal workers' pneumoconiosis) and asbestos-related diseases. Here a range of interpretations exist within what is a hotly contested terrain. At one end of the spectrum are those who make a case for corporate irresponsibility (economic violence; corporate killing). At the other are those who defend industry, shift the blame elsewhere, and castigate left-orientated historians and other researchers for inappropriate use of hindsight and failing to contextualize occupational illness in the period and the prevailing state of knowledge and existing work-health cultures in the past. The historiography of asbestos illustrates this contested terrain very well.[17] Company records, court files, and state papers and enquiries were amongst the core

**Figure 1.2** Female workers in the Atlas Glass Works in Lancashire, c.1950.
Courtesy of Getty Images.

source materials for such studies. With some exceptions, the debates tended to pass over or neglect the lived experience of disability and disease and to gloss over the agency of victims and their individual and collective responses.

The shift in research towards the personal and to discourses, influenced firstly by socialist and feminist ideas, then by postmodernism, changed this landscape. The history of work was an early focus of oral historians but the body was rarely a point of focus until fairly recently. A growing number of studies have turned to oral evidence to elucidate work and occupational health. These include Bloor, Perchard, Walker,

McIvor and Johnston, Rogaly and Burns, Almond and Esbester which focus on the UK, High and Storey on injured workers in Canada, Portelli on coal miners in Harlan County, USA, and Mukherjee on Bhopal, India.[18] Mukherjee's oral history of the Bhopal disaster gets behind the bare (and contested) statistics of death and injury to explore the human story of what was one of the world's worst occupational and environmental health disasters. By providing a view from the workplace we gain valuable insights into the limited effectiveness of regulatory frameworks, whilst also getting a sense of the complexity of work-health and body cultures, the interplay of identities (such as gender, race and class), and the agency of workers negotiating paths through hazardous, exhausting, dusty, dirty, stressful and toxic work environments. Economic violence and damaged bodies are recurring motifs in these studies.

These investigations have taken place and have been influenced by concurrent developments in the discipline of oral history. Partly in response to criticisms over what was deemed as the unreliability of memory, oral history has morphed from what has been termed 'reconstructive' or 'positivist' oral history – typically where testimony was uncritically accepted at face value – towards more 'interpretivist' approaches. The latter was influenced by the postmodernist turn and by the influential work of Italian oral historians, notably Luisa Passerini and Alessandro Portelli.[19] What emerged was a phase of introspection in the discipline, and the outcome was a more theoretically informed and methodologically rigorous oral history. Ideas were borrowed from a wide range of social science and other disciplines (including sociology, anthropology, psychology and linguistics) and tested against the empirical evidence. Memory studies analysed the working of memory, basically confirming the fundamental reliability of long-term memory whilst the subjective nature of the evidence – formerly criticized as a weakness – became recognized as a strength. Silences in life stories and misremembering were identified as being significant in their own right and judged to be full of meaning. Inter-subjectivities also became a focus. Testimonies were observed to be composed and shaped both by the interviewers' subjectivities (such as gender and class) and in a dialogue with the interviewee as well as by the prevailing wider media and culture – hence 'the cultural circuit'.[20] The present thus impinges upon the past in oral interviews. It was established that repetitions, metaphors and anecdotes in oral testimonies have significance and that personal storytelling is subject to prevailing narrative structures and 'rules' within particular societies and cultures. In recalling their past in an interview context, narrators are filtering and sieving memories, constructing and composing their stories, and mixing factual evidence with their own interpretations as they try to make sense of their lives in an active, dialogic and reflexive process of remembering. As mentioned already, Lynn Abrams seminal book, *Oral History Theory* (2010; second edition 2016), provides one the best guides through such developments in the oral history discipline.

Oral history scholarship and methodologies have thus become more sophisticated and have contributed to widening understanding of working-class health experience and health cultures. The unique nature of oral evidence is now widely accepted and its veracity recognized. Oral historians are now much more reflexively critical of their material and

## Jobs and Bodies

acknowledge the influence their own subjectivities have upon the interview and how informants position themselves in the narrative, on occasions using the encounter as a way of projecting a sense of self. Oral historians have postulated that *what* is remembered and *how* it is recalled are significant in its own right. The 'new oral history' influenced by postmodernist ideas has challenged and been fused onto the radical tradition of 'reconstructive' oral history, driven by a desire to give marginalized people a voice and a place, with an equality and democratizing agenda for history. In labour history, the history of the workplace and of deindustrialization, as well as the emerging field of environmental labour studies, this more anthropological, people-centred, gendered and body-conscious oral-history-based scholarship is now well represented in the literature. I'm thinking here, for example, of the work of Steven High, Christine Walley, Alice Mah, Lachlan Mackinnon, Ben Rogaly, Andrew Perchard and Tim Strangleman, to mention just a few.[21] We'll come back to this scholarship at appropriate points in the chapters that follow.

## Contextualizing the stories: Health and safety in post-war Britain

How then did work intersect with the body and health? At a very fundamental level, work is a cornerstone of *good* health, fitness and well-being, for a number of reasons. Employment provides the resources which determine our standards of living and gives purpose and structure to our daily lives, things that are essential for mental health and well-being. Undertaking work can be life-enhancing, contributing to a real sense of purpose and fulfilment, undoubtedly improving self-esteem, physical and mental health, as work-life interviews invariably demonstrate and the studies of the deleterious effects of losing work and being unemployed clearly show. The therapeutic value of work has long been accepted, for example in prison rehabilitation programmes and the treatment of those with learning difficulties and other mental health disabilities and illness, including depression.[22] Workers felt valued and significant as a consequence of their employment, of being associated with productive and purposeful lives and of actively contributing to society. Moreover, thinking jobs could sharpen the intellect, whilst manual jobs could hone a muscular and fit body – as Orwell famously observed of the Wigan miners in the mid-1930s.[23] Robert Gladden, a Middlesbrough steel worker from 1942 to 1989 observed: 'You felt very fit after a shift. It was hard, enjoyable work. It was like body-building, shovelling for eight hours a day. You didn't feel tired; you stayed nice and slim.'[24] The valorization and positive body-sculpting capacity of work are expressed clearly here in phrases like 'very fit' and 'nice and slim'. Tracey Carpenter was one of the first female train drivers for British Rail in London. In an oral interview in 2011 she commented on the hard physical graft of working her first job as a freight guard speaking of the 'oil everywhere. Everywhere was dirty, every engine stank of cigarette smoke and diesel fumes and there was ash all over the desks of the locomotives. It was just everywhere' then reflected: 'and so everything was dirty but you kept really fit. As a driver now I find it very hard to keep my weight off but then you were constantly thin, you walked around in the cold and rain but you kept very fit'.[25] Similarly, a Harlan County (USA) coal miner reflected in an interview with Alessandro Portelli on the older generation working in the pre-mechanized pits:

> In those old pick and shovel days, they were pretty tough men. I mean, the men's lifestyle, the way of working, the arms, the hands, the muscles, the big shoulders. Now what we would consider very hard work, those men could do with ease, because the kind of work they did at the mine, really developed, developed them. My father weighed two hundred pounds and he was five feet eight, and he could bounce a refrigerator on his back.[26]

This miner's narrative deftly observes how the work 'developed' the man in very positive ways, sculpting the fit, honed and powerful body. Skilled craft workers might enjoy being absorbed in the conceptualization and execution of a complex labour process and revel in the relative autonomy they exercised over the pace and rhythm of work, with evident positive consequences for their mental health. The socialist author, Robert Tressell (Noonan) evoked this nicely through his main character Owen when he was planning and decorating a 'drawing room' in the famous novel *Ragged Trousered Philanthropists*. Many professional, academic and creative non-manual workers similarly enjoyed the health-enhancing qualities of work undertaken with much independence, under little direct supervision and overt pressure. Employment, moreover, brought an income which directly impacted upon ability to pay for health insurance, medical treatment and the resources (such as food and housing) which were basic to the maintenance of health and well-being, as well as bringing other non-wage benefits (e.g. holidays and a pension) and opportunities for socialization. Conversely, exit from paid work through retirement, redundancy and long-term unemployment was an important cause for many of social exclusion, isolation and poverty, and has been associated with premature mortality (for more on this see Chapter 4). In almost all its forms, work could *potentially* be good for the body (and loss of work detrimental) – and sometimes we have perhaps been guilty of forgetting this in our haste to brand the capitalist workplace as generically and *intrinsically* unhealthy and dehumanizing.

That said, it is also true – and the evidence is irrefutable – that Fordist production regimes invariably involved an extension of control over and monitoring of the body and, in manual work, high levels of risk, injury, disability and chronic occupation-related diseases. Bodies *were* exploited for profit covertly and overtly. Relatively healthy and safe workplaces in the early twenty-first century have had to be fought for and were (and remain) subject to contestation and a power struggle, as wages and work time have been (and continue to be). To this day there remain many hazardous and health-threatening occupations, labour processes and work environments co-existing with a fundamental neglect of the potential of the workplace as a site of good health practice. Occupational ill-health could be the product of many factors, at the core of which lies an unequal power relationship in which the competitive market system encourages those with power to exploit those with little power, putting profit before health. Managerial pressure *and* the prevailing work culture could also incubate self-exploitation, with a high risk-taking ethos prevalent within manual labouring jobs at mid-twentieth century (especially those that rewarded high productivity with bonus wage-payment systems). The extent of medical knowledge prevailing and the efficacy of the monitoring and regulatory framework are other key explanatory factors. There were also structural flaws, such as the post-war failure to integrate the NHS and the state and private occupational health services, despite hard campaigning by the trade unions.[27] Moreover, sometimes risks were just not known, or poorly understood and it is important that we comprehend risk within the prevailing milieu, knowledge and culture of the time, rather than imposing with hindsight our present-day standards backwards into the past.

Undeniably, work could and did impact adversely upon the body, not least where the profit motive induced managerial abuse, bullying, harassment and work intensification which made it difficult to maintain a healthy work-life balance and the dignity of labour. As two medical researchers reflecting upon the causes of coronary heart disease noted in 1949: 'existing conditions of work impose strains which, when endured too long, are beyond physiological tolerance.'[28] Overwork could lead to physical and emotional fatigue, stress, exhaustion and, in extreme cases, to 'burn-out', breakdown and depression. And the latter may well have been compounded in the recent past as the long-term historical trend in the UK of reducing working hours has been reversed. Whilst working hours fell after the Second World War, the data suggests little change in work hours in the UK from the 1970s to the late 1990s, when male workers in the UK worked more hours than any others in Europe.[29] A long working hours' culture re-emerged from the 1990s, not least amongst professionals where new communications and information technologies (such as the mobile phone; the laptop and easy internet access) blurred the boundaries between work and home, sometimes to the detriment of family life and health.[30] One outcome of longer hours and work intensification in the modern deregulated economy has been rising levels of work-related stress. The Covid-19 pandemic also deepened issues around overwork and stress in sectors such as the NHS and education, whilst creating a massive expansion in home-working under 'lockdown' restrictions which brought its own set of pressures and health issues (we'll return to these issues relating to stress and Covid-19 in subsequent chapters).

Foucault has been influential in positing the notion of the controlled and docile body (utilizing the Benthamite concept of the 'panopticon'), subject to the overt and covert surveillance of management (in the penal system) and this has been applied to the modern workplace by labour sociologists and others. Bourdieu similarly places the body at centre stage in work relations, though he gives more credence than Foucault (e.g. in his deployment of the notion of 'habitus' and 'field') to agency and resistance. To Bourdieu bodies were both subjects and agents; bodies could be passive, but they also could be reactive, dissenting, transgressing and resistant.[31] In reality, power relations in the modern business enterprise subject to the vagaries of the market undoubtedly narrowed the range of choice and patterned people's lived experiences. However, there was a dynamic relationship here and power ebbed and flowed, with market circumstances and the changing socio-political milieu.

## Workers' bodies, war and its aftermath

The structure of the economy and its cyclical nature impacted intimately upon workers' bodies. The interwar Depression and collapse in trade union power associated with mass unemployment and a concerted employers' counter-attack against a resurgent labour movement up to and including the First World War had both a negative impact on health standards at work (clearly demonstrable, for example, in coal mining and iron and steel) and a polarizing effect. The latter can be seen in marked improvement in the so-called 'new' or 'sunrise' industries (such as light and electrical engineering and consumer goods) and deterioration in the older 'staple' heavy industries. The two world wars were periods of challenge and crisis for workers' occupational health and safety on the home front, as the demand for shells, weapons and war production, combined with wartime patriotism, cranked up pressure on workers' bodies. There were increasing levels of fatigue and overstrain through long working hours, rising occupational injury and mortality rates and the exposure of workers to a range of chronic occupational diseases. For example, women workers being exposed to trinitrotoluene (TNT) poisoning in the First World War and male and female workers to asbestos in the Second World War. The twentieth-century world wars were also a catalyst for significant change, and workers were the beneficiaries of some reforms. For example with the acceptance of the concept of industrial fatigue in the First World War and the spread of state-sponsored company welfarism (company medical schemes; x-ray provision) in the Second World War – encouraged by Minister of Labour Ernest Bevin and Secretary of State for Scotland Tom Johnston.[32]

As in other aspects of employment, the Second World War and its immediate aftermath brought significant improvements in standards of health and safety in the workplace. Crucially, the marked growth of trade union membership extended protection over larger swathes of workers at the point of production, whilst the post-war Labour government and full male employment provided a conducive environment to curtail the worst excesses of managerial abuse and exploitation. The National Insurance (Industrial Injuries) Act 1946 brought the Welfare State to the workplace, with streamlined processes and improved benefits compared to the old now rather outmoded Workmen's Compensation Act.[33] Nationalization brought renewed efforts to provide decent medical coverage in the workplace – such as the 'flagship' Mines Medical Service – a pioneer, amongst other things, of preventative x-rays for workers to monitor exposure to and damage from dust inhalation. The social medicine movement attracted a cadre of highly motivated doctors and other medical professionals into the field, determined to extend research and medical knowledge to occupational health. Archie Cochrane, who headed the government's Pneumoconiosis Research Unit and pioneered the mass epidemiological studies of pneumoconiosis and tuberculosis in the early 1950s in the Rhondda Valley in South Wales using the newest x-ray techniques, would be a good example.[34] And the international community had some impact – not least the growing work of the International Labour Organisation (ILO) in information gathering, publicizing work-health hazards and passing basic safety conventions through which it aimed to standardize practice globally. The latter had a limited and uneven impact

## Jobs and Bodies

on countries keen to protect national sovereignty (and competitiveness). However, the UK was one of the leading countries in the world by 1950 – ranked third (after Bulgaria and France) in terms of the numbers of ILO health and safety conventions it had ratified (forty-one out of ninety, compared, for example to the United States which had only ratified six).[35] These initiatives appear to have had a marked impact. The rate of fatal workplace injuries, inflated during the wartime emergency, fell by a half from the wartime peak in 1941 to 1950 and the non-fatal injury rate fell by some 40 per cent.[36]

Nonetheless, despite a focus in the 1940s on the 'healthy factory', which built on a century of pioneering, world-leading work hazard regulation and control, still manual workers in the UK in the immediate post-Second World War period were subject to a wide array of work-related pressures and assaults upon their bodies and minds – both traumatic and chronic.[37] In the period 1945–9 almost 2,000 workers were recorded as killed in Britain each year on average as a result of work-related accidents and many more seriously injured, mutilated and rendered disabled. In the 1950s, deaths ran at an average of 1,564 per annum and by the 1970s the recorded death toll remained an average of 758 per annum.[38] The 'traditional' heavy industries saw the greatest carnage, with the highest death and mutilation rates amongst coal miners, seamen and fishermen, iron and steel workers, shipbuilders, construction workers, and agricultural and forestry workers. Figures provided in the *Registrar Generals Decennial Supplement on Occupational Mortality* for 1951 for accidental deaths (excluding deaths in the home and motor vehicle accidents) provide a rough guide to incidence. Amongst those occupations with more than three times the average standardized mortality rate (SMR) for accidental deaths were slaters and tilers, various categories of underground mine workers and quarrymen, seamen, railway shunters, pointsmen and level crossing men, platelayers, construction workers, well and mine sinkers and tunnel miners. Topping the list, however, were officers in the armed forces with more than twelve times the SMR from work-related injuries. This was an occupational group with obvious risks that tends to get neglected in the literature on occupational health and safety.[39] Not surprisingly, occupational mortality from injury was extremely low amongst non-manual occupational groups. This was another significant – and somewhat neglected – area of class inequalities in health. Clerks and typists, for example, recorded a workplace occupational mortality rate of less than a third of the average SMR, registering something like twenty-five times less risk than coal face workers of accidental death.[40]

Many manual occupations were characterized by high levels of risk to life and limb. Like mining, working at sea was another extremely hazardous job at mid-twentieth century, with a particularly high work-related death rate – indeed in fishing in the 1950s and 1960s the death rate was almost double that of coal mining. Peter Martin – a cook on trawlers out of Grimsby after the Second World War – recalled: 'Fishermen are tough – they've got to be, otherwise they wouldn't be able to carry on and work the way that they do.'[41] On board the men would work up to eighteen hour days, sometimes for several weeks on end, exposed to the elements and vulnerable to injuries as a consequence of outdated and dangerous equipment (such as exposed winches) and low railings. Fatigue was endemic and injuries to the hands commonplace. 'When I look back on more than

## Memory, Context and the Working Body

twenty years on trawlers', Martin commented, 'I can't help being angered that, for the benefit of the country, men are allowed to go to sea to be injured and killed without any thought being given to their welfare.'[42] He was writing this immediately after the infamous Hull trawler disasters in January/February 1968 which saw fifty-eight fatalities from three trawler sinkings (see Chapter 7 for more discussion of this and the civil activism that followed the disaster). Working in the North Sea oil and gas industry was also fraught with dangers – and the site of the world's worst occupational safety disaster in the industry when 167 workers lost their lives on the Piper Alpha platform in 1988. A survivor, Kevin Topham, recalled: 'There were some in the lower accommodation

**Figure 1.3** Piper Alpha oil rig disaster (1988) memorial, Aberdeen.
Courtesy of WikiCommons.

## Jobs and Bodies

cabins. They were trapped in. They never did get out. They were just drowned in there because the doors, the doorframes, were all metal, and these evidently twisted ... and consequently one couldn't open the door.'[43]

Iron and steel works were also notoriously dangerous, though the injury risk differed markedly across the metal-working community. Hot splashes and the incessant inhalation of silica dust were amongst the hazards identified in Patrick McGeown's evocative autobiography, *Heat the Furnace Seven Times Over* (1965). Ralph Glasser referred to the stories of death and mutilation he was told relating to Dixon's 'Blazes' Ironworks in the Gorbals in Glasgow.[44] Dorothy Radwanski, one of very few occupational nurses in industry in the 1960s, described conditions in the foundry at the North British Locomotive Works in Glasgow thus: 'the air was very black; the men were absolutely black. I was absolutely shocked and I said to somebody "it's like *Dante's Inferno*".'[45] As late as the mid-1970s, a Scottish occupational hygienist Ian Kellie commented that conditions in the Scottish steel industry were "appalling" and that he was "astonished" at the high incidence of silicosis.[46] The problems could be heightened in remote areas far from the public gaze. Perchard's work on the Aluminium industry in the Scottish Highlands (in Kinlochleven and Fort William) has shown how bodies were compromised by the furnaces' toxic and carcinogenic emissions, causing occupational asthma, emphysema and chronic pulmonary congestion, and cancers – something denied and suppressed by the company and within the tight-knit community for decades.[47]

The possibility of serious injury in the industrial workplace was widespread: As Sandy Doig (Factories Medical Inspector in Scotland, 1943–70) put it in the late 1960s: 'It is pretty safe to say that there are very few factories without some risk to health.'[48] Bodies were commodified: 'We were selling our health', one textile factory worker commented in 1969, recalling an accident he had where the machine had to be dismantled to retrieve his trapped and mangled foot.[49] Risks varied significantly, however, across manufacturing as the Factory Inspectorate (FI) observed. Those working with metal, in steel works and shipyards, had twice the accident frequency rates of textile factory workers, and four times the accident rate of those in light engineering and printing in 1950.[50] Smaller companies were amongst the worst offenders, as several studies noted.[51] Trauma to the eyes was particularly prevalent in manufacturing, with the FI estimating in 1950 that about 200,000 eye injuries happened in factories each year in the UK.[52] No wonder all major industrial areas had their specialist eye infirmaries to try to deal with this carnage.

Together with the high levels of death and disability through injury in the workplace, workers' bodies were also damaged by a cluster of chronic occupation-related diseases. Endemic health problems associated with work had been identified by medical professionals and in lay epidemiology for centuries and in Britain the most blatant diseases and toxins had been recognized by the state for compensation purposes, starting with a modest list of six occupational diseases in 1906 'prescribed' under the amended Workmen's Compensation Act (WCA). Over time, the list expanded. By the 1950s, the official prescribed list of occupational diseases drawn up by the state for compensation purposes included a wide range of toxins, gases, chemicals, muscular disorders and respiratory ailments. The latter were probably the most significant; indeed coughing was ubiquitous within mid-twentieth-century working-class communities where the inhalation of noxious, toxic and irritating dusts, fumes and chemicals was commonplace. The pneumoconioses – such as silicosis, asbestosis, byssinosis and coal workers' pneumoconiosis – were amongst the most widespread and amongst the most dreaded of work-related ailments. One medical professional estimated in 1958 that over 2 million British workers were disabled to some degree by respiratory illness caused by what they inhaled in their workplaces.[53] Miners, again, suffered disproportionately. Within the coalfield communities, pneumoconiosis caused by the inhalation of coal and rock dust reached record levels post-Second World War, with death rates peaking in the 1945–55 period, and newly diagnosed cases around 1960. The recurrent introduction of new chemicals and compounds also posed unknown health risks, as David Walker has shown, leading to outbreaks of dermatitis, tissue and bone damage and new occupational cancers – such as bladder cancer.[54]

One problem was that doctors were not in a good position to diagnose employment-related diseases such as these because of the neglect of occupational health in their training. The situation was worsened by the compartmentalizing of occupational and public health – the former administered post-war through the Ministry of Labour and the latter the Ministry of Health. Despite wide support from the trade unions and the British Medical Association, the Dale Committee (1951) enquiry determined that the time was not right for an integrated NHS and Occupational Health Service (largely

**Figure 1.4** Will Brown, formerly a fit member of the Aberpergwm Football Club and a miner from South Wales (now totally incapacitated by silicosis, 1945).
Courtesy of Getty Images.

on cost grounds). In the wake of Dale, several industrial health surveys were initiated (to expand empirical research findings) in the 1950s, including the Govan, Glasgow enquiry in 1953, Halifax in 1957–8 and the Potteries in 1959. They uncovered high levels of ill-health and desperately poor standards of cleanliness and hygiene, and health-sapping work environments made worse by poor ventilation and inadequate dust control. Work conditions were deemed particularly conducive to respiratory damage, eye injuries, repetitive strain injury and dermatitis. In Halifax, the Industrial Health Advisory Committee enquiry was particularly critical of the lack of preventative action to minimize risks and share medical knowledge. It found there were no full-time factory medical officers employed in the city's industries, and only four part-timers and twenty-three factory nurses – mostly in the largest factories.[55]

All the 1950s occupational health enquiries found a range of experience, with the worse conditions where workers' bodies were most vulnerable (proportionately) in the smallest workplaces. These types of workplaces were also usually where the trade unions were weakest. And few of the smallest workplaces had anything but rudimentary occupational medicine services. The occupational health expert Donald Hunter estimated in 1959 that only 4 per cent of factories employing less than 100 workers had the services of a doctor on site, whereas about half of the largest factories employed company doctors.[56] What was also evident was a gulf between the relatively unhealthy and unsafe workplaces of the traditional heavy industries, primarily located in the north of England, in South Wales and in Scotland, and the better environmental conditions in the newer 'sunrise' industries in London, the South East and the Midlands. Hammond's study using Factory Inspectorate data showed, for example, a fatal death rate from industrial accidents per 1000 workers in the mid-1960s at almost 25 per cent higher for Scotland, Wales and Northern England compared to London and the South East of England. The amount paid out in statutory injury benefits was three times higher in Scotland, Wales and Northern England than London and the South East and, linked to this carnage, there was a significantly higher proportion of disabled people in the traditional industrial heartlands of South Wales, Clydeside and Tyneside.[57] These spatial elements of body vulnerability linked to the workplace and industrial legacies were elements of the north-south divide that largely escaped wider attention.

In part these discrepancies and inequalities in experience reflected economic structure (a larger proportion of the working population employed in the most dangerous 'heavy' industries), but prevailing health cultures were also important. In Scotland, the particularly bad occupational health and safety record led to a long preoccupation with what became known as the 'Scottish anomaly' by the HSE. One HSE study in 2006 found Scotland's fatal injury rate in workplace accidents was almost 50 per cent higher than England.[58] Deeply entrenched attitudes proved hard to erode, as one Clyde shipbuilding safety officer commented in 1977: 'Safety is always uphill work in a traditional industry like shipbuilding where men are set in their ways … It takes time.'[59] Important here though was that workers were hardly encouraged to act differently. He might have said 'where *management* and men are set in their ways'. There was a lack of knowledge of dangers, lack of support for learning, lack of emphasis on the use of safety equipment and an overall lack of company investment in health and safety training. Before the 1970s health and safety education on the job was rudimentary and usually accrued through direct workplace experience. Safety officers, where they existed, were far from being empowered by their employers to force radical changes in workers' culture on the job.

Occupational ill-health and injury were thus an important source of health inequality in the post-Second World War period, affecting the working class much worse than the middle and upper classes, with male manual workers affected disproportionately, especially in areas of heavy industry, compared to non-manual workers. Unskilled male manual workers in the hazardous heavy industries faced the highest risks, with racial, ethnic and religious minorities also disproportionately exposed to unhealthy work, given the discrimination they faced in the labour market in the post-war decades.[60] Significantly, long before mesothelioma was officially recognized as a prescribed occupational disease, the Registrar Generals data on occupational mortality in 1951 defined labourers and unskilled workers making asbestos goods as having by far the highest SMR for cancer of the lung.[61]

## Gender and the dangerous workplace

Whilst social class, place, race and ethnicity were key determinants of injury and death on the job, gender also fundamentally shaped patterns of health and safety. In the industrial era, there was a marked gender imbalance, a reflection of segregated labour markets for women and men and related patriarchal attitudes which saw men dominate the more dangerous trades. Few women found employment in manual jobs in coal mines, steel works, heavy engineering, chemicals and the docks. Official figures suggest 80 to 90 per cent of all serious work-related disabilities and disease at mid-twentieth century afflicted male workers.[62] The figure for fatalities was even higher: In 1950 the UK Factory Inspectorate reported 799 fatal 'accidents', of which 789 were men and 10 women.[63] Male workers experienced 87 per cent (157,150) of all recorded non-fatal accidents in factories. These figures do not include coal mining. Management bore primary responsibility for this carnage, given their pivotal role in the organization of production. And not least because they invariably failed to challenge prevailing work-health cultures premised on 'macho' behaviours around risk and in many sectors deployed wage payment systems (paying by 'piecework' by results) that incentivized overwork.

Entrenched work habits were difficult to erode. When safety helmets and protective goggles were first introduced in construction, shipyards, steel works and mines, many workmen initially resisted wearing them. In part this was because the early versions of protective clothing were uncomfortable and could interfere with productivity and hence earnings. However, wearing masks, helmets and goggles was also seen by many workers of that era as a sign of personal weakness and an affront to manliness. These attitudes and work cultures became ingrained through peer pressure and socialization from one generation of workers to the next. Workers were also agents in this and were capable of taking decisions that undermined their own health and safety, especially if procedures

## Jobs and Bodies

affected earnings. An ex-miner reflected in the 1990s: 'The safety rules were broken by the men themselves, because they wanted the money.'[64] A 76-year-old retired miner recalled that it was an accepted practice not to put in the necessary number of wooden supports: 'Well, you're supposed to put your wood up at a certain time and a certain measurement and a' that. That didnae happen. Yon never happened.'[65] The regulations were one thing but what actually happened at the coal face, the building site and in the factory was quite another. What is apparent is the co-existence of two important degenerative pressures upon health and the workers' bodies with the intertwining of managerial exploitation and masculine values. Management could have intervened more aggressively to change prevailing work regimes and toxic work cultures.

Sometimes technological fixes were not as effective in practice as they purported to be. Dust provides a good example. The use of masks and respirators made it more difficult to breathe and hence to work effectively and thus to maximize earnings. For many heavy industry workers in the 1950s and 1960s, when the choice came between using a respirator which restrained productivity and doing without, but getting higher wages, the latter course was taken. This was compounded by the fact that the risks of disease caused by inhaling dust at work also seemed distant – a long-term possibility, as one miner noted about masks: 'We did'nae wear them. You did'nae think of the future, we just thought from day to day, well, you did'nae think you were going to get … silicosis or nothing like that.'[66]

Doing dangerous work was to a large extent taken for granted in many working-class communities after the war – when daughters often followed mothers in working in clothing and textile factories and sons frequently followed fathers in coal mining, iron and steel, the docks and shipbuilding communities. What is evident is that taking calculated risks (whilst avoiding obvious 'danger spots') and earning big money were aspired to by most and were especially (though not exclusively) exalted masculine values. An example would be the much lauded 'big hewers' – the 'champion' highest producers and earners – who existed in almost all British mining communities. Exposing the body to significant risk of harm could be justified on the grounds that this was a worthwhile sacrifice for the sake of the family. The wife of a machine operator who worked in the Turner's Asbestos Cement plant in Clydebank for around eight years up to the mid-1960s commented: 'He was frightened to walk out of the job because he was married with a family.'[67] Her husband was well aware that he was risking his health: 'I knew it was dangerous before I went in there 'cause there was people complaining, but when you have two of a family to bring up it was better than walking the streets. I never was idle in my life.'[68] The final comment here is an oft-repeated trope valorizing hard graft and the work ethic. But awareness of danger was also evident here. Bodies were being compromised for the sake of the family but what other choice did poorly educated working men have? Similarly, some miners would try to hide their encroaching breathlessness and where they failed to attain financial compensation or benefits might return to work underground knowing full well that this would worsen their respiratory disability. To such men fulfilling the breadwinner role dominated their thinking, surpassing any concerns they might harbour over the long-term damage that might accrue to their bodies. Some recognized this in later life: 'Silly now, looking back through the years y'know' a retired Clydeside sheet metal worker noted of his propensity to over work.[69] This points to both a deeply ingrained work ethic amongst such male manual workers and a fiercely competitive workplace environment where risk-taking was commonplace and helped to sustain and bolster working-class masculinity. This was so elsewhere too, as Connell has noted of Australian miners and Portelli of the Harlan County miners in Kentucky, USA: 'Pressure from the company hierarchy would meet a cultural disposition amongst the workers.' One union worker recalled: 'I would always think to myself, "let's try to beat that other shift. If they loaded 400 tons, let's get 450."'[70]

Whilst there is a difference in degree of exposure (given the patriarchal patterning of work and the persisting dangerous work taboo for women), female workers' bodies were also vulnerable and women experienced a wide range of health and safety issues on the job. Much of this story has been neglected due to the fixation on male workers' bodies and a widespread sense that female workers were not, or hardly, affected. Data collection was one issue because of the characteristic truncated pattern of female participation in the labour market. Chronic work-related disease could remain undetected in women until long after they had left employment on marriage or childbirth. Lack of separate toilet facilities and inadequate personal protection was a concern in some jobs as women penetrated more of the male-dominated industries as time went on. This was the case on the railways as women entered the service as guards and drivers from the 1970s. Firefighting was another example, where the employment of women increased from 2 per cent in the early 1990s to 11 per cent by 2020. One issue which arose was the inadequacy of the firefighters' uniform, which failed to protect the more sensitive skin tissue on women's breasts, leading to an increased propensity to develop breast cancer.[71]

As Karen Messing has eloquently argued, work, health and safety are deeply gendered, with the sorts of hazards and problems women have faced in the workplace largely disregarded.[72] 'People', Messing has asserted, 'just do not think of women's jobs in connection with occupational health'.[73] She also notes that the data underrepresents accidents, injury and mortality of female workers as these were rarely included in workmen's compensation claims.[74] Whilst science is the main culprit in Messing's thesis, historically trade unions might also be regarded as somewhat culpable. Unions tended to reflect the prevailing ideologies of gender difference and inequality, supporting, in the nineteenth century, the Factory Acts, Mines Acts and other legislation that excluded and subordinated women workers.[75] As Claire Williams has noted about Australia and New Zealand, 'the Factories legislation and the labour movement has privileged the families of working-class men at the expense of working women, and particularly women providers with dependents, and often sick husbands.'[76]

Implicit and at times explicit gender segregation was premised on acceptance by the unions of the prevailing discourse of masculinity and femininity – ideas around who should legitimately be in full-time paid employment (male workers as breadwinners) and who should be homemakers (married women). What was created was a 'dangerous work taboo' whereby women were largely excluded from the most visible areas of work deemed to adversely affect their functions as mothers (or potential mothers), such as underground mining, construction, night work or working with lead.[77] Whilst ostensibly protecting women from risk and harm, this practice ghettoized working women into other more precarious paid work, such as domestic service, clothing sweatshops, low-paid homework and monotonous machine-minding (as in textile factories) and assembly line work. Much of this work (with the possible exception of the textile factories) was less well-regulated, had less exposure to acute life-threatening accident risks, but more exposure to chronic long-term health problems.[78] Barbara Harrison has discussed this for an earlier period (1880–1914) in *Not Only the Dangerous Trades*, reflecting on repetitive strain injuries (RSIs) like telegraphists cramp, musculo skeletal problems like housemaid's knee and fatigue.[79] On top of this was the invariably exhausting dual burden of paid work and unpaid domestic duties that most women carried.

In the UK, gender discriminatory policies like the marriage bar (the sacking of women on marriage, or on pregnancy) and unequal pay were both imposed (as in the Civil Service and teaching) and for a long time a societal expectation associated with

**Figure 1.5** Seamstress sewing together an asbestos mattress, Thomas Ward Asbestos Co, 1961. Note the fibre dust all over the Singer sewing machine and the lack of any PPE.
Courtesy of Getty Images.

working-class 'respectability'. The male-dominated, and male-work oriented, British trade union movement largely neglected female-related OHS issues and not just through gender-exclusionary and discriminatory policies like failure to oppose the marriage bar and to promote equal pay. Many unions also failed to recruit women pro-actively and operated male-preference policies in relation to committee, executive and leadership positions.[80] Women's voices were thus muted within the labour movement – at least up to the 1970s – and they struggled to influence the prevailing OHS discourse. Consequently, the OHS problems and needs of women workers remained largely overlooked. Furthermore, deprived of access to apprenticeships in skilled and well-paid rewarding work where men predominated also denied women the opportunity to enjoy enriching, dignified and well-paid work that had positive implications for health and well-being. We'll come back to the gendering of OHS and explore how men and women workers articulated and narrated risk in their life histories and how they navigated danger and stress in subsequent chapters.

## Public health and occupational health

The boundary between public health and occupational health was somewhat porous, and the workplace could be a significant incubator of germs. Interestingly, the UK's state-prescribed occupational diseases list also included tuberculosis – scheduled under the National Insurance (Industrial Injuries) Act in 1951 for certain specific health workers, including nurses, tuberculosis (TB) sanatoria workers, social workers and asylum officers. TB had long been regarded as the classic disease associated with poverty and overcrowded slums. This scheduling of TB in 1951 created a significant precedent in the UK because no other disease prevalent in the general population had ever been defined officially as an occupational disease – and hence subject to compensation under the Industrial Injuries Act. It marked the culmination of a long campaign going back at least to the 1920s on the part of the TUC and several constituent trade unions to shift medical and popular understanding of the aetiology of TB to recognize that overcrowded workplaces and contact contagion in the course of employment were important causal agents. This campaign utilized growing medical knowledge, including epidemiological studies of nurses, which demonstrated to the satisfaction of the statutory body – the Industrial Diseases Advisory Committee – the markedly higher rate of TB incidence amongst specific occupational groups. This built upon an earlier recognition – going back to the 1920s – that there was a synergistic relationship between forms of pneumoconiosis (notably silicosis) and TB. What happened in industries like slate quarrying, stone masonry, metal mining and cutlery grinding was that weakened lungs with tissue damage caused by dust inhalation at work lowered resistance to the TB bacillus (see Chapter 6).

The scheduling of TB as an occupational disease in 1951 was somewhat unusual – a divergence from an otherwise markedly conservative policy of statutory regulation and monitoring of chronic work-related disease and a tough (i.e. on the workers) regime

**Jobs and Bodies**

of medical surveillance over the damaged body in industry. Tweedale and Hansen have shown how conservative the Pneumoconiosis Medical Panels were in diagnosing asbestosis from the 1930s to the 1960s.[81] These Panels comprised physicians who made an assessment of causation and the degree of respiratory impairment – by the percentage they judged individuals respiratory capacity was diminished. McIvor and Johnston (2007) have shown a similar cautious pattern in relation to the long campaign – from the 1950s to the 1990s – to get bronchitis and emphysema scheduled as occupational diseases (and hence subject to compensation). Here smoking was widely regarded as the major causal pathway – hence blame deflected from the employer and work conditions (dust) to self-inflicted pain and damage to the body from the smoking habit. Insurance companies were embedded in all this and not averse in the 1950s and 1960s to using callous delaying tactics in the knowledge that liability to compensation pay-outs was much reduced if the victim died.[82] What the TB scheduling of 1951 demonstrates is something of the porous nature of occupational health and the difficulty of disentangling causation when bodies drift across different spaces – at home, work and leisure. So diseases could have their origins in employment, or in the home, the family, in personal habits and lifestyle, or the wider environment, and/or be exacerbated by poverty and deprivation. The TB story parallels in many respects what unfolded with Covid-19, discussed in more detail in Chapter 6.

The bladder cancer issue in chemical manufacture was similar in that it can occur quite naturally outside of the dyestuffs sector and to further complicate the issue those affected who worked within the dyestuffs section were exposed to several substances that were all possible causative agents. Multiple causation was recognized later in the case of bronchitis/emphysema and smoking (and enshrined in the compensation 'model' with differential payments depending upon smoking history and a series of other variables), and with stress. Thus the boundaries become blurred. Sexually transmitted infections (STIs), including AIDS, for example, are clearly spread widely within the community through lifestyle choices, though just as clearly these are unequivocally occupational diseases associated with sex industry workers. They have not been and are unlikely in the foreseeable future to be officially recognized as such and scheduled for compensation purposes. This demonstrates the socially constructed nature of occupational disease, as Dembe and others have argued.[83]

## Culpability

So why were work-related diseases, injuries and death rates so persistently high in the British workplace at mid-twentieth century? Interpretations range across a broad spectrum, in part reflecting wide divergences in contemporary views and a range of discourses in the literature from the medical, state, employers and workers perspectives. At one extreme are those that argue the inevitability of 'accidents' or high levels of disease given the intrinsic risks of heavy industries and the lack of medical knowledge at the time. Others have continued a long tradition of 'blaming the victim', drawing upon the ideas of some psychologists about 'accident proneness' or 'careless' workers or, as in the case of the Robens Report into workplace safety in 1972, finding workers' culpable through their own 'apathy' and indifference.[84]

Other contemporary accounts, such as the National Institute of Industrial Psychology's survey of 2000 accidents in the late 1960s, placed responsibility squarely upon employers and management-designed work systems, including payments by results wage systems that placed an incentive on overwork.[85] Some work sociologists – particularly, though not exclusively, those writing in the Marxist tradition – have argued that understanding occupational injury and ill-health is dependent upon locating this 'within the social relations of production' and that capitalist modes of production are intrinsically corrosive of health because of the dominance of the profit motive.[86] Others, interpreting this as overly deterministic and too negative, have argued for a more complex and contingent blending of structural factors with a degree of workers' agency (e.g. in the ways workers express their masculinity in the workplace in varying degrees of risk-taking). There has also been a plea to shift from a general castigation of the system per se, to a more nuanced recognition of a wide range of employer and managerial strategies on health and safety.[87] The latter ranged from the socially responsible 'welfarist' acutely tuned to the health and welfare of their employees (or, more accurately perhaps, to the less dispensable employees such as the skilled craftsmen) to the grossly negligent, authoritarian profit-maximizers who treated employees as little more than commodities. There were also significant differences emerging in the 1950s and 1960s between the extensive occupational medicine services in the workplace in the public sector, compared to the private sector. Provision in the privately owned shipyards, for example, atrophied sharply after the Second World War. On Clydeside the full-time Industrial Medical Officers (IMO) introduced under the wartime Ministry of Labour orders didn't last long. By 1963, it was reported in a Clyde Shipbuilders' Association survey that none of the surviving fifteen Clydeside shipyards had a full or part-time IMO; only six of the fifteen employed a nurse full-time and most only used a doctor on call arrangement.[88]

There were competing discourses relating to the impact of work upon the body and who was to blame. Employers and the state frequently denied responsibility, deflected blame and minimized risk. For example, the Mines Inspectorate (MI) for the Scottish Division claimed in 1953 that of all pit accidents for that year, 'nearly half of the accidents were avoidable by ordinary caution which suggests that workmen were often ready to take a chance'.[89] Similarly, the MI reports detailed many instances of miners being killed through undercutting seams too deep or failing to support their working area adequately.[90] The union leader Abe Moffat castigated the MIs in 1955 for victim-blaming, arguing that the technological solutions to the dust problem underground (including water sprays on the drilling and cutting machines) were not being implemented by the NCB because of the cost.[91] Workers' choices were constrained; bounded in by having to work within a framework dictated by management in relation to investment (or non-investment) in technology and the payments by results wage payment systems which incentivized maximizing production at the expense of health. Not surprisingly, workers cut corners and took risks. Another miner recalled that management turned a blind eye to the practice of not putting in the stipulated number of timber roof supports (and hence compromising safety) – except when the Mines Inspector called: 'See the next day they'd let you go into the same fucking place with no doubties [supports] as long as that fucking coal was coming out, you know what I mean?'.[92]

Historically, perhaps what is critically important is the degree to which workers' choices – however significant – were constrained within an unequal power relationship at the point of production in a context where workers were often undervalued and exploited. Experience differed widely, but this heterogeneity should not distract us from the underlying tendency within competitive, free market capitalism to put shareholders and the profit margin before workers' health and well-being. Nichols work has perhaps been particularly influential here in emphasizing the 'social determinants' of injuries sustained at work – the influence of the business cycle, labour markets, work intensification and the profit motive.[93] Corporate irresponsibility was pervasive, from the boardroom denials of the asbestos multi-national Turner and Newall to the condoning of 'macho' management in the North Sea Oil industry.[94]

One other factor was of major importance in explaining the persistence of high casualty and disease rates in the post-war British workplace: the structural flaws in statutory provision and the regulatory framework. Only about half of the UK's workplaces were covered by the health and safety legislation in the immediate post-Second World War years – agriculture, for example, was not regulated until the Agriculture (Safety, Health and Welfare Provision) Act 1956, despite the sector having injury incidence levels way in excess of manufacturing and second only to shipping and mines. In part, this reflected the historic pattern of government only responding to pressure from public opinion – for example after major disasters involving loss of life – what one health and safety representative referred to as 'tombstone legislation'.[95] But the labour movement also had a marked positive influence. It was no coincidence that the sector with the strongest and deepest tradition of collective organization and strike activity – mining – was also amongst the most systematically regulated in terms of health and safety. Uniquely across UK industry, coal mining included the statutory appointment of workmen's safety inspectors (from 1911). Across manufacturing, however, voluntary workers' safety committees were thin on the ground in the 1950s, despite being recommended by the ILO. Only about 4000 such committees existed across Britain's 230,000 factories in 1960, representing less than 2 per cent of the total.[96]

A number of studies pointed to the way corporate crime was widely accepted and condoned, with low penalties (derisory fines) for breaches of Factory law which consequently failed to act as a deterrent.[97] State policy for its workplace inspectorate emphasized persuasion and education of recalcitrant employers, rather than punitive punishment. In part, as Williams argued in his seminal 1960 study *Accidents and Ill-Health at Work*, this reflected a wide public disinterest in occupational health.[98] In an important recent monograph Long has carefully reconstructed the long campaign, spearheaded by a number of voluntary agencies to establish a national Occupational Health Service integrated into the NHS. As Long has shown, the TUC played a pivotal role in the movement to create the 'healthy factory' and by the 1940s was lobbying for the merging of occupational health with public health in a combined 'service' which would include a full preventative programme within the workplace.[99] However, this idea failed to gain sufficient political support and was never implemented. If successful, it might have done much more to erode the high-risk workplace health cultures that pervaded the heavy industry workplace. Also to have systematically introduced effective preventative public health measures through the workplace (such as x-rays and inoculation) and to have focused research efforts more widely on the work-health interaction (rather than the prevailing narrow focus on specific occupational diseases, like pneumoconiosis). Despite wide support – and precedents in other places such as Scandinavia – the NHS and occupational health remained largely separate. One consequence was the continuing marginalization of occupational health – indicated, for example, in the big discrepancy in the numbers of civil servants employed as factory inspectors (largely focusing on safety rather than health) compared to medical inspectors (a ratio of more than ten to one in the 1950s).[100]

Moreover, an overreliance by the state upon 'scientific discourse' or professionally generated medical knowledge constrained effective regulation. There was a deep-rooted and long-standing belief in the idea that hazards could be regulated and controlled, evident, for example, in the tendency to lay down 'threshold limits' of exposure (measured by particles per cubic inch in the air captured by filters in 'dust counting' machines) – as with silica, vinyl chloride, coal and asbestos dusts. These were later found to be inadequate and revised to be more stringent. In the meantime, as David Walker has argued, this provided workers with a false sense that they were being protected and were secure and not exposed to risk.[101] The very process of getting an occupational disease officially scheduled (and hence subject to compensation) was incredibly restrictive, relying upon positive proof of linkage (and convincing a panel of medical experts: the Industrial Injury Advisory Council), rather than erring on the side of caution and the concept of *reasonable probability* (which the TUC and some experts campaigned for). Medical knowledge was socially constructed and, it has been posited, tended to reflect powerful industrial and corporate interests – as in the case of the Asbestosis Research Council.[102] Significant change in the regulatory regime was not to come until the 1974 Health and Safety at Work Act (HSWA) and that fell far short of what radical reformers pushing for an integrated public health and occupational health service wanted.

## Economic restructuring and occupational health and safety

The relationship between the job and the body changed radically as the British economy morphed from predominantly industrial to non-industrial, dominated by the service sector, offices, creative work and the like. As white collars replaced blue collars, old hazards, risks and dangers declined, replaced by other risks to health and well-being, including stress and overwork. In the early 1950s there were around 2000 recorded work-related trauma fatalities a year, giving a fatal injury rate per 100,000 workers of 10.5. Thereafter fatalities fell steadily. By the 2000s, workers were more than ten times

## Jobs and Bodies

less likely to be killed at work from an 'accident' than in the 1950s. The pattern is confirmed with the less reliable figures for non-fatal work injuries, which according to the HSE fell fourfold from 336,701 in 1974 to 85,110 in 2009/10.[103] That said, workplace disasters continued to occur, though with diminishing frequency. The Hull trawlermen disaster in 1968 saw fifty-eight fishermen die in three separate incidents within a month. The explosion at an ICI chemical plant at Flixborough in 1974 saw twenty-eight killed and thirty-six seriously injured. There were 167 deaths in the Piper Alpha oil platform explosion in 1988. The Stockline plastics factory explosion in Glasgow killed nine and left fifteen seriously injured whilst twenty-three immigrant Chinese cockle pickers at Morecambe Bay were drowned in 2004.[104]

The pattern of declining mortality and improving occupational safety was the product of several factors. Clearly of key importance were the structural shifts in the labour force – the sharp decline of employment in the most dangerous manual trades such as mining, agriculture, shipping and fishing and heavy manufacturing and rise of the more benign (at least in terms of physical hazards) office and professional non-manual jobs. However, the HSE attributes less than half of the improvement to structural change in jobs. They fail to specify what the other ameliorative forces were. However, we might posit that improved vigilance on the part of the trade unions, better health education and awareness, a more critical investigative media, a changed health culture

**Figure 1.6** The Flixborough Nypro Gas and Chemical Plant disaster, 1 June 1974 where twenty-eight workers were killed.
Courtesy of Getty Images.

in the workplace and improved policing and regulation (following the HSWA 1974 and subsequent European Union Directives) all had a positive impact.[105] What is also important in explaining occupational health and safety trends in the UK is the way that risk was increasingly exported to less developed countries where labour was cheaper and regulatory regimes weak or non-existent. This clearly happened, for example, with asbestos.

The most important change since the Second World War in the regulation and control of workplace dangers took place in 1974 with the passage of the HSWA. Prior to the HSWA there were a series of laws which regulated minimum standards of health and safety in specific workplaces such as the Factory Acts (updated in 1961), the Mines and Quarries Acts (updated in 1954) and the Nuclear Installations Act (1965). The law covered such things as temperature, ventilation, lighting, fumes, dust, first aid, washing and toilet facilities, workplace cleanliness and the guarding of hazardous machinery. Some limited regulation had also been introduced for office workers in 1963 after a long trade union campaign. Standing alongside these laws were more specific legal regulations on particular hazards, such as the Construction Regulations (1966) and the Asbestos Regulations (1969). The operation and limitations of this complex and fragmented body of health and safety legislation are beyond the scope of this chapter. However, amongst the weaknesses of the regulatory system were its uneven coverage (with some 8 million workers not covered by any regulation in 1970) and the way specific regulations could be superseded quickly by technological change, such as mine shearing technologies or asbestos spraying, and new products, as in the chemicals sector. There were also issues about the inadequate resourcing of the inspectorates designated with the duty of enforcing the law, the ineffectiveness of policing by inspectorates and criticism of their tactics of prioritizing persuasion and education rather than punitive measures. In part this was a reaction to the law courts who proved reluctant to impose heavy fines, and thus a financial deterrent, upon corporate criminals who breached the law.

The HSWA 1974 rationalized this system by replacing the individual statutes with one that comprehensively covered all employees, designed to encompass all problems of safety, welfare and health at work. It introduced the main institutions currently responsible for British health and safety at work: the Health and Safety Commission and the HSE. Crucially, the HSWA delegated a shared responsibility for workplace health and safety between employers and employees. It was the statutory duty of employers to: 'ensure, so far as is reasonably practicable, the health, safety and welfare at work of all his employees'.[106] Workers had the 'duty' to adhere to the health and safety regulations, work together with the employer, not mistreat anything and 'take reasonable care of your own health and safety and that of your workmates'.[107] The law was enforced by a cadre of HSE inspectors with powers to enter any workplace and issue Prohibition and Improvement Notices stopping a specific job, section or complete workplace. Those breaking the law (employers, workers and manufacturers) could be taken to court by the HSE and fined, or have a custodial sentence of up to two years imposed.

The new system was an improvement, but had several flaws. It allowed alternative arrangements to be made in some special cases – including, significantly, the North

## Jobs and Bodies

Sea oil industry. As Beck, Foster and Woolfson have illustrated, what made this 'new' extractive industry unique was the fact that in many cases the production regime was transplanted almost intact from the United States. This included most of the technology, many of the management structures, and, crucially, a dominant 'gung ho' attitude towards health and safety on many of the platforms.[108] It was also the case that it was the Department of Energy, and not the HSE, which was responsible for safety on most of the oil platforms from 1974. These factors, it has been argued, combined with the emphasis placed on extracting the oil as quickly as possible, led to a neglect of health and safety offshore in many installations, culminating in the 1988 Piper Alpha disaster.

Sprinkled throughout the HSWA section on employers' responsibilities is the phrase 'so far as is reasonably practicable'. The law courts continued to interpret this in the employers' favour, throwing cases out, or imposing small fines which hardly acted as a deterrent. The average fine for health and safety crime was just £99 in 1977–8.[109] Moreover, employers generally insured themselves against this risk. Weak enforcement also continued to be an issue. The Inspectorate was spread thinly, with less than 500 field inspectors in 1980, meaning each covered some 1000 workplaces, making routine preventative visits to every workplace on average only every four years (unless specifically called in). The economic recession from the late 1970s and government hostility towards occupational health and safety, combined with deregulation and public spending cuts in the 1980s only made matters worse. Once again, having the regulations in force and adhering to them were two different things. For example, a heating engineer could remember slip-shod health and safety procedures in his firm well into the late 1980s:

> If we went down tae strip a boiler we just took it [the asbestos] off with a hammer and chisel, you know. There was nae masks or anything at that time, you know. If you came out for a breather they were asking you what you were dain sitting outside, you know. You were spitting up black for maybe a week, you know, when you came out.[110]

Three years after the passage of the HSWA the system was supplemented in 1977 with regulations that permitted unionized workers to set up safety committees with their employers. This had long been an aspiration of the trade union movement and was achieved partly as a quid pro quo for union support for income policies, as part of the Labour government's Social Chapter. However, the sharp decline in trade union membership in the 1980s restricted the impact of this enabling legislation. In 1986, the Reporting of Injuries, Diseases and Dangerous Occurrences Regulations came into operation, compelling employers to report any injuries resulting in absences from work of more than three days. European Union Directives also improved matters somewhat – at least providing something of a protective buffer, despite Tory ambivalence towards such 'restrictions'. In response to growing European pressure, the Management of Health and Safety Regulations 1992 were passed with the aim of addressing some of the shortcomings of the 'shared responsibility' principle. This compelled employers and self-employed to carry out 'risk assessments' of potential workplace hazards and to determine what measures should be taken to comply with the employers or self-employed person's duties under the 1974 HSWA. Criticisms continued, nonetheless, of the shortcomings of the regulatory framework, leading, for example, by the late 1990s in some quarters to a campaign to introduce a new crime of 'corporate killing' to penalize employers more directly. The hope was that this would provide a more effective deterrent.[111] This new offence would mean there would be no need to locate and charge the 'controlling mind' of a company, but that the company itself would be held responsible, with the possibility of its directors being sent to prison.

Whilst serious shortcomings in regulation persisted and economic pressures continued to make workers vulnerable, it would be churlish and inaccurate not to recognize massive progress from the situation prevailing at mid-twentieth century. As Almond and Esbester have noted: 'overall, health and safety has gone from a marginal consideration to a much more central feature of policy and society', adding, 'and, like any other area of social endeavour, the more it matters to people, the more contested or complex its legitimation becomes'.[112] Comparative statistical data (whilst subject to some issues relating to inconsistency in data collection across different countries) certainly suggests that Britain's workplace safety record contrasted favourably with other European countries. By the first decade of the twenty-first century the UK's SMR from fatal accidents at work was joint lowest (with Finland and Sweden) of fifteen European Union (EU) member states.[113]

The situation in relation to long-term trends in occupational health (as opposed to safety) is less clear. Whilst pneumoconiosis was in sharp decline from the 1950s, asbestos-related cancer (including mesothelioma) was on the rise due to the considerable time lag between exposure and the emergence of the malignant tumour. Progress was uneven. The HSE admitted itself in the late 1990s that it had prioritized safety issues and not paid enough attention to chronic ill-health and disease caused by work.[114] New hazards, toxins and diseases – such as those associated with chemicals (like vinyl chloride monomer, benzene and chromates), musculoskeletal disorders, repetitive strain injuries (associated for example with computer use) and stress – replaced old ones. Bronchitis, as mentioned, was only 'recognized' as an occupational disease associated with smoke and dust inhalation at work in 1993. Watterson has identified how 'old, new and silent epidemics' of occupational diseases have co-existed and persisted, arguing that the neglect of workers' bodies has been the product of 'the relative invisibility of occupational health epidemics and the low priority afforded to them'.[115] He commented:

> There are also epidemics that are recognised but are viewed by workers as part of the job, such as back pain for nurses and building workers, damaged knee joints for carpet layers and miners as well as colds and flu for teachers. In times of insecure or poor employment conditions these are likely to remain unchallenged.[116]

Moreover, given the long incubation period for many classic occupational diseases – including occupational cancers – the peak of disability and death rates could occur some considerable time after the initial contact and exposure to toxins and carcinogens.

## Jobs and Bodies

Asbestos-related cancers could emerge twenty, thirty, forty or more years after initial contact to the carcinogen. Hence, death rates from mesothelioma started to accelerate from the 1970s, peaking in the 2000s and 2010s as a result of high exposure rates in the 1950s and 1960s, before really effective regulation kicked in from the UK 1969 Asbestos Regulations onwards (though white or chrysotile asbestos – widely considered to be less carcinogenic than other forms – was not finally banned until 1999). As I have already commented, scholars differ widely in their interpretation of the asbestos tragedy. The evidence strongly indicates, however, that this is a classic example of vested interests in the form of powerful multi-national corporations conspiring to put profit before workers' health, aided by the effective collusion of the state. Whilst the outcome has been the somewhat belated but nonetheless relatively effective regulation of the worst unhealthy working practices in the UK (and other well-regulated economies, such as the United States), in practice the problem has been increasingly transferred to other poorer 'third world' countries where multinational companies could benefit from weaker regulatory regimes, little trade union interference and cheaper labour costs. This happened worldwide with asbestos, as McCulloch and Tweedale have shown in their important study, *Defending the Indefensible* (2008). Chemical manufacture provides another deeply tragic example – with the US multinational Union Carbide responsible for one of the worst occupational and environmental health disasters in history with the lethal gas leakage from its plant in Bhopal in 1984, responsible for at least 3787 deaths (with some estimates as high as 11,000) and almost 4000 severe and permanently disabling injuries.[117]

The recession of the 1980s and Thatcherite policies of deregulation combined with the empowerment of capital and neutering of the trade unions also had degenerative impacts upon occupational health and safety – at the very least slowing down the pace of progress and at worse contributing to overwork, stress and workplace ill-health – as in the North Sea oil and gas sector. More intensive Japanese production methods transplanted to the UK resulted in exhaustion and a rash of new repetitive strain injuries whilst the disciplining effect of mass unemployment facilitated work intensification, insecurity and stress (we return to this in more detail in Chapter 4).[118]

Electronics, another rapidly growing sector from the 1960s, threw up significant health hazards, including exposure to toxic chemicals. In a way similar to some asbestos-related diseases, the health effects of exposure to such chemicals could take a long time to show up. In addition, many of the chemicals used in some of the processes were carcinogenic. Amongst these were chromic acid, trichloroethylene, carbon tetrachloride and other chemicals which directly affected the main organs, such as arsenic and zinc oxide. On top of this were new risks from exposure to gases and vapours, and the even more threatening danger of exposure to ionizing radiation. Fears over the impact of chemical inhalation (ethylene-glycol ethers) in the making of silicon chips in International Business Machines Co. (IBM) led to a media expose which forced the HSE into an enquiry in 2001. The results were inconclusive. In addition, performing detailed repetitive work in electronics under strict time pressure resulted in a high incidence of stress-related complaints.[119]

Ill-health and injury associated with the workplace resulted in massive levels of suffering and hardship, much of it preventable. Williams noted that even the more generous benefits of the National Insurance (Industrial Injuries) Act 1946 only amounted to roughly half the workers' previous salary.[120] As the pressure group Clydeside Action on Asbestos argued this made those affected 'victims twice over' – once as a result of the actual physical harm and disablement, and secondly as a victim of an unfair system of financial compensation. Toxins, carcinogens and injuries (physical and psychological) sustained at work could have devastating impacts upon workers' bodies, with deep ramifications for individuals, families and communities. There were markedly differing levels of impairment, however, and a wide range of experience, with effects and coping strategies varying significantly across a wide spectrum of personal tragedies. Difficulties could be exacerbated, moreover, because rehabilitation services were also very limited in the 1950s and 1960s. At worse, the outcomes could involve quite fundamental mutations in lifestyles, behaviour and identities. Impacts included erosion of physical and mental capacity, loss or change of employment, declining income and standards of living, a collapse of status and self-esteem, a drift towards social exclusion and towards dependency and marginalization as citizens. These transitions were more sudden and traumatic in some cases than others, depending on the nature and pathology of the disease(s) and injuries and the individuals concerned.

Recently, disability studies have done much to establish that those with impairments in our society are socially oppressed, excluded, marginalized and lacking citizenship. This scholarship has developed strong critiques of the state, medical profession and lay policies towards the disabled community in Britain in the nineteenth and twentieth centuries.[121] However, much of this portrayal of the disabled has been constructed from studies of the congenitally impaired, such as those with mental illnesses, those with learning difficulties, and those with loss of faculties such as sight, hearing and speech. Occupational injury and disease hardly feature in the literature.[122] And it is hard to convey the physical pain, emotional trauma and suffering that went along with the damage caused by unhealthy and unsafe workplaces. We examine what this meant for workers, their families and their communities – and how occupational disability stories were framed and narrated in Chapter 3.

## Conclusion

The body was positioned at the ecological core of the workplace and was intimately affected in myriad ways – by the labour process and the toxicity of materials and products, the pressure and intensity of the work, the wider employment environment and the management regime, by relationships with fellow-workers and supervisors, as well as prevailing 'shopfloor' work-health cultures. Employment could be benign, could be profoundly satisfying and health-enhancing, and could be the harbinger of injury, disease and bodily break down. Clearly, at mid-twentieth century when the economy remained dominated by manual labour and the traditional 'heavy' industries remained significant, the workplace could be energy-sapping, dangerous and capable of incubating a wide range of chronic occupational diseases. Perhaps those jobs associated with inhaling toxic dust, chemicals and carcinogens were the most insidious. To a degree workers' bodies were sacrificed at the temple of Fordism – and nowhere was this more evident than in coal mining. The legacy was blighted communities of disabled workers, and of untold and unimaginable pain and suffering as individuals and families coped as best they could with injured and diseased bodies, together with the identity transformations and changes in lifestyles that could entail.[123]

As the economy morphed, so too did the pattern of employment-related injury and disease. Mortality and injury rates dropped sharply as the UK shifted in the second half of the twentieth century to a service sector, knowledge-based economy where non-manual labour predominated in an increasingly deregulated and 'open' market. As an additional 'bonus', the environmental pollution in Britain associated with a carbon-based Fordist economy also dissipated, albeit slowly. Nonetheless, new threats to the body emerged in this changed employment context, with the discovery of new carcinogens in chemical manufacture and asbestos, the growth of repetitive strain injuries (RSI), musculo skeletal disorders (MSD), the epidemic of workplace stress and, latterly, Covid-19. The modern-day stress epidemic in the workplace is just one manifestation of a recurring cycle whereby employment has proven capable of both enhancing health and well-being, whilst making workers ill, disabling and destroying minds and bodies. A recent study has shown how the growth of more insecure and non-standard work since the 1980s has had adverse implications for occupational health, sparking work-related stressors. Stress at work remains a major challenge to occupational health and safety regulators in the UK.[124] The Covid-19 pandemic also deepened pressure at work and stress levels, evident perhaps most starkly in an over-strained NHS where workloads became (and continue to be at the time of writing in 2022/3) intolerable and PPE issues contributed to deadly exposure in the first wave in the UK of March–June 2020. Other sectors experienced sharp upticks in workloads as a consequence of Covid-induced changes in work practices over 2020–2, including teaching in schools, colleges and Higher Education, given the demands of rapidly converting from face-to-face to online teaching of students.

In trying to understand and make sense of this, interpretations range widely within the scholarship on occupational health in what is a hotly contested intellectual landscape. Debates have pivoted around the culpability of corporate capitalism, the extent to which state regulation achieved its objectives, the role of medicine and medical research, whether the trade unions were pro-active enough on health and the extent to which workers' health cultures and attitudes influenced risky and health-threatening behaviour at the point of production. An embodied history of work needs to take account of how workers are positioned within intersecting exploitative systems and cultures which constitute threats to their health and well-being. To understand this we need to explore *both* the mechanisms of capitalist exploitation and managerial pressure within the parameters of a competitive market economy and the prevailing, fluid and mutating work cultures and identities, including how gender, race, ethnicity and age intersect to create an environment of toleration of overwork and risky behaviour which damages bodies. This is where personal testimony is so valuable. It is asserted here that work-life narratives – including oral testimonies and autobiographies – provide eye-witness accounts describing how it felt in this landscape, enabling a window into mutating identities, revealing work and health cultures that became ingrained and ultimately impinged upon the body, and elucidating our understanding of the complex interactions between work, the body, health and emotions in employment, both past and present. This book now turns to such narratives, exploring the ways that those who directly experienced and witnessed such changes navigated and negotiated threats to their bodies whilst at work, and how they told their stories – their ways of narrating – which are so revealing of meanings around the body at work.

# CHAPTER 2
## TALKING DIRTY: NARRATING TOXIC EXPOSURE AND DANGER STORIES

Industrial work left its mark in enduring legacies inscribed upon workers' bodies and minds and in interviews, industrial workers frequently tell accident stories and recall toxic exposures. These speak of the risks and dangers of the work, of witnessing fatal and serious injuries and sometimes reveal their own body scars, mutilations and disabilities. This is what Clyde shipbuilding worker John Allen related in an interview several years ago: 'I've got marks on my body from working in the shipyard.' Recalling working during the Second World War he said: 'You had no safety. They didn't supply you with gloves, they didn't supply goggles. They didn't supply you with helmets. Nothing.'[1] Similarly, London sheet metal worker Fred Hibbs recalled (in an interview in 2010) working in several factories along the Great West Road in London in the 1950s, recounting the hazardous conditions, and how he bore the legacy of his working life, with a permanently injured arm:

> I done this one in, all the muscle's gone. That's supposed to be the muscle but it's gone. I done that one in Danleys in Perivale, lifted up a big block of metal, picked it up ... and this went. It doesn't hurt but I could feel it go, and that was it. ... The bloke, I think he was a first-aider, he says you want to report that. So I said what's the point, it's my fault. There's cranes here, there's lifting tackle here to lift it, so I've gone and messed up me hand.[2]

Fred blamed himself. He also recalled the dust, chemicals and fumes which left him with a respiratory disability: 'I remember that because you had no mask. There was no health and safety there. ... And all of a sudden me lungs went. ... Always bloody working. I wouldn't if I'd known I'd turn out like this.' There is a sense of moral indignation in these recollections. That workers were wronged and harmed by the 'they' Fred refers to – the companies and bosses, who, in hindsight, didn't supply personal protective equipment or care much about workers' well-being. And the legacies of corporate negligence, irresponsibility and economic violence are extensive – as outlined in Chapter 1. This was all *felt* and expressed evocatively in workers' own testimonies. In his recent book on the Park Royal Guinness factory in London, *Voices of Guinness*, Tim Strangleman has acutely observed: 'The workplace environment can make an impression on all the senses – smell, taste, vision, touch and sound – and workers often related their memories through a combination of these.'[3] How industrial blue-collar workers narrated their work experience and their occupational health and safety stories is the theme of this chapter.

## Jobs and Bodies

Emerging from the cataclysm of the Second World War the majority of British workers were employed in manual work, in blue collar jobs. Sixty per cent of the labour force in England and Wales were still manual workers in 1961 (with around 20 per cent non-manual and almost 20 per cent classified as employers, managers and professional workers). However, the job market was diverse. Work experiences ranged across a wide spectrum from the traditional 'heavy industries' and mining, the growing 'sunrise' lighter manufacturing sectors, through to working in shops and offices and the National Health Service and more creative work, such as teaching, to largely unclassified, non-registered (at least as such in the Census) unpaid house and home work – the latter mostly performed by women. And participation in the labour market was changing, towards services and notably with a growing proportion of married women continuing in paid employment in the formal economy for longer periods. How did the last generation of industrial workers relate to their bodies in such contexts and recall their lived experience of work and the hazards, dangers and risks to health that they faced? And how can we interpret this storytelling?

This chapter draws upon work-life interviews of British workers to explore ways that workers remembered and narrated how work impacted upon their bodies, their health and their well-being, including their accident and disease stories. This dovetails with a turn towards the patients' perspective and the personal in medical and health history referred to in the last chapter.[4] The chapter hopefully contributes towards bringing occupational health in line with a historiographical trend towards a focus on discourse, 'lived experience' and the emotional journeys associated with trauma, ill-health and premature death that so often characterized working-class lives at mid-twentieth century. The questions I want to address here are: What kinds of narratives did British industrial workers compose on work and the body? How were risks and dangers remembered? Why were such accident and disease stories constructed? And what can such testimonies tell us about work-health cultures in the workplace; how workers navigated risk and danger? And, can this deepen our understanding of health and safety in the workplace? The argument developed here is that in bearing witness, such testimonies facilitate understanding of the complex relationship between people and their work, the multi-layered effects of work on the body and mind, of the structural violence inherent within the industrial workplace and of prevailing work-health cultures – how industrial work could (perhaps paradoxically) positively forge identities, enhance health and hone fit bodies, whilst simultaneously harming and undermining them.

In this chapter I want to tentatively suggest some ways narrators tell their accident and disease stories, and critically reflect on the themes or motifs that recur in such storytelling. This is what has struck me:

1. *Health-enhancing work narratives*: Some industrial workers' work-life stories emphasized the positive impacts on the body, not the negative. That is the health-enhancing nature of work – especially secure, stable, interesting, decently paid work. Workers tell of the deep attachment to work, a strong work ethic, the intrinsic joys and satisfactions of work, of meaningful and

long-lasting relationships built at work, of their pride and identification in the job and with the product, from making Guinness to making ships. Work thus honed physically fit bodies and enhanced mental health. Perhaps this also speaks to nostalgia (sometimes referred to as 'smokestack nostalgia') in a strand of workers' personal accounts, referring to 'good times', the so-called 'Golden Age' of work, c.1945–75, of relative stability of employment, sharply rising real wages and improving conditions in the context of powerful trade unions pre-Thatcher (1979).

2. *Bearing witness, or social injustice/activist narratives*: Other stories convey a sense of injustice, harm and exploitation of bodies. Here some are framed as morality tales, depicting omnipotent and unscrupulous employers and managers – the 'bosses' – transposed against relatively powerless worker victims in the face of corporate capitalism or narrow-minded small employers in 'back street' businesses – such as the many asbestos insulation contractors that were dotted around port cities. Others in this vein are agency-asserting stories' locating narrators as social actors and representing the trade unions frequently as the 'heroes' or 'guardians' of workers' health and safety on the job, pitted against the managerial 'villains'. Active trade unionists and community occupational health movement activists are most likely to express such stories (but not exclusively so).

3. *Identity building stories and 'graft and sacrifice narratives'*: These are stories that are constructed, or 'composed' to convey a strong sense of self. For male workers, sometimes such stories are expressed in 'macho' ways; risk-taking identifying men as tough guys who could 'take it'. A recurring motif here was maximizing production (and earnings) for the sake of the family irrespective of the cost mentally and physically. Refusing to conform to such 'hard man' values labelled 'others' as lesser men, effeminate and subordinate in working-class culture.

4. *Pragmatism and risk denial accounts*: There were those who argued risks were minimal or non-existent; or 'accidental' and outside anyone's control and could not be avoided. Managers and employers were prone to such risk denial narratives, though some workers also subscribed to variants of this approach to minimalizing risk, or expressed fatalistic acceptance of their lot, or a resigned pragmatism built on long acculturation to the dangers of the work. 'We were brought up with it.' For such workers there was an awareness of risk and danger, but rather than a 'macho' embracing of danger as a marker or badge of masculinity, there was a realistic sense that such risks could be minimized by care, attention and experience on the job – cognizance of the 'danger spots', as oral historian High has argued.[5] So risk and danger were stoically accepted as part and parcel of normal working life. Such workers, as David Walker has argued, were pragmatists rather than tough hard men displaying machismo characteristics.[6]

**Jobs and Bodies**

The range of work-body narratives speaks, perhaps, to the duality, complexity and multi-layered nature of work and its diverse meanings and impacts on health and well-being. Moreover, such ways or styles of work-health storytelling were not necessarily mutually exclusive; rather could overlap, merge and co-exist within one person's testimony. In their health and safety storytelling, women showed a similar range of narrative ways of telling and positioning to men, though there was a tendency to express a markedly more cautious, more intolerant and careful approach to trauma and chronic health risks on the job. Generally, women workers appear to be more risk averse. In part, this appears to be connected to a more gendered familial caring and welfare role, responsible for the reproduction of the family and the general day-to-day health and well-being of the family. The patriarchal exclusion of women from many (though not all) of the most extreme, dangerous and chronically unhealthy jobs through the working of the societal taboo on women doing such work (e.g. working underground in the mines) may also have played a part. Men were more embedded and socialized into prevailing high-risk work cultures in such male-centred work environments, notably in the 'heavy industries'.

### 'Work was a joy': Honing the fit body and mind

Some industrial workers' work-life stories emphasized the *positive* impacts of their work on the body and mind, balancing out the negative. That is the health-enhancing nature of work – especially secure, stable, interesting, decently paid work. This more affirmative narrative, as we've noted, appears to be most evident during the so-called 'Golden Age' of work, c.1945–75 when real wages were growing and trade unions were powerful. Workers tell of the deep attachment to work, a strong work ethic, the intrinsic joys and satisfactions of work, of meaningful and long-lasting relationships built at work, of their pride and identification in the job and with the product, from coal to forging steel, to well spun thread and beautifully crafted woven cloth. And such work could hone physically fit bodies and enhance mental health. Kathy Hind, a wartime worker reflected: 'I worked shovelling coal into the boilers and making sure the heating worked. That was hard work but you kept fit.'[7] Willie Dewar, employed in the North British Locomotive Works, Glasgow reflected: 'Some people said they would quite willingly have worked for nothing in the locomotive industry because it was an interesting, interesting trade to be in.'[8] Similarly, female clothing and textile factory workers invariably expressed a deep sense of gratification in their working lives. Effie Anderson who worked in a Peebles mill from the 1940s to the 1980s reflected: 'Ah enjoyed ma work. I did enjoy ma work.'[9]

This profound intrinsic satisfaction bolstered workers' sense of well-being and was related, in part, to the camaraderie of the industrial workplace; being able to socialize with mates, feeling a sense of performing purposeful work with dignity and a degree of control, earning relatively high and stable wages. For some there was a sense of

**Figure 2.1** Machinists working at Steinberg and Sons gown factory at Hawthorn, Pontypridd, 1969, where, unusually for the 1960s, the company provided a works' nursery for the working mothers' children.
Courtesy of Getty Images.

*relish* working within a piecework payments-by-results wage system where they were rewarded well for working harder. An overwhelming emotion emerging from such accounts is pride. Pride in a job well performed as 'workers not wasters' (as Daniel Wight put it), pride in the role they played in making the final product and confidence in their embodied capacities. 'No kidding you, I was like steel', an Ayrshire miner reflected, 'I was a hard man then'.[10] Scottish miner Tommy Coulter recalled:

> We thought we were the best in the world. We were the elite. When you went tae work at the coal face you, well, we were strong lads, you had tae be … Because of the nature of the work and the nature of lifestyle we could at least hold our own in any, if there was any fisticuffs involved we were quite able to do the business.[11]

These 'affirmative' embodied memories were brought into particularly sharp focus when juxtaposed against workers' reflections on risk and workplace closures, redundancies and premature forced abandonment of work, or transitioning into 'bad' work (lower paid, less skilled, less unionized, more precarious), sometimes with clearly evident health deficits. We will return to such fractured narratives in Chapter 4 on deindustrialization.

## Jobs and Bodies

### Bearing witness: Economic violence and social injustice narratives

Other workers' stories tell of the dangers, hazards and unhealthiness of the industrial workplace, with each industry and even workplace having its own unique characteristics. A recurring motif here is the toll that industrial work has taken upon the body – evident in miners' reiteration of the notion of 'blood on the coal' and anecdotes of accidents and injuries. In their oral testimonies workers also bear witness to the myriad ways in which they have been abused and mistreated by unscrupulous employers and managers seeking to maximize their profit margins. When talking to industrial workers a key element of work-health narratives has been to convey a sense of unfair treatment and moral indignation, of exploitation, of managerial power. In these stories, workers are often expressing an acute awareness of class relations and power dynamics, and of structural economic violence meted out in the workplace: of bodies being abused and profit being put before health. So, bodies are subordinated to the imperatives of production and the profit motive, and workers are induced or incentivized to take risks to maximize earnings in order to make a living – and this had a toll on their bodies, often explicitly recognized, sometimes immediately (with injuries or fatalities from 'accidents'), sometimes long after (as with chronic musculoskeletal disabilities). We are provided with powerful insights from eye-witnesses and those directly affected of the realities of a tough working life in post-war industrial Britain. Detectable here are morality tales of corrupt, irresponsible employers and cunning, villainous managers versus disempowered worker victims and their heroic unions struggling against the odds to protect bodies as best they could.

In telling these stories interviewees are often trying to help us (as interviewers and inexperienced naive 'external' academic observers) understand a different world. As 'outsiders' we are being privileged with these insights from those who directly experienced what it was like. They are taking us on to their shoulders in factories, at the coal face, the shipyard and the steel mill; telling of the prevailing work milieu and work-health cultures. They recall the hazards and how corners were cut by managers, supervisors and workers, and how and why the risks were rationalized and tolerated. Oral historians Portelli and High have both attested to the *frequency* of stories about bodies in very different contexts: the dangerous, health-sapping work of Harlan County USA mines (where 'black lung' was endemic) and the somewhat more benign context of a Canadian paper mill, where, High notes in *One Job Town*: 'accident stories quickly emerged as a major topic of conversation'.[12] The same was certainly true of heavy industry interviewees in coal, steel, the railways and shipyards in the UK – where bodies featured frequently in storytelling. The motivation here by narrators was and is to *act as witnesses* – to put their knowledge, their version of events, into the public domain, on the record. And to identify and call out unfair treatment and injustices. There was outrage expressed here about a lack of reciprocity and a kind of moral economy being breached here, where employers and managers were identified as failing in their responsibilities; in their duty of care to the workers.

In their reminiscences workers are evoking their industrial workplaces. They are recalling and to some degree reimagining and reinterpreting the space and environment they once inhabited – remembering the stench and heat of the pit; the deafening noise of the factory; squinting to work in an ill-lit workshop; the fumes and dust; the strain on their muscles and nerves. In their remembering and through their dialogue they are taking us on this journey, so we can see and understand. Recalling first impressions of the pit or the steelworks could involve admissions of fear and trepidation. John Foley entered the Ravenscraig Steelworks in 1962 having previously worked with the local council, providing school meals. He described the transition to the overwhelming noise and heat of the steelworks as 'frightening … me being [having previously] working wae … 14 women … never, never seen steel being made, anything like that at all. In there, the first week, terrified'.[13] Over time, most workers became accustomed and socialized into toiling within such dangerous environments, accruing experience, recognizing the danger points, taking care, weighing risks carefully. If a worker was killed on the job invariably the work continued – even coal miners whilst they might down tools, almost always would be back on the job the next day.

The 'hell' metaphor crops up frequently in such descriptions of heavy industry – such as steelworks and mines – and the fragility of flesh, muscle and bone within this hostile environment. Entering the furnace of Ravenscraig steelworks for the first time another interviewee commented: 'Ah thought ah wis in hell'.[14] Owen Lilly recalled his first impressions of working in the Turner & Newall asbestos factory in Clydebank in the mid-1960s: 'I'll never forget til the day I die the first impression of that place. It was like walking into Dante's inferno without the fire. It was just hell. The noise was unbelievable. The size of the machinery was awe-inspiring …'[15] Owen went on to recount how they had to work without masks sweeping up despite 'clouds of stoor [dust] everywhere'. Tragically both Owen and his wife Margaret later died of asbestos-related diseases, traced back to Owen's working life.

Such eye-witness testimonies lay bare the realities of irresponsible and abusive power relationships – economic violence – at the point of production and the limited resources that workers could bring to bear upon their situation. The space in which workers toiled and the environment in which bodies were located were frequently vividly recalled, with dust, death and disability recurring motifs in workers' work-life narratives. Miners spoke frequently of the fatalities underground and the occurrence of injuries and chronic, disabling disease. Other workers – dockers, shipbuilders, construction workers – in the UK (and elsewhere) recalled asbestos dust suspended like a 'fog' or falling like 'snow' in their workplaces in the 1950s, 1960s and 1970s, and of playing with the material – for example, making fake beards and moustaches of asbestos and throwing 'monkey dung' (asbestos cement paste) 'snowballs'.[16] Dark humour became a way of dealing with workplace risks and dangers, and was evident within heavy industry workers' stories, apparent, for example, in Billy Connolly's tales of shipyard life.[17] For some, such as dockers up to the 1970s, the insecurity of earnings provided an additional incentive to take the work as it came, irrespective of the risk.[18] For others, danger was something taken for granted. John Hopkins worked in stone quarries in Warwickshire from 1958 to 1972 experiencing most jobs from the stone-processing plant, shot-firing (explosives) to driving the huge excavators and dump trucks. In an interview in 2006 he

**Figure 2.2** Pouring a two ton casting, Osborn Hadfields Steel Founders, Sheffield, South Yorkshire, 1968.
Courtesy of Getty Images.

spoke eloquently of the work as 'beautiful' and 'magical'. He also recalled little regard for health and safety on the job and of workers being allowed to be positioned well inside the safe distance when the rock explosives were detonated. He recalled the fatal accident of a colleague, Babby Adams. The quarries were poorly unionized and there was a bonus system with extra payment for exceeding 1000 tons extracted in a day, providing an inducement to over work and compromise safety. John left the job in 1972 to work in the local Jaguar car plant.[19]

Industrial workers accrued much intimate and intuitive lay knowledge about risks of injury and the toxic nature of the materials they worked with. They knew they got breathless and had persistent coughs from inhaling dust, or burnt from chemicals, or contracted TB or some other infection from someone they worked with. However, medical knowledge was contested and information could be withheld from workers or only selective (and sometimes misleading) information about hazards was leaked out (such as the mythical benign nature of white compared to blue and brown asbestos).

And sometimes the complexities of disease aetiology were hard to fathom, or workers had more immediately pressing concerns preoccupying them. The extent to which industrial workers were informed and knowledgeable on the extent of hazard risk and potential harm to their bodies varied. As Taafe has persuasively argued in her analysis of occupational health and safety at the Chatham Dockyards there were managerial communication and supervision issues and levels of ignorance amongst the workers on the degree of risk associated with asbestos and radiation.[20] In Walker's oral history study of Glasgow dockers, narrators expressed a clear sense that handling asbestos in hessian bags was thought to be harmless up to the 1970s – because that's what they were told. One docker, Thomas O'Conner, angrily recalled, in hindsight:

> The employer had known since 1947 how dangerous it was but omitted tae let us know. And then they started 'oh, it's only this type of asbestos it's blue asbestos that's bad' … But eventually it ended up on pallets with plastic around about it and then eventually [late 1970s] we refused tae work with it at all … They knew from the middle 1940s and never cracked a light … we know the reason, profit, nothing else, it's about money.[21]

Subsequently, as Walker has shown, it was found in court cases that the employers – the National Dock Labour Board – were well aware through their medical branch of the hazards of working with asbestos and other such materials.[22]

The story of asbestos manufacturers, and how long they were aware of the hazards of asbestos, is now well known. Lay knowledge was also extensive – with a sensitivity towards the issue of asbestosis by the middle of the twentieth century and the risk of cancer by the 1980s. Still, those exposed *indirectly* to the materials could be ignorant of the level of risk they faced. This was the case with electrician Barrie Rigby who worked in mills and schools in Lancashire in the 1960s and 1970s (and who later moved on to get an Open University degree and became a lecturer). Barrie was diagnosed with mesothelioma in 2003, aged sixty-one, and died in July 2005. His wife Vera recalled a conversation they had with their compensation claim solicitor:

> Then I remember saying to her [the solicitor], but how can you sue these people if they didn't know asbestos was dangerous? Well then, she laughed you see, 'cause she said they've known asbestos … I think is it first recorded death about 1926 or something. Well we didn't know that. But she filled us in on all this. And she said, it's been known for … I don't think we knew 'cause obviously by this time it was banned in terms of any new stuff in the country. We didn't know that. I remember Barrie saying, 'that is amazing what she told us. To think I was a senior lecturer, lecturing for the Institute of Electrical Engineering [IEE]' – which he was still doing because he still did IEE lectures even after the surgery and the chemo and everything – 'and I didn't know'. That amazed us that it was never … He didn't know and he was teaching. Amazing that. We'd no idea. She gave us more information than we'd ever known, because obviously she was familiar with it all.[23]

**Jobs and Bodies**

Female textile workers also attest to intuitive lay knowledge, but also a lack of in-depth awareness *at the time* of the long-term impacts of their labour processes (e.g. on joint wear and tear) and work environment (e.g. dust and noise) on their bodies over the duration of their working lives.[24] Later in life, narrators bore witness to the impact this had on their bodies, often long after they had ceased to be employed. Environmental historian Rob Nixon has referred to this as 'slow violence'.[25] Industrial workers tell their 'exposure' and accident stories and of the tragic effects – the injuries, deaths, disabilities and the curtailed and destroyed lives that ensued (we will return to this issue of toxic 'legacy' in more detail in the following chapter and in Chapter 4). Legal firms preparing compensation cases collected sworn oral and written statements detailing exactly where claimants were exposed to the injurious products, labour processes or practices. For example, in his mesothelioma compensation testimony Mike Eason catalogued his exposure whilst working as an instrument engineer at the Barton Power Station in Lancashire in 1965:

On the firing floor there were six massive boilers which were fed with very fine coal … I spent a lot of time on the firing floor. In those days they did not have control rooms with panels … the instrumentation and meters would be in place on the relevant plant and you would have to go to the instrumentation/meters to check that they were working and if they were not you would fix them. … You would have to work in cramped spaces and to get things you would have to crawl over or under pipes which were lagged with asbestos to gain access to the instrumentation. You needed to clear asbestos insulation around the instrumentation to get access to the instrument or the meter itself. You needed to check at the site whether it was working and if not whether it could be fixed then and there. If not you would have to remove it from the piping and take it back to the workshop to repair it there and then replace it. You therefore had to clear the asbestos lagging from around the instruments. The lagging would go right up to the instruments and sometimes on to the instrument itself but not so as to cover the face of the instrument or the meter which would prevent you from taking a reading. To remove the asbestos insulation you would try and get an end of the insulation rope material. The material was wound on to the pipework and could be unwound a few inches back so that you could get back to where you needed to work. The material was old, dry, dusty, pieces would come of, it would disintegrate. It was a dusty job. The material would get on to your fingers and on to your arms and on to your boiler suit. It was very dry in the firing floor and the dust that was generated would be inhaled because you were looking closely at what you were doing and working with your hands. … I did not do this sort of job here everyday at the power station but would have done it every week and quite often a couple of times a week. It was a typical job for me to do and that's why they employed me … I have no doubt that I was exposed to asbestos whilst I was working at the Barton Power Station when maintaining and repairing instrumentation and meters.[26]

The testimony provides a frank and evocative picture of toxic exposure on the job. His wife recalled Mike worked at this time with a hard hat and goggles, but not with any mask.

In their oral narratives workers recalled daily abuses of power and the irresponsibility of management. They recalled feeling pressured to work with toxic materials, to 'cut corners', ignore safety regulations and maximize productivity. This might be because of piecework wage or bonus systems – or simply because there was limited alternative employment. The obligations of the family breadwinner hung heavy on many male industrial workers.[27] In this sense these workers were victims of a Fordist, productionist culture that exalted hard graft and the maximization of earnings at all costs. The problem was primarily a structural one, the product of an exploitative system pivoting around profit maximization and the abuse of economic power. Also relevant here is the persistence of a sense of insecurity amongst the post-war generation of workers who could recall the mass unemployment of the interwar economic depression. This diminished over time as that generation died off. Insecurity re-emerges though during the 1980s with increasing mine and factory closures and the acceleration of deindustrialization in the heavy industries in the UK (and elsewhere) and the decline of manufacturing in general.

Another important recurring theme in post-war work-health testimonies relates to the gap that existed between the official statutory regulatory regime and what actually happened in practice on the shop floor and coal face, far away from the regulators' gaze. Coal miners spoke, for example, of subverting the attempts to monitor dust levels in their working spaces, of 'interference' with the equipment, including throwing coats over the monitor. In factories, the Factory Acts provided some protection, but there were ways around many of the provisions. Cleaning whilst machinery was in motion, for example, though officially banned and illegal (in most cases), was widespread.[28] A T&N asbestos employee recalled that in the 1960s:

> When you went in the door of Turner's Asbestos there was a Factory Act with all the stuff. The only problem was that you couldnae see through it with the layer of asbestos cement on the glass you know … You never got any warnings about brown asbestos; you never got any warnings about white asbestos. Ah, you weren't told that when you took it home on your clothes your wife was going to breathe it in as well.[29]

An Electrical Trade Union representative complained in December 1967: 'What we find is that despite the fact that certain statutory regulations are laid down and certain safeguards are laid down, these things are ignored by both the firm and the men.'[30]

On building sites, health and safety regulations were ignored with impunity, whilst sometimes fire regulations were cited to trump safety regulations, as with the demands of some clients for enhanced fire protection in high-rise buildings necessitating in the 1950s and 1960s additional layers of asbestos spraying and panelling.[31] Some joiners clamoured for asbestos work in the high-rise building boom because of the high rates of pay offered to work with the material.[32] Years later demolition work on the same flats

## Jobs and Bodies

could be equally lucrative. In 1984, new regulations were introduced stipulating that those who removed asbestos had to be licensed. A labourer who worked at the time recalled how some firms used the official licensed companies to take away *some* of the asbestos (to appear as if they were fulfilling statutory demands) whilst expecting their labourers to remove the majority: 'these cunts were getting fucking £4 an hour, and we were getting £4 for a shift [a day]. You know that's just to keep their books right. They were just trying to keep it under the carpet sort of thing ...' He added, 'we just carried on.'[33] Lauren Ross, wife of a joiner (Frank, born 1946) who died of mesothelioma, recalled how her husband had been lied to by the company who had convinced him that asbestolux fire doors contained no asbestos (when they had roughly 25 per cent). She continued with a story about a job he had at a local school:

> But he was doing this job removing one of these panels and apparently he thought they were asbestos so he stopped the job. He spoke to his chargehand and said, 'these are asbestos, what do we do'? So he said 'oh don't worry I'll go back and I'll find out. Have your brew and I'll get back to you'. And he came back with a white paper overall and a white paper mask and said, 'this is ok'. Now he didn't tell this to me – he just carried on working – until the following Monday, because the school had been closed for the holidays. And he went back to the job on Monday and they said, 'oh you can't carry on'. He said, 'why'? He said, 'because the children are in and they've had to bring in a specialist team to do it'. When he told me, I went absolutely mad. I said, 'why did you work with it'? He said, 'because they said it'd be all right'. I said, 'but it's really, really dangerous'. I think from that point in his life, because I'd had a bit of a hissy fit, I think he was probably more aware from then.[34]

Peter Lancaster (born 1940) ran a building firm in Bolton that specialized in shop fitting. He recalled that awareness of asbestos grew over time, but that in the 1960s and 1970s there was much ignorance:

> Q. *And you were saying that as time went on you became aware of asbestos?*
> A (Peter): Yes we were more aware. More awareness.
> Q. *So when did that start to happen Peter, when would you start to be aware of the dangers?*
> A (Peter): The dangers of it? Well, do you know, we used to use a product called Asbestolux. Now whether that contained asbestos or not. We used to put it on the stallrisers, that's up by the window on shops, when you're tiling. Now in all honesty yes when you ask me about whether I've worked with it that I have. We used to put this Asbestolux underneath, 'cause it were quicker than wiring and rendering it. Wiring it is putting expanding metal on and then they put coats of rendering on. So that – we did use it then, in all honesty. But what Asbestolux contained I don't know. It obviously must have had some asbestos in for them to refer to asbestos. It was a soft, softish

material, but it didn't absorb moisture on the face of it, I remember that. And we used to seal it and stick mosaic on and all sorts of things. I would say, certainly once my lads had come with me, without a shadow of a doubt, it was known then. In the 1980s I would say, early 1980s.[35]

Peter later in the interview recalled seeing other workers ignoring asbestos on site to get the job done, and, like in the shipyards, those working in the vicinity could be exposed to asbestos dust:

I said to him, 'that's asbestos'. 'Aye it's only a bit', he said, 'and I'm boarding it this afternoon'. And he covered it up. See shopfitters did not want these jobs to stop. If they'd discovered a little bit they'd shut the site down ... whilst he knew the instructions ... what he had to do, he covered it up. It just went on then ... I didn't want my own sons in there exposed to anything. But we were working downstairs. The trouble with shops is the minute they get them they've got to be turned over that fast it's just a mad scramble, everybody's in together and irrespective of whether you are working on floors they can be putting air conditioning up above you and all sorts. It really is a mad scramble.[36]

Another worker who was employed officially by a licenced asbestos removal firm recalled cutting corners at an asbestos stripping job at a coal mine in Fife as the hoses to damp down the dust would not reach down the shaft:

So we were told 'just take it aff [dry], just stick it. You were supposed tae put it in a black bag; then another bag; then a red bag with 'asbestos' on it. But we were told 'just miss out the red asbestos bag. We would wait until they [the miners] were away down the shaft ... That was one thing we kept quiet.[37]

This has to be understood, I think, within a cultural framework – a milieu that facilitated the tolerance and persistence of abusive economic violence. Workers were habituated to undertaking dangerous work, to accepting a high-risk threshold and to being part of a fiercely independent working-class culture that frowned upon those who complained or 'made a fuss'. On the building site of the highest flats in Europe at the time the Transport and General Workers' Union (TGWU) official who warned the men of the dangers of asbestos exposure was told to 'get to fuck', adding 'you're always moaning and groaning about something'.[38] He ended his story with a rueful comment that all of the ten joiners that he warned, nicknamed 'white mice' because of the dust, were now dead. Others took on more dangerous work because there was a financial incentive to do so and they felt they needed the money. Chatham Dockyard boilermaker Tim Robson explained what contributed to his radiation poisoning:

They were asking for volunteers so I agreed ... The money was better than what I usually got. I received £50 a week for working on a frigate, and £100 a week for working on a [nuclear] sub. As a young man hoping to start a family I thought it was a good idea to volunteer. The extra money was a lot then.[39]

Tim died of non-Hodgkin's lymphoma, aged just thirty-nine, in 1994.

A dominant (or hegemonic) mode of 'hard man' masculinity was forged in such heavy industry workplaces and construction sites and many, though not all workers subscribed to this. Gender roles were deeply ingrained. Having to conform to accepted norms and 'man-up' on the job could affect behaviour. As Kris Paap has argued of the US construction industry, the work made 'the worker look and *feel* like a man'.[40] Taafe found a vibrant masculine work culture in her study of the Chatham Dockyard in the UK, with 75 per cent of her questionnaire respondents agreeing this existed and that it could compromise workers' health and safety.[41] Wage payment systems and incentives encouraged this in the dockyards. Taafe argued: 'health and safety measures increased the time it took to complete work and with performance based incentives, such as piecework and payment by results, the temptation to avoid obstructions in order to earn more money was always present.'[42] Stakhanovite grafting was exalted within working-class communities in Britain (and elsewhere), where the 'top producers' and highest earners were lauded and praised.[43] One Clydeside sheet metal worker who started work in 1942 reflected upon his life in a 1999 interview:

> Being a man with no education, the only thing you had was the muscle in your arm and what experience you got with metal, and a very willingness to work. I would go in and say to people, 'Yes I'll do that in that time.' And whatever it took to do that [job] I would do it.[44]

Those who sought to protect and pace themselves could be pilloried as lesser men and subjected to peer pressure to take risks, to compete, to conform and to maximize earnings. Such ingrained gender roles were what was expected of men in the performance of their 'provider' and 'breadwinner' responsibilities that were central to mid-twentieth-century working-class masculinities. Such behaviour was invariably condoned by employers and management, rather than challenged. However, this was also accepted as an integral, immutable part of working-class life in the mid-twentieth century. Workers were socialized into this. As Portelli observed in his wonderful oral history of coal miners in Harlan County, there was 'a cultural disposition' amongst miners to embrace managerial profit maximization through a culture of hard graft.[45] Such risks were part of the fabric of manual working lives in industry, in the UK and elsewhere.

Risk was influenced intimately by the wider context of work, politics, culture and society. In 'Third World' and developing nations, poverty and short life expectancy came into play. As one young Indian asbestos factory worker commented in an interview: 'I am not going to die immediately. Who knows what my future is.'[46] In India, the casual and contract workers were the most vulnerable and were forced to accept risks. Mangabhai Patel worked insulating boilers in Ahmedabad until his asbestosis forced him to quit the job. He recalls: 'As a casual worker you cannot even ask for anything,

**Figure 2.3** Foreman being raised from sewer repair workings twenty-five feet underground in London, 1954.
Courtesy of Getty Images.

your job is very insecure. Casual workers are treated very badly, given low wages and the most dangerous kinds of jobs.'[47] Many immigrant workers brought something of these experiences, different values and work cultures when they relocated to the UK. Power imbalances constrained choices, even in the developed economies. As one postwar Clydeside worker put it: 'It was like fighting an atomic war with a bow and arrow, you know. You hadnae a chance.'[48] Early to mid-twentieth-century trade unionism partly embraced and reflected machismo attitudes – whereas later, from the mid-1970s, unions were more liable to challenge misogyny and provide a counterpoise to a high risk-taking work culture. Again, the oral testimonies elucidate a range of behaviour and ways of telling about unions, resistance and activism. This is explored more in the first section of Chapter 7.

At the point of production there was a tension between protecting the body and conserving labour power, on the one hand, and taking risks and pushing bodies to the

## Jobs and Bodies

limit in order to maximize production (and hence earnings), 'get on' (progressing one's career) and to fulfil managerial expectations, on the other. In some of the interviews conducted with asbestos and chemical workers the tone fizzes with bitterness, resentment and anger; in others, there is a quiet stoicism, pragmatism and fatalistic acceptance of one's lot. David Walker conducted a wonderful interview with a Glasgow worker who was employed in a notoriously dangerous Glasgow chemical plant where his father worked and got him a start. Referring to White's chemical factory in Rutherglen, Richard Fitzpatrick recalled: 'I really didnae think it was a place to be workin' in tae be honest wi' ye ... It wis a job and it wis money'. He was asked if he felt fearful on the job and responded: 'Naw, naw, I wisnae frightened about anything. I was well bred as a worker.' Walker makes the point that Fitzpatrick's testimony shows industrial workers had little choice but to tolerate the hazards of the job, becoming socialized and inured to risk; indeed work and danger were synonymous and had to be accepted in order to earn a living.[49] Both Richard Fitzpatrick and his father lost their septum as a result of inhaling chromate fumes in the plant, for which they respectively received £32 and £75 (posthumously) in compensation.

The idea that employers or managers could be aware of the risks long before workers were told of them were repeated story lines in the oral testimonies, as was the perception

**Figure 2.4** Ex-chemical industry worker Richard Fitzpatrick at the time of his oral history interview with David Walker, August 2004.
Courtesy of David Walker.

that what had happened constituted intentional killing or maiming predicated upon prior knowledge. 'They made us work with poisonous materials and never told us', a Clydeside asbestos insulation engineer recalled.[50] Some used the phrase 'murder'. Clearly, evidence and knowledge that have accumulated since exposure have influenced the way people remember and recount workplace conditions and trauma. Whilst this did not register with my co-researcher Ronnie Johnston or I as clearly as it should have in the late 1990s when conducting the first phase of our research on asbestos, for *Lethal Work*, in retrospect (and from the re-reading of these interviews) there is much evidence of what has been called the 'cultural circuit'. Memories were framed with reference to later media and trade union exposures of the deadly risks of working with asbestos and were influenced by knowledge accumulation that had occurred since the personal experiences being recalled (some of which had occurred forty or more years previously). One landmark TV documentary that clearly made an impact (and mentioned by several interviewees) was *Alice: Fight for Life,* the poignant tragic story of a woman's lingering death from mesothelioma that screened on British TV in 1982. This hard-hitting, prize-winning, ninety-minute film made for harrowing viewing, particularly the interview footage from Alice Jefferson's deathbed. As McCulloch and Tweedale acknowledge: 'It was recognized as a path-breaking work that had put Britain (and other countries) on notice that asbestos was a major hazard. No one would ever look at asbestos in quite the same way again.'[51]

Industrial workers frequently articulated in their oral testimonies accrued lay knowledge and experience of hazards and toxins and of being 'savvy', sensitive and intuitively aware. Older experienced workers would pass down this knowledge to younger, new 'green' workers and apprentices, pointing out hazards and advising care, attention and 'safety first'. In turn, younger fitter workers might help out older workers whose physical capacities were waning with age. These values were not contradictory to working-class masculine cultural norms, but rather co-existed with them. It was accepted that there was a need to look after bodily capacity, not over-work systematically and not take unnecessary risks which might endanger yourself and other workers. 'On the whole', health and safety officer Jenny Constant reflected, 'people have a high level of self-preservation. They don't actually want to kill or injure themselves, however cavalier they may appear.'[52] As David Walker argued with respect to his oral history of dockers and chemical workers: 'The evidence provided by these respondents is that they did not seek risks but rather, where possible, took what limited action they could to avoid the most obvious dangers.'[53] Some voted with their feet and left when they couldn't tolerate the hazards or the harm they perceived being inflicted on their bodies. A Chatham dockyard worker (who started as a rivet boy/labourer in 1937) recalled in an interview with Emma Taaffe:

> I was a person that was conscious of this thing and I was always bunging my ears up with cotton wool right from the very beginning so I didn't become stone deaf, but I left the Dockyard at the age of 60 … I was told that if I carried on for another five years I'd be stone deaf. I was told that by a specialist and when he told me that he

## Jobs and Bodies

said this is just between me and you as my patient, he said, you'd be stone deaf if you carry on with this for another five years. So I retired a week after 60 years of age.[54]

Whilst many dangers in industry were unpredictable, with the guidance of their elders and with the accruing of experience over time industrial workers usually got to know many of the more obvious hazards. For example, from the look and sound of the coal seams and supporting beams, or the sound of machinery not working properly, or the sight of insidious dust floating in the air. James McGrath summed up almost forty years working on the docks:

> See [clears throat] danger was a thing that ye were brought up wi' on the dock. If we worked at plates coming down wi' the garbs ye were always ... we knew it was dangerous but ye were always .... keep yer eye out and most jobs done that ... it was just a thing and it took maybe 5 years but after you were in that dock ye became yer own boss, ye became ... look after yerself. There were some jobs ye couldnae do anything about like .... a wire bursting on a winch, just getting too much pressure, BANG. But other things [clears throat] you could, you always looked after yersel and yer mates, ye know, ye went down there and you looked and if it was dangerous somebody would say 'Watch yer head' 'Watch that bulkhead there, ye might go over it' ye know, things like that.[55]

Still a common, recurring motif was lack of knowledge about the *extent* of the dangers, especially relating to long-term chronic disease – chemicals, radiation and asbestos included. The injustice being meted out here was around knowledge – that the employers had it; knew about the toxicity of asbestos, for example, but kept that from the workers; were dishonest; obscuring the risk; trying to prevent the truth coming out – as in stopping John Todd – 'communist' – getting a platform and being heard.[56] Peter Lancaster reflected on being taken around the local locomotive works on a school trip, in the mid-1950s, aged fourteen or fifteen:

> We even went round there from school, a little trip ... because then employment was plentiful. And they took us round to like show us what it were like to work there. And I always remember looking up, and these guys on this great big platform, and they were stripping asbestos from the inside of this tanker. ... Yes ... About fifteen, fourteen, fifteen, might have been younger. It might have just been an educational trip round there. But yeah I always remember that bit of it, where you looked up and there's these guys ripping out this stuff. You know, I mean such danger. I mean they wouldn't let kids go within a million miles of that now, let alone grown men doing it. So it just shows that even just in my lifetime there's been no awareness whatsoever up to a certain point ...[57]

Many of these accident and disease stories were emotionally charged, and understandably so. Some of the interviews we did with asbestos workers, shipyard workers and coal miners were consumed with rage over illness, disability and fatalities; in others the tone was quiet resignation and fatalistic acceptance of their lot. An asbestos cement factory worker reflected: 'That employment did something wrong to me.'[58] Discovery of and confirmation that employers were aware of the risks long before workers were told – as Tom McGrath commented on – were repeated themes in the oral testimonies. What we are being told is that something could have been done about it, that this wasn't inevitable and that action wasn't forthcoming. This structural exploitation is important to emphasize and weigh in against the 'cultural' arguments. The work environment and conditions were usually imposed upon workers from above – this was managerial responsibility, areas of employers' power and control. Workers might contest this, but their capacity to do so in a great many industrial workplaces in the post-war decades was limited.

Amongst the economic violence and social injustice narratives were those generated by trade union and political activists, advocates and disease movement activists. Here invariably narrators are making the connections between stories of bodily harm and injustice and the need for action, mobilization and change. Here the personal is expressed as political. Narrators emphasize injustice and exploitation and tell us what they did about it or tried to do about it. They are conveying that they didn't just passively accept what was happening, but took action; organized and mobilized and sometimes changed things – from walking out of the job; refusing to work with toxic materials; going on strike, getting organized and campaigning. In these stories, it was usually the trade union or campaigning group that were represented as the protectors or 'guardians' of workers' bodies juxtaposed in a binary opposite against the exploitative employer/manager – the 'villains' in the story who put profit before health. For example, Phyllis Craig, welfare rights officer at Clydeside Action on Asbestos (CAA), shaped her story in this way, as did National Union of Mineworkers' (NUM) President Nicky Wilson. In discussing asbestos exposure and resulting ARD mortality Phyllis Craig squarely laid the blame on exploitative management in the shipyards, construction sites and other exposure points, talking of 'others killing them' and 'greed' as a primary motive, adding government complicity and regulatory caution as contributory factors.[59] Similarly, in a witness seminar on health issues in coal mining NUM President Nicky Wilson spoke of the culpability of the private coal owners before nationalization and then the National Coal Board (NCB) in the epidemic of dust-related respiratory disability that characterized coalfield communities. He reflected on the injustice of this, commenting 'you can't buy back health'.[60] He went on to emphasize and centre the pivotal role of the miners' trade unions historically in campaigning on workmen's compensation, improved prevention in the Mines Acts and on rehabilitation and the welfare of the disabled in mining communities. We will return to this in more detail in Chapter 7 on health and safety activism.

So, a dominant narrative – a way of storytelling – was bearing witness to bodies being harmed and the economic violence, unfairness and injustice in this, breaching (as we've noted) a kind of moral economy where employers and managers were expected to be responsible, to have a 'duty of care' and look after workers' bodies. This was influenced by

## Jobs and Bodies

changing societal expectations and standards. Folk were remembering the past through the prism of a more health-conscious present, with vastly improved OHS standards and regulation by the time they were interviewed. This influenced how stories of *past* risk and exposure on the job were framed. The 'cultural circuit' was evident here: narrators might refer to their being 'no health and safety back then' implicitly comparing the present to the past. With a long history of mine and factory regulation stretching back to the mid-nineteenth century, and workmen's compensation laws in place from the end of the nineteenth century this was patently untrue. However, this was how many narrators saw it – their subjective reality; their 'structures of feeling', as Raymond Williams famously put it.[61] And there is some truth in this if we compare the pre-1974 HSWA scenario with what followed, and take in to account the unevenness of the regulatory regime and the vast gulf between legislation and actual practice on the shop floor, the building site, shipyard and deep underground far from the regulators' gaze in the pits. For others, the modern-day compensation litigation culture made them reticent to admit any individual responsibility or cultural influences on risk behaviour in the past. It is important to be aware (as researchers deploying oral history methodologies) of the 'cultural circuit' and its influence on the construction of memory. Equally, workers in an interview context are perfectly capable of independent reconstruction and differentiating between such influences and their lived reality as they perceive it. Moreover, the reality of their damaged bodies bore witness to the very real physical and mental legacies of industrial work. These are not just imagined discourses. They tell of an almost lost world now, and how workers' bodies were positioned within it, their sensory perception of the work and the impacts of it – joyous and fulfilling; traumatic and chronic.

Interviewees wanted the harms they experienced in post-war workplaces to be recognized; to be on record – hence the prevalence of accident and disease stories in their testimonies; the frequency of embodied stories. This was testament to the ways that heavy industrial workplaces in their heyday could injure, damage and pollute workers bodies, whilst also engendering a sense of joy, pride and fulfilment in skilled, strenuous and productive work. In talking and telling in their vernacular, ex-industrial workers want us to know and understand how it felt; how it was; how it affected them – to take us into those spaces they spent their lives in and were so important in the construction of their identities.

### 'Graft and sacrifice narratives': Identity construction/composure in accident and disease stories

This brings me to another point: some that narrators use their stories to build and project an image of themselves; to convey their identities. We are familiar with theories of 'composure' through the pioneering work of oral historians like Dawson, Thomson, Summerfield and Abrams. Whilst relating the very real damage that work inflicted on bodies and identifying injustice and the mechanisms of economic violence, it is also evident that narrators were projecting a sense of self in their work-body stories;

constructing identities that they were comfortable with to achieve composure. Working-class narrators are invariably very capable of taking control of the interview; exerting their authority; finding ways to tell the stories they want to tell; subverting, when they wish, the interview questionnaire/agenda. In this way they are expressing what Carol Riessman has called 'a performative self'.[62]

Constructing masculinity in discourse or narration was evident in interviews with male industrial war workers, as we argued in *Men in Reserve*.[63] Civilian working men often felt emasculated not being in uniform in wartime, so what we see recurring is the discursive construction of a sense of manliness in stories that emphasized the dangers of wartime work, the risks, the long hours, the ways they put their bodies on the line. Fred Clark, an aircraft wood machinist recalled: 'I collapsed meself. 1941. Ulcerated throat and tonsils. Which the doctor said was the first sign of a nervous breakdown. It was the hours we was putting in ... We wasn't tired, we was just bloody walking dead!'[64] Similarly aircraft factory worker Derek Sims recalled the numbing graft and fatigue of wartime: 'The long, the hours were ... oh they were, they were killers really. When I think about it, we coped with them ... and I'm sure there was an awful lot of illness, that, you know, we never knew about.'[65] D.C.M. Howe, a wartime aircraft fitter at Vickers Aviation, commented: 'Once we started then there were no days off at all. It was seven days a week for days and days on end ... But everyone really got down to it. It was amazing the amount of work ... We used to churn out twenty four, twenty five aircraft in one small place like that ... in a week.'[66]

There was also a tendency in their stories about wartime work to define their masculine industrial bodies as superior to others; to position themselves as more productive than women or 'effete' inexperienced dilutee men drafted on to the shop floor or the mine. Glasgow chemical worker Richard Fitzpatrick, who we have already encountered, reflected: 'They [female workers] were mostly out in the yard y'know, doing odds and ends, but never in the furnace shop or the crystal house or the store. Once the war finished the women all disappeared, y'know, bar the, where you made your breakfast, the women worked in there.'[67] Whilst William Ryder, employed during the war in Woolwich Arsenal, London, said about women wartime workers:

> Ah only they were more or less cleaners. They used to keep the gangways clean and that sort of thing. It was hardly the hardest job in the world. They were a nuisance. Well you could never find them when you wanted them. [laughter] You had to keep your eye on them ... It was all little stuff they were fiddling about with. Yes, little bits and pieces. I was more or less dealing with hundreds of tons.[68]

These men were expressing their manly credentials through performative stories of toughness, stoicism and resilience, of their graft and sacrifice as wartime workers; telling us that they could 'take it'. Men were also responding to peer pressure to conform to societal and work-culture norms. In some cases, for example, workers would refuse to wear safety equipment; harnesses, helmets, masks, goggles, etc. as protecting bodies was deemed to be effeminate behaviour – and likely to be viciously censured by other

## Jobs and Bodies

working men. Willie Dewar asserted that in wartime fellow workers in the North British Locomotive works in Glasgow rarely wore protective gloves, helmets or goggles. He claimed this was to avoid risking slurs against their manliness from workmates: "Oh he's a 'jessie', you know. A 'jessie' was, well, like a woman, you know … The majority of them [workers] that was sort of child's play to wear gloves, 'oh no', or wear glasses. 'No, no, but nowadays you're forced to do that.'"[69] Whilst shipyard worker Thomas Stewart recalled of American shipyard workers: 'you would scoff at them working with gloves … daft!'[70]

Heavy manual work forged masculinities and men developed a complex relationship with dangerous, health-threatening manual work, to some extent embracing the very processes that consumed their bodies – as Connell argues – in order to fulfil manly roles.[71] Peer pressure determined that men should act in certain ways, including taking risks or taking work to fulfil the breadwinner role even when this work was known to be dangerous. Those unwilling to take risks to maximize earnings might be castigated and pilloried – as effeminate, 'cissies', 'glundies' and needing 'iron jelloids' – as a Yorkshire miner recalled in his autobiography.[72] This is tied to a powerful, pervasive and enduring work ethic. Fulfilling the breadwinner role conferred status in working-class communities, as Wight's important ethnographic study elucidates.[73] The risks taken and the 'sacrifice' of men's bodies could, in turn, legitimize male power within the home and family. Whilst most industrial workers strove to avoid or at least minimize risks, it remained the case that bodily damage in this productionist and competitive work culture was economically *and* culturally incentivized.

Gendered inter-subjectivities were also evident in such interviewing. In a revealing critical reflection on two separate interviewers talking to two of the same men in separate interviews (Willie Dewar cited above and Harry McGregor), Alison Chand (young female researcher in her twenties) argued that intersubjectivities in the interview encounter are important, though not the only dynamic in a complex encounter where wartime memories are being composed and influenced by the cultural circuit. She comments on how two elderly male ex-SWW Reserved Occupation veterans she interviewed played down their tough, hard man, superior masculinity image to her, whilst playing it up in their narrative reconstructions of their lives for me (an older male interviewer, in my fifties at the time).[74]

Oral history interviews can throw up unexpected stories. Stuart McIntosh was interviewed in 2003 by my colleague and co-author Neil Rafeek for an oral history of our University where he was a student (Strathclyde, Glasgow, Scotland). He spoke (at length) in one section of his prior employment (before going to University as a mature student) in a local steelworks in the 1960s:

> It was great, it was like Billy Connolly always says, when they shut the gates it was just a big laugh inside. It was a very macho culture but at times the work could be very hard, but it's not like a production line so it was never boring, never boring, it got very exciting when the furnace was operating and that kind of thing, it could also be quite violent too. But it was, you would say very much an old fashioned West of Scotland man's world, definitely.

> Q: *How do you mean it could be violent at times?*
>
> Well … when the work was there, there was such a demand for men that they would take in *anyone,* so guys quite often recently released from prison, and they include the occasional psychopath, literally, would wind up working beside you. So that could be a bit uncomfortable but … you had to be able to look after yourself
>
> Q: *Were there much physical problems there? Violence amongst …?*
>
> Not a lot but you had to be prepared to stand up and say that you *were* prepared to fight. A couple of times I was in fights and *I didn't choose them* but if you backed down, that would be it, you would, you wouldn't, *everyone, everyone,* would stamp on you from then on, so you had to do that. But once you'd done that, that was okay.[75]

McIntosh evokes quite brilliantly the toxic masculinity of this Clydeside steelworks – including a reference later to the venomous work environment linked to sectarianism (Catholic Celtic vs Protestant Rangers). Myriad risks to the body and mind are evident here in this testimony.

This was their world and workers were socialized into this. Such risks were part of the fabric of manual working lives and rarely questioned at the time. When I worked with my older brother Kevin in his painting and decorating outfit in the early mid-1970s I didn't question how we used illegal 'cripples' (L-shaped metal devices clipped on the rungs of ladders) to support planks whilst painting windows (for speed) or question defecating on the job when you needed to go in empty paint tins. Crucially, the bosses (including in this context my older and unhealthy brother!) could have intervened earlier and more aggressively to change the high-risk work culture which prevailed in many manual workplaces like building sites and shipyards.

That's not to say that all employers and managers acted the same, or that change did not occur in management health and safety regimes over time. At any one time a wide range of managerial strategies on the body at work co-existed.[76] Moreover, not all male industrial and manual workers were 'macho' men, demonstrating their masculinity in displays of bravado and in 'heroic' storytelling that emphasized the dangers, toughness and hardships of the job that had to be endured. Hegemonic forms of 'hard man' masculinity were never absolute, and masculinities were fluid, subject to challenge and subversion. Workers may have positioned themselves in relation to the hegemonic masculinity of their communities, but sometimes uncomfortably and in opposition. Masculinity was complex and fluid, characterized by a range of prevailing masculinities at any one time, whilst behaviour differed widely and changed over time. What was tolerated on the shop floor in the 1950s and 1960s in terms of risk and of health and safety regimes was no longer tolerated later in the century. Older, more experienced workers could demonstrate a more 'canny' and careful approach, showing (and teaching) a recognition of workplace 'danger points' and attention to the need to preserve their capacity to function by avoiding danger or exposure or stress levels that might threaten their ability to earn a livelihood. Taafe has identified in her study of OHS

**Jobs and Bodies**

in the Chatham Dockyards that it was young men and those men with young families that were most likely to embrace a high-risk work culture.[77] Trade unions and workplace health and safety officers played a part in challenging such toxic work cultures and shifting this 'risk threshold' terrain, notably from the mid-1970s (see Chapter 7).

## Risk denial accounts

These myriad ways of telling accident and disease stories – in injustice and exploitation narratives, activist accounts and identity-composing 'graft and sacrifice' stories – were not mutually exclusive – interviewees could switch between and embrace all these ways of telling. And there were also other stories that diverged from these; stories where significant risk was denied, or at least downplayed as manageable. Some suggested accidents were inevitable and that no one knew the extent of toxic harms. This is most evident in stories from employers and managers, company doctors and some regulators. We see it, for example, in the argument that coal dust was good for you (even protecting against getting TB), and that only some forms of asbestos were harmful, with white asbestos being benign – a fallacy still widely pedaled in Asia. In 1967 a T&N Asbestos company doctor was dispatched to John Brown's shipyard to assure the workmen that the asbestos insulation boards (a product called Marinite) they were working with were not dangerous (despite the cancer link being indicated a decade earlier by Richard Doll's research).[78] A Brown's shipyard spokesman confidently asserted: 'It is true to say there is no constituent of Marinite that has any cancer producing agent in it.'[79] A decade or so later a Clydeside lagger with advanced asbestosis reported to a company doctor only to be told that he (the doctor) did 'not believe in asbestosis' and that a spell in the Belsen concentration camp would have done him good as he was overweight.[80]

Michael King, training in 1970 to be an occupational nurse with the National Dock Labour Board (he was their first male nurse), attended a conference and recalled how the asbestos risk had been persistently ignored and denied:

> I'll always remember it because a chest physician was lecturing us. There was a lot of people, over a hundred people, all nurses, at university and – and this guy was lecturing and he said, A lot of people here won't know the dangers of asbestos. But he said, I can tell you there is a place called Barking – my ears! – just outside London, he said, which has been responsible for many, many deaths caused by asbestos. But at that stage, 1969, 1970, 1970 that was, it was kept very quiet of course, you know. Now we always thought as training to be a nurse, we always thought that white asbestos was perfectly safe. And it was always blue asbestos that caused the problems.[81]

Michael's ears pricked up because he was raised in Barking and attended school close to the asbestos factory being referred to by the chest specialist. He continued: 'But people didn't bother at that time about it. It wasn't – But here was a guy, the chest physician, telling us that many deaths had been caused by the asbestos factory in Barking. So he was well aware of this of course.' As Geoff Tweedale's wonderful study of the Turner & Newall company has shown, asbestos companies consistently spread misinformation and denied and downplayed the risk of asbestos exposure right through to the 1980s, despite accruing and incontrovertible scientific medical knowledge to the contrary. The same was true of other asbestos companies (like Cape Asbestos) and most asbestos users (such as the small insulation lagging firms) dotted across the shipyard and port cities of the UK.[82]

Risk denial was not uncommon elsewhere and persisted in some places for a long time. When I interviewed Belgian ex-asbestos worker Eric Jonkheere in 2013 he recalled that risk denial was very much the attitude of his grandfather and father who worked in the ETERNIT asbestos factory in Flanders, Belgium, before him. His father Pierre was convinced the stories about the carcinogenic nature of asbestos were untrue. This is perhaps indicative of the embedded and deferential nature of these workers in the company culture of this single factory village. Pierre Jonkheere died of mesothelioma in 1987, aged fifty-nine, and a decade or so later Eric's mother Francoise also died of the disease, followed by two of Eric's brothers.[83] The company doctor, who had misdiagnosed Pierre Jonkheere's cancer as an infection and prescribed antibiotics, also died of mesothelioma. In the town of Asbestos, Quebec, there was what was once the world's largest open cast asbestos mine. Van Horssen's wonderfully crafted recent book tells of how one interviewee threw a lump of chrysotile (white asbestos) on the table in a meeting to demonstrate he was not afraid of it. Four ex-asbestos workers even travelled from Asbestos, Quebec, to France in 1997 to run a marathon to show their lungs were not affected by asbestos.[84] Over time, attitudes changed and eventually, in December 2020, the town's name was changed after a town-wide poll to the more benign Val des Sources.

## Women's work stories, risk and work-health cultures

As noted in Chapter 1, women have relatedly rarely been the subject of scholarly research on occupational health and safety.[85] Karen Messing's research in Ontario, Canada, has been one of the stand-out exceptions. This has been the consequence of a preoccupation with industrial male workers as the 'breadwinners' who occupied and monopolized the most hazardous jobs – a product of the sexual division of labour and the persisting dangerous work taboo. This was enshrined and legitimized in legislation and customary practice in many industrial workplaces – as with the legal ban on women working underground in the UK (from 1842). Women were excluded from working in most jobs in the heavy industries and in construction prior to the 1970s – and only penetrated such dangerous jobs slowly thereafter. Taaffe has shown how the radiation regulations of 1969 enabled men to be exposed to more than twice the level of women, hence no women were employed directly in the nuclear section in submarines in the docks.[86] Even women cleaners on the submarines were not allowed to work near the reactor. All the known cases of radiation-induced cancer deaths by the 2000s were male. The focus of research

## Jobs and Bodies

has been on health and safety as a male issue: one survey in 2000 found only 7 per cent of epidemiological studies of OHS related directly to female workers.[87]

Women still had significant engagement directly in dangerous and unhealthy industrial work, for example in textile and clothing factories. And also with exhausting work regimes (e.g. in wartime, taking over men's jobs) and exposure to toxins and chemicals on the job, as well as debilitating work and stress-filled lives given the double burden of unpaid home work as well as paid employment. In coal mining, for example, women who worked on the surface at collieries faced risks of accidents from the wagons being shunted, moving machinery, coal-carrying conveyor belts and drive bands. They also worked in a toxic dusty environment. Surface worker Janet Chapman described conditions to oral historian Ian MacDougall: 'Ye were black, ye were really black ... It wis roofed, ye were a' enclosed. Sometimes, sometimes it wis so bad ye couldnae see each other, ye know, for the ... for the ... stour [dust].'[88]

Textile factories were invariably noisy (especially weaving sheds) with dangerous machinery, and in these workplaces women could be exposed to a range of respiratory ailments, including byssinosis (brown lung). With post-war shifts in manufacturing in the UK women found themselves facing new sets of hazards and exposure to a range of toxins, chemicals and carcinogens in the workplace, for example in the electronics sector. Evidence from 'silicon valley' California in the mid-1980s found occupational illness amongst microelectronics workers to be three times the level of those working in manufacturing.[89] How did women narrate work-health cultures? What do these stories reveal about how women assessed risk and how they situated and articulated their bodies within the workplace? Did patterns of labour market participation shaped by gender discrimination and 'protective' legislation affect women's responses to danger and risk in the mid-twentieth-century economy in somewhat different ways to men?

During the Second World War women found themselves drawn into replacing men in dusty and dangerous factory and other work. But there continued to be limits on this 'dilution' of labour, with the enduring existence of the taboo on the most hazardous employment even during the emergency (and, of course, the continuation of the 'combat taboo' that prevented women even in the armed forces to engage directly in combat). This continued to prevent, for example, women being employed underground and the novel process of the recruitment of 'Bevin Boys' to coal mining from a one in ten ballot of the enlistment draft. Edna McDonald took work in a steelworks during the Second World War and recalled (in an interview in 1991) the shock of first starting (in 1941 aged twenty), and evoked the atmosphere:

> And the noise ... I just couldn't stand it. No, the noise was terrible, really terrifying. So, we was really petrified, until we got used to it. But once we got used to it, we started to use sign language. I'm a very good lip reader. It's a good job, 'cause I'm pretty deaf now, so it's quite handy, because we used to use sign language like deaf people because you couldn't talk to each other for the noise, but, ah, it was very very terrifying ... We were like coal miners, because in them days, as I said,

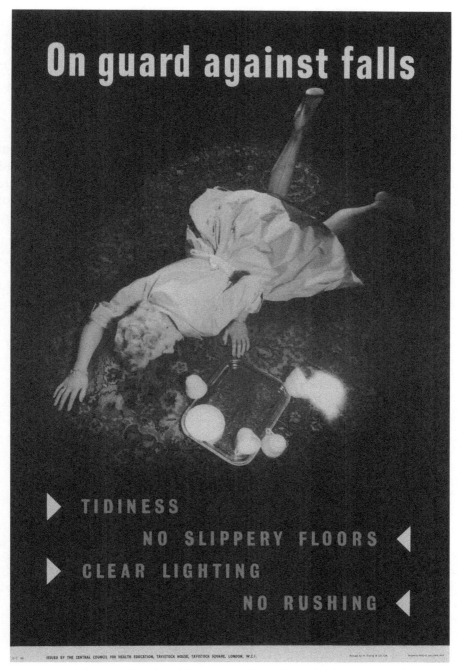

**Figure 2.5** Poster issued by the Central Council for Health Education, depicting a waitress. Outside of wartime, this is a relatively rare depiction of a female figure in a health and safety poster.
Courtesy of Getty Images.

## Jobs and Bodies

it wasn't clean. There, there was a lot of blue dust flying around. Of course, it got in your eyes, it got in your skin, it got everywhere, but we went out, back home, covered in this dirt ... it really broke our hearts because we thought we were pretty when we went out, but, ah, when we came back, we had to walk home, 'cause there was no showers. You didn't get a wash or anything. You walked home in all your dirt.[90]

Edna added: 'You had to be in a union because it was very very dangerous down there ... you were absolutely roasted. You were burnt to death really, and it was dangerous ... You had to have your wits about you all the time you were down there ....' And Edna testified to the painful graft and bone-weariness of her wartime work, commenting: 'you were really tired when you went home at night. It was really very hard work. We had a lot of pain, you know, a lot of pain in your arms too, trying to pull these levers. It was very very hard work.'

Amongst the gender-specific hazards that Edna identified resulting from her wartime work was the loss of babies in the first months of pregnancy. She recalled:

At that time, a lot of the girls were starting to get married, and there was eight of us, before we left, were having babies, and seven of us lost our babies, and only one girl managed to keep it, and we said it was with the weight, with the strain of pulling these heavy levers, that we lost our babies, because in them days, when you were having a baby, and the war was on, ah, you couldn't go to a doctor for three months, 'cause the doctor just wouldn't have anything to do wi' you for the first three months. In them days there wasn't the testing they do now. You practically know the next day if you're having a baby nowadays, but in them days, no way. There was none o' them tests going about, so the doctor wouldn't examine you until you were three months pregnant, and then she would give you a certificate to say, 'right, you're allowed to leave work', but up 'til then you weren't allowed to leave work, 'cause the war were on. You couldn't just walk out on it. You were, you were there, so by the time three months had come, and all this heavy work we were doing, the damage was done, and as I said, on my shift alone, there was seven of us out of eight of us lost our babies.[91]

Edna demonstrated an acute awareness of the relationship between work and the body, sharpened during the extraordinary demands of wartime. She told a story of a friend who worked in the local munitions factory shell filling:

They got a lot of illnesses, the women that worked in there. They got a lot of illnesses. I had a friend there, and she was, she was never the same woman. She went, oh, in a wheelchair, and she went yellow, and ... but you never found out ... in them days everything was secret in the war [...] they wouldn't own up they were poisoning people, but we said all along she was poisoned with the, you know, stuff they were working in.[92]

Talking Dirty

It's very likely the reference here is to TNT poisoning. Edna continued with her observations on how the work assaulted and penetrated the body, returning to the steelworks and her own experience:

> It was the same with us, we used to breathe all this steel, ah, dust into our lungs and our eyes, 'cause I remember my father going to Carlisle and getting his eyes cleaned out, and I remember at the time he said that they lifted his eyes out of the socket, and he said they cleaned, and he could feel this steel, blue steel running out of his eyes as they were cleaning it, they showed him it. Terrible [...] the stuff we breathed in, you know. It was like a blue steel, blue, very very fine steel, yeah. A lot of us are deaf through the steelworks, because you didn't have hearing things, you didn't have to wear things over your ears like you do now for noise. We never did anything like that. A lot of us are deaf through that. I'm deaf in one ear through that and all. My husband was deaf through it, and we never had any compensation or anything like that.[93]

At a couple of points in her story, Edna referred to transgression during wartime, breaching the customary gendered division of labour, saying: 'It wasn't a woman's job at all. It wasn't a woman's work at all. No way ... no comfort at all. No, there was no comfort at all. It was very very hot, very very dirty.' That said, it was not uncommon for female wartime workers to downplay their role and emphasize the higher risks that male workers took. Another female wartime steel worker, Betty Saffill, commented:

> Some of the lads got burnt ... and they used to go to first aid ... Harry [boyfriend] used to get sparks on his face, burnt sparks from the ingots when he was pushing them down, you know, they would maybe bounce or something, a bit, and then, and then they used to, ah, spark up into his face, and then there was a few foul words came out, you see ... Like, you took no notice of that because that was all in your job. If you took any notice of that, well, you might just as well pack up and leave it, which ... You thought of the money, actually.[94]

Edna also expressed a sense that it was the men in the steelworks that had faced the greatest risks. Edna spoke in awe of the men manipulating the hot metal through the rollers whilst she asserted 'we were the weaker sex' needing more of the milk and the salt tablets that were provided by the company to try to replenish what was being taken out of their bodies in the steelworks. In Summerfield's seminal classification of female wartime oral narratives, Edna fell into the category of a 'stoic' rather than an 'heroic' female wartime worker, largely accepting her subordination to the imperatives of wartime production and the dangers that went along with it. She commented: 'You just went to work and worked, and you did as you were told ... You were just like a second class citizen, women in them days, you know. We did our bit, and that was it.'

Women were also employed working with asbestos in wartime, replacing men who were enlisted – a process which resulted in spikes in ARDs decades later. One woman

65

## Jobs and Bodies

**Figure 2.6** Women workers at an iron and steel company at Park Gate, Rotherham, c.1940. Courtesy of Getty Images.

described working as an asbestos beater in T&N, Clydebank, as a young eighteen-year-old during the war, replacing a man who left for the Navy. Her job was to lift and tip up heavy twenty to thirty pound (around 10–15 kilos) bags of asbestos fibre into the 'mixer' to create asbestos cement. 'It was quite interesting. It was a hard job', she said, adding 'It was quite a good job. I quite enjoyed it anyway.'[95] A colleague in the same department recalled: 'Dust was flying all over the place … You look up and you wouldn't even see who was working in it. Like everything else if you don't do it somebody else will. The firm didn't care if you jacked [left] or not. Oh no, no.'[96] A sense of fatalism is evident in this testimony as well as disempowerment given the attitude of the company and the feeling that others would do the job if you did not. The female wartime asbestos beater went on to reflect on the lack of personal protective equipment during the war:

> I don't remember a mask or anything. No. First time I ever remember wearing a mask was when I went back into Singer's after the war was finished and I became – trust me to get all the dangerous jobs – a paint sprayer, and it wasn't paint it was laquer for the sewing machines you know. But no, I don't remember any safety precautions at all … You never thought of danger. I mean asbestos was nothing. Just never gave asbestos a thought, you know.[97]

Other women workers spoke of having to organize rudimentary personal protection themselves in the face of lack of provision by the company, using sacks tied around themselves and scarves around their faces and heads.[98]

Where women worked in industrial jobs, work-health cultures, including risk-taking, could assume levels not dissimilar to male workers. There was a degree of gender convergence or blurring here, rather than significant difference. This wasn't all about macho men proving their superiority in a competitive work environment. Wartime studies provided evidence of this, including the wonderful oral history-based investigation of women workers in South Wales munitions factories by Mari Williams.[99] Whilst wartime propaganda, including films, painted a rosy picture of war factory work for women (to facilitate recruitment), the reality was very different. Amongst the many enhanced hazards faced by female wartime workers were risks of TNT and phosphorus poisoning (as referred to in Edna's testimony above) and explosions in the shell-filling factories. The detonator shop at Bridgend Royal Ordnance Factory (ROF), nicknamed 'the suicide club', in South Wales was particularly dangerous, as one of Williams interviewees noted:

> I remember working down in pellets, in the yellow powder and we used to have our hair going yellow in the front. Then I volunteered to go into the detonators where they were making the dets. to go for the bombs and that. It was a dangerous section. Well, I had a blow-up there ... the last one blew up in the air. It blew the box up. So, I remember I had that [top of thumb] hanging off, stitched all around there, and all these steel splinters through the eyebrows. But, otherwise, I was lucky, I was, because the poor people that was down there had limbs blown off and blindness. It was terrible down there, mind.[100]

Fear and unease were amongst mixed emotions expressed in Williams cohort of twenty-two female wartime munitions interviewees. That said, Williams concluded: 'The evidence of former employees of Bridgend ROF suggests that many workers took unnecessary risks when handling explosives and ignored safety regulations in a bid to reach production targets.'[101] Patriotism contributed to this attitude – with risk-acceptance thresholds widely recalibrated during wartime on the Home Front in order to contribute to the war effort. As with men in the coal mines, the Welsh women's efforts were also spurred on by financial inducements and the award of prizes for the highest output, which Williams argued incentivized negligence.[102] A Welsh woman who was awarded the prize of being the fastest wartime worker admitted she did it by breaching safety regulations: 'But of course I used to do it *not* the safety way.'[103] Some women also compromised their safety by taking in feminine 'contraband' (such as rings, lipstick and hair clips which were an explosion risk) or refused to wear protective head coverings, resulting in accidents when hair became entangled in the machinery.[104] In this sense for more 'heroic' wartime women workers (to return again to Summerfield's classification) the performance of femininity represented a risk not dissimilar to the performance of masculinity through peer pressure noted in other studies of male coal miners, building workers or shipbuilders.

## Jobs and Bodies

Other wartime stories attested to exposure to danger and profoundly unhealthy work environments. Maureen Holdsworth was one of those women who recorded their story for the BBC People's War Archive website:

> Government call up was compulsory. I wanted to join the Women's Air Force but I was sent to Ministry of Labour Munitions at Hapton. It was grim but we were forced to go. They made magnesium metal here. My first job was shovelling peat into a machine but then I worked on the Kek Mills – these were about 30 to 40 feet high and full of magnesium. The dust was so bad you couldn't see the person working opposite you. We had to wear little masks – but if you coughed it was always black. The conditions were terrible. There was a hospital on site for people who were gassed in the chlorinators. There were leaks. I was gassed one day as I walked through the chlorinator plant to clock on. I remember my eyes streaming and I panicked and ran to the wrong door to try and get out. I only worked there for two years. Sir Stafford Cripps came and closed the place down and then I went to work at Mullards in Blackburn. However when I was given an X ray, the Doctor wouldn't pass me as fit for working there – 'you've had enough,' he said.[105]

A degree of gender convergence in occupational health and safety cultures has been argued persuasively in studies of the Second World War and in two oral history-based studies of post-war textile workers in Northern England and in Paisley, Scotland.[106] In reconstructing their past working life, female workers articulated tolerance of risk and danger. Abenstern et al. (2005) engaged directly with Johnston and McIvor's earlier work (on masculinity and risk-taking) arguing that there was similar high-risk taking behaviour amongst female textile weavers (to male heavy industry workers), notably cleaning machinery whilst it was in motion, in clear breach of the 1937 law banning such dangerous practice.[107] The main motivations of the women, cited in their oral history interviews, were to placate management and to maximize piecework wages. As one weaver commented: 'You were supposed to stop your frame when you were cleaning … but you didn't because you were grabbing. You were keeping your money going.'[108] Crucially, management did not allow any specific time when the full mill engines would be stopped for such cleaning to take place and when they did (half an hour at the end of Friday's dayshift) this was still ignored by the women weavers, who preferred to leave early. Burns's recent oral history-based analysis of occupational health and safety practices amongst Paisley's female thread workers came to similar conclusions. Burns explores how female workers reacted and adapted to noise and to the piecework payments regime that incentivized maximization of output and earnings. And the effects these had in relation to stress and pressure on the job and on their bodies in later life, causing a series of disabilities, including musculoskeletal damage (knee replacements were common amongst the doffers) and hearing loss. Based on the oral interview evidence he argued: 'women engaged in risky work practices not only as victims of the industrial work process but with agency in their desire to earn increased wages. This agency was framed within the inevitability of the absorption of risk.'[109] 'But that was all just part of the job' one textile worker recalled in a revealing reflection on risk-taking in relation to accidents, noise and other such hazards in the Paisley mills where rate-fixers were referred to as the 'cruelty men.'[110] Interviewees also expressed ignorance of the long-term effects of their labour processes (such as doffing which involved repeated uncomfortable postures) and work environment. This indicates, Burns notes, 'that physical harm to working class bodies was an acceptable price to pay to earn a living'.[111] And the female work-health narratives were overwhelmingly positive, in that the women expressed support for the piecework wage system that allowed them to earn relatively high wages (compared to many other female jobs), and a great deal of job satisfaction and pride in their work.[112]

Other female industrial workers evidenced grim conditions, including dangerous and intensely dusty work environments. Vera Rigby was a female weaver in Lancashire. She recalled her parent's respiratory impairments, visiting her father in his mill when she was young and reflected on the dusty atmosphere in cotton mills:

I mean my dad had byssinosis. My dad worked in the cotton mills and I can remember as a child going to see him ... And you couldn't see in the room. I mean my dad had a terrible, terrible chest. My mum had worked in the cotton mills but she'd come out because of a bad chest and gone to Oldham Elastic, because although it was noisy there wasn't the cotton or the fluff. Oh my dad used to come home covered in cotton ... I can remember looking in at that door and you couldn't see my dad. Somebody would say we were there, me and my mum, and he would come to us. But he was just covered. My dad's chest was terrible. Really, really, really bad. As with many people that I knew.[113]

Other narratives suggest awareness of danger points as well as a degree of risk-taking on the job that would be intolerable today. Tracy Carpenter was one of the first female railway freight guards in the 1980s (and later an engine driver) in London. She recalled:

But we did feel that we were doing quite dangerous, dirty, heavy work and it was dangerous: there was a lot of walking around very dark yards that were in very poor condition at night. You were quite likely to hurt yourself and there was a lot of walking along the track. ... The wagons were dirty, they were dark, they were black, they moved silently at night, you didn't see them coming ... the locos didn't have headlights on, the signals were dim, the yards weren't lit, the lamps would go out ... You had your hand lamp but it was cumbersome to use it a lot of the time and you took risks. You took foolish risks more then ... there's more of a safety culture now – that irritates us but they're right .... And the wagons weren't designed to be user friendly, they weren't soft cornered and gentle, they had hard, sharp, catchy corners, catchy edges, they were rusty, dirty and they didn't get maintenance if they didn't need maintenance ...[114]

## Jobs and Bodies

Tracy continued, with an anecdote: 'There was a dreadful accident where a freight guard got his foot cut off and that was absolutely horrifying and people were very aware that this could have happened to any of us. The man it happened to was very conscientious and careful, so there was a realisation that we were in quite a dangerous environment.'

Another female London Transport worker, Pam Singer, identified the lack of toilet facilities for women at railway depots and inadequate personal protection equipment (PPE) for women (no steel capped boots in her size) as problems in the 1980s. She reflected on the additional pressure that came with privatization in the 1990s and much more intensive work regimes which necessitated a 'different work culture'. She also highlighted the deleterious impact of shift-working, nightshifts and mixed shift-working on the body:

So earlies you'd start any time between 4:45 and 8:30-ish. You had sort of middle turns, 13:00 or whatever. You would have lates, where you could start at 16:00, 17:00. And then nights, where you'd start 22:00, 23:00. And that was the killer. The killer is we would do ... you'd start 17:00 one week, then the next week you'd be starting 06:00, and then the week after you'd be starting 14:27, and then the week after that you'd be doing nights, and then you'd have a few days off. And so there wasn't a shift pattern that was in any way sympathetic to your body rhythms. Nobody thought of that in those days. There wasn't any circadian rhythm technologists in those days. And they had these swing shifts like that and it was kind of like, well, of course. It's part of the job and you do it, right? And that's what I found most distressing.[115]

Linda Read started her apprenticeship as an electrical fitter in 1973 at the Chatham Dockyard and in an interview with Emma Taafe commented on her workplace exposure to asbestos and her awareness of its toxicity: 'Electrical breakers on submarines have these asbestos pads and I had to file them and shape them and because I commented about it, you know, I wasn't too happy about doing it ... I got a bad report remark from that.'[116] She was asked if masks were provided and replied: 'No nothing whatsoever, and I used my own file tool from my own toolkit to file it so the dust was carried into my toolbox.' In such workplaces the dangers and pressure might be eased by joking and banter. Humour became a distraction. Sally Groves worked between 1975 and 1980 at the Trico Wiper Factory, Great West Road, London, which employed 1600 workers, and was an activist (on the strike committee) during the 1976 Trico Equal Pay strike (twenty-one weeks out). She recalled:

Yeah, people would chat a lot, yes, there was always a lot of jokes. Banter. Yes, but it was hard work, it was really hard work. Piecework. Yeah, that's right, you couldn't just do things at your own pace, you had to work, you know under a lot of pressure. I think the women had always been treated with quite a lot of contempt in the factory, not only by management, who really looked down on them, ... a lot of the men also had that same attitude.[117]

Mary Spicer started work during the war in the local foundry, Sterling Metals (Attleborough near Coventry – one of the largest foundries in the UK employing 1500 in 1951 and over 3000 at peak in the 1970s – and remained in employment there for forty-six years, doing, as she describes it, 'a man's job'. In an interview on her working life in 2006 she constructs a narrative that on the one hand oozes with pride and identification with her work and on the other recognizes the vulnerability of the body in the workplace. Her testimony is peppered with anecdotes of dust, dirt and noise, of injuries and ill-health caused by the work, from scalds, burns and trauma, to deafness and fatalities, including an explosion that killed two workers and injured several more. She describes a workplace in the 1950s and 1960s with little effective health and safety provision, including no PPE – masks or ear defenders. She survived this largely unscathed, with only a couple of relatively minor accidents, but her husband (who also worked in the plant) suffered severe industrial deafness and had to stop working in consequence.[118]

Another female metal worker Joyce Igo provides a wonderful example of evocative storytelling on work and health, sensitively positioning the body in employment. Joyce was exceptional in being one of the few women to be employed on the shop floor in a steel mill in the 1950s, following her wartime work experience in the Rover car factory. Born in 1923 Joyce worked in the Warrenby steel plate mill as a plate marker from *c*.1952 to 1957 and recorded her story in 1991.[119] Her oral testimony focused on the heat, dirt, sweat and exhaustion of the mill, as well as referring to the 'double-burden' on their bodies that women faced: 'The dust in the mill. I mean, it was filthy really … it was a dirty job. … We had a rest room. We could go and just sit in it, and sometimes nod off to sleep if you were too tired, because you had your work to do at home as well as going to work.' Joyce used phrases like 'disgusting' and 'scandalous' to convey her moral indignation at the polluted work environment: 'We were filthy. I mean, you felt ashamed going on the bus, like, when you had to, if you were dirty. We didn't wear, we weren't forced to wear anything on our heads, like. Like, in the war, we were, ah, on the machines.' That said, Joyce also articulated a sense of being socialized over time into accepting the heat and noise. 'You just learned to live with it, just learned to live with it […] and I mean, the big mill, it used to make awful noises, and then when they threw the salt, as I say, it was like a bomb dropping, BONG, and the scale flying.' And like many male narratives, Joyce dwelled on the dangers and accidents, telling of a fatal accident of a male worker who fell into the rollers. She reflected:

Oh yeah. You had to be careful. You see, these plates, when they came down, they came on, like, ah, railway lines, I would say. A bit like that. And then there was drops, you know, ah, but I wouldn't go on when they were moving. I wouldn't go on them at all when they were moving, but, I mean, there was sometimes breaks in these mesh things. There was like mesh in between for the scale to drop through, you see, 'cause, through a bank, as they called it. The bank dropped right down. I think, I don't know whether they had to clean that out every now and then, like, but, um, oh yeah, there was dangers if you didn't watch what you were doing … but the girls had to watch what they were doing, you know, because sometimes the

**Jobs and Bodies**

marker and his assistant and the, the stamper lad, would ride the plates, you know. They'd jump from one to the other, but I didn't like it. I wouldn't do that.'[120]

Joyce was making the point clearly here that she accrued experience, was aware of the danger spots, that care needed to be taken and that it was fellow male workers who were taking undue risks that she was averse to and would not tolerate. Her husband also worked in the mill and Joyce reflected ruefully on his propensity to tolerate unsafe work practices, recalling that though he adapted reluctantly to the use of a safety helmet he was more ambivalent about ear defenders and goggles. She explained though that this was partly for practical reasons as both could adversely affect his ability to do his work effectively:

But the [ear] muffs, he wouldn't wear them because he couldn't hear the mill working, and he had to hear the mill working. He says, he could tell straight away if anything was going wrong with the rolls or anything like that, and that's why he wouldn't wear them ... You see, he even, they had goggles to wear over their glasses. He used to go through a lot of glasses. They were pitted, but he couldn't wear them for the heat. You see, plastic goggles, over the top of your glasses ... they just used to sweat up, and steam up, when you were having to go right up to the heat of the slabs.[121]

Lived experience and the realities of working lives are indicated in such sensory eye-witness testimony. Workers attuned to such work in steelworks, coal mines and the like felt they needed to deploy their senses without interference, so PPE covering ears and eyes could be a problem to use and could be discarded if they interfered with production.

Women also faced a series of gender-specific risks in the post-war workplace, which could include sexual harassment, physical and verbal abuse. Sexual harassment and physical and verbal abuse were pervasive. Bus conductor Sheila Emmanuel spoke of her experience being dragged off her bus and physically assaulted, as well as racially abused in the 1970s in London, recalling: 'it was a good thing that traffic was slow because if the traffic was going fast I would have had a lot of injuries.' She continued: 'you just grit your teeth and take it as it comes. You don't always say well you're gonna make a big uproar about what happened ... I enjoyed my job on the bus apart from when you find some people are aggressive.'[122] Eileen Magee recalled an experience in the early 1960s that was seared into her memory:

One job when I worked in an office in Belfast, it was a very small office; a furniture company, they did hire purchase, and the boss there he was really, I don't know if you remember somebody like Max Bygraves, he was like him. You know the check coat and a big tie and a scar, and he used to come up and he used to touch all the girls, you know, put his arm around them and give them a squeeze. And I was 17, and I was horrified; and he came up to me and tried to [do it to me] and I just stiffened, I was almost in tears. And he said: 'Oh, she's only skinny, anyway!

There's nothing!' He said, 'there's more flesh on a hare's lip', or something. And, you know, he had been a friend of a friend of my father's, and that's how I'd got the job. I couldn't even tell my father about it, because there was a tight lip, then, about sexual matters. You couldn't say. I probably couldn't even have said it my mother. You were just frightened. It was stupid, really.[123]

Eileen left Belfast within a year and moved to London.

Female work-health narratives were also more likely to reflect on the porous and invasive nature of dust and dirt – how toxic industrial detritus could infiltrate the home and the neighbourhood. Joyce Igo told another story relating to the 1970s when she and her husband were living in the vicinity of the British Steel plant in Grangetown, NE England. She was approached by an environmental health inspector looking for information because of the prevalence of bronchitis in the area:

So I said, and just at that, that BOS [British Oxygen Steel] plant gave out its belch, and all that, and I said, 'see that there', well, I said, 'take it down to London and show them down there what we, the conditions we're having to live in'. I says, 'it's scandalous'. Never mind about what you smoke, what you drink and what you eat, I says, 'we're breathing that in'. It was disgusting, that BOS plant, when it comes out. My husband bought a white car, brand new, when he retired, and I lived down Grangetown, and we went out this morning, and you should have seen the state of it, 'cause we hadn't got a garage built then. We'd moved, and we hadn't got the garage up, and it was disgusting. All like that silver, silver stuff coming out of it.[124]

There was also the chance of contamination brought from external workplaces into the home – the domain of unpaid work for most married women in the post-war years. Housewives could be exposed to the inhalation of carcinogenic fibres from family members entering the home with asbestos contaminated clothing and overalls. As one Clydeside joiners' wife attested, recalling a conversation with her husband about her son: 'I used tae say tae him "was Peter there today at his work?". And he used to say "I couldnae tell you, I couldnae see him". He couldnae see him for a' the dust. And then I used to tae take his overall and take them out to the stairs and brush them before I could wash them.'[125] Lauren Ross, the wife of a joiner in Manchester (who died of mesothelioma), recalled:

Every bit of skin that was exposed was covered with – I suppose like when you see pictures of miners, probably not quite so black, because normal everyday dust in houses isn't as black as coal dust, so it would be a lighter shade, but in exactly the same way. He could come home absolutely full of dust. But you don't think anything of it. He'd give us all a hug then he'd say, I'm just going in the bath.[126]

Mavis Nye was diagnosed with mesothelioma in 2009. In an interview with Emma Taafe she recalled how she had been exposed as a child with her father bringing in asbestos

## Jobs and Bodies

dust on his work clothes, and similarly as an adult from her husband Raymond.[127] Like male workers, most female housewives would have been socialized into acceptance of such behaviour, thinking nothing or little of it at least prior to the 1970s and 1980s when the true hazards of asbestos exposure became more widely recognized within working-class communities. Washing and cleaning were ingrained gendered roles assigned to women, and the brushing down in the 'stairs' – which was a communal area of the tenement close – would have further spread contamination, contributing to wider environmental exposure to this deadly carcinogen.

## Conclusion

Worker narratives on health and safety in industry range across a spectrum – and here we have identified and reflected on some of the different ways stories relating to risk at work and work-health cultures were told. These stories recall intimate sensory experiences at work and speak to how industrial work profoundly affected workers bodies, and how toxins could be transferred from the industrial workplace into the home. In their narratives in oral histories and other personal accounts, working-class interviewees – men and women – elucidate prevailing (and changing) work-health cultures, the power dynamics of the workplace and the complex impact of gendered identities, including the impact of masculine and feminine performance, of ingrained gender roles. What comes through powerfully is the prevailing pragmatism and socialization of the post-war generation of industrial workers into high levels of risk and danger.

These worker stories show an acute awareness of the complex, multi-layered impacts of industrial work on the body, good as well as bad. And, a clear sense of who was responsible and cognizance of how things have changed over time. For most this represented improvement in how bodies are protected in industrial work, though for some there was a sense the regulation of work had gone too far: 'health and safety gone mad'. In these stories it is evident that worker-narrators are (a) bearing witness to harm and injustice, (b) composing their identities; their sense of self in the process and (c) identifying as social actors – whether as victims or as activists spurred to action and mobilization in industrial accident and disease movements. As Steven High has argued in *One Job Town*, storytelling has 'an important political function … transforming private hurt into public knowledge'.[128] We explore OHS activism in more detail in Chapter 7.

Clearly, there are a multitude of ways of telling, including more positive stories about the body-sculpting and health-enhancing nature of industrial work (and the devastation felt at its loss), and risk denial accounts, by employers and managers, and those taken in by management-influenced control over the flow of knowledge. These narratives from those directly involved tell us much about how 'good' industrial work within a 'moral economy' of reciprocal obligations could positively forge identities, enhance health and hone fit bodies and minds. They also speak of risk-taking cultures, pragmatism and agency and degrees of pressure equating to economic violence which simultaneously harmed, disabled and killed industrial workers.

The dominant strand of industrial-era workers' stories, however, positioned the body at work, identified the risk and 'danger spots' and demonstrated how acculturated industrial workers were to high levels of risk in relation to both trauma and chronic disease from their work. For many men seeped in this culture, this was an integral part of their way of doing masculinity in these post-war decades. This was what you did being a working man in industry, and young workers brought in to this tough environment were expected to conform to the work-health cultures that prevailed on the building site, deep underground in the mine or in the steelworks and shipyards. And masculine work cultures persisted and transcended the shipyard, mine and building site. In an interview, ex-Scottish firefighter Scott McCabe reflected on his work in the 1990s noting how a 'machismo culture' persisted. He recalled misogynist attitudes towards the small minority of female firefighters (around one in fifty at this time), how dirty kit was 'a badge of honour' and how he walked across a roof ridge 120 feet up with no safety harness, wires or rope.[129] Exposure to toxic chemicals and contaminants was common and average life expectancy of a firefighter after retirement in the 1990s was seven years, with a disproportionate number of premature deaths caused by cancer.[130]

Many bent to the pressure of such hegemonic masculinity in the industrial workplace, conforming to what was expected of them. Others transgressed, so a range of masculinities was ever present. Women in industry appear to have been subject to similar pressures and narrate the dangers of work in similar ways. In the context of wartime and in post-war industrial spaces (such as textile mills) women workers recalled being absorbed in a productionist work culture, where risks were traded for higher productivity and wage maximization. However, female industrial workers appear more immune to cultural expectations on the job to take risks, and more conscious of maintaining health and well-being. It appears from industrial workers' narratives that work-health cultures remain complex, multi-faceted and fluid over time and space.

Whether interest is in the discourses or the material reality, talking to and listening to those who bear witness in these stories gets us closer to lived experience, the work-body interaction – how work was felt through the senses – and what this meant and signified to those involved. To use Raymond Williams phrase, 'structures of feeling' are elucidated in these workers' memories. In bearing witness, such testimonies facilitate understanding of work-health cultures, agency and of the subtle acculturation to damaging sets of values and embedded structural violence inherent within the industrial workplace. And they show acute awareness of how employers and managers motivated by profit or the pressures and imperatives of production deadlines were culpable in ignoring health and safety protocols, sustaining work-health cultures that were inimical to health and well-being, causing stress, injury, long-term disabilities and premature mortality. In the next chapter we turn our attention to what it meant to be living with such harm, disability and death caused by industrial work in working-class families and communities and how those directly affected remembered this.

# CHAPTER 3
# INDUSTRIAL LEGACIES; DAMAGED BODIES

Fred Brady worked in the shipyards in Sunderland for thirty-seven years from the 1950s. In an interview in 1999 for the British Library Sound Archive he spoke of the embodied legacies of a working life in industry recalling there were:

> ... very few welders over 50 who do not have asthma, bronchitis etc. I have about nine things wrong with me. I consider myself lucky. I saw a man in the town last week only a year older than me ... two sticks ... eyes going, deaf ... arthritis all over his body ... tennis elbow. At least I am mobile. I spoke to him ... all he talked about was the price of the beer going up in the club. He did not moan once about the afflictions he had ... I really felt for him. This is endemic with Sunderland people.[1]

Dangerous and toxic industrial workplaces left a grim legacy of disability, ill-health, curtailed lives and profound grief across traditional working-class communities dependent upon coal mining, steel-making, shipbuilding and the like for employment. This chapter focuses on workers' experience of disability and sickness and how this was narrated in their personal stories. For many seriously injured and sick workers this meant identity disintegration and degrees of social marginalization or 'estrangement' as Wing-Chung Ho has argued in a recent study of China.[2] The analysis here tracks industrial workers from the point when they are injured or contract an occupational disease, reconstructing the lived experience of being disabled and sick. I explore how individuals, families and working-class communities articulated loss, injury and chronic disease, and coped with this. Oral testimonies are relied on extensively in this chapter to explore how men and women were affected by disability caused by work and how they remembered, narrated, reacted and managed trauma and chronic disease. Such personal sources provide a window into a world rarely glimpsed. As recent histories of occupational disability that have focused predominantly on the pre-Second World War period have noted, it is difficult to reconstruct lived experience because of the lack of autobiographical material – with resulting dependency upon institutional records, such as the Poor Law and hospitals.[3] Drawing upon Blaxter's classic thesis around disability and 'social exclusion' it is argued here that working-class experiences and narration of occupational disability and sickness are diverse and complex.[4] These ideas are fleshed out through case studies of the discourses around and impact of two of the most significant of occupational disease epidemics in the UK (and in many other countries), comparing experience in two communities – asbestos-related diseases (ARDs) in UK shipyards and port communities and breathing-impaired disabled coalminers in UK coalfields.

## Jobs and Bodies

The gendered aspects of such experience are a key focus here. Women suffered from a range of workplace injuries and risks, and occupational diseases, including asbestos-related diseases (as for example with direct exposure during wartime and indirectly, for example from exposure from washing relatives work clothes) as noted in the previous chapter. The family context is important here as women also played key roles as carers for working-class men afflicted with occupational sickness and disabilities (usually as wives or mothers, but also professionally as social workers and nurses). These are experiences that have been neglected in the literature. In coalfield communities disabled ex-workmen were perhaps the most visible of all post-war working-class communities. In bearing witness, oral accounts relate something of the pain and suffering involved, the economic and social costs of losing a breadwinner, phases of convalescence, rehabilitation and adaptation, as well as the personal identity mutations that loss of paid work and disability meant for many individuals. Here workers, wives and family members are poignantly describing prescribed lives, difficult adaptations, bereavement, loss and navigating transitions into ill-health, dependency and in some cases poverty as family income declined. Post-traumatic stress disorder (PTSD) is evident from some of these stories, though for many British working-class men of this immediate post-war generation the stigmatization of mental health left this unspoken and hidden. Silence on mental health is common in their autobiographical accounts. The range of personal testimonies, however, do also speak of resilience, adaptability, individual and family coping strategies, collective organization and community mobilization, activism and advocacy (e.g. around reparation and compensation) that went some way to mediate the economic impacts of disability. Coal mining communities perhaps exemplified this mobilization around the politics of the body and disability in the second half of the twentieth century.

## Living with death and occupational disability: Coal miners

It is near impossible to convey the physical and psychological pain, emotional trauma, grief and suffering that went along with the damage caused by unhealthy and dangerous industrial workplaces. A trade union official in South Wales noted during wartime that conditions were far worse in coal mining than in the local munitions factories, yet earnings were higher in the latter. He observed: 'The miners have rotten working conditions, artificial ventilation, the stench of the water, smoke and its effect on chest and lungs, most miners get some kind of bronchial trouble at an early age.'[5] There were markedly differing levels of impairment across the mining workforce and a wide range of experience, with effects and coping strategies varying significantly across a wide spectrum of personal and community tragedies. At worse, the outcomes could involve quite fundamental *mutations* in lifestyles, behaviour and identities as disabled workers and their families adapted to new realities with the loss or curtailment of a breadwinner. Impacts included erosion of physical and mental capacity, loss or change of employment, declining income and standards of living, a collapse of status and self-esteem, a drift towards social exclusion and towards dependency and marginalization as citizens. These transitions were more sudden and traumatic in some cases than others, depending on the nature and pathology of the disease(s) and injuries and the individuals concerned. That said, coal-mining communities were amongst those with the largest numbers of disabled men of all mid-twentieth-century working-class industrial communities. Those affected articulated a sense of this wide range of experience in their oral testimonies and autobiographical accounts.

Because of fears over loss of earnings, some workers opted to hide the extent of their disability and continue to work, sometimes risking further damage to themselves. It was traditional in coal mining for the coalowners and later the NCB to accommodate disabled workers where possible with other more suitable employment, away from the more strenuous and dusty jobs on the seam to elsewhere underground, or better still moving disabled men to work on the surface at the colliery. Others found work outside of coal-mining, though adapting to different work could be a challenge for ex-miners. Bodies became shaped and hardened by manual work in the pit. During the Second World War some found work in munitions factories, though this could be problematic, as a forewoman at the Bridgend Royal Ordnance Factory (ROF) recalled:

I remember having some retired miners, they had retired through dust or something because they weren't that old. … The fuses then, on the naval side, well … they had tiny little screws that you screwed in and had to seal them up, and I always remember this gentleman saying to me … 'it's a shovel I want in my hand, not this little screw-driver. I can't feel it'. And his hands were hard with the coal and that, and it was true, he just couldn't feel that screw-driver in his hand. It was so tiny compared to his shovel that he'd been used to having.[6]

The age limit of fifty-five years for employment in the wartime ROFs also made it difficult for disabled ex-miners, alleviated somewhat in 1943 when this restriction was relaxed. Still, high levels of unemployment and under-employment characterized the experience of disabled miners during the war and from 1943 miners diagnosed and certified with pneumoconiosis were banned from further employment in mining. This was linked to paranoia that either pneumoconiosis was itself infectious (as some believed, as it turned out erroneously) or it predisposed those affected to tuberculosis (as with silico-tuberculosis) and hence was a real risk to others coming into contact through their employment with germ-riddled pneumoconiotics. The stigma attached to having 'pneumo' at this time (like with TB) discouraged many from admitting it or seeking a medical diagnosis or medical treatment (limited though the latter was).

After the war the situation for disabled miners improved somewhat, but still a doctor described re-employment efforts in lighter, more suitable jobs for disabled miners after the war as 'unsuccessful' and commented in the early 1950s: 'They are compelled by economic pressure to carry on with their job.'[7] A South Wales miner (whose father had died of pneumoconiosis in 1969) continued to work for nine years after being diagnosed with pneumoconiosis in 1971 and after being advised by his GP to leave the

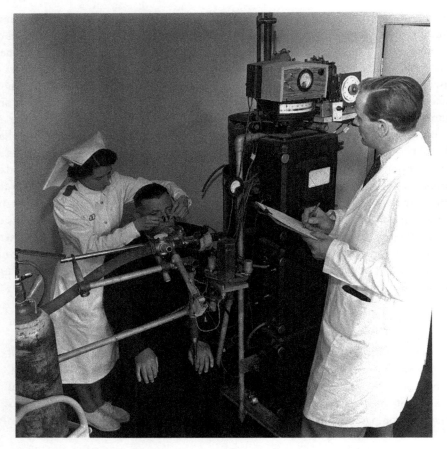

**Figure 3.1** Testing for pneumoconiosis by Charles Fletcher, Director of the Pneumoconiosis Research Unit in South Wales, 1951.
Courtesy of Getty Images.

coal face. When asked 'when you were told in 1971 that you had pneumoconiosis why did you not want to leave the [coal] face then' he replied, after a long pause: 'Young family. Money. Not greedy but just, y'know. No money. It was a big drop in the wages see. Yeh. A minimum wage compared to a coal face worker or a hard heading man. A hell of a big difference.'[8]

A common well-established practice was to move older and disabled miners from work underground to less strenuous and less dusty conditions working on the surface screening and sorting the coal, or other such jobs. However, earnings on surface work for adult men averaged around half the wages that coal face workers could earn – and there was also a massive downgrading in status and prestige associated with being a surface worker compared to a coal face worker. Proud disabled miners encountered being shamed, embarrassed and stigmatized as well as a sharp loss of earnings.

## Industrial Legacies; Damaged Bodies

The process of sudden and sustained injury from accidents or longer-term encroaching disability from chronic occupational disease could trigger mutations in identities. Men felt diminished not being able to work and earn. *Emasculation* occurred as male workers experienced loss of independence, a sense of failure as a breadwinner and a profound displacement during injury, sickness and recuperation from an external male-dominated work environment to the feminized space of the home. And loss of income and dwindling financial resources (compensation, if granted, ran at around half the average coal miners' wages) made it difficult to sustain a consumption pattern commensurate with a normal miners' lifestyle, never mind keeping up a hegemonic 'hard man' image – invariably involving heavy drinking and smoking. Mildred Blaxter described this in her pioneering mid-1970s study of disability as a process of 're-evaluating identity', which could be either a sudden discontinuity or a longer-term process of 'drift'.[9] Disabled unemployed miners experienced loss of a package of intrinsic and extrinsic rewards that were associated with work (such as camaraderie; pride in the job; self-esteem) and the experience could be felt as degrading and humiliating. Ex-miner Tommy Coulter recalled: 'It was a *stigma*. And then it was even worse if they'd to go to the surface. Like ma dad, he was bad wi' he's chest, he'd tae go tae the surface and it was a big blow to his prestige.'[10] And Fife miner William Dunsmore reflected:

> Being a leading man I never ever asked any man to do anything that I could not do myself, and I was embarrassed walking in the tailgate in the 1970s. ... I tried to get in before the men got in because if they hear me panting they'd be saying 'he's done', which I presume I was, but I was embarrassed.[11]

The repetition of the word 'embarrassed' signified the deep emotional impact of disability for this particular miner. Similarly, Durham miner Marshall Wylde described his father's condition:

> The horrible thing about it was that my father was a big strong stocky man ... but when he used to go upstairs, he used to go down on his behind and when he used to go up he used to crawl. It was all right medical, but mental, he was such a proud man and that he had to get things done for him. It was hard seeing my father deteriorate because he was a healthy man and always took an active part in his family life.[12]

In some workplaces the mutual support system saw younger and fitter fellow workers supporting older and disabled workers. As one Scottish miner noted: 'You carried lesser men, gie them a hand, wee dig out and that, but you couldn't cover them all but by and large did a good job covering the weaker elements in society in them days.'[13] Another said: 'When you get older in the pit the younger men kind of looked after the older ones.'[14] This could only be sustained for so long. Increasingly those affected were housebound, isolated and increasingly less able to operate as independent citizens as their age and disability progressed. Convalescence and rehabilitation helped some, but was often

**Figure 3.2** Paraplegics arriving by bus at the CISWO Paraplegic Centre, Pontefract, Yorkshire, 1960.
Courtesy of Getty Images.

only of limited impact for the more seriously injured. The Coal Industry Social Welfare Organisation, established in 1952, played an important role in supporting miners disabled by their work, including through the CISWO paraplegic centre in Pontefract, West Yorkshire.[15]

As the pace of industrial contraction accelerated and pit closures mounted from the 1950s and 1960s opportunities for disabled miners declined. A Durham mining union official, David Guy, reflected on the restricted opportunities that faced those with lung impairment as the pits closed:

> As long as they were able to work, or get to work in some shape or form, the management were pretty sympathetic to people in poor health, especially if it was caused by the work at the pit and there was a tendency for the union and the management to work together to try and fix them up in jobs which they could cope with. Once the pit closed and that type of sympathetic approach wasn't there any longer by employers outside the industry – I mean the first thing they make you do when you apply for a job is to get you medically examined and in the vast majority of cases people were told 'You're not fit enough to work for us, how the

## Industrial Legacies; Damaged Bodies

hell did you manage at the pit?'. So that's resulted in a high percentage of people in the mining communities relying upon sickness benefits, industrial injuries benefits. So I think we've been able to monitor that much better than what we would have done had the pits still been operating. I think the pits *masked* a lot of that, whereas now they're out there now, the reality is there isn't any sympathy for you if you've got a form of disablement. Employers want to take on people who they are going to be able to exploit to the maximum, so they don't want anyone who's got a bad chest or who have spinal injuries or neck injuries or arthritis, there is a reluctance of employers to employ people in that category.[16]

A South Wales miner, Mostyn Moses, suffering from a combination of pneumoconiosis, bronchitis and emphysema commented: 'I have been spitting up dust like black lead from my lungs, like black slurry. Then I started seeing blood and now they tell me I've got tuberculosis as well.'[17] Death could ultimately occur through respiratory failure and/ or cardiac failure. There was and remains no cure for pneumoconiosis.

Miners' bodies could be curtailed many ways. In his autobiography Abe Moffat talked of his younger brother incapacitated with pneumoconiosis and emphysema: 'a physical wreck before he reached the age of fifty'.[18] Some noted the impact of occupation-related disability on their sex life. A 65-year-old miner admitted bluntly that his lung condition meant he was 'too fucked to have sex'.[19] The diminution of libido is a documented consequence of loss of employment for some male workers, recognized as early as the 1930s.[20] However, coupled with this is a loss of pride brought about by not being able to perform as a man in other senses associated with the loss of independence and the 'provider' role. A fifty-year-old miner made this clear:

It was a big blow to me to be told that I'd never work again. Eh, your pride's dented, ken. I mean when your out and your wife's to come out and say to you 'Come on I'll get that …' Wee jobs outside eh, that you're no fit to do, and your son or whatever eh will say to you 'Right come on …' It definitely hurts your pride.[21]

Impacts varied across a wide spectrum, however, depending on a range of factors, including degrees of disability, capacities, age, resources and support networks. One of the recurring themes in the oral testimonies, however, was the curtailment of normal social activities, such as walking, dancing and sport as physical capacity deteriorated and mobility became restricted. A Scottish miner reflected: 'You've not got the capacity to do it. And it restricts you … Like decorating a house, I cannot hold a machine to take wallpaper off, and you get frustrated.'[22] Rita Moses, the wife of a South Wales miner suffering from multiple respiratory diseases noted: 'There's no quality of life for him. He loved his garden and to go for a walk and a drink. Now he can hardly do anything … We've got three sons and two daughters. My Mostyn was a fit and healthy man then.'[23] A 58-year-old disabled miner from Ayrshire remarked: 'I swam a lot. I played golf. I wasnae a bad golfer … And eh, you cannae do them things now. You cannae compete in these things anymore.'[24] The reference to not being able to 'compete' is significant, given

## Jobs and Bodies

the importance of this to the maintenance of masculinity. Competing to produce the most coal or cut the longest roadway were features of many coal mining communities – and some pits rewarded prizes for being the 'top dog', a source of much pride amongst fellow-miners. An ex-coal miner from Durham with emphysema also commented on how his condition constrained his independence and confined him to the home:

> Well for a start, it's stopped us from getting out and I only get out once, once a week and I've got to be took in a car and brought back. If I walk about twelve yards, I've got to stop. That's how it's affected me. And then I've got to go to bed with that [tube] … stuck up me nose all night [laughs], so, I've really – well that's how it's affected me anyway. Before, I was an active bloke, you know.[25]

Clearly, serious occupational disability (caused by injury or by chronic disease such as pneumoconiosis) impacted upon pride, identity and self-esteem, so the effects upon mental health could be as devastating – sometimes more so – than the physical impairment. A Durham ex-miner with chronic bronchitis reflected: 'I shouldn't feel like that but that's my nature and I take it badly because I could do it and when suddenly you can't, I think "well, I'm a bloody write-off here, waste of time really" … It's hard to accept, it's so hard.'[26]

What is being recalled in oral testimonies is frequently an intimate, personal story of damage, loss, pain, adjustment – and of mutating identities. Ex-miners and their families are articulating how it felt in their own words, bringing us closer to understanding their worlds and the range of emotions they experience as they transition from independent breadwinner to being dependent, in varying degrees, upon the state and their families for support. If the traditional heavy industries like mining provided a habitat where historically masculinity was forged, they also had the potential to *emasculate* as injuries and advancing disability curtailed men's capacity to perform as men – as providers, as sexually active partners, as supportive husbands, parents and grandparents. Lives invariably became narrowed and diminished as a consequence, with individuals, partners and families having to readjust their lifestyles as injuries or chronic disease disabled workers.

To some extent the social exclusionary impacts of disability were mediated by the highly supportive, tight knit coal mining communities, where miners and their families could also draw upon the support of their trade union and, from the 1950s, the pioneering welfare work of the Coal Industry Social Welfare Organisation. We come back to examine advocacy and activism in more detail in the final chapter of this book.

## Asbestos-related disease

As with coal miners, Blaxter and Wing Chung-Ho's assertions that disability triggers social exclusion applies to other occupationally sick, disabled and dying people, although with important caveats.[27] Illness, disability and premature death from asbestos-related disease

## Industrial Legacies; Damaged Bodies

(ARD) followed a somewhat different trajectory to that of the coalfields, though there were many parallels. In a similar fashion, economic violence destroyed lives, leaving in its wake a legacy of indescribable pain, suffering and premature death, and deep psychological distress not unlike that found in other PTSDs. As a 64-year-old electrician with cancer (mesothelioma) caused by asbestos reflected in an interview in 1999: 'Until now I thought trauma was a fad imported from America and reserved for the middle classes. I am now wiser.'[28] Oral interviewing methodologies enable us to explore and to elucidate this experience, to get behind the sterile body counts to the human dimension; the lived reality of what this felt like for the individuals and their families behind the numbers. Each case was an individual tragedy that affected all those close to them. Oral testimonies of those suffering from ARDs illuminate a hidden world of private grief, sadness, anger, frustration, disappointment, pain and suffering. In *Lethal Work* we reported on the 'blighted lives' of ARD victims in Scotland and argued that people were invariably marginalized by their illness.[29] We probably under-estimated the extent they were so. Narrators recalled the encroaching social isolation, the reconfiguration of lives around the domestic space of the home, and restricted social and physical activities (as with miners). Victims spoke of relative economic deprivation associated with income reduction, of the trauma associated with being diagnosed in a GP's office or at a hospital, and of living and coping strategies as they struggled to adapt to the news that they were going to die from an incurable cancer. As Castleman and Tweedale show, the majority of mesothelioma victims did not get any financial compensation – even in industrialized countries with statutory Workmen's Compensation systems in the twentieth century (including the UK and Canada).[30] There were economic costs as well as socio-cultural ones. And, these asbestos disease victims and their families did not benefit to the same extent from the strong community and trade union support that characterized coal mining.

Speaking directly to victims and their family members, those directly implicated, enables us to provide a refocused history that reveals much about the emotional journey (in what was often a hidden and personalized space) involved in the transition from fit and able worker to disabled and dependent person, with all that this represents for gendered identities. Janet Ross spoke movingly in 2003 about her ex-shipyard worker husband's experience with mesothelioma:

> I find it impossible to separate the physical, psychological and social. They are interlinked. He was robbed of his normal daily life, he was so breathless, tired, lethargic and general malaise. The impact of that was quite shocking as he was devastated at feeling so bad so soon and then getting the diagnosis and realising it would only get worse. I think this impacted psychologically with the finality of it all sinking in. We would have our wee moments together when he would break down, he just couldn't believe in this age nothing could be done to help him. It gave him a sense of hopelessness which affected his whole way of life, his thinking including his relationship with myself and his family. On the social side he couldn't go out and about and because he was mentally alert he realised what he was losing. This made it worse, he was very aware of his condition and how it was impacting on his life.[31]

## Jobs and Bodies

As noted previously, if the traditional heavy industries provided an environment in which working-class masculinities were forged, they also had the potential to emasculate as encroaching disability curtailed men's capacity to perform as men. An asbestos worker reflected on how difficult it was adapting to the disabling impact of his respiratory disease, and of the reversal of breadwinner roles: 'My wife's got a wee part-time job three mornings a week. And I've seen her going out about half past twelve and I've just finished the last bit of my washing, just ready to put my clothes on.'[32] In an interview in 2003, Julie Blair recalled her father with an ARD and on oxygen sixteen hours a day and in a wheelchair at the end of his life: 'My Dad was a very proud person and his attitude changed very much. He was ashamed that his body was failing him and that he was breathless and he really did not want to meet anyone and he became quite reclusive because of his illness.'[33] Reflecting on the lack of support and counselling in her father's case, Julie continued:

> They were very proud ... and also my father yes it was, he wouldn't even claim any compensation for his illness at all. It was just how people were brought up all these years ago. They did not want to talk about their feelings and that kind of thing. Yes, very much stiff upper lip and keep your thoughts to yourself. Which can be unhealthy. Yes, very much so.[34]

Disabled male working-class ex-industrial workers often found it difficult to discuss what was happening to their bodies, especially older men steeped in the values and cultural practices of their generation, which included stoically containing their emotions. Like disabled miners, asbestos disease victims also found it hard to sustain heavy drinking and smoking consumption patterns commensurate with working-class male identities (though this could have some health benefits). They had this in common with unemployed workers, as Daniel Wight's beautiful ethnographic research revealed.[35] Such disruptions could lead to tensions within the family. Again, however, there was a degree of agency here, albeit prescribed. As with miners, some workers with asbestosis or early stage cancer chose to hide their disability and to continue to work for as long as they could, despite knowing this could further damage respiratory function. To some extent this emerged out of desperation at their plight. The economic and cultural imperatives to act as men and to provide for their families influenced such decisions.

What we perhaps failed to see and to convey adequately in *Lethal Work* two decades ago is how dying a premature and unnatural death, one that was preventable and caused by an outside party, increased psychological distress and discomposure. Signs of PTSD are evident across many of our (and others) asbestos disease interviews. In a recent interview, I asked Phyllis Craig, the Welfare Rights Officer for Clydeside Action on Asbestos since 1995, about the impact of mesothelioma on the lives of her clients. She responded:

> I think the physical and mental go together; the mental is torment; that's the only word. It's torture. They have severe breathlessness to the point they feel they are

## Industrial Legacies; Damaged Bodies

suffocating … they can't breathe. And the fear and anxiety brings it on more. And they try to do things, and they can't walk; they can't do anything. They need somebody to do it all for them. The physical side is terrible. There's fear; there's pain; there's suffering; there's all sorts of anxieties; there's coping, there's worrying and if you add to that that someone else did this, such an anger because they are taking that person away from their partner; their children … Their careers are ended; everything ends because they know they are going to die. I think it's ten times worse, or a hundred times worse if you know someone else has done this. And the families feel it too; they feel a hundred times worse because their personality does change. They are angry. It's devastating … It's horrendous for them. They think about their family; they think about their own mortality and they think about the anger inside them because someone else has caused that … If you think that someone in your work has done something and caused you to be terminally ill and have a horrific death and you're thinking that's what I'm facing because of someone else and because of greed … People have terrible anxiety and difficulty coping because this was not something natural that's happened to them. Someone did this to them. So the physical pain for them is torture but this is intertwined with the mental picture, losing their family, losing their life and not because they have a cancer that has come and they know that's what happens to everyone … but that someone else has killed them; that someone else has taken my life.[36]

In Phyllis Craig's heart-felt narrative the repetition (eight times) of the point that an outside agent was responsible serves to emphasize the significance of this issue. This was believed to be something done to them and outside their control. 'They killed us.' Mary Poole, widow of Terry who died of mesothelioma aged just sixty-six, spoke similarly of this:

But for it to be something that he's died off that he didn't need to have died of that's the awful part of it. That it was known years before anything was ever done about it … They expose you to asbestos and you know that it's still going on now. And that the numbers haven't even peaked yet. And it's alright people saying, Oh well then it'll go down. Yeah but still people are being exposed.[37]

Bitterness and raw anger feature here and are evident in other mesothelioma narratives. Vera Rigby spoke of her husband Barrie, an electrician who moved to college lecturing, who was exposed to asbestos on a range of contracts, including in textile mills and working in schools, and her rage over him not being informed:

Never. Never. Never at all. It makes me really angry because when I think he was a senior lecturer at the end, and even then we didn't know. Never, never ever mentioned. We'd no idea why they were saying, 'have you ever worked with asbestos?' And a very, very good friend and still is – Neil who my husband met when he went into lecturing – he'd done a similar thing. Been an apprentice motor mechanic and he was now in motor vehicles at Mostyn College. And only through us now, Neil knows because brake linings and stuff. But you see like Neil said, 'nobody ever said anything to us as apprentice motor mechanics'.[38]

Recently, in a mixed methods doctoral dissertation that incorporates oral interviews of patients dying of mesothelioma, Helen Clayson (a GP and hospice manager) undertook the most comprehensive study in the UK to date of the effects of this incurable cancer. She refers to the 'complex emotional turmoil' that diagnosis with a fatal asbestos-related cancer induces and comments: 'Bereaved relatives' emotional accounts reflect witnessing severe suffering, express anger and blame around the potentially avoidable asbestos exposure, and present the deaths due to mesothelioma as "mass murder"'.[39] Clayson emphasizes the prevalence of stoic reactions in the face of severe breathlessness and pain and how 'the disease burden is high' even compared to other forms of cancer, usually necessitating multiple visits to GPs, hospital outpatients clinics and hospital admission in the last year of their lives.[40] Severe breathlessness and pleural effusions (lung draining) to release fluid build-up are common and often distressing symptoms. There is also a stigma attached to having a malignant disease and much 'anticipatory anxiety' about the cancer risk amongst those without any symptoms, or with pleural plaques or pleural thickening, who are aware of their exposure to asbestos throughout their working lives.[41] Joe Cowell, a trade union activist and asbestos worker in the UK, comments: 'I started with 25 [fellow workers]. There's two of us left. The others are dead with asbestos. The graveyard is full of my [trade union] members. I have a black tie I constantly wear, attending funerals of asbestos cases.'[42] But the overwhelming reactions that Clayson finds in her investigation are those of stoicism and fatalism, with respondents emphasizing how they are coping with their terminal illness. A 55-year-old woman diagnosed with mesothelioma reflects, 'I've been perfectly healthy up to 55, so I've had 55 [years], a lot of people don't get that long.'[43] A 66-year-old shipbuilding millwright comments: 'I've had my upsets, I've had my tears [...] and after that I just said, "Sod it, I'll just take each day as it comes". I even go back to work once a fortnight.'[44]

Another issue that we did not sufficiently explore in *Lethal Work* is the impact that serious chronic occupational disease had upon women. We neglected the effect on women's lives of directly contracting mesothelioma. The disease challenged women's femininity, corroding their capacity to act as nurturers, carers, mothers and wives – quite apart from the obvious economic ramifications associated with any loss of their earnings (dual-income families were increasingly the norm from the 1960s onwards). Asbestos welfare-rights expert Phyllis Craig commented:

Women even if they are working are generally still the homemaker; generally still the person who the family comes to; the Dad usually goes along with it ... And to have that missing, or for her to know that's going to be missing for them would be the biggest concern. For the man it's more financial. They want to make sure they [the family] are financially stable. That's the difference. The other one is emotional stability. They [women] fear for their children.[45]

Whilst statistically women were less prone than men to contracting ARDs (given the sexual division of labour and dangerous work 'taboo' that existed within working-class culture), as Gorman's and Clayson's work shows, a significant number of them did, and their lives were blighted in similar, if somewhat different, ways than were those of male ARD victims.[46] Women were amongst the earliest diagnosed cases of ARDs (including Nellie Kershaw) but continued to face an uphill struggle to get *diagnosed* with an occupational disease and hence to get proper and proportionate levels of financial compensation. The wars raised exposure. For example, around 1500 women were employed by Boots in Nottingham making gas masks in the Second World War. From the 1960s, case after case of these ex-Boots female workers were diagnosed with the deadly cancer mesothelioma – one, Hannah Meres, after working just five weeks during the war.[47] The gas mask filters contained around 15 per cent blue asbestos (crocidolite). Female factory workers exposed directly to asbestos in their working lives post-war also contracted deadly ARDs. The case of Alice Jefferson was exposed in a powerful, harrowing TV documentary, *Alice: Fight for Life*, in 1982. Consumed with anger, Brenda McKessock narrated the experience of her mother Ellen, a Scottish ex-factory worker in *Mesothelioma: The Story of an Illness* (1995).

By the 1990s, women were beginning to get damages for mesothelioma where it was proven that environmental exposure had occurred, notably as a result of washing their husband's overalls and work clothes or living in the vicinity of an asbestos factory. Still, as Gorman argued (writing in 2000), women faced 'fundamental discrimination', the Department of Health and Social Security (DHSS) refused to believe low-level exposure was responsible, and women 'are pushed to the margins of inclusion by a male-dominated interpretation of legislation in social security adjudication and at civil law'.[48] The proportion of female ARD cases to men being diagnosed continued to increase in the twenty-first century, including female teachers, exposed to asbestos in schools and shown to have significantly higher mortality rates from mesothelioma than would be expected.[49]

For men, disability caused through a work-related injury or disease could be deeply emasculating, as previously noted. A sixty-year-old railway track worker disabled by a work injury which left him blind in one eye commented on being taken off his job as a track supervisor: 'They've changed the rules now; they've took all that off me. What it is, because they've more or less made me impotent in the gang, do you know what I mean.' Significant in this narrative, as Kirk (the interviewer) noted, was the deployment of pronouns – 'them and us' and reference to 'impotent', suggesting something of a crisis of masculinity.[50] The oral evidence brought to light (as noted in Chapter 2) the existence of an individualist element in workers' culture that coexisted, sometimes uneasily, with the collective, mutual, class-conscious character of traditional working-class communities.

Men responded less directly to health education and hazards-awareness campaigns than did women and were generally more reluctant to admit they had a health problem and to seek medical intervention. And, when they became ill, some would refuse to allow help or to admit that they needed it.[51] The wife of a quantity surveyor with mesothelioma reflected, after his death, that 'he never made a fuss [...] I was the one that used to see him sitting on the edge of the bed with his arms around himself rocking back and forward in

## Jobs and Bodies

pain'.[52] A 61-year-old shipyard engineering worker with mesothelioma commented: 'A lot of it's my own problem. Too macho to be shouting out when I should be, you know, when I'm in pain.'[53] Diseased and disabled workers unable to compete and to perform as men invariably felt belittled and devalued. Those affected narrated how this was lived in their everyday lives and how it felt to them. An ex-marine engineer with an asbestos-related disease reflected: 'I led a very full social life ... I no longer do that. I have shut myself off from life completely.'[54] Another reflected, 'I'm buggered',[55] and a Clydeside asbestos sprayer quite aptly described ARD victims as 'industrial lepers'.[56] An occupational asthma sufferer interviewed in 1998 reflected on the impact his disability had: 'I've had no social life since about 1980. Eh, people unfortunately don't want to know you when you're, you're ill like, y'know. People stopped coming. I was very disappointed.'[57]

Emotions might be controlled by many men, except in private moments, as the wife of the quantity surveyor cited earlier recalled:

> You do your best to bolster them and keep going for them and make light of things. And he took my hand and said: 'I'm not going to see ... as a bride.' Then we went up to bed together and we just cuddled and we both cried. And it's the one and only time that I saw my husband crying.[58]

She told of how her husband insisted on driving the car out of the drive 'and then we would pull in and stop and I would take over'. 'Men, eh', she pondered, 'don't like to

**Figure 3.3** International Asbestos Memorial, Clydebank.
(Photo by Arthur McIvor).

give in'. A pleural plaques sufferer related: 'The depression's bad. You get that something terrible. You just want to greet your eyes out and everything, you know … You can get a violent one. You just flash up stuff.'[59] 'All my thoughts are negative', the wife of a 64-year-old electrician with mesothelioma stated: 'I cannae see a future.'[60] Of course, coping capacities and strategies ranged widely, but the oral testimonies consistently referred to the psychosocial distress and disruption to lives, commensurate with trauma, experienced by ARD victims and survivors. The human disaster of asbestos has been memorialized recently, with the erection in 2015 of the haunting international asbestos memorial (designed by Jephson Robb and commissioned by the Clydebank Asbestos Group) in Clydebank, near Glasgow (Figure 3.3).

## Caring for the sick and injured

If women less frequently experienced a severe workplace injury or chronic industrial disease than men, they did feel the impact acutely as invariably it was female family members who bore the brunt of caring for the sick, injured and impaired. Their lives could also be changed as a consequence – and this has not been acknowledged as much as it should have been. Several years ago the Scottish Oral History Centre received a deposit of seven interviews conducted by Nigel Ingham for the Greater Manchester Asbestos Victims Support Group. The main focus of these recordings was the wives of ARD victims telling their stories of living through their husband's diagnosis with mesothelioma, their treatment and their untimely deaths.[61] Sharing their deeply personal stories for posterity they provide a unique perspective, through the lens of family and loved ones of the impact of contracting a serious occupational disease and of the care and support role provided by the wives and families of victims. They told their stories to deepen understanding and help others. As Margaret Poole put it: 'So now whatever I can do to help somebody else … I'll try and do. That's why I agreed to do this [the interview]. And I'll keep going to the group. And maybe somewhere along the line I can help somebody else …'[62]

Lauren Ross recalled the mesothelioma diagnosis of her husband Frank (a joiner) when he was aged just fifty-nine:

> We went into this room and somebody had just come out, and we went in straight away and there was an x-ray on, you know those light boxes. And I just remember thinking, please don't let that be his. You know which now is probably quite selfish, because it had to be somebody's but I just thought, please don't let that be his. And it was. And they said straight away, we think you've got mesothelioma. And if you have, you've got eight months to twelve. And it was just like the bottom fell out of your world. In fact it was so bad you couldn't even comprehend it. In some ways you did. But in other ways it didn't hit you. It's just like it's so bad you can't – because I think my eyes filled up with tears and I did a bit of a gulp. But I think if I had actually realised at that minute I wouldn't have been able to speak. I would

have just been uncontrollably on the floor I think. But it is just such a shock I don't know whether your adrenalin kicks in but you do actually ask questions and things. But it is just unbelievable.[63]

Lauren went on to describe having to relay to her husband later that he did have mesothelioma and her concern over him suffering:

It's the worst thing you can be told that you're going to die. Because we all know we are going to die but we don't put a date on it or a timescale on it, we're just going to go when we go don't we? Everybody lives with that knowledge. But having a date, you just think, What am I going to do in that time? Is he going to suffer? I suppose from a wife's point of view it's, is he going to suffer? You know, and the family. Because it's bad enough going but you don't want to see them suffer on the way, and they do, unfortunately.[64]

The incredible, indescribable pain experienced by those with mesothelioma is related in these testimonies from wives, who invariably managed the chemotherapy tablets and pain relief regimes, usually involving morphine and radiotherapy. Despite being in what Lauren described as 'agony' (even with the morphine) her husband tried to maintain some semblance of a fatherly role to their children:

He still got up early with the kids. And he still – right up until he went in the hospice, he used to still get up in the morning and make them a piece of toast if they wanted it, or make them a cup of tea, because that's what he liked to do, but then if he wanted he could sleep all day or however he felt. But he felt that getting up and making the kids a cup of tea, he was contributing. And I think it is something that they will never forget. I know it seems little but to him he was looking after his children even then.[65]

Wives usually accompanied their partners through this journey, experiencing much anxiety, stress and secondary trauma along the way. They played the main role as carers, navigating the medical services, treatment and pain relief and having to cope as their loved one's health deteriorated. The job of caring was another ingrained gender role, usually performed by women. The Manchester group interviews include really harrowing descriptions of weight loss, emaciation, pain and suffering, which worsened through the final stages of the cancer. Mavis Tong described her husband as 'skeletal' near the end, 'like you see in the camps'.[66] Terry Poole's pain was so intense they tried a cordotomy (cutting nerves in the spinal cord to relieve pain) and a local nerve block after morphine, ketamine and oxycodone.[67] His wife felt it made little difference. Barbara Eason reflected on her part in the final stages of her husband Mike's struggle with mesothelioma:

I did everything for Mike. I washed him. I mean he was getting to a stage he couldn't do anything for himself. He might just manage to go to the bathroom, just

## Industrial Legacies; Damaged Bodies

try and walk there but he didn't have the strength to – He'd sit on the toilet seat and I had to wash him. He hadn't got the strength. He'd manage perhaps to shave himself because as he looked in the mirror … he went just like – You see he was only very slim to start with … Well at first he'd lay here but then after that he was just in bed all the time. And he just looked like something out of Belsen. His face was was – Oh it was just in. He looked so bad … I said in here that Mike said he didn't like to look in the mirror because he looked like something out of a prisoner of war camp, because he'd gone so thin.[68]

Barbara continued later in the interview:

I've missed all that, all what he suffered with – night sweats and all sorts. But I could have gone on and on. Couldn't lie down in bed because of his breathing. I've missed all that, things I had to do for him. He couldn't do anything. Couldn't sleep. Couldn't lie down. Had to just sit – Absolutely terrible what he had to go through. And pain like gnawing, like a rat gnawing. When I think of all the – I had to rub cream on his back all the time 'cause he was itching and oh! It was terrible.[69]

She managed this awful period stoically, supporting her husband through his last days with as much composure and dignity as possible. Barbara recalled:

But once I was stood at the kitchen and it was once when he wasn't too bad. I can see him in his green dressing gown. I sometimes put that on sometimes. And he was stood in the hall. I had my face to the sink. And I was crying. He says, 'are you crying?' And I turned round and I said, 'yeah'. I says, 'I'm just upset'. I says, 'I'm trying to imagine you not being here'. Now I think what it is when they're dying you're just kind of going through it, but it's not sinking in until they've actually gone. And I said, 'I'm trying to imagine you not being here'. And do you know what he said to me, 'I'll always be with you'. So – ! But when he did die, oh God it was awful. Absolutely awful.[70]

Vera Rigby, cited previously, cared for her husband for over two years after his diagnosis with mesothelioma. She spoke of the difficulties of misdiagnosis, the ineptitude and lack of experience of doctors and medical wards, the struggles with compensation and her supportive role and the quiet stoicism of her husband (who was super-fit before becoming ill, aged just sixty-one, in 2003) as they navigated through encroaching breathlessness, experimental surgery (a lung was removed), chemotherapy, pain and suffering. The gap left in her life when her husband died was tangible. Vera spoke movingly of his loss, his absence from subsequent holidays and from the family, including seeing the grandchildren grow up; how she was dependent upon him for doing all the practical jobs around the house (he was trained as an electrician) and how she sold up their family home soon after he died because she couldn't cope. These emotions of profound sadness and despair are difficult to comprehend. Vera also made a key point, reflecting that, in

## Jobs and Bodies

retrospect, she felt she had coped reasonably well compared to others in her asbestos victims support group, noting that some remained deeply bitter and angry and could not come to terms with their loss for a very long time, if at all.[71] Margaret Poole expressed her deep sense of guilt that she couldn't do more and came to challenge her own Catholic faith as a consequence of what she witnessed with her husband's horrendous death from mesothelioma:

> Watching him and not being able to make it right, you know, not being able to help him and keep him comfortable, or give him comfort even. 'Cause it was awful. Awful. I wouldn't wish it on my worst enemy. ... So I think that's the end of my tale really. I wish I could have done more than I did. I wish I could have brought him home [from the hospice]. I know I did the right thing not doing that but it doesn't make me feel any better or less guilty about not bringing him home. I would have loved to have been able to bring him home and care for him here.[72]

A sense of anxiety around their own health due to possible asbestos exposure also emerged from some of the wives' interviews. Mavis Tong, who herself had a persistent cough, remembered being concerned:

> I mean Jim obviously wore overalls because he's a painter, and I used to shake them out, 'cause there was all bits in, you know, you know, in the pouch whathaveyou, and I hated putting them in the washer really. And it said in this literature somewhere, that family could pick it up because of bringing things home. And I thought, Oh yeah I used to shake his overalls. And I thought, ... Oh I think I'll see a doctor ... I think I'll ask the doctor if I can go for a chest x-ray.[73]

Thankfully Mavis's x-ray was negative.

Capacities to cope and 'move on', as Vera Rigby put it, ranged widely. Some of the wives of mesothelioma victims could draw upon family and friends for support. Others relied on health and social workers. For some the Macmillan nurses were a godsend. Lauren Ross commented:

> We had a fabulous Macmillan nurse at the hospital, but unfortunately they don't come out. If I phoned her up and I used to say, 'look he's taking all this oral morphine'. She used to say, 'right. Up his MSTs and see how you go'. Or I would go and have counselling with her. I'd just go down and – Well Frank would take me, because he drove and I don't. He'd take me down and he'd chat away with the nurses in the unit, and I'd go and see Vicky and cry my eyes out. I'd come outside and he'd go, 'you alright?' I'd go, 'Yes I am'. She was brilliant.[74]

Where some financial compensation was awarded this could bring some consolation to victims concerned about their spouses financial circumstances going forward and the

## Industrial Legacies; Damaged Bodies

family's well-being. In reality, however, this meant little given the enormity of the loss. Lauren Ross explained what this meant to her:

> He wanted justice and he wanted to see that I'd be alright. And I do understand it … The day you get it you think you'll be happy but you're not. It's the worst day of your life. Well it's not the worst day of your life but it's horrible. It's absolutely horrible. Because it's like blood money … I suppose it's like when somebody that you are very close to dies, and they say, you've got this money. It doesn't actually mean anything. I think sometimes people think, she's going on holiday again. She must be loaded. She must be happy. I go on holiday because I don't have, I don't have Frank. I could sit in day after day after day and be with Frank and never go on holiday. But I don't have anyone else, I'm not looking for anyone else. So me and some of the other widows go away … And we keep each other company because at the end of the day we all know what we feel like. But that's all I do. Most of it is protected so that my children will get some of it, which is what I think he would like.[75]

Raymond Nye, ex-shipwright at Chatham Docks, and husband to Mavis, diagnosed with mesothelioma in 2009, expressed his deep sense of guilt about bringing home toxic asbestos dust and exposing his wife to risk:

> Worst thing is. I must put this down to me. I have helped to kill the most precious thing in my life. How can I cope with that? The poison dust was on my clothes in my hair, asbestos. A job that I took to earn money for wife and family … I don't want to go on. Life can be cruel.[76]

This situation was reflected in the wonderful novel *Waterline* where the main character Mick went off the rails consumed with guilt at having brought home the asbestos dust from his job in the shipyards that led to the death of his beloved wife Cathy from mesothelioma:

> Always the same question coming back at him. How is it no himself? Him that was working with the stuff every day, brushing against the laggers and their buckets of monkey dung, walking under scaffold planks with great showers of it floating down like snowstorms … Fucking lies, all of it … And he should have known. Even if no at first, way back, then he certainly could have done later on, when there was the warnings and the newspaper reports …[77]

Others reflected on their anxieties that they could be diagnosed anytime with cancer because of their work histories and what their loss might mean to the family, as with Thomas Henry Wright, a former Chatham Dockyard worker who penned a poem in 2002 about potential radiation exposure titled 'The Next to Go': 'Nobody told us the work might cost lives … Who'll be next to go Jack, Ben or me?'[78] These are deeply

## Jobs and Bodies

emotional, personal stories, shared by those who care about their loved ones which bear testament to the unfairness and injustice of asbestos-related diseases. They speak of the agony and heartbreak of living with such disease, and of the pressures, anxieties, worries, guilt, frustration and anger of victims and their carers. They want others to know about their pain and the suffering of those with such occupational diseases; to understand; to help others; to learn lessons.

## Beyond the workplace: Environmental pollution stories

Another aspect of the damage to bodies done by industrial toxins, chemicals and materials is the way that the factory and workplace fails to completely contain the hazard which can and did spill over and contaminate the community. Industrial cities cast a long shadow of pollution and environmental damage that emanated from the workplace – the steelworks, chemical works, asbestos factories, abattoirs, shipyards and the like. The dangers of radioactive contamination in the vicinity of nuclear power stations are well known, but polluting toxicants, fumes, dust, glare, noise and dust in the environs of factories were commonplace. In the 1950s, before closure, for example, folk commented on the glare coming from the giant iron and steel works on the south side of Glasgow – in the Gorbals – nicknamed 'Dixon's Blazes'. Reputedly, people could read their newspapers outside at night the glow was so powerful. But steelworks also belched out polluting dust, as Kajeca documented in her wonderful film, 'Red Dust' on what was once the largest steelworks in Europe – Ravenscraig in Lanarkshire.[79] The documentary writer deployed oral testimonies of ex-Ravenscraig steel workers and local community activists campaigning on the deleterious health effects of the pollution. Industrial chemical plants also belched pollution into the surrounding urban environment. The notorious White's chemical plant in Rutherglen, Glasgow, provides another example where workers' health was poor but pollution affected the wider local environment and the community. This happened during the working life of the plant, but also continued in the decades after the plant closed in 1968, right up to the present. The issue, similar to that exposed in the movie *Erin Brockovitch*, is with chromium IV seepage from chemical dumps around the factory and contamination of the water table.[80]

Beyond direct workplace exposure, asbestos left a grim environmental legacy, belching dust from factory, building site and workshop extractor systems into the air in the neighbourhood and widening contamination via their asbestos dumps in the vicinity of the asbestos factories like T&N in Rochdale and Glasgow and Cape Asbestos in London. Michael King (born 1943) grew up around the Cape Asbestos plant in Barking, near Dagenham, London, and recalled:

> I can remember the dust that used to come out and everybody talked about the dust and what have you. Particularly landing on the playground at St Ethelburga's [school].
> *So what was it like?*

## Industrial Legacies; Damaged Bodies

Like cotton wool type. I can remember that. Settled in the playgrounds ... Other people since I have been diagnosed with this, other people I have spoken to – from school – remember a lot more than I do about it. One chap, little bit older, he was my brother's age, he remembered clearly the trees were never the same in the area of Cape Asbestos as they were in other places. He said they was always a brownish tinge to them. I can't remember that ... I remember it on the ground of course. Yes I can remember the stuff on the ground and you scrape it up with your feet. And something I never did, and again people have talked about it, gathering it up and making snowballs in summer with asbestos ... Near the sports hall there used to be a sort of dump where people – where waste material was kept as well. That's clearly in my mind, the waste that was there as well. This was asbestos waste. Asbestos waste, yes, yes, yes, yes. And all the time we never thought anything about it. We never considered it to be a danger or anything. When I left school in 1958, so I was 15 and 3 months [...] I worked at the co-op butchers in Barking. A mile or so away from the factory.[81]

Michael was diagnosed with mesothelioma in 2013, aged seventy, with his exposure traced back to living around the Barking plant. And he was not alone:

And I believe, I think they said there was something like 245 people per 100,000 from Barking. I think it's the worst area in the country ... Talking to a friend of my brother's, my brother was 7 years older than me, and this lad who I met recently, he knew quite a number of lads of his age who had died through it – people who I didn't know from Barking, from the church, because they're Catholics as well ... Very sad. Very, very sad ... It's awful isn't it? When something that you know full well could have been avoided. They knew it could have been avoided. I didn't need to go to that school in that situation had they done the right thing.[82]

Other cities and neighbourhoods were affected in similar ways. Glasgow and the West of Scotland were a particular asbestos 'hot spot', as were other industrial and port cities. Asbestos dust from factories, shipyards and building sites, as well as from asbestos waste tips blew into the neighbouring streets. One estimate in the mid-1970s indicated that urban areas had around ten times the asbestos fibre content free-floating in the air compared to rural areas.[83] In the immediate environs of asbestos processing plants, the asbestos content in the air was more than double the average urban air asbestos contamination level. Streets adjacent to Turners asbestos factory in Clydebank were covered in white dust which settled on cars and on window sills. Turner and Newall's own company medical adviser, Dr Hilton Lewinsohn commented on this environmental exposure as early as 1968, referring to 'spillage' from vehicles within and around asbestos plant premises:

Not only are the drivers of the tractors at risk [directly moving the material around the site], but also the warehousemen, the office workers and others as well as the community living in the neighbourhood of the factory, especially in the direction of the prevailing winds. The association of mesothelioma of the pleura with non-occupational exposure to asbestos dust is now well recognised – this is an unnecessary risk to the community and all possible measures should be urgently implemented to stop this hazardous procedure.[84]

Whether anything was done following this information is not known. Asbestos was also brought home on the skin, hair and work clothes of employees. Several years earlier a survey in London identified the first cases of secondary or 'bystander' exposure, with eleven cases of mesothelioma amongst people who had a separate family member working directly with asbestos.[85] Most were housewives. One recalled: 'I said [to her husband] "why are you all white"? ... Your black hair was pure white with the dust ... the man came home and he was pure white, actually white with dust. It was a nightmare, a pure nightmare.'[86]

Other exposure points occurred in workers' transit from workplace to home, in local shops, cafes, pubs, fish and chip shops and on trains, trams and buses. An employee of Turners Asbestos Cement factory in Clydebank commented ironicallly how workers 'were very popular with some of the bus conductors'. He recalled: 'We nearly all carried newspapers just tae sit on in the buses so it didnae affect too many people. But we didnae know we were killing them.'[87] Indeed bus conductors are amongst those subsequently known to have died of mesothelioma. However, it was not until 1995 that the first successful legal action to claim compensation for a 'bystander' asbestos-related disease took place. June Hancock was awarded £65,000 in Leeds High Court in 1995 against Turner & Newall.[88] Until the end of the century the DHSS found it difficult to officially recognize mesothelioma as caused by such low-level secondary contact and women suffered because of their ineligibility (unless directly employed) to qualify for Industrial Disability Benefit.

Asbestos also proved to be an environmental hazard emanating from indiscriminate dumping on factory and other sites during the heyday of manufacture. Children were found to be playing on asbestos tips (e.g. in Falkirk), and exposed to asbestos dust blowing around school playgrounds (e.g. in Drumchapel, Glasgow).[89] The Turners Asbestos Cement factory in Clydebank left a massive uncovered asbestos waste pile on the site after it closed in 1970 as it had dumped all its waste from 1938 down at the river bank and mudflats adjacent to the factory. An ex-Turners employee responsible for waste disposal from the plant testified to this in 1987 recalling that 'all the ground between the factory and the river along the whole frontage was reclaimed by dumping asbestos waste', estimated at around 1000 yards long by 40 yards wide and 7 yards deep.[90] Several years before (in 1980) the Director of the Cancer Prevention Society had exposed what he called the 'scandalous contamination' of the community and the heightened cancer risks in Clydebank.[91] The local council subsequently funded the covering up of the asbestos on site in 1985 at a cost of £400,000 of taxpayers' money after failing to recover any money from the site owners (Monaville Estates) due to their insolvency.[92] Several years later a more extensive site remediation scheme cost Clydebank Council

£8 million (four times the original cost estimate), with all the asbestos waste moved from the site and dumped in a dredged and deepened nearby disused dock basin and concreted over. Ironically, an American-owned private hospital now stands on the old site of the T&N Asbestos factory.[93]

Epidemiological studies have found significantly higher rates of mesothelioma and cancer amongst those who lived in such communities adjacent to asbestos factories and mines.[94] Deprived and impoverished working-class neighbourhoods were the worst hit, deepening existing health inequalities across industrial cities and nationally. And asbestos exposure continues to be an issue long after its use was banned (in the UK in 1999) because of its insidious existence within the infrastructure of public buildings, workplaces and homes. It is now routinely identified in house purchasers 'home reports' (Scotland) and buyers' surveys (England), not least in the artex (patterned plaster) used widely in home decoration from the 1960s to the 1980s. Given such environmental exposure, the 'magic mineral' is going to be causing untold damage to people's bodies for many more years to come yet.

## Conclusion

Industrial work in the post-Second World War era continued to damage bodies – in some cases, as with the case studies here of coal mining and asbestos, very severely, causing sickness, injury and premature death. Much of the harm caused by this economic violence meted out on working people was both tragic and unnecessary, given the state of prior knowledge. And it occurred across both nationalized (e.g. coal mining) and privatized sectors of the economy. Managerial exploitation geared towards maximizing production and profits could seriously undermine workers' health and well-being – as we've seen here in these investigations of coal workers' pneumoconiosis and asbestos-related diseases. Serious injury, encroaching disability, old-age, premature death and/or the removal of employment could have deep social, physical and psychological effects. This manifested as social exclusion, 'estrangement' and emasculation, trauma and enormous pressure and emotional turmoil for carers, notably the wives of victims. It appears that the impact upon the male psyche could be even more damaging where loss of the provider role was combined with physical deterioration in health as a consequence of industrial injury, disability or disease. Massive adjustments had to be negotiated in this forced transition from independent provider in a male-dominated work environment, to socially excluded dependent, often confined within what was still perceived by members of this generation as the woman's domain in the home.

The oral testimonies of such disabled workers and their close family members help us to understand how work could impact upon the body and upon identities, and how individuals and families navigated the transition from fit, independent and capable worker, able and willing to carry their own weight, to a slower unfit worker, increasingly dependent upon others. Partners and wives – most frequently women – might have to adjust to becoming full-time carers, with limited state support and much emotional stress on top of the financial hardships. This *emotional history* has hardly been explored, clearly merits more attention and hopefully will become an important research focus in the future. Bitterness, frustration, embarrassment, anger and violence as well as stoic and even heroic toleration and resignation to one's fate all feature significantly in the worker narratives investigated here, with a wide range of emotions evident in the oral testimonies and other narratives of disabled workers and their families.

There is also, however, a further and very different identifiable impact of such experience. For some workers, and some wives and carers of victims, the experience of chronic illness and premature death was radicalizing, enervating and politicizing. Knowledge of bodily damage, pain and premature death, and perceptions of injustice and exploitation, drew many, like Vera Rigby in Manchester, into political activism in the occupational health and injury movement – to campaign to punish those responsible, to prevent the same thing happening to others and to get decent levels of compensation. We go on to examine in more depth such occupational health and safety advocacy and activism in the last chapter. We turn our attention next though to industrial legacies and the health impacts of losing work in the era of deindustrialization.

# CHAPTER 4
## 'FIT FOR THE SCRAP HEAP': REMEMBERING LOSING WORK AND HEALTH

Industrial work in the post-Second World War era was multi-faceted and complex in its impacts on health, well-being and the body. It could be fulfilling and a source of pride and identity, but at the same time was invariably physically demanding, dirty, dangerous, unhealthy and, for some, precarious, demeaning and uncertain. Exploitative management in the sector caused injury, sickness and premature death. However, it is important that we keep this in perspective. In post-Second World War Britain negligible levels of unemployment, powerful trade unions and a post-war political consensus contributed to humanizing work in a mixed economy (with substantial nationalization, including the coal mines from 1947) where basic human rights in the workplace were enshrined in a comprehensive legal labour code. Whilst older occupational threats and diseases persisted in industry and new (or newly discovered) health hazards replaced old ones, the trend was clearly towards a safer and healthier work environment. And the more dangerous jobs were declining fast. The risks of a serious disabling injury and losing life in a workplace accident fell more than tenfold between 1950 and 2000.[1] Workers benefitted from clear rights to organize and to picket during strikes, and from access to a wide-ranging National Health Service, as well as to a comprehensive workplace health, safety and welfare regime, with (albeit limited) financial compensation for job loss, work-related injuries and a cluster of industrial diseases, as we've seen. By the 1970s, bodies at work had protection at unprecedented levels. And industrial work in the UK after the Second World War provided a profound sense of purpose, pride and identity and a source of enduring friendships and meaningful social relationships, and contributed to a vibrant if complex working-class culture. Workers' relationships to their work of course varied widely across a spectrum from alienation and boredom, to intense joy and satisfaction. But, with some exceptions, industrial work in the post-war era and the tangible material rewards it brought had a positive impact on well-being and was health-enhancing in profound ways. Such well-unionized jobs with rising real wages for fully three decades post-war enabled houses to be purchased and working-class families to be reared in relative comfort compared to pre-war.

A growing threat to workers' bodies emerged, however, as a result of the *loss* of their work through economic restructuring. The dismantling of industry with plant downsizing and closures, and the shift to a post-industrial economy based on office and service sector jobs, was a long, drawn-out process in the UK, as elsewhere, but a profound shock to those experiencing it nonetheless. The pace of change accelerated in the last quarter of the twentieth century, as a consequence of politically induced workplace

## Jobs and Bodies

closures associated with Thatcherism and the emergence of neo-liberal economics. A primary underlying motivation here was to break the trade unions. The idea of a 'Golden Age' of work in the post-war decades is exaggerated and an over-generalization, of course. Nonetheless, it is evident that the accelerated phase of deindustrialization in the 1980s and 1990s ruptured this relatively stable work milieu and associated social order in fundamental ways. And, the long-term unemployment, underemployment and labour market insecurity that followed had massive adverse impacts on workers' health and well-being.

Much scholarship has been devoted to exploring the impacts of factory and pit closures and of work loss.[2] Debates over deindustrialization and 'smokestack nostalgia' have identified a tendency to uncritically romanticize and sentimentalize the industrial workplace.[3] In this selective remembering, the lived and embodied experience of the people who worked in these spaces and were directly affected by deindustrialization has sometimes been airbrushed out, and the industrial workplace can appear benign, shorn of the class and power relations in which it was embedded. The occupational hazards, risks and bodily harms industrial workers faced discussed in previous chapters are an important corrective to this view. That said, there is space I think for elucidation of the impact of what were concurrently corrosive, traumatic and, for some, emancipating processes upon workers' bodies as deindustrialization progressed. After a short section providing some context on economic restructuring, job loss and the debates on unemployment and health we move in this chapter to bring in the voices of those workers and their families that were affected, exploring their lived experience and narratives of job loss and the effects of such rupture and destabilization on health and well-being. This involves discussion of, firstly, articulations of loss of livelihoods; secondly, the lived experience of heightened pressure and stress on the job and in the labour market as unemployment increased; and, finally, a comment on the more positive narratives of release, adaptations and escape, for some, from industrial jobs to more benign, healthier and rewarding employment. Plant, yard and mine shutdowns and loss of work, as many studies have revealed, were deeply inimical to both physical and mental health. Moreover, in deindustrializing communities, the *legacy* of the work previously undertaken remains evident in, for example, high levels of disability, injury and ill health (as we discussed in Chapter 3). Layered on top of this, in the 1980s and 1990s were the ill-health impacts of loss of work, combined with the stressors and pressures that went along with labour market insecurity and deepening precarity.

## Deindustrialization, unemployment and health

The UK experienced a particularly rapid and steep rate of deindustrialization in the second half of the twentieth century. In 1979, manufacturing employed 6.8 million workers and accounted for some 30 per cent of the GDP. By 2010, this was down to 2.5 million workers and 11 per cent of national income. Some regions experienced a faster rate of decline than others. Taking the 1931 Occupational Census as the base point, by 2001 Scotland had lost 47 per cent of industrial jobs, whilst England had lost 30 per cent.[4] In coal mining, contraction began in the 1950s. In 1957, 822 pits employed 704,000 across the UK; by 1975, this was down to 241 pits employing 245,000; and between 1981 and 1994, the labour force contracted to just seventeen collieries employing 8518 miners. The last deep mine in the country closed in December 2015, though some employment continued thereafter in open-cast mining. Following pit closures, few middle-aged and elderly miners found alternative jobs, and fewer still, *good* (well-paid and unionized) different jobs. In the mid-1990s, just one in four of those who had been miners a decade earlier had a full-time job.[5] Some industrial workers retrained, transitioned into new careers and adapted to change. Others witnessed a downward spiral, well documented in the deindustrialization literature. A *Mass Observation* participant who told his story in 1997 (when aged sixty-nine and retired) had been a time-served engineer working at a cotton mill in Paisley, followed by a spell in the Rolls Royce factory in Hillington, Glasgow:

> I myself have been made redundant four times during my working life and had to do other things to tide me over. And as you get older it becomes more difficult to get another job, if at all … If you have a fairly well paid job and become redundant, the chances of getting another job at the same salary becomes a remote possibility.[6]

Amongst his subsequent post-redundancy jobs were as a clerk, a salesman and as a driving instructor.

Deindustrialization in the UK was a complex process, associated with large-scale job losses *and* changes in work organization in contracting industries, rising levels of work intensification, job insecurity, and worker disempowerment in mining and manufacturing. The transition from an industrial to a service-based economy involved direct plant closures, redundancies and rising levels of unemployment, but also a shift in response to market pressures towards lower cost, more flexible labour and a concerted managerial offensive to increase workloads, attack trade unions and undermine the labour contract. These processes impacted negatively upon workers' bodies in a myriad of ways.

The impact of job loss on health is a controversial topic and has been debated intensely since at least the interwar depression.[7] Mel Bartley has argued that this discussion was characterized by 'a loop of claim and counter-claim'.[8] Whilst the evidence strongly indicates a clear correlation between high unemployment levels and ill-health, the case for unemployment as a *direct* cause is more contested. Region and environment are important variables (as there are long-standing regional differences in health standards) whilst a primary complicating factor lies with 'the healthy worker effect – the tendency of healthy workers to survive in employment while the unhealthy lose their jobs'.[9] It has also been argued that sickness rates in areas of high unemployment have been artificially inflated by the benefits regime which provides a premium for those claiming for long-term sickness or disability benefits as opposed to the dole.

## Jobs and Bodies

Because health standards correlate directly with income levels, loss of work and falling income inevitably impacted adversely on morbidity and mortality. Studies of the mortality rates of the employed and unemployed have demonstrated reduced life expectancy with long-term unemployment, even when behaviour (such as alcohol consumption and smoking) and social class are allowed for.[10] Unemployment impoverished individuals and families, and poverty was a driver of ill-health and premature death. Morbidity was clearly associated with unemployment and labour market insecurity – with symptoms including high blood pressure, ulcers, weight loss, weight gain, heart disease and alcoholism.[11] As Shaw et al.'s study demonstrates, districts with the highest levels of unemployment also had the highest recorded levels of ill-health (measured by those on permanent incapacity and sickness benefits). In some districts of Glasgow, for example, male unemployment rates in 1991 ranged between 20 and 25 per cent and in the same areas those on incapacity benefits reached 12 to 16 per cent. In more affluent areas of the UK – such as Buckingham, Wokingham, Chesham and Amersham there was less than 5 per cent unemployed and less than 2 per cent permanently sick.[12] 'Clearly', Shaw and her colleagues asserted, 'being out of work in such large numbers damages the health of men of working age in these places' as it did for women, though the relationship was not so clearly defined.[13] The coalfields exhibited similar patterns. Around 750,000 people of working age in the coalfields self-reported as having 'a limiting long-term illness' to the 1991 Census. Losing work clearly impacted upon ex-miners bodies, resulting, for example, in higher levels of obesity due to inactivity and in some cases higher rates of smoking and drinking.[14]

A consensus has emerged that *long-term* unemployment directly contributed to degeneration in psychological health, defined as 'the emotional and cognitive state, including a person's mental health, happiness, work and life satisfaction'.[15] Work loss was felt and experienced intimately in workers' bodies, constituting a primary cause of widening health inequalities.[16] Sociological, ethnographic and psychological studies have clearly identified a range of mental ill-health consequences of job loss, including depression, anxiety, negative self-esteem, eroded self-confidence and insomnia.[17] Unemployment was stigmatized and embedded identities as workers and breadwinners 'spoiled'.[18] A middle-aged working-class Mass Observer (male born 1940s) responded to the Summer 1983 directive on unemployment, reflecting on the ambiguous meanings of work to him:

> What I have enjoyed about jobs in the past is the sense of companionship that some of them brought, especially labouring jobs. What I began not to enjoy was the sense of futility and humiliation and waste that I also felt. Also the sheer physical discomfort of many of them ... I am affected by unemployment in several ways. A grinding lack of money is one. Just as important is the way I cannot admire myself, and the fact that others cannot. Yes it is important to have regular work but it is also important for the work to matter. Make-work is probably nearly as bad as having no work at all.[19]

'Fit for the Scrap Heap'

Recovery from psychological ill health caused by unemployment was possible and could be alleviated by medical interventions (such as antidepressant prescriptions), counselling and psychiatric treatment, although the latter was rarely obtained by British blue-collar working-class men. Two British studies put suicide rates amongst unemployed men at around double the rate in the general population.[20] Some industrial areas were worse than others: in Scotland, suicide rates for men rose sharply in the 1970s and 1980s, at 40 per cent more than the suicide rate in England and Wales.[21]

Where there was considerable debate, however, was over whether mental ill-health was the consequence of poverty (as studies of the 1930s had tended to stress) or the result of the loss of the cluster of intrinsic rewards which employment provided, such as status, identity, time structure, esteem, social contact, control and power. Much of the research in the 1980s stressed the latter, whilst Fryer has argued a strong case for unemployment poverty as the primary stressor and cause of mental ill health.[22] In a British study covering 1971–91, Mel Bartley and Ian Plewis demonstrated the cumulative impact of spells of unemployment on higher rates of heart disease in later life.[23] And studies of the geography of unemployment and health demonstrate a close correlation between deindustrializing districts and the highest recorded levels of ill health (measured by those on permanent incapacity and sickness benefits).[24]

Most investigations have also emphasized, however, that unemployment is likely to be one of a number of contributory factors in both mental and physical ill health and that frequently causation is difficult to pin down. There were some positive health benefits to leaving some types of employment for some people – including relief from work pressure, exposure to toxins and carcinogens, alienation, fatigue and stress. Interestingly, in Martin and Wallace's study of unemployed women, more of those interviewed self-reported that their physical health had *improved* since leaving work than those who reported a deterioration.[25] However, the same study found unemployment triggered a range of mental health problems.

The argument that loss of work is detrimental to health and well-being is irrefutable and strongly supported by the empirical evidence. Depression is a common outcome of job loss. In Martin and Wallace's study almost half of the unemployed women reported being depressed as a result of losing their jobs, with loneliness a recurring trigger.[26] It might be argued that unemployed people might 'self-assess' as more unhealthy because they wished to avoid the stigma of being unemployed. This was discounted by Bellamy and Bellamy in their study of unemployment and health in the period 1984–91. They found that when allowances had been made for 'the healthy worker' effect still: 'high levels of unemployment exert an adverse effect on the relative chances of poor health, whether subjective or objective, across a national population of working age.' They further contended: 'high levels of unemployment generate ill health that leads to more irregular employment and more frequent early exit from the labour market' and that 'rising rates of unemployment adversely affect job stress.'[27] We'll come back to this final point about the labour market and on-the-job stressors later.

Peter Warr's influential 1987 investigation argued persuasively that job loss was a significant primary stressor responsible for deteriorating mental health.[28] A tool-maker

105

## Jobs and Bodies

compulsorily made redundant when Joseph Lucas's Birmingham factory closed in 1986 noted years after that he suffered from 'endogenic depression' and added: 'I live in modest poverty on occupational and state pension.'[29] Other studies have implicated insecure, precarious work – common before and in the aftermath of plant and pit closures.[30] The impact on men is connected to deeply entrenched notions of masculinity and their threatened breadwinner status. Goodwin's quantitative analysis (of a 1991 data cohort) supports the view that unemployment caused a range of emotional problems and mental ill health amongst male workers due to 'a societal mis-match between men who do not work and the masculine ideal'.[31]

Space and place undoubtedly mattered. The industrial conurbation of Clydeside, dominated by coal mining, shipbuilding, docks, textile manufacture, metals and heavy engineering, provides an example. Clydeside working-class communities had a long history of deprivation-related ill health (including tuberculosis) and of radical protest – hence the tag of 'Red Clydeside'. This was associated with relatively low wages (compared with England), job insecurity, economic volatility (e.g. in shipbuilding) and notoriously overcrowded tenement-style slum housing. Occupational health and safety standards were also low, sometimes referred to as the 'Scottish anomaly'. One study in 2006 found occupational injury rates to be almost 50 per cent higher in Scotland than the national average.[32] The negative health impacts of deindustrialization were layered on top of already poor health standards in the Glasgow and Clydeside region, as happened in other heavy industry dominated areas, like Tyneside and Merseyside. Recent research by the Glasgow Centre for Population Health has focused on what has become known as the 'Glasgow effect'. This sought to explain why the city had such poor health and high mortality and why such health deficits persisted compared with other conurbations with similar levels of unemployment and deprivation. Of twenty deindustrializing conurbations across Europe, Clydeside had the worst health record. This remains unexplained but, significantly, the authors speculate that the 'severity of deindustrialization' may well have been a significant factor.[33] Whole swathes of Glasgow and West Central Scotland became desolated and 'ruined' communities, with high levels of consolation-seeking unhealthy and risky behaviour, including smoking, alcohol and drug abuse. For example, Craigneuk was the community adjacent to Ravenscraig, Scotland's largest steelworks that closed in 1992. Around a decade later (2004) unemployment in the area stood at 34 per cent and Craigneuk featured in the worst 10 per cent of wards in Scotland for various indicators of deprivation and ill-health.[34] This was also manifested in increasing levels of long-term limiting illnesses and a sharp increase in those receiving incapacity benefits in Glasgow in the 1980s and 1990s.[35] In some deindustrializing districts of Glasgow, male unemployment and incapacity benefits were over five times higher than in affluent areas in the south of England.[36] The despair and hopelessness were evocatively represented in cultural media, including novels like Ross Raisin's *Waterline* (2011), and outstanding recent examples in Douglas Stewart's, *Shuggie Bain*, 2020 and *Young Mungo*, 2022, as well as films, such as the haunting Cranhill Arts documentary *Clyde Film* (1983).

Coal-mining communities had similar experiences to deindustrializing urban areas. As already mentioned, in the 1991 census, around 750,000 people of working age in

'Fit for the Scrap Heap'

British coalfields self-reported as having 'a limiting long-term illness', and higher rates of obesity, smoking, alcohol and drug abuse, including heroin, were associated with unemployment.[37] In deindustrializing communities, young people were denied opportunities to progress into adulthood, expected and customary job and life-courses were dislocated, and certainty and security were replaced with a void. In the UK, one response of some younger miners was to move and transfer to remaining viable pits, resulting in increasingly aged mining communities and the rupture of family support networks, including for the disabled (we'll return to this). In the UK, coal-mining communities recorded the highest levels of sickness and disability benefits, with persistent unemployment-related poverty. One report in 2013 found that, on average, Scottish coalfield communities had 33 per cent higher levels of deprivation than non-mining communities, with the worst on a par with the deindustrializing working-class urban areas in Glasgow (such as Shettleston and Springburn).[38] Moreover, *long-term* unemployment has continued to directly contribute to degeneration in health and earlier death. A recent report by NHS Scotland estimated that unemployment increased premature mortality by 63 per cent.[39]

In some areas open cast (or surface) mining replaced the deep pits. However, open cast provided few local jobs compared to the pits and damaged the landscape, worsening the environment for those who remained living in these communities. In a powerfully emotive voice, retired coal-mining engineer Sam Purdie (born in the small Ayrshire mining village of Glenbuck) commented (in 2015) on Ayrshire's mining legacy:

Now all that is left are the scars left on the landscape where a new generation of profiteering coal exploiters have left seventy-five metre deep death-trap ponds. Nothing but hundreds of hectares of sterile black sub-strata exists where once there were green hills. Sheep and cattle once grazed here and the sky was full of the sounds of the skylark, lapwing, curlew and grouse. The profiteers took the coal, pocketed the money, refuted responsibility for the despoliation and left … Now the communities, who gave their lives to coal mining, are isolated in their enforced redundancy in a dangerous nightmare moonscape. Those in the local communities who voiced their concerns were completely ignored …[40]

Concurrently, the shift towards a post-industrial economy meant that more workers were employed in safer, more benign jobs than during the industrial era. Consequently, workplace fatalities and self-reported injuries continued to fall, the former by over 80 per cent from 1974 to 2018.[41] At 0.8 deaths per 100,000 workers, the UK's occupational fatality rate was comparable to Scandinavia and amongst the lowest in the world in 2018 – half that of Japan and Australia; one quarter that of the United States.[42] The continuation of legislative controls under the *Health and Safety at Work Act* (1974) and the European Union OHS directives were important in this respect. What will happen as a result of Britain withdrawing from the European Union remains to be seen, but there is the real potential of deterioration in OHS standards as a result of the removal of a raft of European protective regulations.

**Jobs and Bodies**

**Figure 4.1** Derek Case (age twenty-two), holds a 70/80 lb. piece of coal that has just been dug from the seam behind at the open cast mine at Mitcheson's Gill, near Durham, 1976.
Courtesy of Getty Images.

## 'Scrap Heap' Stories: Narrating unemployment and health

Turning then to the oral testimonies: Workers involved in downsizing and plant closures narrated their lived experiences of how the loss of their industrial jobs and resulting unemployment impacted on their health in many ways as they struggled to interpret and make sense of their working lives and draw meaning from it. What is evident is the degree to which workers understood this process, were aware of who or what were responsible and the degree to which their industrial work and its loss were associated with their declining health and well-being. Industrial work, as we have seen, was central to the lives of most men and many women in the post-1945 generation and a source of pride, dignity and identity. The loss hit workers and their families in the pocket, financially, but the impact was also deeply socio-psychological. Charles McLauchlan was just twenty-three when he lost his job when the Ferguslie mill closed in Paisley in 1983, a year after his wife lost her job in the same mill as it wound down. He recalled in an interview in 2018:

> I didn't work for fifteen year … Poverty stricken, you had no wages every week, no work, there was no sign of work anywhere. You could walk out of one job into

# 'Fit for the Scrap Heap'

another one in the seventies but around the eighties it just didn't happen. So you were left on the scrap heap. ... It was hard, we were getting married and after that [the redundancy], no future. We were going to buy a house and we can't do that if we are getting paid off. I was straight out of school into the mill, then seven year later you're back on the street again.[43]

Older workers felt the loss directly, but also mourned the loss of opportunity for their offspring. Frederick Brady was laid off after thirty-seven years working in shipyards in Sunderland. In an interview in 1999 he commented that there was no work to be had so:

We became industrial gypsies... travelled ... Aberdeen ... Southampton... Hull etc. Germany ... Holland ... Belgium. I feel very bitter towards it. I was robbed of many years of our working life ... compensation was a pittance ... I got seventeen thousand pounds. Sunderland was the biggest shipbuilding town in the world ... more shipyards on the Wear than anywhere else. ... I am bitter not just for me but for the young people of Sunderland who would be working in the shipyards. Most young people here have never had a proper job. That was never considered. ... [the] River was a liquid motorway ... ships all the time ... tugs hooting ... you feel the river has died now.[44]

He added that the pollution was less, the riverside 'much prettier' and Sunderland 'improving' as a city, but concluded 'I would rather have the shipyards'.

Some laid-off workers adapted more easily than others and many found other jobs, albeit often experiencing deskilling and income reductions in the process. This could be diminishing and demoralizing. To lose steady, stable (and often well-unionized) industrial work was traumatic and plant closures could be met with shock, disbelief and a range of emotions. Davie Higgins was one of the last men on site at the Killoch Colliery in Ayrshire when it closed in 1986. He recalled:

At the time of the Killoch closure [November 1986], the suddenness of it all was to be witnessed to be believed. I was one of the three Deputy Chief Electrical Engineers on site. All the lads knew that the future was bleak. They had given up. Most had accepted that it would be better to take the redundancy payment on offer ... At a meeting in Edinburgh, the closure was announced. The very next morning, we were instructed to keep as many of our men as possible on the surface for immediate redundancy interview. It had all been set up well in advance. I remember one of the interviewers boasting, 'you supply the bodies, and we will supply the money'. I remember the first of our lads being called. He was back in our midst within barely a few minutes. Confirm your name, this is your redundancy sum, sign here, go and get washed, the bus will be here to take you home shortly, that's it, you're finished, cheerio, you don't need to come back.

## Jobs and Bodies

The lads were stunned by the suddenness of it all. It was no longer a laugh. They did not even have time to say farewell to old friends. We staff members felt somewhat sick. In an instant we realized that possibly the finest group of dedicated capable tradesmen were to be scattered and dismissed with utter contempt. Within a week the workforce was gone, another week and almost all staff had also gone. On 1 Nov, it was my own hand that threw the final circuit breakers to shut off all electrical power below ground level. A long poem was written, I have it somewhere. It began:

> It was bitter cold that morning, the first day of November
> Another working day we say, but one we long remember
> Mr Mackin & Mr Higgins who chose to throw the switch.
> And the pit born proud in sixty-three has died in eighty-six.

I found myself alone on the premises, a sole employee, almost like a watchman for a few months. Until I refused the British Coal proposal for my future. On the last day of Feb 1987, I too took the payoff and walked away from an industry that had given me so much to enjoy.

It was over. The bridges were burned, and there was no road back … At the time there were also thoughts of bringing the towers down by controlled demolition. When it happened much later, it was publicised and there was even provision for the public to view the spectacle, but I was far away by then. No bad thing. It would have broken my heart. The death of an industry that had given so much to our forebears, but it took from them more than it gave. We remember with pride and regret just the same.[45]

The shock of closure and redundancy seeps through David's heart – felt reminiscence, revealing something of the callousness, insensitivity and 'contempt' of management contrasted against the mixed emotions: the 'pride' and joy, and the 'regret', shock and sorrow, of the miners.

Some metal workers' testimonies scream with the loss and damage caused by redundancy. Ex-steel worker Martin Kerr said, 'I never saw so many men cry at the demolition of the Ravenscraig plant [Scotland's largest steelworks] in 1996.'[46] William Baker worked most of his life at the giant Sterling Metals Foundry near Coventry before being made redundant when the place closed in the mid-1980s. Crackling with emotion, he recalled him and his brothers expecting 'a job for life'. He spent eight months on the dole drawing unemployment benefit 'which', he commented, 'was hard', clearly feeling the stigma after never having been unemployed in his life. Then he articulated the degradation of moving 'from job to job, getting crap jobs … nobody would touch them', including in smaller foundries where OHS standards were poor. He ended up having an accident at work which left him disabled and on incapacity benefit. He recalled how his grandfather had also been made redundant from his job after which 'he flipped and lost his mind … he couldn't cope with it'.[47]

'Fit for the Scrap Heap'

Others laid emphasis on the devastation wrought upon working-class communities. Margaret Cullen described Springburn (in North Glasgow) in its heyday in the 1950s when she had her first job at the local cooperative store:

You would see the men comin oot, oot the factories, Cowlairs Works and eh one or two different works. And they used to come up three deep coming up Springburn Road ... when they heard the horn, aw the men coming from their work you know. The place was black with people ... It was a busy, busy place then. Industrial. But then it just ... once they closed all these places, then Springburn died.[48]

Irene Dickson was laid off from the Bryant and May match-making factory in Maryhill in the north of Glasgow in 1981 and described the impact on herself and on the community as 'devastating' – repeating that word three times. 'I never, ever recovered from that', Irene added, 'right up until I retired.'[49]

The death of the community is a common metaphor in workers' eye-witness testimonies. When the BMC Leyland truck and tractor factory in Bathgate closed in 1986 with over 2000 redundancies, one worker (Jim Bilsborough) declared: 'I just could not believe that they would shut that plant. I kept saying to myself, and I wisnae alone, how can they shut a place like this?'.[50] Another (John Cooper) reflected: 'When the plant closed I was absolutely shattered. I'd never, ever been paid off before.' A prevailing theme in the stories of plant closures was loss; a deep, profound sense of bereavement, of mourning for lost skills, opportunities (for themselves and their kids), relationships, income and security seeps from the testimonies. Another BMC Leyland factory worker (Tam Brandon) reflected about the closure:

Don't mind telling you I cried because I was looking forward to my family getting work there. The Leyland had a tremendous input in the social life of people. You've got to understand how many thousands of people worked in there ... and their skills were unsurpassed. I got that word and I came home and I sat and I held my wife's hand and I said 'we're finished'.[51]

The workers built a coffin to display in protest on the final day before closure to denote their acute sense of loss.

Losing work was invariably articulated as a disturbing and health-eroding experience for this generation of blue-collar workers brought up within a powerful work culture in communities that exalted hard graft and honest toil and stigmatized laziness. This was expressed in stories emphasizing the work ethic, the joy of work, pride in the job and the close social relationships and camaraderie developed over the duration of working lives. In these articulations of the meaning of work, narrators often emphasized pride in their skills, as Tam Brandon did, and demonstrated their awareness of risks and dangers in industrial work, the physicality of it, as well as the positive health and welfare connotations of being in stable, secure, enjoyable work. They recognized the innate duality of work: its frustrations as well as its joys; its risks to health as well as the benefits

111

## Jobs and Bodies

to health and well-being conferred by work. But, a recurring motif in their stories was the *deterioration* that came along with plant run-downs and closure. A whole gamut of emotions bubble to the surface in the telling of these job loss stories: sadness, frustration, bitterness, outrage, anger, pride, stress, embarrassment, shame – and sometimes a sense of relief and escape. These issues were reflected variously in popular culture. For example in Ross Raisin's Glasgow and Clydebank-based novel *Waterline* the main character Mick reflects on redundancy and its implications:

> In the end it came to nothing. That's exactly what they got. Nothing … See that was a worrying time. The severance cheque didn't solve anything, and the wife's job obviously wasn't going to keep the four of them for long. The arguments they had. 'So ye won't even consider it [going on the dole; drawing unemployment benefit], well? It's the damn pride, is what it is … this frequenting of the Empress [local pub] every afternoon and sitting about the house like a pound of mince isnae helping anybody'. She [his wife] was right, obviously. And her taking on more hours at the store, it was hardly fair, plus on top of that having to come home knackered after work to him there on the settee, grumbling and drunk. Again. … I am a shipbuilder. That right eh? So what are ye now the shipyard has copped its whack and the job is away? I am a shipbuilder. Once a shipbuilder always a shipbuilder, and all that tollie they'd told themselves. No just the jobs that went, but the life … He wouldn't let it go. Couldn't cope with the idea that things had changed.[52]

Oral testimonies of workers speak revealingly of the stigma of unemployment and the journey through identity disintegration as traditional breadwinner masculinity was challenged by the loss of the provider role. Corrosion of self-esteem; a sense of being on the 'scrap heap' pervades the narratives of workers displaced by plant closures. One Cumnock ex-miner commented on being 'a drain on society'.[53] A Kilmarnock woman recalled her father 'felt absolutely worthless [after] being made redundant' whilst another recalled of her husband after being laid off: 'he became really depressed and he was on sleeping tablets for a long time.'[54] Taking alternative lower paid, subordinate work could also be demeaning, stigmatizing and embarrassing. Shame was one of the salient emotions expressed in these stories. 'I hated being unemployed', recalled Alex Moffat after being laid off from BMC Leyland, Bathgate in 1986. The writer Farquhar McLay, who started work in 1951 in an iron foundry, commented forty years later on the 'workerist and productivist notions we were brought up on' – continuing, 'having pride in our role as indispensable (though cruelly exploited) units of production, taking identity from the jobs we did and suffering a terrible kind of shameful death with its loss'.[55]

This crisis of identity was also a recurring motif in the oral testimonies of former male steelworkers in South Wales collected by Walkerdine and Jimenez.[56] Unemployment impacted on identity and well-being in many ways, and workers' own oral narratives suggest a clear awareness of this. Ayrshire miner 'Tommy' argued that work had kept miners fit and focused and when unemployed 'your system's shutting doon'.[57] Sedentary

## 'Fit for the Scrap Heap'

post-industrial lifestyles contributed to obesity whilst rising para-suicide and suicide rates were linked to trauma and to mental illness induced by job losses. Ayrshire coal miner George Montgomery recalled two suicides, asserting: 'When they close pits, and dae these things, these are the effects it has on people.'[58] When the Govan Kvaerner shipyard announced redundancies in 1999, it pushed one of the workers over the edge. A colleague recalled:

> We came in to the yard the next morning [after receiving their redundancy letter], sadly Eddie had committed suicide the night before, he had hung himself and they thought it was due to – well we dae – due tae the letter he got the day before that he was getting paid off. It was a sad time in the yard. Eddie was a good boy ... a good lad.[59]

Another shipyard worker reflected on the closure of Robbs shipyard in Leith in 1984, commenting: 'Ah mean, we saw people who were fit strong men after the closure of the yard basically doin' the shoppin', shovin' prams around Leith ... And a lot o' them went downhill very quickly, because their life had been taken away from them wi' Leith closing.'[60] This narrative alludes to identity and health disintegration, to what Angela Coyle has referred to as the 'unsexing of men.'[61].

Emasculation from job loss was a recurring motif in oral testimonies. We've argued earlier how heavy industrial work forged masculinity, and a 'hard man' style of hyper masculinity. This was particularly evident in working-class communities like Clydeside and Merseyside.[62] As a Scottish ex-miner noted: 'This idea, "I'm the man of the family". Whether you've got a family or not doesnae matter, you're supposed to be a macho man, like, go out and earn a wage, like, you know. When you cannae do that it makes you less of a man in other people's eyes.'[63]

Going 'downhill' (as John Keggie put it) could lead to depression, self-harm, alcohol and drug abuse, sleeping tablets and tranquilizer dependency. A Clyde shipyard worker recalling the 1980s remembered the explosive growth of heroin use in Govan (and his own addiction at the time) and reflected on the lack of job opportunities as a contributory cause: 'Disaffection. Know what I mean? They're wanting something, you know? Like there's nothing here so they want something to belong tae, something that means something.'[64]

Work then provided meaning and a sense of belonging. Another fundamental thing that could be lost as plants closed were relationships, both personal and collective. Betty Long from Springburn, a chronically deindustrialized community in Glasgow, reflected: 'It hurt a lot of men. Not just not getting their money but just missing all their colleagues.'[65] An ex-miner reflected on the impact loss of work had on relationships: 'They'd nae work, nothing else to dae in the morning, got up, go to the pub, come back hame, go to the pub. It ruined ma brother's life. His wife left ... An awfy lot of men seemed to just go aff the rails.'[66]

Trade union shop stewards, company welfare officers and industrial chaplains all played a role in the pastoral care and welfare of workers during run-downs and plant

## Jobs and Bodies

closures and their testimonies relate a range of impacts, attesting to the disintegration of the social fabric in working-class communities. One Glasgow industrial chaplain reflected on the 'savage' nature of unemployment, noting: 'when you're unemployed you almost become a leper in the eyes of a lot of people.'[67] Deploying the 'leper' metaphor to denote a sense of mutation from inclusion to exclusion and evoke the devastating impacts of loss of work is indicative of how the process could be profoundly shaming. Job loss could mean being outcast, a 'waster', not a worker.

This harrowing sense of loss was connected to the deep attachment to their work. This was very evident in mining, shipbuilding, steelmaking and other 'heavy' industries. For example, Glasgow shipbuilding worker Danny Houston commented: 'I don't think I would change anything [...] Proud to be a Clyde shipbuilder.'[68] He went on to reflect on the social relationships forged at work, the solidarity and the banter, reflecting, 'everyday a came intae work, even if I come in pretty sad, a went hame laughing'. Losing work could be overwhelming, especially perhaps for those in middle and older age groups. Gerry Slater, made redundant from the Harland & Woolf shipyard in Glasgow in 1963, commented on a long-serving older colleague's reaction on hearing the news he was being laid off: 'I turned roon and the tears wur running doon the man's face. He didnae know wit tae say because it was new tae ye, ye know wit a mean? That kind a scenario was new tae ye.'[69] Another shipyard worker recalled his redundancy: 'I was actually shattered because that's aww I had ever known. I had stayed in Govan, educated in

**Figure 4.2** Coal miner at Bentley colliery, South Yorkshire, after news of its imminent closure, October 1992, as part of a new mine closure programme with the loss of 31,000 jobs.
Courtesy of Getty Images.

'Fit for the Scrap Heap'

Govan, served ma time in Govan, worked in Govan, so I was sitting saying, "Where do I go from here?"'.[70] Andy Perchard has recently identified in his oral-history based study of coal mining 'the prevailing psychological and deep cultural scars of deindustrialization', where a recurring motif in oral testimonies was that of 'broken men'.[71]

Some unemployed workers tried to suppress their emotions as a coping strategy, or withdrew from social contact. An out-of-work electrical engineering worker (male) from Sunderland commented:

> You have to divorce yourself from your own feelings all the time; otherwise it would be too painful. You lead a sort of double life: the pointlessness of the reduced daily round, and the knowledge that you are still a feeling, thinking human being whose skills and talents are lying unused for the time being. I'm lucky. I have nerves like steel. But with people of a more nervous or introverted nature it's different. They lock themselves away, they're ashamed. There have been one or two suicides; people jump off the bridge. The police play these things down, naturally. They say there is no connection between being out of work and doing away with yourself. Those who are out of work know better.[72]

According to Clare Bambra, 'paid work, or lack of it, is the most important determinant of population health and health inequalities in advanced market democracies'.[73] During industrialization, bodies were worn out and discarded, mangled, poisoned and diseased in the workplace to varying degrees, and this systemic economic violence left a lasting legacy of premature death and disability, scarring deindustrializing communities long after the work had disappeared. In such places, therefore, the deleterious impact of job-loss trauma was overlaid upon an already unhealthy population, in turn a product of deprivation and working in unsafe, toxic and heavily polluted work environments.

Certain groups, including older workers, migrant workers and people with injuries and disabilities, were particularly vulnerable to the long-term unemployment, work rationalizations, and intensifications generated by deindustrialization and the adverse effects these had upon health. In the UK, the number of people claiming sickness and disability benefits rose sharply in the 1980s and 1990s as the recession resulted in a shakeout of workers with disabilities, who found it more difficult thereafter, as Lindsay and Houston have argued, to find alternative work in competition with able-bodied workers.[74] Some unemployed workers also claimed disability benefits (quite legitimately in most cases given the bodily damage accrued through their industrial work, such as respiratory ailments, back problems and loss of fingers) because these were rather more generous than the prevailing basic unemployment benefits.

Considerable awareness of this deepening discrimination and widening of inequalities was demonstrated in workers' oral testimonies. After nationalization in 1947, the National Coal Board (NCB) initially had a progressive inclusion policy of reabsorbing employees who had been disabled from their occupations in light work underground or on the surface.[75] As pits closed and job opportunities shrank, however, workers with disabilities found themselves more marginalized. The emphasis on production and the increasing

115

## Jobs and Bodies

pace of work together with the growing pool of unemployed able-bodied miners meant fewer job vacancies for those with disabilities. These latter ex-miners were less mobile than younger, fit miners, and were more dependent on family support networks embedded within the community, which were themselves diminishing as younger family members left these communities to search for work elsewhere. National Union of Mineworkers (NUM) president Nicky Wilson started work in 1967 at the Cardowan pit in Ayrshire, which employed 1800 people, including a 'substantial proportion of disabled men'. He recalled that at that point the NCB and the miners ensured that disabled workers were re-employed, including those with mental health problems: 'These guys were always looked after as well'. Wilson continued: 'That unfortunately disappeared as we moved into the 1980s, when things got harder and there was more tension between the employers and the unions and a lot of those good things that had been there for years disappeared.'[76] It seems that deindustrialization resulted in growing social exclusion and marginalization of the disabled in disintegrating coalfield communities.

This may well have been the case in other traditional working-class communities too as deindustrialization accelerated. Female train driver Tracey Carpenter recalled 'the walking wounded ... if any joint goes, your eyes, your heart .... There are so many things that can stop drivers driving'. In this eventuality ex-drivers and others injured on the railway found themselves moved to easier work within their capabilities, most at railway depots. However, privatized train companies mostly withdrew the traditional 'green card' employment of the industry's disabled railwaymen at depot and shunting yards in the 1990s.[77] One study in 2002 found employment rates of disabled persons as low as 30 to 40 per cent in the deindustrializing regions of Wales, Scotland, and Northern Ireland, and the big northern cities (such as Manchester and Liverpool), compared with 70 to 85 per cent in other service sector-dominated local economies (such as in London and South East England).[78] This exclusion of disabled people was worsened by the withdrawal of the Thatcherite state from direct regulation of the labour market. The outlawing of job discrimination for disabled people in the UK had to wait a further two decades (1995) after such legal rights were won by women. Ann Borsay has shown how at the peak in the 1960s only around 60 per cent of employers were complying with the provisions of the Disabled Persons (Employment) Act, which established an employment quota of 3 per cent disabled in all workplaces employing more than twenty employees.[79] By the early 1990s, that proportion had plummeted to around 20 per cent of employers, with widespread evasion of social and legal responsibilities towards disabled people evident amongst big business in Britain.[80]

A series of oral interviews undertaken with male and female workers at the Johnnie Walker whisky plant in Kilmarnock just prior to closure in March 2012 provided revealing insights into how working lives and job loss are narrated and felt, and the psychological scars of redundancy.[81] The Johnnie Walker Kilmarnock plant employed 1800 workers in 1970 and 707 in 2009 when the closure was announced.[82] The oral interviews suggest similarities in the ways that men and women narrate job loss but also divergences, especially in the case of older, long-serving employees. The male employees at Johnnie Walker were more likely to mourn the demise of skill, job knowledge and

116

'Fit for the Scrap Heap'

experience, and identity, to mark corrosion of working-class breadwinner masculinity, and to express a sense of moral outrage at the loss of their right to work. The Johnnie Walker women's narratives focus more on lamenting loss of personal independence and the fracturing of close relationships forged at work. Perhaps partly these differences were connected to the types of jobs men and women did in a gender-divided labour force where the men did most of the skilled and supervisory jobs and the women the lesser skilled (and lesser paid) jobs in the plant. Impacts were differentiated and experienced through the lens of the acculturated values of femininity and masculinity. Several of the female narrators referred to social relations at work being like 'family': 'it is like an extended family'.[83] 'Coming in here every day it's like coming home to your family', said Rhona Roberts, continuing, 'It's been interesting, exciting and sad. It's been all of those things, and it's a massive end to think that they're going to close it. Because this is all we've been used to and suddenly it's not going to be here.'[84] As with many male 'scrap heap' stories, here we see articulated a clear sense of profound loss and rupture; of a changed world compared to 'all we've been used to'.

In these female work loss narratives, the meaning of work was defined as so much more than just the labour process and a wage. This was an all-inclusive community where life was centred in the workplace around close friendships and communal shared experiences which had a deep significance at a personal level. Humour – joking and 'banter' – mediated the monotony and grind of the working day and that too was fractured with factory closure. Stride has argued of female workers laid off at Templeton's carpet factory (Glasgow) that the transition to new work was 'less severe' but that nonetheless this represented a 'profound rupture'.[85] Whilst there may have been differences in how the experience of plant closures was felt and expressed by men and women workers, the demise of personal networks, mutual support and the health deficits were evidently felt deeply by all in the aftermath of plant closures. A married woman in her forties in the Northern town of Bolton made redundant in 1978 articulated this in an interview conducted by Jeremy Seabrook in the early 1980s:

> Being without work was a horrible experience. It came to me as a complete surprise … After a number of rejections I started to think 'well, whatever's wrong with me?' Your self-confidence goes lower and lower. You start to think that even applying is a waste of time. You're sure you won't get it. Then you get diffident and start to avoid people. I felt I was worthless and useless … My finances soon led me to look for any kind of job. I wasn't choosy … For most people, their job is their main reason for living. If you can't do that, you feel you're on the scrap-heap; you feel a burden to society … Even though I've got a job now, I'm not using myself to my full capacities, nor anywhere near it. This happens to a lot of women. It's being stretched that gives you satisfaction. Not using the skills you have, you feel it's such a waste … Here I'm the lowest of the low.[86]

Mrs Tysoe's evocative narrative oozes with what work signified to her – in both financial and intrinsic terms (job satisfaction and independence). One gets an impression of

**Figure 4.3** Some of the 300 Berlei factory workers made redundant in South Wales filling in application forms for new jobs, January 1986.
Courtesy of Getty Images.

just how central fulfilling work was to this woman's life and how diminished that life was without it. Expressions such as 'useless', 'burden', 'worthless' and 'waste' combined with the deployment of the 'scrap-heap' metaphor indicate a profound sense of loss of self-esteem, autonomy and purpose and the hit taken to her health and well-being as a result of being unemployed.

Another less-mentioned and often adverse health impact of job loss associated with deindustrialization was the effects this destabilization had on family life, relationships and roles. The pressures on family incomes could lead to strains upon marriages and relationships, sometimes recalled in oral testimonies. And a more insidious impact was the incidence of domestic violence in some households affected by redundancies and long-term unemployment. In Douglas Stewart's recent novel the character Mrs Campbell is beaten badly by her ex-shipyard husband. She explains to her young rescuers that it is nothing to do with drink and football rivalry, but has its roots deeper:

Ye're too wee to know anything about men and their anger … Every day for twenty-seven year that man went to the shipyards. Girders as big as corporation buses flying around on chains, a ton weight of steel dangling above his heid, and at any time it could've dropped and kil't him, and left me with nothin' but three weans and a divot in the mattress. And he *knew* it. Aw those men knew it. … Imagine all that fear and disappointment clogged up in there, and nobody stopped to ask him about it, to ask if he was happy in his life, if he was coping. None of the men would tell ye how they really felt … And whut did they get for aw their troubles eh? They got laid off by some suit-wearing snobs in Westminster who couldnae find Glasgow on a map, who didnae give a flying fuck if the men had families to feed. They get telt that they're the problem wi' this country, that they're haudin' back progress because they're no afraid of hard work. Then some uppity ginger bitch that's the end of them with a stroke of her fountain pen. Done, finito, kaput.[87]

The connections made here between the structural violence of the job, being thrown on the 'scrap heap' and made to feel worthless and emasculated and increasing levels of violence within the home also seeped through some oral testimonies. Laura (pseudonym), brought up in the shadow of the Glenarnock steelworks in Kilbirnie, Ayrshire, commented:

My uncle uh was a steel worker and so he worked there until uh, it shut and then of course with the steel work shutting and with em Chrysler shutting he became unemployed and that, that was like the early eighties and I'm sure there's a lot more domestic violence happened around that time because of the poverty and em injustice and class hatred em against em working people in Scotland … I had just seen the trauma still continuing, I expected somebody would write a history of what had gone and they never did and the people that surrounded me, ex-steel workers, the devastation. I mean when they knocked down the steel work in a weekend, I was utterly visually traumatised so making sense of all of … I mean the whole town was traumatised, so many women were getting beaten up. Adults were depr …, it seemed as if the whole town was depressed. I was terrified and also the degree of hatred and abuse the Thatcher Government had for everybody I mean it's abuse. Ahm … so that was horrendous.[88]

In this narrative we hear clearly of the devastating rupture and trauma of job loss, and the connection being made by a witness of the surge in domestic violence that was linked to this dislocation in people's lives. And there is a clear sense of the culpability of the Thatcher administration in the 1980s. The rise in domestic tension and gender-based violence has been noted in other studies of deindustrializing communities, for example in France, India and Romania.[89] It remains one of the indirect, often hidden and under-explored aspects of the embodied impacts of deindustrialization. Undoubtedly, there was a cumulative effect here on the mental and physical health of women, many of whom were carrying the 'double burden' of unpaid work in the home and the added pressure of often being the sole breadwinner where men (especially those over fifty) struggled to find alternative employment.

## Jobs and Bodies

## Under pressure: Downsizing, insecurity and worsening conditions

The deindustrialization literature has tended, I think, to focus on the trauma of plant closures and resultant redundancies and unemployment, somewhat neglecting the longer, more drawn-out process during downsizing and rundowns of the cranking up of workloads, disempowerment, stress and pressure imposed on many of those who managed to cling on, survive and hold down fast-disappearing industrial jobs. Protracted downsizing really characterized industrial decline in the UK from the 1970s to the present. Typically, plants contracted, cutting their labour force back, as they struggled to survive, before eventually closing. Deindustrialization brought a sense of insecurity, destabilization of customary patterns and of precarity. Narrators elucidate how this felt; how working in restructured and downsizing mining and manufacturing companies struggling for survival with rising unemployment and insecurity invariably involved an intensification of work, higher working hours, taking on more risk and rising stress levels testing physical and mental capacities to work. National Union of Mineworkers' President Nicky Wilson, for example, recalled the re-emergence of a 'long hour's culture' as working shifts rose, for some to twelve hours, after the defeat of the 1984–5 miners' strike; 'the work-life balance just disappeared completely for a period of time'.[90] The wider context was public spending cuts to the HSE and an increase in fatalities and serious injuries at work. Tombs has shown how OHS standards in some sectors deteriorated sharply in the 1980s UK recession: between 1981 and 1985, fatal and major injury rates increased across British manufacturing by 30 per cent and in construction by a staggering 45 per cent.[91] With regulatory degradation, workers' rights were eroding, including rights to compensation for injuries and disease.[92] Disempowerment marked this process. A Govan shipyard worker recalled the failure of a strike in 1999 at the downsizing Kaeverner (formerly Fairfields) yard which resulted in a four-night shift being extended to a run of five nights:

> They just broke the unions then. I thought the unions let us doon there, pretty badly. To me, that put a lot a people aff the unions because after that, we wir never really the same. Any grievance we had wae the company, the guys oan the shop-floor would say, 'Wits the point!?' because the unions cannae dae anything anyway.[93]

A profound sense of loss is articulated in this narrative; loss of power as exemplified in a strong trade union capable of protecting workers' rights, and a sense of hopelessness: 'Wit's the point'. A Clydebank mother articulated this in a similar way talking of her son who 'desperately wants to work', reflecting 'they just lost the whole will [...] don't know how to motivate themselves anymore. They're like "what's the point"'.[94] Established working patterns and support networks were uprooted, and 'protective practices' that enabled bodies to be shielded in the workplace and energies conserved were eroded.

Another aspect of this assault upon workers was that some companies used the threat of closure to increase workloads, encouraging workers to accept dangers and risks. This

'Fit for the Scrap Heap'

happened at the Imperial Chemicals (ICI) plant in Dumfries, which claimed it would not be viable if it had to implement expensive health and safety reforms. A worker there commented: 'if it cost the company a lot of money, there was very little change ... they just ignored oor comments on likes a' noise and ambient temperature and stuff.'[95] He commented that there was little the men could do but accept this: 'You've got young guys in there with mortgages and families ... the argument [to stop working] was blown oot the water ... that happened so many times, so many, many times ... By this time I was married and we were planning families and a' the rest o' it.' This was inherently destabilizing. Trade unions fought a rear guard battle to protect workers under pressure, but struggled in this context, as membership collapsed. By the 2010s, trade union membership density (at 24 per cent of the total labour force) in the UK was down to less than half the level it had been at peak in the 1970s. One outcome was slippage in occupational health and safety standards in many industries.

A number of empirical studies have demonstrated deleterious impacts on psychological health and well-being as a consequence of deepening 'work stressors' associated with longer work hours, managerial pressure, and lack of autonomy and control of work under changing production regimes, such as forms of Taylorism, Fordism, 'lean' production and 'total quality management'.[96] Managerial power was bolstered by growing unemployment and a raft of Thatcherite neoliberal economic policies: deregulation and privatization combined with anti-labour legislation in the 1980s and 1990s that eroded workers' rights, including rights to compensation for injuries and disease, a process paralleled in Canada, as Robert Storey has shown.[97] This was frequently described in workers' narratives as disconcerting and destabilizing change, and sometimes as a threat to cherished craft skills and independence on the job.[98] Interviewed workers reported that 'corners were cut' and risks to health were taken, such as handling of asbestos without protection, not using machine guards, and cutting coal 'dry'.[99] Some unemployed Clydeside workers took the option to migrate to work in the North Sea Oil industry despite its notoriously dangerous conditions and 'gung ho' long hours work culture – what one narrator described as 'physical suicide'.[100] Workers who did not go along with this risked being censured as effeminate within the peer group and dissent could be met with savage labour discipline, including replacement. The names of 'Strathclyders' who migrated north for work and were killed in the Piper Alpha oil rig disaster in July 1988 are commemorated by a monument in Motherwell.

In this context, migrant workers were amongst the most vulnerable to bodily damage and were clustered in the most dangerous and unhealthy jobs – as with Pakistani migrants in toxic heavy chemical plants in Glasgow and Indian migrant workers in decrepit iron foundries in the Midlands. An Indian migrant worker, Chudar Singh Jandu, recalled conditions in Coventry in the 1980s: 'The general working conditions were very bad – there was not much point complaining about health and safety. We were just happy to be here. Generally, in the foundries and other engineering factories around Coventry the working conditions were atrocious. The wages were low, long hours, and dirty working conditions.'[101]

## Jobs and Bodies

Disempowerment led to more risk taking and, in the 1980s, more accidents in some industrial sectors. The outcome was that in the deindustrializing industries during the rundown period, working conditions could deteriorate and inequalities widened between occupational health and safety standards in the older, obsolete and declining heavy industries and those in the newer 'sunrise' sectors, such as light engineering and electronics. This repeated a pattern evident in the 1930s. With regard to the 1980s and 1990s, Wichert has argued that 'there is consistent, international evidence for the detrimental effects of the experience of *both* job insecurity and work intensification on psychological health and well-being'.[102]

In coal mining, as Perchard's seminal work has shown, management felt pressure to produce and reach NCB targets, and invariably transmitted such pressure downward to the coal face.[103] Studies of pits in the 1990s by Waddington and colleagues found 'a bewildering variety of changes in working practices and management'; they argued that 'the intensification of work and job insecurity had produced its own kind of stress'.[104] Ex-miner Alec Mills testified to the impact of such change in the Ayrshire coalfield in an interview in 2000: 'New development everywhere. We had a lot of men that were injured there. Because they brought them in from the other collieries without giving them the requisite training. Because it was intense mechanization that they had introduced onto the face lines. It was different from the conventional method'.[105] The period after the defeat of the miners' strike in 1984–5 witnessed the emergence of a new pattern of industrial relations and work practices, with management (now British Coal) empowered and the National Union of Mineworkers neutered.[106] Employment of outside contractors increased, non-unionism grew significantly and the union was undermined by internal divisions. This was intensified with privatization and the fragmentation of ownership from 1994, with the growth of local bargaining and the refusal of some companies to recognize trade unions entirely (e.g. Midland Mining). The traditional protective role of the miners' unions atrophied in this environment, which saw rising stress levels and real disincentives to accurately report injuries, whilst the true level of industrial disease remained obscured by the haemorrhage of workers from the industry.

At the coal face, the prevailing productionist ethos undermined health and safety measures, including dust control. Ayrshire machine coal shearer and 'leading hand' William Dunsmore commented that they worked in dangerously dusty conditions because 'the management was on top of me for production. Production, production, production'.[107] Another Scottish miner, John Orr, commented that inhaling dust after shot firing 'was very much a contributory factor on the lung damage ... you're under pressure to get progress'.[108] Alec Mills reflected that 'they did increase the production, but again that was at the expense of men's health'.[109] Significantly, pneumoconiosis and chronic obstructive pulmonary disease cases rose from the 1990s.[110] Emma Wallis's study in 2000 found that health and safety standards had deteriorated markedly in the privatized era of coal mining from 1994.[111] Significantly, only the single worker-controlled pit in South Wales (Tower) maintained health and safety standards similar to those in the nationalized era before 1994. This idea that the privatization drive over 1979–97 (which saw half of all public-sector workers switch to privately owned companies) led to a deterioration in OHS standards has recently been confirmed by detailed quantitative research, with Beck and Watterson concluding that:

> During its period of aggressive privatization, the UK has seen an increase in the number of multi-fatality disasters, and, perhaps more importantly a statistically significant abnormality in the number of deaths resulting from these disasters. This pattern can be evidenced both in terms of a comparison with UK data for earlier and later years, as well as on the basis of comparisons with other large European countries.[112]

These developments were part of a wider process of growing levels of precarious, more insecure employment, accompanied by the weakening of unions and collective bargaining, which contributed to poorer standards of occupational health and safety in Britain in industry in the later twentieth century.[113] One study of the literature found that 'of the more than 50 published articles and monographs identified all but a handful found precarious employment was associated with a deterioration in occupational health and safety in terms of injury rates, hazard exposures or worker (and manager) knowledge of OHS and regulatory responsibilities'. The researchers argued:

> There is also growing recognition that the health impacts of organisational downsizing may be masked or complicated by the over-representation of older and less healthy workers amongst those displaced and a reluctance of surviving workers to report illness or take absence for fear this will endanger their job.[114]

## Adaptation and escape narratives

Whilst privatization, deregulation, economic restructuring, plant run-downs and redundancies had a series of negative health impacts, and the dominant way of narrating referenced these, a minority strand of workers' narratives focused on the positive impacts of escaping from dangerous, polluting and unhealthy work in mining and manufacturing to more environmentally innocuous services and professions.[115] Sometimes a range of effects were remembered and articulated in sophisticated and critical analyses which weighed up the pros and the cons. Released from physically exhausting, dangerous, noxious, contaminated and alienating work environments, some bodies could recuperate. In her autobiography, writer Deborah Orr reflected on the benefits to her father of being made redundant from the Ravenscraig Steelworks: 'John was a gentler, less angry man when he was not so bone-tired, when the sensory assault of his work, six days a week, fifty weeks a year for forty years, had finally abated and when the disruptive rhythms of shift-work had stopped.'[116]

## Jobs and Bodies

And a sense of 'relief' and 'escape' from 'bad' work was expressed in some oral narratives. Jim McCaig, an ex-steelworker from the iconic Ravenscraig Steelworks (the largest in Scotland), retrained as a teacher and reflected in a recent interview:

> I used to make jokes every day of my life with my [teacher] colleagues who were complaining about their conditions of employment and their salaries and I would stand up and say: Look, you guys don't have a real job, this is not a job, this is a vocation ... you're never gonnae get an explosion, you're never gonnae get killed, you don't breathe foul air and you're better paid than we were in the steel industry.[117]

In such narratives, deindustrialization and plant closure were articulated as liberating; as escape, as an opportunity and as a respite from 'bad' work; as health-enhancing. Tommy Brennan, Ravenscraig union convenor, reflected several years after the closure how 'diversification' had created many better jobs, noting 'Lanarkshire is a healthier place now in every way ... You can see the green in the parks; when the plant was going, the fields were all orange-coloured with dust'.[118] Such stories, whilst contradicting the dominant ruination and loss narrative, also merit our attention. Glasgow writer Farquhar McLay reflected back in 1990 on his early working days in the 1950s in a Glasgow iron foundry, commenting: 'I could easily understand why the working man would be suicidal. He was trapped in a nightmare.'[119] He continued:

> The old jobs are vanishing. Nostalgia for these outmoded forms of production – now a marketable commodity in art and culture – is surely misplaced. It was hard, miserable toil in deplorable conditions. People forget the crude anti-Catholic discrimination operated by management and foremen which kept workers at each other's throats; as well as the callous indifference which led to an accident rate which is hardly credible today. Ships were built on the Clyde because labour was cheap on the Clyde and the people in work were for the most part too cowed and too terrified of unemployment to make any real trouble.[120]

Some welcomed the opportunity to get a substantial redundancy pay-off, using the money to invest in a new business, like window cleaning or a taxi, and expressed a sense of enjoying the job change. Shipbuilding worker Danny Houston, who was made redundant at the age of twenty-nine from Kaverner in 1987, recalled: 'I thought it was great; paid a holiday, got a wee car and that but I got a job right away. I done driving, labouring, done window fitting ... I did a bit a joinery work. I'm quite good wae ma hands, but then, the wages were dreadful compared to the wages in here.'[121]

His oral testimony was probably more sanguine towards his experience because he was one of the lucky ones and had been successful in getting another job and in getting back into the shipbuilding industry eight years later (at Yarrows). But there were others who embraced the change in roles and adapted to different jobs without any overt sense of trauma or emasculation, as recent work on deindustrializing communities has shown – such as James Ferns work on ex-steelworkers.[122] And new roles based around

'Fit for the Scrap Heap'

expanded domestic and family responsibilities, caring, as well as more leisure, could have positive impacts on well-being. A married retail worker in Yorkshire told in an interview in 2016 how her ex-miner husband was made redundant more than a decade before. When asked how that affected them she replied:

> He became a househusband ... It was a shock, at first. I am so used to my space. Our children have grown up now. I have a lad in the army. Daughter has got married. Always used to my own space. To have him at home 24/7, it was like I could murder him at times. But you get used to it. You just get used to it. Then his mother got diagnosed [with dementia] and it was like it happened for a reason; why he got made redundant. It was a good job that he did, because we would have really struggled. I would have had to pack in work to look after her. Because there is no way I could have had her put in a home. It's not what I want for her. Unless it gets to the stage where it's really bad. We can cope now better.[123]

Whilst we get no glimpse here of how her ex-miner husband felt, we do get a sense through the lens of his wife's story of how over time the family adapted to a reconfiguration of gender relations. And, how in this case the sharing of caring duties for his ill mother facilitated the health and well-being of his wife, enabling her to continue her career.

Amongst coal miners, there was definitely a multilayered response to the demise of the industry, which was mourned at one level and welcomed at another, based on recognition that there was 'blood on the coal'. One miner reflected that Thatcher, almost universally reviled in mining communities, 'saved his life' by closing the pits. He didn't think he could have survived another fifteen years working underground.[124] Asked how he felt about pit closures, a Scottish miner interviewed in 1999 commented: 'Looking back noo, ah mean, wi' the health problems that all miners had ah think it's the best thing that ever happened. It should all have been open cast years and years ago.'[125] Another responded to the same question: 'Well, mind you, anybody that worked in the pit, the parents used to say, "I won't have my son working in the pit." So it would be a false philosophy to say it was a pity they disappeared.'[126] Miner Joe Bokas, interviewed in 1999, said: 'Glad it's forgotten about ... Death traps ... Oh, no, ah'm delighted tae see it's finished.'[127] Another weighed the costs and benefits carefully, reflecting:

> Well, ye see, in one sense it's a sad business, loss o' livelihood. In the other sense, there's a hell o' a lot of deaths in the pits, a hell o' a lot of disease – pneumoconiosis, silicosis, bronchitis, emphysema, all that carry-on. And in one way ye look at it, miners, people are living longer now ... A miner used tae be an old man at 42. Ye see, ma father wis 42 when he died.[128]

In this commentary James articulated a sense of the range of emotions that could be generated by job loss associated with deindustrialization – registering a sense of relief, almost of joy from escaping exhausting and dangerous work regimes, tempered against the sadness of 'loss o' livelihood'. His testimony was undoubtedly affected by

125

## Jobs and Bodies

the premature death of his father, aged forty-two, of pneumoconiosis. Heavy industry, as we've seen, could also pollute neighbourhoods, leaving a toxic environmental legacy behind. One local resident reflected on the Ravenscraig Steelworks: 'The Craig, it was good when it was there, but you should have seen the muck that came out of it at night, it was ridiculous. All this shit came out.'[129] The coke oven waste was later discovered to be carcinogenic. In these testimonies, the lived realities of participants who had experienced the toxic and dangerous work first-hand temper any sentimental nostalgia as they evaluate and reflect upon the positive and negative impacts of the loss of industrial work.

Oral narratives of job loss and its embodiment could, therefore, be multifaceted, with some, albeit a minority strand of voices, identifying retrospectively the *benefits* to health and well-being of job displacement. And some industrial workers, as in Jim McCaig's case, did adapt to losing work and successfully transitioned into more creative, interesting and less health-threatening occupations – for example, as social workers, into local politics and into nursing and education jobs.[130] This does need to be kept in perspective, though. First, the data indicate that it was difficult for most displaced industrial workers (especially middle-aged and older ones) to make such transitions into the 'new', better, cleaner and more benign (on the body) service-based economy. The most common route was into lower-paid, more precarious and less skilled manual work, or on to state benefit dependency – with all that implied for self-esteem. Second, what was invariably being recalled in these industrial work 'escape narratives' was an insidious regime of managerial economic violence perpetrated upon workers by irresponsible public corporations and private employers who put production and profit above workers' health and well-being. It is perhaps not surprising that some might view escaping from such grim work environments as a positive move. The thrust of the dominant narrative, nonetheless, was to document, to express (often very poignantly), and to mourn in 'scrap heap' stories the loss of work that was so absolutely central to identity construction, to social relationships and to the maintenance of livelihoods, however dangerous and unhealthy the work might be.

## Conclusion

This chapter has argued the case that an ethnographic oral history approach can add really significantly to our understanding of the impact of deindustrialization and the connections between job loss, identity, health and welfare. The rich detail, thick description and often intense articulated emotion help us as academic 'outsiders' to better understand how working lives in industry (like my father's) were profoundly affected by plant closures, getting us beyond statistical body counts and overly sentimentalized and nostalgic representations of industrial work to more nuanced understandings of the embodied meanings and impacts of job loss. The 'spirals of destruction', as Christine Walley so beautifully put it, associated with deindustrialization led to widening social inequalities, and British industrial workers' oral narratives speak directly to this lived experience of rupture, loss and deterioration and their awareness of who and what was responsible.[131] In this evolving conversation, however, we must be aware of a wide range of voices and narratives and try to encompass these different voices and perspectives in our analysis. It may be tempting to see one set of narratives as representative, but plant closure stories sieved through the collective trauma and dislocation of the event are characterized by their diversity. We might identify a dominant or hegemonic strand of 'scrap-heap narratives' where workers felt deeply shamed, emasculated and diminished by unemployment, felt through their bodies, which including deterioration in health and well-being and awareness of premature mortality. There were others who expressed their agency and resistance in classic, heroic 'activist narratives' where injustice was a core motif, whilst others still articulated forms of 'liberation narratives', describing the loss of industrial jobs as positive and health-enhancing, providing opportunities for change, expressing a sense of relief and escape. And these understandings are not necessarily mutually exclusive. In narrating their lived experience of job loss and plant closures, interviewees are informing and interpreting, projecting a sense of self in the process and drawing meaning from their working lives. We need to listen attentively and learn from those who bore witness and try to make sense of these diverse, different and sometimes contradictory stories in our interpretations. That includes taking cognisance of silences and transgressing voices as well as dominant, hegemonic narratives if we are to understand the complex but profound impacts that deindustrialization had on traditional working-class communities, families and on workers' bodies. Moreover, wider knowledge and awareness of this experience and causal pathways to ill health could help to inform and shape public policy in nations, regions and communities currently undergoing deindustrialization, support more healthy ageing strategies, influence regeneration policies, and facilitate a more sustainable, more equitable, and less traumatic transition to postindustrial economies.

# CHAPTER 5
## STRESS AND BURN-OUT: NARRATING THE MODERN WORK-HEALTH EPIDEMIC

'Work-related stress', the UK HSE asserts, 'is defined as a harmful reaction that people have to undue pressures and demands placed on them at work'.[1] With globalization and the accelerated shift to a service-sector dominant post-industrial economy in the UK from the 1970s on, the emphasis in occupational health shifted from physiological impacts to psychological ones; from the body to the mind. Backache, stress and burn-out are now the top three workplace-related complaints. That's not to say that stress caused by work didn't exist before in the industrial era. Overstrain and mental exhaustion certainly did, usually expressed in somewhat different terms, as 'fatigue', 'neurosis', 'nerves' or 'nervous breakdown', as the research of Kirby, Jackson, Melling, Haggett, Schaffner and others has shown.[2] In Vernon's classic text, *Health in Relation to Occupation*, published in 1939, there is a section on 'psychological disorders', covering 'nervous debility, nervous breakdown, neurosis, neurasthenia, nervous exhaustion and anxiety states'. Vernon references two studies over 1936–7 that found around a third of all sickness absence from work was linked to 'psychoneurosis', with school teachers identified as a particularly susceptible group to work-induced nervous breakdown. After years of trade union pressure (from Ernest Bevin's TGWU) another 1937 study investigated bus drivers and conductors, finding considerable 'nervous strain' associated with 'speeding-up' of routes and irregular meal times. The main symptom was gastric sickness, and as Vernon commented: 'emotional stress is very likely to upset digestion'.[3]

The two world wars drew scientific and public attention towards mental health, as a result of the trauma of 'shell shock', bombing and fatigue on the home front. This provided the context for the formation of the aptly termed government agency, the Industrial Fatigue Research Board (1915–48 – renamed the Industrial Health Research Board). This body conducted several of the workplace 'psychoneurosis' studies in the 1930s. They identified women as more susceptible than men in a 1936 study of shop assistants where amongst the causal factors were 'rush periods of rapid and harassing work' and 'fear of not earning enough commission' and 'fear of complaints'.[4]

Jill Kirby refers to a 'linguistic shift' arguing that the 1970s marked a 'transitional period' between the older discourse of 'nerves' and the new language around 'stress'.[5] Stress in the modern workplace was more ethereal and less visible than physical injury, accidents or even chronic industrial diseases which manifest as tangible damage to the body, in flesh, tissue and bones. And as researchers have shown, mental ill-health, whether associated directly with work, or not, was widely and for a long time gendered, in that this was considered to be a 'problem' that women were particularly susceptible

## Jobs and Bodies

to (and affected more by than men), as the 'weaker sex'. This argument was made by Vernon in 1939 and a version continues to be subscribed to by the UK HSE, led by the data.[6] This has sparked a debate in the literature. Antagonists here have rightly indicated that the data is unreliable because of the propensity of men not to report mental ill-health, in part because of the stigma attached to this. Haggett has argued this case in her recent study of male psychological disorders over the period 1945–80, commenting that men under-reported mental ill-health, found it harder to articulate their feelings (alexithymia), carried their 'distress' privately and did not seek help to the same extent as women did.[7] This was the product of a prevalent and dominant masculine culture, built upon a set of values that denied expression of weakness or inability to cope, that stifled emotions and that validated being (at least outwardly) tough and stoic. These were core values of masculinity across the social classes until the later twentieth century. As Bellaby noted, men were more reluctant than women to admit their work made them vulnerable, whilst stress and anxiety 'were rarely admitted to in company'.[8] Mental ill-health was particularly stigmatized and rarely openly spoken about, hence rendered virtually invisible. In an interview in 2022 a UNISON health and safety representative responded to my question on the gendering of stress, saying:

> Women are more likely to come and tell you; a man won't really admit to it. We've had a couple of cases where I've had to dig really deep with members to get them to admit that 'I am really stressed and it is work' ... Men won't really tell you, you have to really dig to find out ... Eventually they'll disclose.[9]

Men had three times the suicide rate of women, three times the alcoholism rate and almost four times the drug-related death rate than women in the 2010s.[10] Not surprisingly the gender gap in life expectancy persisted.

This chapter explores the story of workplace stress and its 'discovery' in the later twentieth century. The first section provides background and context, referring to some of the data, the shifting attitudes of the UK HSE from its foundation in the mid-1970s and the ways that stress has been understood in the literature. The following section draws upon personal testimonies to investigate how workers' stress stories were told and what such oral and other personal accounts can inform us about jobs, bodies and mental ill-health caused by employment in the modern workplace. Of particular importance as sources have been individual responses to the *Mass Observation* 1998 part two directive 'Staying Well and Everyday Life'. A total of 123 responses that mentioned stress were read and some are cited below. *Mass Observation* started in 1937, ran through to the 1950s and was resurrected in 1981. The organization generated 'directives', asking its panel of volunteer citizens to comment on a wide range of social, cultural and political topics. One historian who has used the collection to explore and analyse people's responses to the AIDs epidemic in the 1980s has described the source thus:

> The data are awkward and eclectic. While some MOers followed the directives fairly systematically, others addressed them only partially, and some not at all.

130

## Stress and Burn-Out

Unlike opinion polls or surveys that ask direct questions and demand direct answers, MO sought discursive responses guided by general themes and loose questions. These responses allow us to see something of the complex texture of thought, opinion, and feeling (rather as an oral history interview might).[11]

Another key source for this chapter has been the wonderful recent collection of interviews conducted by Emily Grabham for the project, *Balancing precarious work and care: Interviews with women workers 2015–2017*, now archived, with open online access at the UK Data Service.

### The body and mind at work: Contextualizing the stressful workplace

Stress due to work is not a new phenomenon and has always been an issue, at least since industrialization. It's just that the mental health aspects of occupational health and safety were less visible, submerged and downplayed, compared to the physical carnage of working in the pits, factories and building sites. And the prevailing culture facilitated this silence, and working-class folk had little choice but to be pragmatic and 'get by', at least before the NHS and the boon of free medical treatment. 'You never thought about stress then', commented a Second World War home front 'reserved' worker, 'you just carried on'.[12] 'Fatigue' and overwork, though, were ubiquitous. Stress and exhaustion-induced anxiety were particularly evident on the home front during the pressure points in the two world wars, as we've previously commented on.

The deployment of the body at work fundamentally changed in the late twentieth/ early twenty-first centuries, as Wolkowitz has shown, from extraction, building and making goods to 'interpersonal interactions', with a heavy emphasis across a number of employment sectors in 'emotional labour' – employment that required interaction with people and the expression or suppression of emotions.[13] Women were disproportionately employed in such public-facing sectors (such as social care work, hairdressing, flight attendants, call centres, cashiers) and hence, as Lesley Doyal has argued, were particularly prone to the stresses and pressures associated with what has been termed 'emotional dissonance'.[14] For women, low status jobs (with little autonomy or control) and sexual harassment in the workplace by men, in myriad forms, added to the stressful environment, as a series of studies have shown, including of nurses and clerical work.[15]

Concomitant with Britain's changing employment landscape, old occupational illnesses were gradually replaced by 'new' illnesses, such as repetitive strain injury (RSI), sick building syndrome and the inchoate complaint of stress. There has also been a growing recognition that traditional studies of work and health interactions have frequently been rather narrowly conceived, neglecting mental health and the experience of marginalized groups, for example the health experience of female workers and of unpaid work such as domestic household labour and caring.[16] Isolation has emerged as one of the deleterious mental health impacts of a range of work situations, including homeworking for wages and unpaid domestic labour – something which Oakley identified as associated with

## Jobs and Bodies

the work of the 'housewife' in her seminal study in 1974, together with monotony and lack of intrinsic interest.[17] More recently, isolation is an issue for the growing cadre of self-employed workers exploiting the opportunities provided by computer, mobile phone and internet technologies to work from home The shift to home-working has also been accelerated recently by the Covid-19 epidemic (explored further in the next chapter).

Several processes are at work here. The increasing preponderance of professional, or white-collar-related occupational diseases reflects the country's changing employment structure. On the other hand, the slow recognition of new occupational diseases demonstrated the historical reluctance of corporate capitalism and successive governments to acknowledge that certain ailments were work-related and therefore potentially liable for compensation. This has been the pattern with, for example, lead poisoning, asbestos-related diseases, coal workers' pneumoconiosis, and with emphysema/bronchitis caused through working in mines (the latter not legally recognized as a prescribed occupational disease until 1993). The case of RSI suffered by many typists, sewing machinists (e.g. featured in the recent 2021 Sky TV drama, *American Rust*) and keyboard operators and linked to the diffusion of word processing in the 1980s illustrates the contested nature of such work-related disorders. As with stress in the immediate post-war years, workers claiming RSIs were widely considered to be malingering work-shy shirkers – the illness was believed to be imaginary, rather than real. It was not until the 1990s that RSIs (now classified commonly as musculoskeletal disorders; MSDs) were officially accepted as occupational ailments.

It is clear that new industries and new types of work brought with them unforeseen hazards. After musculoskeletal disorders, stress-related complaints formed the second most commonly reported group of work-related ill-health conditions in the UK at the end of the twentieth century, with the rate of reported stress at work doubling between 1990 and 1999.[18] After flattening out from around 2000–15, rates of work-related stress, anxiety and depression have jumped again, with recent figures showing an increase of around 50 per cent in cases from 2015 to 2020.[19] In 2020 stress at work accounted for 18 million lost work days in the UK, or over half of all working days lost through occupational health and safety issues, affecting 828,000 individuals. To put that in perspective, the highest number of working days lost to strike activity over the period 1990–2022 was in 1990, when 1.9 million working days were lost. Workers in the NHS and in education were reported to be amongst those particularly prone to work-related stress.[20] A 37-year-old male nurse *Mass Observer* in Liverpool noted in 1998: 'I would say that the mental stress of my work is the part that makes me feel unwell.'[21] And stress had a range of psychological and physical symptoms, being associated, for example, with depression, anxiety attacks and other forms of mental illness, as well as heightened risk of coronary heart disease, stomach ulcers and some cancers. Stress was also a contributory factor in unhealthy behaviour such as cigarette, alcohol and substance abuse.[22] In 1998 a major study by the HSE in the UK called *The Stress and Health at Work Study* (SHAW) found that one in five of the UK working population believed their jobs were extremely or very stressful, such that this level of stress was making them ill.[23] This marked a major departure for the HSE from a previously sceptical and

## Stress and Burn-Out

equivocal position regarding work stress.[24] It followed shortly after the first successful legal case (in 1994) in which a social worker was awarded £175,000 in damages after suing Northumberland County Council for a career-ending stress-related breakdown.[25] In the NHS Staff Survey of 2020, 44 per cent of those surveyed reported feeling unwell as a result of work-related stress.[26]

However, as with many other occupational health epidemics, work-related stress is a contested concept. There is a persuasive popular discourse, backed up by many empirical studies, that levels of work stress have been rising since the 1980s. Dalton provides an example of this position, arguing in his 1998 study that 'stress is bad and getting worse', for both workers and managers, whilst a TUC study in 1996 (of 7000 union safety representatives) identified stress as widespread and the main occupational hazard for their members.[27] It led to a rash of trade union 'work stress' audits to raise awareness and a call for tighter regulation. Compensation cases were also increasing, supported by trade unions such as UNISON (public sector workers), establishing the principle that employers were responsible for psychological ill-health caused by their work practices.[28] Taylor and colleagues' studies of call centre workers found work-related stress to be endemic and posited three interconnected factors influencing health and well-being in work: 1. 'proximate' (the labour process and work station); 2. 'ambient' (including lighting and temperature); and 3. 'social' (including management behaviour and the management of labour, such as deadlines and work quotas).[29] Stress affected both female and male call centre employees and Wolkowitz has called for more attention to be focused on the gendering of workplace stress, as unlike most previous occupational epidemics, this was as prevalent amongst women workers, for example as care workers and in the NHS – where self-reported stress levels reached their highest levels.[30] An ongoing stressor was the combination of paid and unpaid work in the home (including housework and care roles), where there is persisting evidence of women carrying an unequal burden of such unpaid work compared to men.[31] We will come back to examine this in a bit more detail in the final section of this chapter.

Stress levels were also greater amongst more insecure immigrant workers and non-standard contract workers than 'core' permanently employed staff – though the latter were certainly not immune. Managers – an initial focus of early stress-at-work studies – were particularly at risk, as were professionals, such as teachers and lecturers, subject to ever-increasing levels of paperwork, monitoring and 'accountability' performance reviews.[32] The contemporary epidemic of workplace stress appears to be breaking new ground in being less tied to social class and to gender than 'classic' industrial disease epidemics have been in the past. Stress could also be a killer.[33]

The forces identified with the rise in work stress have been diverse. One theory is that this is connected with the fundamental shifts in workplace power from the 1980s, with the empowerment of management and neutering of the trade unions, and the increase in workloads and pressure in work that resulted. Increased pressures were being felt in the UK workplace from globalization, rising unemployment, greater job insecurity, more non-standard work contracts and tighter managerial control and a revival of 'coercive' discipline (the 'prerogative' to manage) with privatization, cost-cutting, downsizing,

## Jobs and Bodies

contracting out and new human resource management systems (focusing on individual responsibility for workloads and greater surveillance). Wolmar, for example, has shown how pressure and speed-up associated with the privatization of British Rail from the mid-1990s led directly to poorer standards of maintenance and a rash of accidents.[34] The loss of an experienced cadre of older railway workers and the deskilling of railway labour further contributed to this additional risk[35] Reorganization or 'rationalization' of work was often cited in workers self-reporting as significant in causing workplace stress, together with bullying and harassment by management. The most self-reported cause of stress at work, however, was increased workloads.

On the other hand, many employers and managers continued to be dismissive, challenging trade union claims about the extent of the work stress epidemic and, importantly, contesting culpability, claiming stress to be linked to individual susceptibilities and to pressures outwith the workplace (such as home, family life and relationship breakdowns). Responsibility was thus deflected from issues associated with workloads, work intensification, wage incentives, job design, increased monitoring and surveillance and rising job insecurity – causal factors that figured prominently in trade union campaigns and the popular discourse. Wainwright and Calnan's recent study of the work stress epidemic has posited that this 'problem' needs to be kept in perspective and that the reality has been misrepresented and sensationalized because levels of stress may well have been more significant historically, but under-reported before the 1990s.[36] Whilst incidence was never quantified, work-related stress 'neuroses' were a recurring theme in the annual Factory Inspectors Reports at least from the growth of mass production from the 1920s, and recognized as widely prevalent by some occupational health experts – such as Vernon (as we've noted) and Donald Hunter in 1959.[37] Popular perception – evident in work stress 'victims' personal oral testimonies for example – of a 'golden age' of work before the 1980s may be partly down to nostalgia and somewhat exaggerated.

Wainwright and Calnan argue that the rising self-reporting of stress has coincided with the marked reduction in trade union and labour power since the 1980s and in part represents an individualized alternative to the neutered collective tactics of strikes and industrial action to tackle workplace grievances. This is part of a growing 'culture of victimhood and the therapeutic state' where workers translate what they see as worsening work conditions into 'emotional distress' with reporting swelled by the possibilities of compensation.[38] It also became more acceptable by the end of the twentieth century for men to express such feelings and self-report stress, whereas previously this would have been considered an affront to their masculinity, policed by peer pressure. One of the difficulties, therefore, is that whilst most physical injury, toxins or carcinogens had clear and unequivocal health impacts, stress is mediated much more by subjectivity and consciousness – with different responses, capacities and variable resilience: 'one person's stressor may be another person's challenge'.[39] Some research has shown mild or low-level stress to improve health and well-being, enhancing cognitive performance, resilience, our immune systems and healthy ageing.[40] Hence the concept of 'positive stress'. Wainwright and Calnan's study does

# Stress and Burn-Out

help to question assumptions, puts workplace stress in perspective and provides an antidote to uncritical accounts that implicate modern work systems wholesale as inimical to health – just as previous accounts based on wholesale deskilling or 'dehumanization' within Fordist work regimes have done. They conclude: 'It [work] may not be the pathogenic destroyer of health and well-being portrayed in the work-stress discourse.' They continue, however, to insist: 'but for many people the experience of paid employment is one of boredom, unfulfilled potential, frustration, uncertainty, dissatisfaction or alienation'.[41]

Whilst Wainwright and Calnan provide a useful counterpoise to exaggerated claims about work stress, and historicize and contextualize the epidemic, they do, nonetheless, rather tend to lose sight of the material impacts of work upon the body in their preoccupation with discourses. There is, as Wolkowitz has argued, an 'organic as well as the symbolic level of work experience' and 'each of us has only one body and it feels the pinch'.[42] Phil Taylor and colleagues' recent investigation of stress in call centres, studies such as Bolton and Boyd's of 'emotional labour' in airline flight attendants work, evidence of growing levels of violence at work (e.g. in buses and taxis), ill-health associated with nightwork and studies of stress levels by the HSE, TUC and in the NHS and in Higher Education all convincingly point to a worsening of work-related stress incidence since the 1980s.[43] We have seen already, in the previous chapter, how deindustrialization played out in increasing work-related stressors for those still holding down a job in the contracting industrial blue-collar sector. The evidence points towards this being connected to changes in work with restructuring and to an all-pervasive *intensification* of work in response to market pressures brought on by recession, neo-liberal deregulation and globalization. And for women, the transition to the modern norm of the dual wage earner family, whilst it may have raised family earnings, also created more pressure due to the slower pace of change in men's contribution to domestic work and child-rearing. Hence the 'double-burden' continued to contribute as a causal factor in the high levels of stress, depression and anxiety experienced by women (for more on this see the final section of this chapter), whilst what Oliver James has referred to as 'affluenza', or 'selfish capitalism' may have also contributed to additional pressure to conform to consumerist aspirations.[44] Newspapers, magazines and social media may well have played a role in this too. To some commentators, workers have increasingly become unwitting 'slaves' in a modern 'overwork' culture that is damaging to health and well-being.[45] This interpretation may well underplay the extent to which workers are capable of resisting and mitigating the imposition of stressful work regimes. The recent (2020–1) 'right to disconnect' (from mobile phones, laptops, etc.) campaign by the union PROSPECT (of scientific and technical staff) – inspired by developments in France where legislation was introduced in 2017 – would be an example.[46] Nonetheless, the evidence indicates that whilst old workplace hazards and diseases associated with physical impacts on the body have declined, new ones have emerged and that chronic work-related stress was the most significant of these by the end of the twentieth century. Amongst other things, chronic stress was a causal factor in heart disease, diabetes, depression, obesity and Alzheimer's.

## Jobs and Bodies

### Narrating breakdown: Personal accounts of work-related stress, anxiety and depression

In a wonderful recent book (2019), Diane Kirby examines personal stories from a range of sources, including the Mass Observation Archive and archived oral interviews, to examine stress in the twentieth century. She argues that for much of the century work-related stress was framed as 'strongly linked to the individual's inherent weakness or predisposition, rather than their circumstances, environment or the demands placed upon them'.[47] Structural factors, work processes, work hours and workloads, and management rarely featured in such conversations before the 1970s. Kirby also acutely observes how in many of the earlier personal accounts of work-related stress, pre-1970s, sufferers placed emphasis on physical symptoms – such as ulcers and other digestive complaints – and how they tended to convey their distress within the domestic setting of the home, rather than the public setting of the workplace. This reflected the stigma attached to mental illness and an attempt to hide the shame frequently attached to it. An example Kirby analyses from the British Library Sound Archive was an interview in 1998 with Peter Allen who recalled that in the 1970s whilst working for his local authority:

> I didn't know what it was, there wasn't anything broken or twisted or anything, your lungs weren't bad, it was a nervous breakdown ... In those days, well people just used to say, 'he's had a nervous breakdown' and for the first two hours they were very sympathetic, but after that it was, you know, it's not like a broken leg, if you can't see it, if it's not manifest, then people, if it's in your head, can't quite understand it.[48]

This hints at a widespread playing down (even silencing) of stress as mental illness, profound ignorance of the issue, lack of understanding and a dearth of compassion within society in the immediate post-war decades for those experiencing work-related stress. For working-class men of this generation, moreover, this was associated with inadequacy and weakness, an emasculating failure to cope. This could manifest in embarrassment and shame in the presence of stress and fear over what peers thought of them.[49] Tracey Carpenter became one of the first female railway freight guards in London in 1984. Recalling that era in an interview in 2011 she reflected on mental health issues at work in the 1980s with an anecdote:

> And people [workers] would have suicides [members of the public throwing themselves in front of trains] and not be able to afford to go sick even though they were traumatised and that's all changed now because we're fully salaried, we get sick pay ... now and if people have suicides they get counselling. When I started a friend who was a driver at Stratford had depression and we couldn't tell anyone – I was sworn to secrecy – and he was seeing a psychiatrist and we couldn't tell anybody because he would have been sacked. The fear was that if you

136

had depression you would drive a train into a wall, there was no tolerance of any mental health issues at all whereas now there's counselling and it's just joined the modern world more.[50]

Unlike many of the 'classic' industrial diseases, such as pneumoconiosis, chronic stress affected female workers as much as male workers. One issue for women, Langhamer argues in her research on emotions and women's work in the 'long' 1950s, was the emotional distress of the 'double burden' of trying to balance paid work with their role as mothers responsible for childcare and domestic duties when women's formal employment increased rapidly, especially in part-time work.[51] One divorced woman recalled in a *Mass Observation* Report in 1983:

I tried working full-time but sometimes one of the children fell ill and I had to leave. This happened several times. Or, I would receive alarming 'phone calls from a worried elder child to say that little brother had not arrived home from school and what should she do? I was a nervous wreck by the time I reached home to find him safe and sound.[52]

For some workers it was shift work, including night shift work, that was a significant stressor and caused disruption to family life. One woman recalling the 1950s observed:

My parents' work often affected the family life quite strongly. My father often worked shifts and quite often night work so life never really had a strict routine. When I was older my mother also went out to work. She always worked in the catering business so quite often the hours were unsocial. In fact in my father's mid years he had a nervous breakdown and this was attributed to the fact that he worked irregular shifts. I can't remember my parents really enjoying their work, my father was a manual worker although he didn't really seem suited to it, being a gentle person. My father worked as a necessity, constantly worried about money.[53]

Mass unemployment in the 1980s forced some to take jobs for which they were unsuited and this contributed to cumulative pressure and stress. A male NHS clerk expressed a sense of this in a statement in response to a *Mass Observation* (MO) directive in 1998 on 'health and well-being' arguing that he 'loathed' his work (but it was all he could get) and felt undervalued: 'I felt trapped, humiliated and overwhelmed.' He continued: 'This situation made me increasingly depressed and overwrought, leading to an initial dependence on tranquilisers just to get me through the day. But when even these failed to work to a lengthy period of sick leave and consultations with a psychiatrist, who eventually recommended retirement on health grounds.'[54] The stress affected him so badly that he had faked illness and had self-harmed (attacking himself with a hammer) to avoid going into work. His retirement on health grounds was in 1988, aged forty-one, and he was still unemployed at the time of writing for MO ten years later. Others took

## Jobs and Bodies

early retirement to escape stressful and unhealthy work environments. A female ex-retail sales assistant reported to MO:

> While I was going out to work I did feel a certain amount of stress, but not all the time, it depended on how busy I was at home and at work. The last job that I had was a very hectic one, working evenings in a mini-market and off-licence store, mainly on my own, and it eventually became too much to manage, because I was having problems with my legs and could not be 'on' them all day and during the evenings as well. So at the age of 51 I called it a day.[55]

She switched to what she termed 'unpaid work', looking after her grandson. Faced with such stress some sought medical advice and for a period the common response was to prescribe tranquilizers and anti-depressants, including valium (first licensed in 1963), the 'little yellow pill' immortalized in the Rolling Stones song (1966) 'mother's little helper': 'And it helps her on her way, gets her through her busy day'.[56]

Over time, attitudes and prevailing cultures shifted, with a growing recognition that chronic work-related stress had complex causes, was primarily the product of structural factors and power dynamics within the workplace, not the fault of individuals, or linked to personal susceptibility. And gender identities morphed and became more fluid, enabling easier articulation of mental illness, especially, perhaps, for men. In relating personal stories of experiencing stress at work a range of narratives are evident by the early twentieth-first century. In one recent (2014) study that relied upon fifty-one personal one-to-one interviews the researchers argued that: 'Participants reported adverse working conditions and management practices as common causes of work stress. Stress-inducing management practices included unrealistic demands, lack of support, unfair treatment, low decision latitude, lack of appreciation, effort–reward imbalance, conflicting roles, lack of transparency and poor communication.'[57] They added:

> The narrative data on participants' understanding of factors that may cause stress at work suggested working conditions, management practices, nature of job, life events and financial factors. ... The majority of participants ($n = 42/51$) referred to working conditions as a main source of stress. Working conditions were mainly related to factors such as workload, the physical environment (e.g. noisy offices, lack of windows, small rooms, and offices in which the temperature was either too low or too high for comfort), long working hours, heavy workloads and understaffing.[58]

Digital monitoring and surveillance systems were also identified as primary stressors. As information scientist Karen Levy has argued, growing workplace monitoring has eroded workers freedom and autonomy, with such systems constituting 'a managerial tool facilitating power and control over workers'.[59] London train driver Tracey Carpenter reflected on a series of changes that came with privatization and 'restructuring' on the

# Stress and Burn-Out

railways in the 1990s, including the introduction of the 'black box' monitoring unit in train cabs – derisorily called 'the spy in the cab'.[60] These reduced the autonomy and independence of the drivers and were viewed as a 'policing' mechanism which piled on the pressure:

> We've got data recorders in the trains now which can be downloaded at any time ... It's just like a black box on an aeroplane. It records data. It used to only record 24 hours but now technology's got better, it can hold months as far as I know, of every train journey and its times. You can tell how far the train has gone along so all you need to do is find the date and the time and you can work out what that train was doing at that time and who was on it, who was driving it. So if you make a mistake they can see, they will then download your train and look what you were doing through that journey. And probably the guy who drove the train before you is sweating too in case he accidently went a few miles an hour too fast somewhere because they could be looking around at his trip too. Any mistake you make they'll download the data recorder, but you get random downloads also a certain amount of times a year and if you make a mistake you then get looked at more. So you can get into a downward spiral where if you make a mistake you get looked at more, and the minor mistakes you make because you're human, that wouldn't have been noticed, now are. It has become a much more stressful job ... than it was. There weren't data recorders till a few years ago. You would just do the best you could and you wouldn't worry if you were a few miles over the speed but now they are so prescriptive. There's no sense that there are lots of right ways and safe ways of doing the job.[61]

This led to greater stress:

> They've got to the position now where the black boxes have gone from being not a spy in the cab and just for accident investigations to being a routine tool by which they will monitor drivers' performance, and there are automatic downloads to make sure. What happens is you make a small mistake and then you live on your nerves ... you are aware that you are on a cliff edge to a certain extent. But however careful you are and however conscientious you are you will make mistakes. You can't maintain high concentration levels all the time: the job would be too tiring if it was like that ... I think it's a lot more stressful really, looking back it's a lot more stressful than it was isn't it. Oh god. They're looking over your shoulder all the time. Kafkaesque ... I really think it's Kafka land now on the railway, but I think that's the same across a lot of industries.[62]

Call centres perhaps epitomize the almost apocalyptic vision of meaningless, degraded, monotonous and dehumanized work, with intrusive levels of surveillance. As Taylor and colleagues have shown, call centre workers oral testimonies frequently incorporated this alienated, disconnected, work-as-drudgery narrative.[63] Recalling her

139

**Jobs and Bodies**

work at a utility company call centre in the 1990s/2000s a 56-year-old worker from Leeds reflected in an interview with researcher Emily Grabham:

> When I think of the times, you know … when you wake up on a morning and think oh my god, I've got to go in and be shouted at and do these complicated bills that somebody has messed up and just go, oh, I don't think I could do it now to be honest with you … I couldn't go back into an office, it would drive me crazy.[64]

A particularly scathing and emotional indictment of such work came from a former Abbey National building society call centre manager in Glasgow, Catherine McBean, who recalled of the late 1990s:

> This was supposed to be making less work for all the branches and you were to take all the calls. But I remember [pause], when we set the call centre up, it was exciting to begin with, but then we saw, when I saw what was actually happening in the call centre, people were monitored every second of the day. And they were rated on their call rate and the duration of the calls, you had to make the calls as short as you could; how many calls they had answered, and that was all monitored, in computerised monitoring of the calls and the terminals – they all sat in front of a terminal on the phone. And [pause], I remember one day being in my office and watching this girl. She had her headphones on and she was tethered, with the headphone wire to the phone and she got up off her chair and started pacing up and down the floor. I thought to myself that's like a dog in a yard, in a kennel pacing up and down there. And I thought, this is not right. People can't go to the toilet, they don't feel they can go to the toilet without having an impact negatively on their performance levels. And, the pressure of the situation. I thought we shouldn't be treating human beings like this. I really, really didn't like it. And I began to have problems dealing, living with that. So, there came an opportunity for me to take voluntary redundancy. I didn't have to. And I'm not blowing my own trumpet when I say I was quite a star in the place. I could have gone on, but I said [pause], 'I don't want to be a part of this'. And I took the voluntary redundancy and left.[65]

This narrative strongly evokes the *panopticon* nature of this employment, with the high level of performance monitoring and self-exploitation evident, as well as the assault on personal dignity, expressed powerfully through the deployment of the 'dog and kennel' metaphor. Some simply couldn't take it: call centre worker Chloe English killed herself in May 2021 following high levels of anxiety and chronic stress on the job.[66]

For others stress derived from the work environment and relationships in work, and especially from poor management. A female office worker in London reflected in 1998 on the difficulties of working in an air-conditioned 'open plan' office with no windows that opened, whilst asserting: 'It is very stressful because our boss is a very poor people manager and engenders low morale.'[67] And age may well have played a part, with some older workers finding changes in labour processes particularly stressful. For example, a recently retired monotype printer told *Mass Observation* in 1992 in response to their directive on 'the pace of life' that he had faced 'demanding work ... [and] ... extreme high pressures' over a long fifty-five-hour work week (seventy hours including travelling time) and that his capacity to cope had dwindled over time:

> Before I retired eighteen months ago, I was finding new equipment, such as fax machines, radio phones, photo-copiers, calculators, computers and electronic machine controls, had so speeded the turn round time for orders it was difficult to keep mentally abreast with the workflow ... At that period in my life I could tell when I was overtaxing myself by physical signs ... without them I could have worked myself into a nervous breakdown. This was the doctor's diagnosis and always appeared when overworking.[68]

A 55-year-old female journalist spoke about similar stressors associated with technological change, new ways of working and a switch of management in the 1990s:

> One factor in well-being, which would be underlined by all my colleagues around the sub-editors table, is the stress resulting entirely from the introduction of computerised newspaper production. We did, of course, have deadlines in the pen and paper, hot metal days. But the computer has pressures that we never knew before due to its propensity for crashing, locking, losing copy and even whole pages. In addition, new owners and a less considerate regime mean we are seriously under-staffed and can never take the requisite screen breaks. We all suffer from tension and eye-strain.[69]

Deborah Collins, a London-based journalist, recalled the technological changes in the late 1980s, the attack on trade unions and higher stress levels and its effects:

> So we had, for instance, a colleague of mine who was head of the art desk, the graphic designers, who I knew was getting up at three o'clock in the morning to come in and deal with the teething problems of the new technology, and without him there would have been disasters and I don't think what he did was noticed, let alone appreciated. And we had staff members grappling with this who were on antidepressants and taking time off with stress and everything.[70]

For others the problem manifested in insomnia. A 56-year-old newspaper executive manager commented on his 'worry about work': 'When things are pretty "hairy" at the office I can wake up at one or two o'clock in the morning and start turning things over in my mind ... I get a bit panicky and start to perspire.'[71]

Oral testimonies and other personal accounts such as those reported by Mass Observers from the late twentieth century on show how some narrators were constructing and conveying a positive sense of self in their stories. They were composing narratives that showed awareness of culpability beyond themselves, expressing that their

## Jobs and Bodies

deterioration in health was not a consequence of their personal failures but that the fault was structural – caused by the systems and work regimes imposed upon them. A Scottish police officer Ian Millar recalled in an interview in 2017:

> I was a police officer and I finished as an inspector although I also did a spell as a chief inspector for a time and the stress piled onto us around 2012 onwards, it was massive. When I was doing my bit as chief inspector, which I did from November 2011, to May 2012, em … I mean I was getting up … I was arriving into work at half five in the morning and getting home at five o'clock at night. Getting no breaks, just getting absolutely hammered. And it was very mentally draining. And that was in the run up to Police Scotland. And it's hard to say … it's not that the work didn't care but it did seem to me like they didn't care. It was like … well I mean there was quite a lot of my peers who went off with depression or burn out. But myself, when I reverted back to being inspector I went to a role which was community policing so effectively what happened was I ended up being the deputy chief inspector and it just had a massive workload as well and eventually I just kinda crashed. I mean I didn't go off sick but eh … I remember getting home one day and I woke up twenty-nine hours later. And I was struggling a wee bit at work and I eventually got brought in to be spoken to and I just told them what had happened. Now they did refer me to occupational health and they were actually quite surprised that I was still working but I had it in my own mind Rachel that if I'd of gone off sick I would have never gone back … there was a lot of pressure.[72]

To deflect from any sense of personal weakness Ian was keen to insist that he was a 'grafter' with a strong work ethic, not allowing himself to lose any work time, continuing to turn up despite his exhaustion. He also suggested a wider structural problem in indicating he was not alone, reporting 'quite a lot of my peers' … 'went off with depression or burn-out'. He proceeded to assert that it was the chronic stress at work that led to physical ill-health and attributed his diabetes to his breakdown:

> And I think that's what triggered the shingles. I know the nurse at my practice … I think when I was diagnosed with diabetes there was a recognition that 'you've probably had this a wee while'. You've had this for a wee while and something has triggered it. And I know I can never say with any definition that it was pressure at work … I'm pretty sure it was. It was either pressure at work or pressure at home or a combination.[73]

Such personal testimonies suggest a growing awareness of stress across society by the end of the twentieth century and support the argument made by Kirby that people were subjectively articulating that they *felt* worse, facing more stress linked to 'modern life' in 'burn-out' Britain.[74] These stories resonate with Kirby's observation drawn from similar accounts that these are 'narratives of victimhood', contrasting with earlier (pre-1970s) articulations in which self-blame and personal responsibility dominated.[75] They also,

## Stress and Burn-Out

however, are a barometer of real, tangible deleterious changes in work associated with the post-1980 decades of deepening deindustrialization, worker disempowerment and pressures associated with instability, uncertainty and increasingly precarious employment.

Ben Rogaly's recent oral history-based work on migrant workers in Peterborough provides a powerful case for migrant labour in the food-processing and warehousing (including Amazon) sector in the 2000s and 2010s being particularly susceptible to chronic stress and anxiety at work within the context of what he terms 'racial capitalism'.[76] Rogaly's migrant narrators identified the main workplace stressors in the 2000s and 2010s as production target setting, recurrent revision of targets upwards and the close monitoring of work through digital surveillance technology, combined with sanctions which could lead to dismissal.[77] Polish warehouse worker Sabina recalled:

> Some people, bless, were running to do their targets, they still couldn't achieve them. And that was quite brutal because you knew and as later on – I didn't know that from the beginning – but later, management, they knew very well that these people were working very hard and … whatever they had achieved was very low just because they had rubbish stuff.[78]

Target-setting and bonuses as incentives for working at a 50 per cent over target rate could compromise health and safety rules as Azwer, one of Rogaly's narrators, noted after an injury to his back. Another, Armins, commented on feeling demeaned by the work regime and how little management cared about workers' bodies and health and safety:

> Because they had orders from somebody above and the supervisors were there just to keep pushing us, like push, push, push. And the guy who was the supervisor, he was a football trainer, so his attitude, like standing in the front in the middle of the warehouse and shouting … It was really annoying and degrading, like talking you down, constantly shouting at you.[79]

Rogaly concluded that migrants faced a politically induced 'hostile environment' in the 2000s and 2010s, mirroring a recurring cycle we have commented on previously where migrant labour frequently faced the harshest work regimes and worst occupational health and safety conditions. Moreover, as Rogaly argued, for UK workers in the early twenty-first-century work-related stressors included: 'a decade-long decline in average real wages, increasing in-work poverty, job insecurity and intensification of workplace regimes'.[80]

This wasn't just a feature of the modern UK workplace. Jessica Bruder's anthropological account, *Nomadland* (2017), now a movie, brilliantly depicts such brutal conditions in the United States, in places like the giant Amazon warehouses where the strong work ethic of older workers was exploited in conditions that tested the fittest of bodies. Workers were encouraged to prepare their bodies beforehand with regular exercise and then underwent 'work hardening' as part of their training for work shifts that could cover ten to twenty miles of walking.[81] Overstrain and mental ill-health caused by stress were ubiquitous and well documented in the Amazon warehouses in the 2010s.

## Jobs and Bodies

'There's nothing to describe the misery', one of Bruder's narrators commented. The main protagonist, Linda, added: 'If I live through this I'll be in great shape.'[82] Amazon was and remains a fiercely anti-trade union employer and in such circumstances it was difficult for workers to push back. Nonetheless, industrial action for union recognition, improved wages and conditions occurred in the early 2020s at an Amazon centre in Staten Island, New York and one in Coventry in January 2023 – the first known strike at a UK Amazon plant.

In the UK, the NHS and teaching were 'burn-out' professions where work-related stress was particularly acute in the late twentieth and early twenty-first centuries.[83] The case of Kate Rawnsley provides an example. Kate was an art lecturer at Bradford College, where she started working in 1992. In the mid-2000s she experienced an acute period of bullying and harassment, followed by being allocated an unsuitable room for her art teaching by management, the 'reallocation' of a colleague who shared workload with her and, finally (unbelievably) the arbitrary disposal of her work desk (to a skip). As a consequence, she experienced acute anxiety, depression and insomnia, reported to occupational health on campus, worsened by further ongoing 'intimidating and aggressive' behaviour by management. Kate commented in a 'case meeting':

> I came to this meeting with the thought of a realistic outcome that we've something positive to go on, but in my heart of hearts I know … that my voice is never heard, and I know my voice is not being heard now … And it just breaks my heart. All I've ever wanted was to teach art and to take people from quite impoverished backgrounds, to put them into a degree and for them to get great grades … You've tried to railroad me into this situation and it's made me ill and it's had a dramatic effect on my family, on my little girl, on everything. I don't know what to do. I really don't know what to do about this at all because, it's … it's really, really made me very, very poorly, I just feel totally undervalued.[84]

Kate's sense of intense frustration, hurt and disempowerment seeps through this testimony. In the later stress compensation claim case in court the College lawyers tried to shift the blame to Kate's mental health and factors outside the workplace as causes. This replicates tactics used by employers previously that we have commented on, such as asbestos-related disease compensation cases where 'blaming the victim' was commonly deployed and employers and insurance companies delayed claims as long as possible in the hope the complainant would die before settlement. In Kate's case the judge condemned Bradford College management as 'callous' and their responses to Kate's well-documented work-related stress breakdown as 'cavalier'. After a long struggle, supported throughout by her trade union, the UCU, she was awarded £159,000 in damages in 2017. Kate commented:

> I couldn't sleep, I still have problems. I became suicidal at times. I cried at work a lot. I'd worked so hard and been treated so badly. I was terrified of going to work. Terrified of my managers. I didn't know what they were going to do next. I was on

antidepressants until a month after I won the case ... but I feel vindicated. I am glad it went to court. I feel believed.[85]

Others reported similarly inflexible and unsympathetic attitudes on the part of management towards mental health issues. A female social historian (aged fifty-one) reported to *Mass Observation* in January 2000:

The last time I had to take time off work was in 1994 and I ended up being granted early retirement on the grounds of ill-health. I was seriously depressed at the time and close to breakdown. I simply didn't have the energy, will or desire to return to the stress and waste of the place where I worked. It was a straightforward decision to take time off – I felt so dreadful there was no alternative. I had a supportive doctor who could see the state I was in (at first I wasn't fully aware of it) and ensured I got time off. Thoughtfully she entered as my illness on the certificates 'general debility' – if she'd entered 'depression' it could have been very damaging to me had I returned to work. My employer was very unforgiving to mental illness, as many are, I understand.[86]

NHS administrator Michelle McBride attested to the undervaluation of workers and lack of sympathy in her workplace in the 2000s and 2010s towards stress amongst NHS office support workers (who were predominantly women):

You are quite far down the food chain ... admin. don't matter ... You're the equivalent of the cleaner ... You're in a stressful position as an administrator. They don't recognise you as an important piece of the work. Clinicians come first. They just put the workload on you and you kind of have to muddle through.[87]

She continued:

It's definitely got worse, definitely. There's a lot more people off with workplace stress and they're actually willing now to say it. Before it was, 'no, I'm fine'. Now definitely they are more willing ... there are a lot more people willing to put workplace stress on a sick note; they weren't before, because management were coming down on them: 'what are you stressed about'; 'how can you be stressed you're only admin.'[88]

Michelle had her own breakdown with stress in 2010, as a result of a particular manager abusing and bullying her. She recalled:

I walked out and I was actually sitting in my car crying; and I'm not one of those people that do that; I would rather fight with you, I'll take anyone on ... I was so intimidated and so low. People should be respected for what they do. They should not be frightened to go to work every day, or frightened to say I'm stressed at work. But if a manager is just not willing to help it's not fair.[89]

## Jobs and Bodies

In other employment sectors post-traumatic stress disorder (PTSD) was an issue, increasingly recognized over time. PTSD has come to be seen as the product not just of military service, domestic, sexual and other forms of abuse, but also due to extreme trauma at work. Whilst rarely admitted or articulated as such before the 1980s (the 1988 Piper Alpha oil rig disaster was a watershed of sorts), PTSD would have been a common reaction to experiencing or witnessing serious and fatal accidents at work. This is now well documented in the case of modern-day mine disasters, for example in the case of the entombment (and rescue) of the Chilean miners in 2010.[90] In firefighting there was exposure to what were known as 'critical incidents', including tragic deaths of members of the public and colleagues. Scottish firefighter Scott McCabe recalled the trauma associated with the death of a female colleague after a wall collapsed on her and how a colleague with PTSD had panic attacks hearing engine sirens or passing a fire station. He recollected that in the 1990s he and others found it difficult to talk about stress, referring to the ineffectiveness of measures such as what was known as 'the cuddle club' where those affected by 'critical incidents' were encouraged to open up and talk about their feelings. 'It was awkward', Scott recalled, 'it was uncomfortable and people didn't share their feelings at all'. The system was reformed after pressure by the Fire Brigades' Union (FBU) facilitated the employment of an occupational stress trained clinician Jean Bruce leading to more effective treatment, therapy and rehabilitation.[91] Scott survived his twenty-three years in the Fire Service with no serious mental health 'episodes' only to have a stress-related 'nervous breakdown' several years into his new job as an FE college lecturer:

Working in FE is more stressful than working in the Fire Service … It's a business and it's run like that. You're given so many hours of teaching and that equates to so much money so you have to perform and that's where the problems come … it's when you are not hitting your targets; you're not performing. The pressure that exerts on people is unfair.[92]

He associated his breakdown and contemplation of suicide in Autumn 2020 with overwork, 'pressures put on myself', and family responsibilities during the first phase of Covid-19. Fortunately, he had the strong support of colleagues and the College and effective treatment, including 'talking therapy' which he found 'cathartic' and described as 'brilliant'. Still, he was months in recovery and reflected, a year or so later in our interview:

Now I'm acutely aware I have mental health issues … I still feel I'm not back to 100%. There's a line somewhere where you can break again, and I don't know where that line is. I'm really cautious that I don't over-commit to things and I get my work-balance just right and I don't be doing things at night or at the weekend.[93]

Clearly, understandings of the causal roots of stress shifted and most of those experiencing work-related stress and recalling this in written or oral evidence over the past two decades or so had an acute sense of the underlying structural stressors that were

## Stress and Burn-Out

causing their physical and/or mental ill-health and distress. When asked in 1998 'what makes you feel unwell' a 55-year-old medically retired male nurse commented: 'The environment that we live in accounts for a lot of today's illness. At work management who do not care about those under them putting these people under undue stress to further their own ends.' He continued: 'Usually my wife tells me when things get out of control and then I go to the doctors.'[94] Scott McCabe was scathingly critical of management, identifying inadequate training leading to poor risk assessments and a 'dysfunctional safety committee' packed with managers at the FE college he worked at.[95] And societal attitudes moved too in this direction, aided by shifting discourses in newspapers and on television where managerial negligence was identified rather than emphasizing individual responsibility. A growing strand of more progressive management came to accept the culpability of modern work regimes, and initiate organizational stress control and occupational health schemes, genuinely more flexible work arrangements and appreciate the need for a better work-life balance. Kirby has traced these shifts towards 'stress management' within Lloyds Bank PLC (later Lloyds Trustee Savings Bank) and the emergence of a 'stress management industry'.[96] These shifts in understanding and corporate policy were linked to scientific and medical advances, activist campaigns from the 1980s (headed by the TUC) and progressive changes in employment law (influenced by European Union directives). These also contributed to profoundly shifting the OHS discourse away from personal culpability for mental ill-health, identifying the primacy of structural factors that underlay the tsunami in work-related stress associated with the post-modern workplace. The first successful prosecution for substantial damages (£175,000) for a stress breakdown in 1994 also had an impact. Nonetheless, this remained a contested terrain and these battles were, and continue to be, fought within the wider destabilizing context of deregulation of labour markets, increasing work casualization and employment precarity, the end of the idea of a 'job-for-life' and the pervasive undermining of trade unions and their dwindling capacity to sustain the protective matrix they brought to the workplace.

Michelle McBride and Kate Rawnsley's cases are indicative of both the empowerment of management in recent years and of the resilience and agency of individuals facing stressful work conditions, as well as the central importance of trade unions in a supportive role in the modern workplace. Michelle commented on the UNISON representative (Steven) who helped her deal with the stress that came from an abusive and bullying manager saying: 'I've never been so grateful to anybody.'[97] And Kate noted: 'Everyone should be a member of a union. You've no idea what is around the corner, and you need that assurance. You insure your car, your house. You should insure your work life.' Individual trade unions, such as UNISON and the UCU, supported by the TUC and STUC, played important roles in supporting individual members in disputes over stress and excessive workloads, as well as in stress compensation cases. The radical occupational health and safety magazine *Hazards* (established in 1976), under the editorship of Rory O'Neill, also played a key role as did, more recently, the National Work Stress Network (1997) in publicizing cases, shifting the discourse and in advocacy for victims of work-related stress.

**Jobs and Bodies**

## Gender, the 'double burden' and stress

The gendering of stress, anxiety and mental health merits more attention. We have noted already how historically, for employed women, the 'double burden' of paid work combined with unpaid household duties and family responsibilities could undermine health and well-being. A sense of overwhelming pressure may well have been especially the case with female single parents, a group which grew as a proportion of the total from the 1950s on. Smaller families were to some degree compensated by older relatives, living longer, adding to women's caring responsibilities. The particular pressure points of wartime brought the strain upon mothers to public attention, but this became an issue that more and more families grappled with as levels of female participation in the labour market shifted sharply upwards from the 1960s on and the 'dual earner' household became the norm. For married women and mothers this could create stress and tension within the home, particularly where male household members were reluctant to change ingrained habits of little or no participation in family caring responsibilities or domestic duties and chores, such as shopping, cleaning and cooking. The larger the family the worse could be the pressure. The personal responses of women to a *Mass Observation* directive in 1998 on 'staying well and everyday life' shed some light on this. One woman in her fifties from South-West England who was holding down several part-time jobs reported wryly in 1998:

> Basically what makes me feel unwell ... just overburdened, is having too much to do ... just tired and pissed off having too much to do. On a day-to-day basis the overburdening usually comes from me having to do everything that needs doing to keep the show on the road. For although I only have a part-time job I still do the majority of the household duties. I wouldn't mind so much if it was just me but there are usually two very large capable male type things in front of the telly who could be lending a hand ... Their principle of leisure being more important than things that have to be done doesn't quite tally with mine.[98]

Changing work patterns and lack of control over work were other stressors. A 54-year-old married woman who had worked in a frozen food factory in Suffolk for thirty years commented on how the work regime changed fundamentally in the mid-1990s. This saw the scrapping of a regular eight-hour day, five days a week, and the introduction of four twelve-hour shifts on a pattern dictated by management (including over weekends and bank holidays), with the loss of any discretionary control over when holidays were taken. She reflected on the pressure her paid work put upon her:

> Working twelve hour shifts is awful, especially on nights. I feel absolutely shattered when I leave off ... I get so tired that I start crying when I'm at home. If it was possible for me to leave I would, but with my husband unemployed I need the money. Except for 1997 when I had my breast removed I have had no other time

## Stress and Burn-Out

off work. It would be so easy to give in when I feel ill but if I am off work more than twice, I don't get paid.[99]

Another younger Mass Observer (unemployed; aged thirty-three and disabled with ME – myalgic encephalomyelitis, or chronic fatigue syndrome) responding to the 'staying well and everyday life' directive in 1998 ruminated on the burn-out and exhaustion she saw all around her:

We're expected to work long hours in demanding jobs with the constant fear of redundancy and unemployment pushing us to our physical and psychological limits. We're not encouraged to listen to our bodies and read the warning signs. We're frowned upon for taking time off work when we're ill. The psychological stresses are huge – money, jobs, the family, the future, and society is more disparate, families spread far apart, people not knowing their neighbours. The support networks are small and emotional support often not forthcoming ... the warning signs are clear.[100]

There was also a sense of malaise and a drifting work-life balance in some of these responses to the 1998 MO 'well-being' directive. A 44-year-old female museum assistant noted: 'I feel much less tough than I used to be, or than I always thought myself! I imagine a time ahead where the general level of pressure eases off and there is more time to sleep and enjoy leisure etc. But sometimes I think this time will never come.'[101]

The demands of the job could impact on the body at home and encroach into family time. A 46-year-old school secretary reflected on her persistent exhaustion:

The only problem I have is tiredness after work. I often fall asleep in the chair or even sitting at the table after our evening meal following a working day. During school holidays this happens rarely. Mine is a very stressful and demanding job requiring a lot of concentration because of the huge number of distractions, so I think this is mental not physical tiredness ... the last time I had time off work was about ten years ago ...[102]

A 34-year-old married Liverpool woman gave up her paid job in a factory because of the work environment, having suffered from what she termed 'psychosomatic' headaches because of the noise and extremes of temperature. The latter was reported to the 'health and safety people', but nothing was done because the workforce was small and fell outside the regulations. She reported: 'Health-wise I'm much better now since I gave up employed work ... It was exhausting ... I'm much, much happier now.' This choice was facilitated by having a self-employed husband earning a good wage. For others this was not possible.

Stress from paid and unpaid work could coalesce and be exhibited in physical symptoms. A 36-year-old male nursery school teacher with domestic caring duties at home (father and mother) commented on how this would manifest in migraines and

149

## Jobs and Bodies

'stomach trouble'. 'These have blown up', he said, 'when things have been difficult at home and also at work when I've had difficulties with staff etc. I have come to realise that if I take on too much, or listen to too many problems, then I myself start to become ill.' His coping mechanism was to withdraw and disassociate – 'I've tended to become quite hard over the years, but only to preserve my physical and mental well-being'.[103] A 55-year-old female prison probation officer noted, in 1998: 'The main result of what is fairly stressful work is headaches and stomach upsets.' She added that monitoring was overbearing and that: 'We are aware that we are constantly having to improve efficiency'.[104] A woman who worked as a florist commented on the physical impacts of her work – including chronic arthritis – before talking about the primary stressor: 'The thing that makes me so unwell is the relationship I have with my boss … she makes life very difficult for me.' This combined with pressure from her home life, including an alcoholic husband. On medical advice she was encouraged to get out of the toxic workplace she was in, but she reflected: 'I have difficulty with that as my daughter has a mental health problem and learning difficulties, my mother had a stroke.' She added: 'My boss hates me and my husband is a drunk. How can I not get stressed?'[105]

A series of interviews conducted by Emily Grabham in 2015–19, now archived at the UK Data Service (previously Qualidata) Archive, highlighted how the burden of paid work combined with unpaid work servicing the needs of families could generate unhealthy stressful conditions for women in the modern post-industrial economy.[106] A retail sector worker in her sixties in London told how she tried to get more flexible working hours after her caring role increased significantly following her husband having a stroke in 2005.[107] The lack of support from the store manager caused her to have a breakdown:

> They told me that I would probably have to do a late night and a weekend, because I wasn't a registered carer. This is one of the managers. It caused me to be off work for 3 weeks with work-related stress. I couldn't cope with it. And then they say, don't worry, it might not happen. But hang on, you've planted the seed in my head and there is me thinking well, I can't do late nights. I can't ask my daughter with the little ones who are 5 and 6 to leave here at 10, 11 o'clock at night and then take them to school. At weekends it's her time with the children. I just think sometimes they just don't think what they are doing to people. I think it is just a number on a pay roll or a pawn on a chess board, and they will move you where they think you should be.[108]

She continued:

> The mental scars, the pressure is still there. Because it can't go away. They know that I can't do it … It's awful … It gives me stress and depression, because they say, don't worry about it. How can you not worry what is going to happen … it got to me so much that I was off work with the work related stress, because of it all on top of everything else. But they don't seem to worry. The person [store manager] told

me I may have to work evenings and that was the same person that told me I would have been better off if my husband had died, because I could have got on with my life. Then she said, if you say anything to anyone, I will deny it. But again, you know, my husband had just had a major stroke, you know, and he was in hospital for a month and they were telling you this … A lot of people won't say anything. This is what I was saying, you know, I'll speak out because I am not afraid to … A lot of people won't speak out. They will just take what they are told … They are frightened for their job.[109]

This testimony speaks vividly to what happens 'behind the scenes' with inflexible and bullying managers, of accumulating stress and anxiety, of adversarial relations – 'them and us' – intense frustration over the lack of control over work and resentment at the arbitrary power of management – a 'pawn on a chessboard'. And of the insensitivity and inhumanity of bosses telling her it would have been better had her husband died. Later she commented on her own sense of dehumanization in this workplace: 'You are just like a robot.' Another recurring motif in the narrative is a sense that many people would take such treatment in silence, without protest, but that she was not frightened to push back. She got the union involved, threatening to take it to an employment rights tribunal:

You get to a stage with work where you think you know, like enough is enough. I had just had it. You can threaten all the time and I said to her, just don't threaten me, do it. I said and you will see where it goes … I think now that's the only thing you can do. They just want to walk all over you. All companies are the same. If you don't want your job, out the door, there is somebody else that will walk in, no matter how many year's service you have done. I've done a lot of years … I've been there twenty four years. In the same place, in the same store. So, there is no loyalty any more as far as I am concerned. I go there, do my job, and come away.[110]

This section of the narrative ends with a sense that she was wronged by management who treated her with a lack of respect and with contempt – and in return she is left alienated, again, 'like a robot', and feeling no sense of joy anymore doing her paid day job. Later she reflected on this being an issue of basic dignity and her human rights being ignored with impunity. The balancing of family responsibilities, a caring role and paid employment took its toll on the body and on well-being, and was recognized as such: 'Yes, it is a strain on me. I've lost my independence, and that is one of the big things.' She pilloried her employers for not offering 'flexibility and understanding' when she was trying to juggle additional pressures at home with the pressures of the job: 'they want so much of you that I can't do it.' And she showed an acute awareness of shifting power dynamics and how the labour market had made matters worse: 'I don't think it helps when you've got so many people unemployed. Because before if you was in a job, you were relatively safe … but now a lot of the companies don't want to compromise.'

**Jobs and Bodies**

Others in the retail sector reported on profoundly stressful working environments, compounded by women's personal unpaid caring roles and responsibilities within the home. An Asian mother of two children who worked in HR for a supermarket chain for sixteen years recalled how difficult it was for workers with caring responsibilities to avoid the disciplinary procedure when they took time off when dependents were ill or in need, or children needed looking after, for example at Christmas. Also how the procedure and the insensitive attitudes of some managers just deepened anxiety and stress on the job.[111] One fellow worker was told in a disciplinary hearing by management she shouldn't have had children if they interfered with her ability to work. Head Office might align themselves with more progressive 'flexible' working policies but in the workplace, shop managers, under pressure themselves to hit performance targets, could be more brutal. Workplace bullying by retail managers appears to have been widespread. The narrator was issued a formal disciplinary notice herself when she took time off to care for her mother-in-law, recalling:

> Yes, it was the worst nightmare, because it was like, you know what, why do we work? Where has humanity gone? I suffered from stress, depression, but I thought to myself, I'm not going to give up. I need to fight. And it took five months for the appeal hearing to be heard. The manager taking it turned round and said, I can't believe you are here. I said, if you look at my record and my absence, if I've been off a lot, I could understand. But I've never gone sick in sixteen years. At the time it was like fourteen years, fifteen years.[112]

She suspected racism as management failed to understand the caring Asian culture she came from:

> Maybe he [the manager] needed to learn about different cultures and maybe he didn't respect his mother-in-law, but where I come from, when I got married she became my mum. The minute we decided we were going to get married, she was my mum. She may not have given birth to me, but she's my mum. He was like, well, your loyalty should be with the company. And I was like, I don't think so.[113]

The appeal was won, eventually, but only after what was described as 'the most stressful five months'. With her other hat on as a trade union health and safety rep. she described how much of her union role was to try to manage the stress levels of her members, something she knew from her own experience.

Other stressors in retail were the labour-saving technological innovations like the self-scanning tills and the diffusion of performance monitoring systems, such as automatic counting of items through the person-operated till:

> I think the fear is keeping me going, because technology is taking over. So if you take just my company, for example, if you walked into a store, five, six years ago you'd never seen a self-scan till. It was all about cashiers. You were treated like you

# Stress and Burn-Out

were a member of the family. You knew one another. Now, we are almost robotic. We have to get x number of items through a till in a minute. I have to scan twenty seven items in a minute. If I fall below twenty seven, I will be on the red page. It gets flagged up, didn't hit twenty seven.[114]

The loss of control and de-humanizing of work seeps through this evocative testimony of a transitioning workplace regime from 'family' to 'robotic'. Another insidious surveillance method common within retail was called the 'mystery shopper':

They will get somebody ... to come along and they would be told what to look for and then they write a report out. The report comes down and they mark you. Each of the bits would be out of ten. So they look at the environment and the toilets and all the rest of it, car park. So the first thing that the manager looks at is the score. Is it over eighty per cent? The next thing they go is right at the bottom to see who has been named as failing. And then they end up with warnings ... There wasn't enough warmth in the smile. I thought, how do you measure a warmth in a smile? Do we have thermometers? Do we have a smilometer? We all have different ways of smiling and the colleague got disciplined.[115]

She continued:

The report adds to their bonus. So what happens is ... if you hit over eighty per cent every one, that's good, because it means you would get your three per cent bonus. But the managers actually get more than we do. So, to a manager it's really important, because it, they get something like eight or nine per cent, so that's a huge amount for a manager on their wages ... It's, "Right, we've just had this, you know, we've done an observation and we gave you a red, because you weren't smiling. We expect you to smile." There is no questions asked. They don't want to understand what that person is going through. And it's basically, this is what we are doing. If we don't see an improvement you will end up in a disciplinary. That's more pressure for someone who has got something going on.[116]

Intensifying stressors have characterized a range of workplaces, from social work, through the NHS to teaching at all levels – schools, colleges and higher education. Avril Brunton, a London social worker who retrained as a teacher, could only manage nine years in the job (1991–2000) before she felt 'worn out' and switched to part-time working.[117] Anne Bromwich taught at the well-unionized Holland Park comprehensive school in London during the 1960s and '70s and reflected on the changes that followed Thatcher's education reforms noting:

I wasn't there in that period I'm pleased to say, because I would have found it very distressing. What I understood Holland Park to become in much later years, the mid-nineties onwards, from various things I read or people told me about, was

153

**Jobs and Bodies**

that it was much more a school where there were managers and there were all kinds of rules. It was rules, managers, therefore efficiency, and the things I heard broke my heart.[118]

Christine Rowe became a health and safety officer at the FE College she taught at in London and recalled the 'trauma' and 'burn-out' associated with the educational reforms of the 1990s:

I was teaching counselling in the college and outside the college. I thought the whole college was suffering from post-traumatic stress, from the managers that had been delayered, from the changes that had been imposed on us and from the punishing, punishing, punishing exam schedule. Like I say I had eleven different classes doing eleven different exams, with eleven different sets of paperwork involved in each, and it was just intensive in that sense, and there didn't seem to be any let up from it at all. ... yes, it was death by a thousand cuts. Yes, the whole lot, yes, certainly was, very stressful. ... I tried to do work that was meaningful for me.[119]

Whilst such work regimes could be devastating for professional secure-contract workers, like Kate Rawnsley, those on short-term, temporary and precarious contracts probably felt the intensifying workload pressure more. One casual contract college teacher reflected on the long, unsociable working hours grading papers and preparing classes, combined with shabby, 'shameful' treatment of her by the students: 'You get abused. You get sworn at. You get threatened.'[120] At the extreme, inability to cope with excessive workloads could become intolerable. A number of suicides have been directly attributed to overwork, including that of the Cardiff University Business School tutor, Malcolm Anderson, aged forty-eight. He was reported to be working on the grading of 418 exam papers over a twenty-day period and that he regularly worked seventy- to eighty-hour weeks.[121] He had complained of excessive workload in annual performance reviews in the years leading up to his suicide, without redress. He left a wife and three young children.

The 'operational' staff in universities and colleges felt the pressure too. A Black Caribbean cleaning supervisor in one of the Glasgow universities provided a damning indictment of the bullying and harassment she faced from management when she requested and was refused personal development support and more flexible working hours to care for her two children during the school summer holidays.[122] This led to a mental breakdown on her part. She equated her treatment to that of being 'shackled' as a slave on a 'plantation'. Micro-management and inflexibility piled up the stress: Concurrently, a colleague with a disabled child who was refused time off for caring purposes was reported to 'be suicidal'. 'Somebody suffering from depression', she asserted, 'is going to sue [the university] for mental health, because of the depression that affects them over the years'. She asserted: 'they work in the colonial days ... it's like working for a slave master':

I have never suffered depression until I started working for [the university]. I am always a happy person. I had it bad with them. I had it bad. I always say to them

# Stress and Burn-Out

that, you made me realise I was black. I didn't realise I was black. I know I am black, but I am not conscious of it. I am not one of the, I am confident. I walk into a place and I don't think whether I am black or white. But they make me conscious. This is my line manager make me conscious of my colour. I says, so, I says, apart from all your bad management staff, I said, you are racist as well on top of it.[123]

Related themes emerge from other eye-witness accounts, where respondents spoke at length of dehumanizing work regimes and the stress of having to 'juggle' with the responsibilities of a caring role whilst trying to hold down a paid job. Sometimes this was because husbands, some ex-manual workers, had lost their jobs with economic restructuring and so wives had 'stepped up' into the breadwinning role.[124] A primary carer for three children spoke of having to work harder to attain the position of 'favourite' with the employment agency she was registered with and hence get asked to do more shifts. Others spoke of the overwhelming sense of guilt as they felt they were neglecting their children's needs.[125] 'Juggling' childcare responsibilities when employed on unsocial work hours outside of 9 to 5 pm and during the long school holidays could be particular stressors, as a number of interviewees pointed out.[126] Some felt stigmatized for being young and having children and discriminated against.[127] One betting shop worker with a young child found herself being moved from shop to shop (with longer and longer commute times) and under intense pressure being on a stage two disciplinary, meaning one more incident could result in being sacked.[128] Another reported being sacked for taking time off to visit her sick adult daughter.[129] Stressors intensified for those on precarious contracts because they usually had no holiday entitlement or holiday pay, no sick pay and no pension. 'There is no safety net at all', one female worker noted.[130] And the disempowering impact of the labour market added to the stress. As an experienced female trade union representative in retail recalled:

It's a crazy world. It's really awful. It's difficult, because people, we are not vocal like we used to be. I think it's that fear of losing jobs, because the job market is not secure, hence why, when you tell somebody to put in a grievance or appeal a decision, they don't want to do it because they think god, if I do that, I am going to be out of a job.[131]

## Conclusion

With the shift towards a modern economy health and safety issues at work morphed from physical to psychological, most evident in the chronic stress epidemic in the workplace from the later twentieth century. The personal narratives deployed in this chapter from Mass Observers and oral interviews clearly demonstrate a discursive shift from individual blame for 'nervous breakdown' to recognition of underlying structural factors outside of the control of individuals. Managerial bullying, excessive workloads and a dysfunctional work-life balance were recognized as stressors in many workplaces.

## Jobs and Bodies

The personal testimonies also provide rich texture around what individuals thought, felt and experienced, giving voice to the marginalized and subordinated in the modern workplace. And these personal reminiscences demonstrate the gendered nature of workplace stress.

Clearly paid employment and unpaid work in the home and for the family were porous: stressors in one spilt over into the other, especially so for women with children, given the prevailing culture which identified women as the primary carers and homemakers. This gender asymmetry left an emotional toll with the pressure of the 'double burden' impacting adversely upon bodies and minds, manifesting itself as stress, anxiety and depression, of feeling overwhelmed, 'knackered', burnt-out and unable to 'unwind' and 'recharge', as oral interviews and other personal accounts (such as *Mass Observation*) attest. A recent paper by Seedat and Rondon in the *British Medical Journal* in 2021 argued that women's poorer mental health – 'depressive and anxiety symptoms' – was partially caused by the disproportionate burden of unpaid work in the home and that poorer women felt this fatigue and chronic stress more acutely (they were less able to pay to outsource some of the 'drudgery'). They argued: 'Transformative change for women requires policy that recognises, reduces, and redistributes unpaid care work.'[132] Their research also showed how women's stress levels and mental health were worsened by Covid-19 over 2020–1.[133] We examine infection at work, culminating in Covid-19 in the next chapter.

# CHAPTER 6
# INFECTED BODIES: FROM ANTHRAX TO COVID-19 IN THE WORKPLACE

Workers' bodies were also exposed to a series of infection risks associated with invisible microbes – bacteria and viruses ranging from the common cold to killer infections like anthrax, TB and, recently, Covid-19. Here the dividing line between occupational and public health becomes blurred. Causal pathways are not always clear and can be difficult to determine with certainty; was an infection caught at home, outside in a café or pub, or at work? Was it a consequence of lifestyle behaviour or choices, or outside personal control, the result of structural factors, with higher risks associated with deprivation or race/ethnicity, for example? Some occupational diseases, such as silicosis, caused by dust inhalation at work, resulted in tissue damage that predisposed workers to infection by germs, such as TB and pneumonia, as we have commented on in an earlier chapter. In other cases infection was direct, via inhalation of germs from fellow workers or contact with the public at work, or absorption through the skin, as with anthrax (with for example wool sorters) from organic materials. With tuberculosis (TB), medical laboratory workers, doctors, nurses, social workers, sanatorium staff and prison wardens were amongst those occupations that were particularly (but not exclusively) susceptible. Pandemic diseases, such as influenza in 1957 and 1968–70, and recurring epidemics, like seasonal flu, also affected workers and could be spread via contact at work.

The workplace was perceived as a potential site of infection and could act as a site of exposure and an accelerant, as recognized, for example, during the Second World War with TB on the 'home front'. The infection risk was highest where workers were crowded together in enclosed and poorly ventilated spaces, as, for example, during the wars in munitions factories, in some typing 'pools' (see the front cover image of this book) or in 'open plan' offices, call centres and the like. This potential for infection risk at work could stoke fears and anxieties (sometimes misplaced and irrational) – as occurred, for example, in the paranoia surrounding the initial stages of the AIDs epidemic in the early 1980s. These issues have been very evident in the current (as I write in 2021–2) Covid-19 pandemic.

A difficulty here is distinguishing between what was a public health issue and what was the domain of occupational health. In reality, the boundaries were permeable as the same bodies occupied homes and workplaces, and, as we have seen, the home was also the unpaid workplace of many, predominantly women. This chapter reviews the literature and examines the issues around infection in the UK workplace in the twentieth

## Jobs and Bodies

century, ending with some reflections on Covid-19 as an occupational health issue. A series of personal testimonies are drawn upon to explore how workers have narrated and navigated infection risks in the modern workplace.

### Germs in the workplace; infected workers

In the kinds of manual labour that characterized industry during the nineteenth century and much of the twentieth century, workers were widely susceptible to cuts, flesh wounds and burns at work and this gave bacteria an entry point to the body. Septic infection could follow – and in extreme cases sepsis (or 'blood poisoning'), where the body reacts to the localized infection and it spreads through the bloodstream. Sepsis was life-threatening before the widespread availability of antibiotics after SWW. Given the level of dirt, limited availability of washing facilities on the job, the lack of basic hygiene knowledge and the cultural practices of workers (referred to already) in industry up to mid-twentieth century septic infections were perhaps inevitable and were widespread. Sepsis could be serious in these circumstances, even deadly, unless treated quickly and effectively with antiseptics and antibiotics. An example of female workers who were susceptible were the Scottish herring gutters who travelled as far south down the East coast as Great Yarmouth following the herring fleets. The gutters attempted to protect their vulnerable fingers against cuts binding them in cloth bandages called 'clooties'. Nonetheless, cuts leading to blood poisoning and time off to heal were common amongst the gutters.

Septic infections, or sepsis, however, were not contagious so could not be spread to others. First Aid systems in the workplace – supplemented with the St Johns Ambulance voluntary service – made a difference here, whilst antibiotics were an important breakthrough in the 1940s. First Aid boxes, initially developed in the 1880s, usually with sterile gauze and antiseptic, became crucial in stabilizing wounded workers and minimizing the risk of infection, including in serious injury cases which were moved on to hospital. Industries like mining, the docks and the railways were relatively well-supplied and benefitted post-SWW from extensive occupational medical services, nurses and doctors. And many big industrial employers had medical clinics on site to treat cuts and injuries. However, first aid provision and medical services were much more patchy, even non-existent, across the vast swathe of smaller industrial workshops, units and the self-employment sector (e.g. in construction).[1] It only became a *statutory* requirement on all employers to have first aid provision in the workplace with the Health and Safety (First Aid) Regulations of 1981.

Perhaps the first *specific* work-related infection to receive significant attention was anthrax, amongst the most serious of the animal-to-human transmitted diseases (which included glanders from infected horses and Weil's disease from infected rats). Anthrax was known and existed around across the globe for centuries, but the biological agent – *bacillus anthracis* was only recognized in the 1850s. Afflicted workers had usually inhaled spores from infected animals (usually cattle), or more commonly their wool

158

**Figure 6.1** Scottish herring gutters at Great Yarmouth, 1948. Note the protective waterproof boots and oilskins, as well as the finger 'clooties'.
Courtesy of Getty Images.

and hides, or had the germ pass into their system from an open cut on their skin. In the UK woolsorters in Bradford (and other places like Kidderminster) were amongst those most susceptible in the late nineteenth century, with the germs coming via imported contaminated wool and cattle hides, especially from the Far East. The death rate was particularly high from inhalation of the spores. After official government enquiries into workers' deaths some attempts were made to address the problem, primarily through import controls and the establishment of disinfection stations at the ports where the materials came into the country, with a major disinfection station at Liverpool. Deaths continued though at a rate of between ten and twenty-six per year through the 1900s, and rose significantly during the First World War.

The occupational health expert Donald Hunter noted how exhaust ventilation introduced in factories and workshops made a difference and how some shipping

## Jobs and Bodies

firms provided protective gloves for workers: 'but' he observed 'the difficulty of getting the men to wear them is great'.[2] Carter and Melling argue that trade unions played a significant role in pressurizing to get change, led by the TUC.[3] One notable achievement was the inclusion of anthrax in the first listing of six occupational diseases subject to financial compensation under the Workmen's Compensation Act of 1906. Preventative measures had only limited success, however, with the anthrax 'control regime ... patently limited and uneven in the years before 1939'.[4] Commercial interests were prioritized over workers' well-being and the vulnerability of women to anthrax was largely ignored with the focus in infection control upon the relatively well-paid male woolsorters.[5] Antibiotics, including penicillin, provided effective treatment after the Second World War, and that, combined with cattle vaccination, saw cases decline rapidly.

The last recorded case of respiratory anthrax in the UK was in 1974, though clusters of fatal skin lesion anthrax cases have occurred subsequently amongst drug users injecting heroin, including fourteen tragic deaths in Scotland in 2009 (linked to mixing the drug with infected bonemeal). Its toxicity led anthrax to be developed as a biological weapon. The UK experimented with it on Gruinard Island in Scotland during SWW and it has been used in terrorist attacks (e.g. in the United States in 2001).

**Figure 6.2** Three policemen carefully destroying a cow with anthrax, Gloucestershire, 1954. Courtesy of Getty Images.

Tuberculosis was on a completely different scale. Pulmonary TB was a major public health killer in industrial-urbanized nations like Britain in the nineteenth century, spreading like wildfire in congested urban housing, including the overcrowded tenements of Scotland where TB rates were amongst the highest and most persistent through to the Second World War. Recent research has refined our understanding of TB *as an occupational disease*; the ways that workplaces were also sites of TB infection and diffusion, including the work of McIvor, Greenlees and Newman.[6] In her comparative study of air quality in work environments in textile factories in the United States and UK, Greenlees has shown how mills in New England, Massachusetts, were the first to regulate the unhygienic practice of 'shuttle-kissing' (using the mouth to suck the thread through the shuttle, deployed in the weaving process). This was implicated in the passage of microbes from one worker to another, including, it was thought, influenza and TB germs. The practice of 'shuttle-kissing' in New England (USA) textile mills was subsequently banned by public health officials in the 1910s – just before the First World War. Germ-consciousness was not so well developed in the UK mills, where 'shuttle-kissing' was rejected as a source of contagion by mill owners and many (though not all) Medical Officers of Health in the Northern England textile communities. A UK Home Office enquiry in 1928 declared cotton mill workers to have 'no particular predisposition to tuberculosis'.[7] The suction shuttle, banned in Massachusetts in 1911, was not banned in the UK until forty years later in 1952.

But the workplace *was* implicated in TB infection and TB was recognized by many experts in the UK as an occupational disease. Certain groups of workers were identified as particularly susceptible, due either to their respiratory capacity being undermined by dust inhalation at work – recognized in the 1920s as silico-tuberculosis – or by direct contact through their work with the germ or those who were infectious. Stone masons and miners, laboratory workers, hospital, asylum and TB sanatorium staff (including nurses and doctors) and health visitors were amongst the most at risk. In the 1920s a quarter of all members of the Asylum Workers' Union were reported to have died of TB. Nurses implicitly accepted the risks of contracting deadly diseases from those they treated – that is until the Prophit study (1935–44) unequivocally demonstrated the disproportionate risks of contracting TB. However, any public-facing workers were at higher risk, including bus and taxi drivers, firemen, publicans, waiters and waitresses, and police and prison officers. And overcrowded and poorly ventilated factories and offices were demonstrated to be sites of local TB epidemics in the 1930s and 1940s, as in studies of boot and shoe workers, tailoring, printing and book-binding. Clerks had three times the TB rate of those who worked in farming between the wars, despite higher average earnings. And TB rates jumped up in wartime, with munitions factories and other wartime workplaces implicated in the spreading of harmful germs. In response, in 1944 a mass campaign was initiated to detect early signs of TB, with mobile radiological units touring around wartime factories. This was repeated after the war, with a campaign based around large factories, starting with a radiological unit set up at the giant Ford car factory in Dagenham.

It was in this context that TB was eventually prescribed, after a long campaign, as an occupational disease in 1951, under the National Insurance (Industrial

## Jobs and Bodies

Injuries) Act (1946), specifically for certain groups of workers who came into 'close and frequent contact with a source or sources of tuberculosis infection'. The Second World War was important in raising germ-consciousness in the workplace, with the government and factory Joint Production Committees playing their part in raising awareness and changing what Newman has referred to as 'everyday germ practices'.[8] And I've argued elsewhere that the trade union movement played a key role in the 1951 'landmark' success with TB, the first time that an infectious disease widely prevalent in the community was designated officially as an occupational disease which merited compensation under the Workmen's Compensation Act or the National Insurance (Industrial Injuries) Act.[9]

Other germs derived from or penetrated the workplace, or were thought to do so. Sexually transmitted diseases such as chlamydia, herpes, syphilis, gonorrhoea and AIDs/HIV were (and continue to be) unequivocally occupational diseases for those working in the sex industry. This was not officially recognized, however, through the process of scheduling occupational diseases for compensation purposes either under the Workmen's Compensation Act or the National Insurance (Industrial Injuries) Act 1947. Indeed, sex work was largely 'invisible … unrecognised and unregulated work'.[10] As such these workers were denied basic medico-legal rights and, as Wilton argued:

> In the case of sex work in particular, its status as a 'non-occupation' and the moral approbrium attached to those who carry it out, have led to increased risk of HIV infection among what is often a particularly disadvantaged group of women.[11]

Studies in the 1980s found 24 to 44 per cent of sex industry workers to have had episodes of chlamydia and/or gonorrhoea.[12] The rate of STIs amongst sex workers in 2021 was up to sixty times the rate amongst the general population, something described as an 'ignored epidemic'.[13] Illegality and stigmatization curtailed efforts to control infection, though more widespread awareness, condom use and vaccines have made a difference. This reminds us again of the ways that occupational health and safety have been gendered, and OHS discourse framed, with a neglect of the health risks faced (in this case predominantly, but not exclusively) by women. Sex workers organized themselves in the English Collective of Prostitutes to campaign for safer conditions, control over violence and decriminalization of prostitution, taking to the streets, for example in March 2018.

Laboratory and health workers could be exposed to microbiological hazards, with outbreaks of smallpox, hepatitis and TB in the UK traced to laboratories or hospital staff or health workers. For hospital nursing staff, exposure points for hepatitis B (from infected blood) were accidental needle jabs and infected blood in the renal dialysis units, where there were several fatalities.[14] These events led to the creation of the government's Dangerous Pathogens Advisory Group in the mid-1970s, which was later absorbed within the UK Health and Safety Executive, created in 1974. Greater awareness and safety measures led to a rapid fall in cases, though the risk remained. One recent study estimated a one in three chance of contracting hepatitis B after a needle accident with an infected hepatitis B patient.[15]

**Figure 6.3** Sex workers demonstration in Soho, London on International Women's Day, March 2018.
Courtesy of Wiktor Szymanowicz/Future Publishing via Getty Images.

Epidemic diseases continued to provide a threat to workers' bodies and generated a series of workplace initiatives to try to control the spread of germs. Mask-wearing at work was known during flu outbreaks in the 1930s, and during the war the government encouraged face-mask wearing (not the gas mask) to try to keep flu levels under control where people congregated in workplaces, shelters and the London tube stations.[16] During the 1957 and 1968–70 influenza epidemics some workplaces insisted on their workers wearing personal protective equipment (PPE) to try to prevent or at least control person-to-person contagion. There are photos of masked typists verifying this practice in 1957 and 1969–70 (see front cover picture). The design of these masks may have been influenced by the longer practice of 'smog masks' (going back at least to the 1920s) which we have photographic evidence of being worn in London and other cities in the 1950s and 1960s until the Clean Air Acts proved effective. *The Beatles* were photographed wearing their smog masks before a concert in Manchester in 1965.[17] Unfortunately, we don't know the extent of the workplace face-mask protection measures across the economy in the post-war years, or the effectiveness of such mask-wearing. The whole history of PPE at work merits further systematic research.

Some workplaces also encouraged and sponsored flu vaccination campaigns, with jabs being offered and delivered at work.[18] Mass workplace vaccinations in the 1960s included some London breweries, Selfridges in London (where 1400 workers were reported to have volunteered) and, apparently, the 'bunny girls' at the London Playboy

## Jobs and Bodies

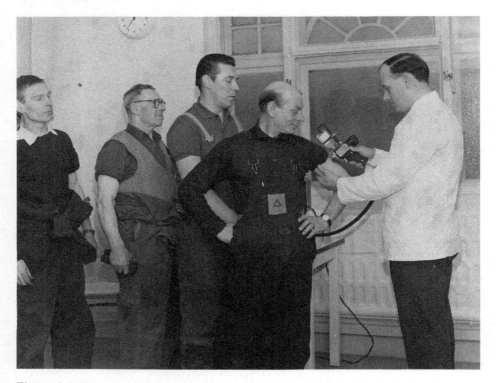

**Figure 6.4** Flu vaccine being given to Courage Brewery workers, London, January 1968. Courtesy of Getty Images.

Club.[19] Previously, in October 1957 the British government acquired flu vaccinations for key hospital workers most at risk – including doctors and nurses, and before that groups of workers had been used as guinea pigs for flu vaccines, including the army and coal miners.[20] However, as Mark Honigsbaum has argued, fully effective vaccines were not developed in time to have any appreciable impact on the flu epidemics of 1957 or 1968–70.[21]

The control measures appear to have been uneven and at best of only limited effectiveness – not least because of the ability of the flu virus to mutate. During the 1989 flu epidemic 26,000 were killed across the UK; in Scotland, in 1989, flu deaths (at near 2500) exceeded the peak of the first Covid-19 wave in 2020. It was reported that infection rates were high in schools and hospitals, affecting teachers and nurses, amongst others. Mike Walsh, a Scottish nurse, recalled: 'There were days during the flu epidemic of 1989 when I was turning up for work feeling really unwell but I had to go because there was nobody else actually left to care for patients.' He continued: 'We had no personal protection equipment [PPE], no masks, no self-isolation.'[22] Health services were pushed to near breaking point. Elizabeth Shaw from the Lothian Health Board commented at the time about nurses: 'They are being very stretched because of the influenza epidemic and I think they are very tired.'[23] These issues of heightened infection risk (and mortality) in the workplace, problems with PPE, stress and fatigue from overwork and the pressures of coping when understaffed were all to recur with Covid-19 thirty years later.

In the 1980s, sensationalized media coverage and 'New Right' reactions to the AIDs/HIV epidemic during public health campaigns in the Thatcher era fuelled a moral panic and irrational fears around infection in the workplace. Explicit and covert discrimination and victimization of HIV-infected individuals ensued. Watt has shown how this was the case through a detailed examination of employment tribunal unfair dismissal cases brought under UK employment protection legislation (1978).[24] Whilst tribunal judgements varied, there was a pattern in the 1980s of upholding job dismissals of homosexual men on subjective standards, including fear of losing customers, fellow-workers refusal to work with a known HIV infected person and the inflexibility of prejudiced employers (as in some cases in the construction industry).[25] The principle or 'formula' established was that a person posing 'a significant risk of communicating an infectious disease to others in the workplace will not be qualified for his or her job'.[26] Much of this transgression of human rights went unrecorded, never reaching an unfair dismissal case (which was premised usually on trade union support), or settled by agreed financial compensation before the hearing. By the early 1990s there were signs of a more liberal and progressive position within the employment tribunals hearing unfair dismissal cases – moving towards decisions based on objective medical assessments and full prior consultation, as well as consideration of the duty to redeploy HIV infected persons to other work where the risk of infection was deemed insignificant.[27]

In his wonderfully reflective study of *Mass Observation* respondents' commentaries on AIDs (replying to a directive in 1987), Cook has described the 1980s through the lens of these 'intimate lives' as a period of 'vicious homophobia'.[28] Recruitment restrictions were introduced in the armed forces and some HIV-positive health care workers had certain roles restricted, notably engaging in what were considered exposure-prone procedures like administering injections. In prisons, the response of the Prison Officers' Association was to threaten strikes over fears of contagion (after Greg Richards, a prison chaplain, died of an AIDs-related illness in February 1985) and to support a policy of segregation and isolation for inmates diagnosed with the virus.[29] The stigma associated with the 'gay plague' affected homosexual men, with (quite justified) anxieties around being passed up for promotion, not being employed or being sacked if their sexuality and/or AIDs/HIV status was discovered.

It is clear that workers and employers expressed a wide range of responses to what they perceived as a threat of HIV infection in the workplace in the 1980s and 1990s. The fear of being dismissed from a job was a very real one, especially when paranoia over contagion was widespread during the early years of the epidemic (*c*.1981–6) when hospital patients with AIDs were typically being segregated and isolated, and nurses and doctors treating them were using full PPE. Of nine cases of gay nurses with AIDs reported to the RCN in 1985, two were dismissed by private employers.[30] As knowledge and awareness deepened, and anti-viral treatments for HIV improved in the mid-1990s,

**Jobs and Bodies**

attitudes and policies changed, morphing into what Virginia Berridge has called a 'Liberal response', based on empathetic counselling and a 'consensus which stressed education rather than exclusion'.[31] In fact, no cases of HIV transmission by health care workers with the disease were ever recorded in the UK (and only four ever confirmed and recorded worldwide). It is now widely accepted that HIV/AIDs cannot be transmitted by normal everyday contact in the workplace.

## Covid-19 in the workplace

Covid-19 is very different from AIDs/HIV in that like other infectious respiratory diseases, such as TB, and other coronaviruses, such as severe acute respiratory syndrome (SARS) and the common cold, it is easily transmissible within the workplace (as elsewhere). Covid-19 is transmitted primarily through directly inhaling the germ in the air (from infected persons' breathing, coughs and sneezes) or picking it up on the hands from surfaces and transferring it by contact via mouth and nose. The *workplace* infection risk of Covid-19 over 2020–2 reached levels not seen with an infectious disease for decades, possibly not since the 'Spanish' flu pandemic of 1918–19. This was particularly the case with workers in the NHS and social care sector (including care homes for the elderly) who had the most contact with patients with the highest viral load. However, other groups of public-facing workers were more prone to becoming infected, such as teachers (in schools, further and higher education), shop workers, distribution workers, police, firefighters and drivers (including bus and taxi drivers). There were also workplace outbreaks in some factories and offices where infection control measures were lax, including in food processing plants and, notably, at the massive Driving Vehicle Licencing Agency (DVLA) offices in Swansea. In a study by the Glasgow Social and Public Health Sciences Unit on the first Covid lockdown in 2020 it was shown that healthcare workers broadly defined (including nurses, doctors and pharmacists) had a seven-fold higher risk of being infected by Covid-19 than 'non-essential workers'. 'Essential' social care workers and teachers had an infection rate 84 per cent higher than non-essential workers, whilst transport workers had a higher infection rate of 60 per cent.[32] Nestling in the top ten occupations with the highest death rates according to the Office for National Statistics (ONS) in the first three months of the Covid-19 pandemic were police officers, ambulance staff, taxi drivers, bakers and food processing workers, security guards, care workers, and waiters and waitresses.[33]

In the case of healthcare workers this confirmed what was already well-known – and repeated a pattern of higher exposure to infection through the experience of other contagious diseases, such as TB. The high rate of healthcare staff deaths made headline news – for example *The Observer* in December 2020 reporting that over 600 NHS and social care staff had died with Covid since the start of the pandemic.[34] The first two months of March and April 2020 were the most chaotic, as a junior hospital doctor's memoir recounts. Roopa Farooki kept a daily diary through the first forty days documenting the experience of poor preparation, government prevarication, negligible testing and inadequate PPE, colleagues getting the virus from workplace exposure and the harrowing death of one young colleague in their own hospital intensive care unit (ICU).[35] A GP, Tom Templeton, recalled: 'In our clinic, left to our own devices, we mocked up an infection control room, saw patients in cars, improvised PPE and rotated shifts in clinics and on the phone to reduce infection.'[36]

In part, the higher risk amongst health workers was a product of the older average age profile of the NHS workforce.[37] It went further. Like previous pandemic infections such as TB, the impact affected people inequitably. In explaining high Covid rates amongst nurses, Ann Hemingway, Professor of Public Health at Bournemouth University and a registered nurse, has made the point that nursing is a job that is relatively poorly paid and disproportionately attracted those from certain communities where the risk of hospitalization and mortality from the virus were highest: Black and minority ethic (BME) groups and those on low incomes with a higher propensity for 'high blood pressure, coronary heart disease, lung disease, type 2 diabetes and obesity'.[38] In deindustrializing communities with high levels of plant closures and soaring unemployment and resulting deprivation, employment in the health sector expanded rapidly to cope with the expanding health needs of economically challenged and multiple-deprived families. It was the wives and daughters of ex-blue collar workers who disproportionately took the expanding low paid and precarious jobs in hospitals and care homes in the second half of the twentieth century – forming what's been termed 'the new working class'.[39] A Royal College of Nursing (RCN) study found that BME nursing and care staff were more likely than white nurses to be working with inadequate PPE, and more likely to be pressured to do so.[40] Hemingway argued convincingly:

Nurses are at the forefront of trying to reduce existing health inequalities which are being made worse by Covid-19. We are also victims of those inequalities – a feminised, racialised workforce dealing with poor conditions and lacking a political voice. Care and prevention of disease are not perceived as being as important as finding a cure or a vaccine, but in the global recovery from Covid-19, all these elements are equally vital. We have already lost too many colleagues in the fight against this disease.[41]

But not only were healthcare workers putting their bodies literally on the line due to infection risk, they also felt the embodied impact acutely as a result of the chronic under-staffing of the NHS and the immense workload pressures healthcare staff were put under coping with the sheer numbers of infected patients entering clinics and hospital. Like many others, NHS Consultant Ami Jones worked virtually three months solid during the first wave of the pandemic, sleeping mostly away from home so as not to risk infecting her family. She described this period as 'very dark; very disturbing'.[42] Dr Tom Templeton noted ill patients were left with 'a new emotional scar; an invisible tattoo'[43] – and the same might be said for the healthcare workers who treated them. Intensive care units and designated Covid-19 wards were the worst. The Covid-19 emergency exposed long-term structural problems, including issues around the

## Jobs and Bodies

standard twelve-hour work shifts of nurses. New research in Autumn 2020 highlighted poor working conditions:

> Staff stress, absenteeism and turnover in the [health] professions have reached alarmingly high levels ... This has been compounded by the Covid-19 pandemic, which has laid bare and exacerbated longer-term issues including chronic excessive workload, inadequate working conditions, staff burnout and inequalities, particularly amongst minority ethnic groups.[44]

The pressure was cumulative. Palliative care doctor Rachel Clarke commented in January 2021: 'Staff have gone into the second wave already exhausted. Many are suffering from clinical depression, anxiety, post-traumatic stress disorder. I've seen colleagues break down in tears in the hospital ... staff are just burning with frustration and grief.'[45] Two Liverpool hospital surgeons reflected on the long-term mental health impacts on health workers:

> In Liverpool, we and our teams have also had sleepless nights. On sharing our stories, it is obvious that some of our insomnia relates to guilt. This can be guilt over potential transmission from us, healthcare workers, to vulnerable patients because of inadequate or inappropriate PPE, or being off work and untested for the virus. Guilt, anger, anxiety, fear, shame and depression were all shown to lead to resignations and poor work performance in healthcare workers during the SARS outbreak. Sadly, in our personal experience, a stiff upper-lip mentality persists among the medical profession, especially in the UK. Although not actively discouraged, an environment in which our feelings and fears can be shared is not actively nurtured. Indeed, there have been reports of suicide in healthcare workers in Europe during the Covid-19 pandemic. This is unacceptable. Sometimes the best response is not to keep calm and carry on, but to speak out. We will see "burnout" among healthcare workers during this pandemic. Many healthcare workers are working to excess and performing activities outside of their normal duties. ... For all the reasons above, it seems clear to us that working in healthcare during the Covid-19 pandemic will be associated with both short- and long-lasting psychological effects. For some of us, this might include post-traumatic stress disorder. Healthcare workers need to recognize this. Rather than being invincible, we are actually highly vulnerable. We are already at higher risk of drug and alcohol abuse than workers from other sectors. This risk may ramp up during a pandemic as did mental and social illnesses during the SARS outbreak.[46]

Issues around childcare during lockdowns added to the stress for many healthcare workers, especially women on whom this burden fell disproportionately. A Glasgow GP reflected in an interview in June 2020:

> For me the stress of work has been harder because I've been trying to do everything [paperwork] in lunch breaks and rushing to do it before I'm getting

home for childcare or switching over childcare or getting home for dinner, um, whereas I used to have a few hours after my work before I picked up the little one from childcare so, um, that has made it worse. In a way although I'm doing less hours it actually feels a lot more stressful because I'm always rushing, um, and I'm not in as much, I'm able to just drop into work if I need to follow someone up or, um, do a quick job or something that I've missed. So, so I find that probably the biggest change. Um, work itself has completely changed, um, and I think the first few, well first few months really of lockdown but particularly the first few weeks what we were doing was literally changing day-by-day as everything was evolving and guidance was coming out day-by-day. So especially for working part-time as a mum then I found I was just getting every time I went to work you just had hundreds of emails with, um, all the different guidance and all the changes and what we should and shouldn't be doing. So just keeping on top of that in itself was, um, quite a nightmare as well as everything else going on.[47]

Working all day or large parts of the day in full PPE could be stifling and made matters even worse for some healthcare workers. And this also affected nurses working outside of intensive care. For example, Hazel Gibson, a Glasgow paediatric nurse, commented in an interview in May 2020:

From a personal point of view as a staff nurse there we're having, we've changed the way that we work um, for example PPE … from the minute I walk into the department I have to wear a facemask for my full shift [laughs]. We're not allowed to have any bottles of water out at the nurses' station now so we're actually all drinking less than what we would have been on our shift because it's not there in front of us, it's not just there easy to grab. Um, and trying to keep our social, you know, distancing [laughs] is quite difficult in a small nursing station. Um, so … from my work life kind of point of view that's what's the, the big changes that we've noticed.[48]

A staffing crisis ensued. In April 2020 it was reported that around a quarter of all NHS staff were absent either with Covid-19 or self-isolating as a contact of an infectious person.[49] This came on top of an existing staff shortage. This piled additional pressure on those still working. In 2020, 28 per cent of all nurses and health visitors had left their posts within three years in England and over a third of RCN nurses surveyed in 2020 indicated they were considering leaving.[50] The pandemic added to existing high levels of stress, deepening levels of post-traumatic stress disorder and burn-out. A report for the Engage Britain charity found a record number of NHS workers – more than 400 a week – leaving their jobs in 2021 to improve their work-life balance.[51] An occupational therapist commented: 'I think people generally feel overworked and undervalued in the NHS. The stress levels in under-resourced teams is massive. Ultimately, people make the decision to leave, to take early retirement, or seek other careers.'[52] Amanda

## Jobs and Bodies

Smith (Intensive Care Unit nurse in Belfast) commented on the situation in the Covid Nightingale wards in the city:

> We've lost something like fifteen nurses since the first surge ... If you've got an unstable patient, the other ICU nurse could be left with three or four patients to look after on their own. You're worried you'll miss something ... People are getting very stressed at trying to combine their home lives with work. If they have young children who are hearing all the talk of how dangerous Covid is, they worry about their Mum going to work ... And when you see somebody in a bed who's 44 years old, you think, 'that could be any of us'.[53]

And exposure to high disability and death rates from Covid took its toll. Another report concluded that around 20 per cent of staff working in intensive care experienced symptoms of post-traumatic stress disorder.[54] Scottish nurse Louise Poplar had more than twenty years nursing experience, but caught Covid-19 in the first few weeks of the pandemic in April 2020. She recalled in an interview with Alison Chand in May 2020:

> I honestly thought, and I'll, I'll put my hand on heart, maybe it was a stupidity thing, I honestly don't know, but I went in and thought, 'I never pick up any bugs in work'. We can have norovirus, we can have whatever ... other staff go down with, with norovirus, whatever. I, for whatever reasons, my immune system seems to be really really good, and I don't pick, well, touch wood, I haven't picked anything up up to now in work, um, of whatever variety, some a lot more milder things than other things that you can normally pick up in work. I am absolutely OCD usually about hand hygiene and whatever else, but it's an airborne virus, so there's, it doesn't matter how, as much as you wash your hands and don't touch your mouth as the best way, you're still inhaling at times, and because of the, the climate I work in, there is, there is periods that you are going to be, I'm not saying exposed, but, yeah, there's periods.[55]

She remembered vividly the fear she felt as her health deteriorated:

> I do remember thinking at one point, 'this is it', I'm, I'm in serious trouble here, and I think it was just at the point where the first couple of deaths from nurses was hitting the news, and, um, ... you would want to watch the stuff about Covid and the government's plans and stuff, just to, and you were seeing that nurses were dying and I remember saying to Scott [husband] on the Thursday, 'I'm in trouble here, I'm really in trouble here', and I had been hallucinating through temps of 40 and above, ... I remember saying to Scott, and it was when I was coming out of the last of the temperatures, 'you need to hold on to me', and he was like that, 'I'm not touching you' [laughter], um, because, um, we did have a very strict, when I was back in the house, we had a very strict, I lived upstairs, everybody else lived downstairs, and there was no, there was nobody coming up the stairs. I used the

170

# Infected Bodies

toilet upstairs, used the bathroom upstairs, and the only person that came up the stairs was Scott with my meals on a tray. It got totally disinfected and then got back, brought back downstairs, but I remember saying to Scott, I shouted him, and I was like, 'you need to hold me'.[56]

She also articulated something of the deep stress and pressure experienced by many health workers, worsened by Covid-19:

It, every day is different. Every day is different. You get staff, there's a lot of staff that are quite teary just now, there's the staff that are quite emotionally drained. Um, I think it depends on … our specific ward, I think we're, we're kind of struggling in the fact of, of what we would normally do and how busy we normally are, has totally … it's, it's a different kind of busy-ness … it's very difficult to describe. Although we don't have the numbers of patients, the patients that we've got are very very sick, so our care's totally different, but I think mixing community life, or home life, with hospital life, is probably the biggest thing for all of us. We're all terrified that we bring it home to our families. We're all terrified. The, that wrong move, that wrong little bug that's sitting on you that you've not, you can't see it … I think a lot of the staff are finding balancing … we're still obviously still working full time, um, for a couple of weeks in the mid-point of the crisis, we were all working extra hours. Every single person was working extra hours to try and get us through what was, um, the, the main part of the pandemic, and that alone was causing … likewise, we're all trying to do home schooling, we're all trying to, we're all in the one environment, you can't, you can't go out, you're not segregated. We're going to work, coming home exhausted, then you're trying to have to deal with a family at home, so I think there is a lot of people that are emotionally and physically drained at this precise moment. I know one of the wards that they allocated as actual Covid, they were dealing with four, five deaths a day, um, and their staff were just in pieces. Their staff are just absolutely devastated, because these are people, and I think, what's, what's the hardest thing for us, as a nursing point, is we're always told, you nurse, you hold hands, in death, whatever. You, you, you support that patient as best as you can, and families. There's no family there. You're left, um, you're left not … initially, at the start, we were told that you're only allowed ten minutes in a room maximum with a patient due to the fact of, or you've got to come out, change your PPE, and go back in again. Um, and patients are dying. There was a wee elderly gentleman who had no family with him. We had let the, he was unconscious, um, and we, we took a, a DECT phone into the room and the son said goodbye over the phone. That's, that's, that's not right. Do you know what I mean? The, the family should be there holding their hand and supporting them, and we're watching the gentleman deteriorate over the next half hour, and I was like, I'm just going to go in and sit with him, 'cause you can't leave somebody dying on their own, and the staff were like that, but, but … you can't. Ah, and I was like that, 'I am not leaving …' … now I went into the room, I did have full PPE on,

I was totally protecting myself, protecting my family. The gentleman passed away, like, about five minutes after I went into the room, without his family round about him. That's hard, because they're scared. They want their family. They don't want a stranger, and because they've just come into hospital, it's not as if they've been up on the wards for a couple of days where they've got to know the staff, they've come in, they've been very very sick, they maybe see us for a few hours, and then the, the shift changes over and then the next lot come in, so it's different faces again. That's draining for a nurse, because you want to provide the best care that you can for these patients, and you know that their family not being there ... they've, they've relaxed a bit with the families coming in now, but initially, at the height of the pandemic, nobody was allowed near the hospital, so these wee souls were dying with a stranger holding their hand, or, in some cases, nobody holding their hand, so I think we're all feeling a bit drained.[57]

This honest and heart-felt testimony from Louise speaks volumes about how this felt to nurses directly experiencing Covid illness and deaths: the trauma and the emotional toll this took upon them, captured in phrases such as 'terrified', 'exhausted', 'devastated' and the repetition of 'drained'.

Schools, colleges and universities were other important sites of infection for workers during the Covid-19 pandemic over 2020 and 2021. Within teaching contexts there appears to have been a greater chance of staff infection and periods of absence through illness with the virus, but statistically no greater risk of hospitalization or severe ill-health for teachers and lecturers from Covid compared to others.[58] The relatively low average age of school teachers (forty-two) contributed to this. The uncertainties over infection risk, especially in the early phase of the pandemic, and the burden of staff illness and absences, however, undoubtedly contributed to increased stress, anxiety and higher workloads, exacerbating existing issues of staff exhaustion and burn-out across the education sector. With two staff members shielding and several off or self-isolating teaching support staff team leader Hannah Cardona recalled of the first wave: 'during that, the first sort of four to six weeks I was working ridiculous hours'.[59] Scottish teacher Chris Naylor reflected on the extra work associated with the cancellation of exams and the 'emotional pressure' to get it right when trying to juggle home-care for their two children, commenting: 'So, there's been this important work to do to get those grades right, um, and it's, it's challenging doing it when you've got two small children in the house in what is a relatively small environment'.[60] Teacher Debbie Taylor similarly reflected on the extra pressure of trying to assess student's grades without exams and the difficulties of what she terms 'major juggling' with home schooling and teaching. However, she highlighted another issue that piled pressure on her: the transition from face-to-face teaching to learning all the aspects of remote teaching delivery online, which she described in May 2020 as 'horrific':

Because it's all online, everything's new, everything's a new process, and, like, I mean I've been teaching for a long time, so I can walk into the classroom and, and teach lessons quite easily because I've done it for so many, done it so many times, done it for so long, um, but when it comes to the online stuff, um, I'm finding it quite hard to work out how some things work, so I'm having to just do extra bits and pieces on that.[61]

Learning and adapting to these new technologies and ways of working was also identified as one of the key stressors associated with Covid-19 in the Higher Education sector.[62] This may well have affected older teachers and lecturers acculturated to 'chalk and talk' teaching rather more than younger ones more attuned to and comfortable with online and 'blended' teaching methodologies. Some voted with their feet and left their jobs, whilst others expressed an interest in doing so. Despite evidence of young children under five having low susceptibility rates to Covid-19, nursery and pre-school teachers were reported to be under intense pressure, dealing with the stress and anxiety of working in close contact with the children, with little PPE, or testing, during the first year of the pandemic. In one survey in January 2021, 10 per cent of these workers reported having taken time off for stress linked to Covid, and 20 per cent were considering leaving the sector.[63]

Outside of the health care sector and teaching there were other workplaces where infection risk was significant and sometimes heightened by managerial ignorance, or negligence and regulatory inaction. According to figures released by Public Health England almost a year into the pandemic there had been 3549 'outbreaks' in workplaces outside of the health and teaching sectors, including factories, offices and building sites. The food processing, manufacturing and distribution sectors were amongst the worst hit, with 440 workplace outbreaks reported.[64] Public-facing workers were also more at risk, including transport workers doing the key job of providing a service for essential workers, such as health workers and teachers, to get them to their jobs. London Transport bus drivers, for example, were found in a specially commissioned investigation (by the Mayor of the City of London) to have three times the standardized mortality death rate over the first months of the pandemic. This was double the average death rate if factors such as socio-economic status and race are factored in.[65] Over half of the fifty-five all-male deaths of London bus drivers in the early months of the pandemic were of BME workers. Most deaths occurred during the first three months of the pandemic and the delay in imposing the first lock-down and lack of PPE and regulations on mask-wearing contributed.[66]

The London bus drivers scandal was exposed in a BBC Radio 4 documentary podcast, which focused on the first month of the pandemic, when, as Mayor Sadiq Khan commented, the Westminster government rules were that: 'transport workers should not be wearing PPE'.[67] One London bus driver (Kevin; previously a Health and Safety Officer with the GMB union) testified to the long delays in getting bus drivers' cabs sealed up and Covid compliant and the initial lack of hand sanitizer. Drivers resorted to using selotape, cling film and plastic sheeting as 'fixes', notably over 'speech holes' in the perspex panels that divided drivers from the passengers when paying fares. There were also risks from switching cabs with other drivers following shifts, communal depots and mess rooms and direct contact with potentially virus-laden NHS workers alighting buses at hospitals en route. Kevin reported being forced to do his own risk assessment as the company one was inadequate. An experienced (thirty-eight years) female driver also reported another risk associated with 'ferrying' bus drivers in her car from the depot to the terminus to connect with their bus. She wanted to remain anonymous indicating that some London bus workers feared for their job if they raised safety concerns. At the Cricklewood Bus Garage in London alone there were forty-six cases reported in the first month of Covid. One worker (anonymous) voluntarily decided to stay off his work on health grounds and encouraged others to do the same. He was sacked as a consequence.[68]

The HSE stepped in and cranked up workplace inspections and regulation as the pandemic progressed, dealing with more than 100,000 Covid complaint cases in the first year. However, the capacity of the HSE (like the NHS) had been undermined by two decades of public sector spending cuts from the 1990s. Moreover, their regulatory enforcement powers were restricted by the official classification, with government support, of the workplace risk as 'significant' rather than 'serious'. The HSE issued few Covid-related prohibition notices closing any workplaces down and there were no prosecutions in the first year of the pandemic. The downplaying of workplace risk, so evident with earlier occupational diseases (see previous chapters) recurred again with Covid-19. As the shadow employment minister Andy McDonald commented: 'It's undoubted that citizens of our country, of working age, have gone to work and lost their lives.'[69] TUC Health and Safety Policy Officer Shelly Asquith described Covid-19 as: 'the most serious workplace safety hazard in a generation' claiming it had taken 10,000 workers lives in the first year.[70] Whilst most companies complied with the rules, a significant minority breached them with impunity. A TUC safety representatives' nationwide survey in March 2021 found a third of UK reps reporting inadequate PPE provision and almost half reporting lack of enforcement of social distancing at work.[71] The position was invariably worse in non-unionized workplaces. Half of non-unionized food factories were reported to not have enough PPE in March 2021 and 25 per cent of managers in these places were not aware of the need to undertake Covid risk assessments.

Because of the inadequacy of compensation for those self-isolating, low-paid, insecure, 'gig-economy' workers were tending to return to work whilst still potentially infectious before the quarantine period was officially finished. Those on zero hours contracts were less likely to get tested and more than twice as likely than others to return to work early.[72] A total of 1.3 million workers were employed in call centres across the UK and there were a number of workplace Covid outbreaks, including at call centres in Doncaster, Motherwell and London. Taylor's study of Covid-19 in call centres in Scotland during the first wave of the pandemic demonstrated 'poor social distancing measures, hot-desking, poor cleansing and a lack of remote or home-working options ... [and] concerning levels of anxiety and fear among call-centre staff regarding their risk of catching or transferring Covid-19 in their workplace'.[73] For some there was the fear of losing their jobs, or being discriminated against in work allocation, that drove them back to work, however ill.[74] And this climate of fear and disempowerment deterred 'whistleblowers', especially in work environments such as call centres where trade unions were so weak. 'Too many workplaces', the TUC General Secretary Frances O'Grady asserted, 'are not Covid-secure'.[75] Unsafe workplaces were clearly playing a significant role in spreading the virus.

This was very evident in the case of the Driver and Vehicle Licensing Agency (DVLA) offices in Swansea, which employed just over 6000 people, where there occurred the largest single workplace outbreak of the Covid-19 pandemic over 2020–1.[76] More than 600 DVLA workers at this government agency tested positive for Covid-19, with one death, over the first year or so to March 2021, prompting front-page news in *The Observer*.[77] Whilst the DVLA and government spokespersons downplayed the incident and claimed all safety procedures were followed, it was evident from a local public health briefing that DVLA management were culpable for several breaches of legal requirements and public health recommendations. These included demanding more workers work on site than were required in a twenty-four- hour a day shift system with 'hot-desking', and poor enforcement of social distancing. Management also provided misleading case numbers to Parliament, something the DVLA chief executive Julie Lennard publically apologized for. Commuting to work added to the risks. Vulnerable workers reported having been refused requests to work at home, whilst workers reported being pressured to return to work before the end of self-isolation and to turn off test-and-trace apps. This amidst an atmosphere of fear and anxiety. One DVLA worker reported: 'We are all worried. We are all scared', and another: 'It actually started in my zone … It just spread like wildfire. Loads have tested positive. More than I can count'.[78] The local MP reported that the fundamental problem was the archaic IT system at DVLA which made home working difficult. Letters from constituents indicated they were bullied and scared to speak out in case of repercussions.[79] Most comments to the press by DVLA workers were anonymous.

Much of this was confirmed in a survey by Phil Taylor of University of Strathclyde, including that 87 per cent of workers felt pressurized to go in to work and near 70 per cent of workers worked within two metres of those seated in front of them.[80] Proximity in the office and occupancy levels became the key issues, with the Public and Commercial Services' Union (PCS) initiating industrial action in the summer of 2021 to force management to provide a robust health and safety regime that protected workers from risk. Thirty-seven days were lost to targeted rolling strike action between April and August 2021 – the longest strike on record on a workplace Covid-19 health and safety issue.[81] The PCS General Secretary Mark Serwotka commented that this action 'shows how badly DVLA management have failed in their responsibility to keep staff safe'.[82] The incident and the resulting backlog of work on driving licences prompted an official enquiry by the government's Transport Committee in the summer of 2021.[83] In giving evidence Serwotka asserted:

> DVLA management have operated in a way that is clearly worse than any other management in the civil service; why [have] they have not been able to have their staff working from home when Departments such as HMRC have delivered furlough, with over ninety per cent of people working from home throughout the pandemic … I have never encountered in twenty one years the level of incompetence and mismanagement that it is on display at the DVLA in Swansea.[84]

## Jobs and Bodies

The counter-narrative from management was that there was compliance with government guidance and legal requirements, but that the site and the work required, including confidential work with individual's medical evidence, created challenges and that it took between March and July of 2020 to make the site fully Covid-compliant.[85] Management blamed community transmission, not the workplace. The point was also made that the HSE enquiry into the single Covid death exonerated the company from blame, finding no lapse in Covid-safety compliance implicated in the fatality.[86] The fact remains, however, that a strike occurred and was sustained over thirty-seven days – evidence of a disillusioned and embittered workforce that were convinced enough to vote for and pursue sustained industrial action because they felt threatened by what they perceived as the failings of the work-health and safety regime in place at the DVLA offices in Swansea. And this appalling health and safety incident at DVLA was confirmed in Taylor's independent investigation. He observed:

> It's deeply concerning ... We know that there are workers here, who have experienced illness, ill health, anxiety, worry, a fear of coming to work, deteriorating mental health, which really, I would say, is unnecessary, should never have happened and the employers have a really big question against them in whether or not they have carried out the duty of care in respect to their employees. It would seem they have absolutely not done so.[87]

## Conclusion

The workplace was a potential site of contagion, and infection at work has long been an issue in the UK workplace for some workers, going back to anthrax and TB. For others, as during the AIDs outbreak in the early 1980s, paranoia about infection at work deepened discriminatory practices. Covid-19 exposed serious gaps in regulatory provision and hit certain groups of workers particularly hard, notably health and social care workers. Other public-facing occupations had significantly higher levels of Covid-19 incidence and deaths, including transport workers, whilst lax workplace rules led directly to thousands of workplace outbreaks, of which the DVLA was amongst the worse.

The oral testimonies and personal stories of those working and living through this bear witness and speak to how this was felt and experienced, from the early crisis months to the ongoing staffing shortages and changes in work practices which were so critical to destabilizing work norms. This was especially the case in the NHS and social care – contributing to deepening the ongoing epidemic of workplace stress and burn-out. Beyond the direct infection risk in the workplace, Covid-19 has had a major indirect impact on working lives, health and well-being. For those on the 'front line', in the NHS and social care services, the additional work treating and caring for those infected, pushed these services to breaking point. This was exacerbated by the context of spending cuts over the two preceding decades, the staffing shortage from those becoming infected or having to isolate as a result of contact with infected persons and the accruing backlog of routine operations cancelled during the emergency. In rehabilitation services in Glasgow, for example, clinicians and physiotherapists were reported to be doing more than double the usual workload in the aftermath of the Covid-19 pandemic.[88] The workload crisis in the health services (as far as paediatrics was concerned) was brilliantly captured in Adam Kay's book, adapted for a TV drama aired in February–March 2022, *This Is Going to Hurt*.[89] This workload crisis affected education workers too, perhaps especially the school teachers, and was one factor behind a series of strikes in Higher Education over 2018–22.

The lock-downs of schools and workplaces at the worst stages of the pandemic over 2020–1 in order to control the spread of the disease changed the ways many people did their work and its location. Many were 'furloughed' (laid off) on 80 per cent of their wages, whilst there was a sudden shift to working from home, rather than the office. And this resulted in more 'hybrid' working, mixing working from home part of the week, with commuting to and working in the office. This had its advantages and disadvantages. One survey in a Higher Education institution in summer 2020 reported 56 per cent of respondents indicating Covid had a 'negative' or 'very negative' impact on their health and well-being, whilst 30 per cent reported a 'positive' or 'very positive' effect.[90] Home working enabled production and services to continue and provided more flexibility and the removal of the commute (with useful environmental consequences). However, it could be more isolating losing the social contact of the office workplace, and there were the additional pressures for many of childcare and home schooling. This burden proved to fall disproportionately upon women, as did the increase in intimate partner domestic violence that occurred in lock-down circumstances.[91] The impact of Covid-19 widened existing gender asymmetries and inequalities. As the August 2020 HE report cited above concluded: 'those who were already more disadvantaged were likely to be impacted more severely.'[92]

Offices have been perceived as relatively benign. However, for some, including some of those with serious underlying illnesses, disabilities or co-morbidities making them more vulnerable to infection, the return to the office was met with trepidation, such were the effects of two years of the pandemic. Michelle McBride (an NHS administrator since 1999 with serious underlying health issues) commented in an interview that she was 'anxious' and 'nervous' about returning to the office to work, where she had contact with colleagues and the public: 'the office environment for me is quite terrifying', she said.[93] At the same time, homeworking for Michelle, complicated with two bouts of serious injury and ill-health, had proven alienating. She recalled:

I feel a bit isolated … nobody cared … It's like as long as you turn up and switch that computer on they know you're alive. But they don't pick up the phone and ask 'how you are doing'; 'are you managing ok?' 'I know you live by yourself – are you ok?' I felt a bit isolated … ostracised by my team … I know how much I am not valued by my team mates and my manager now … It proved to me, … I know nobody is indispensable and I'm under no illusions, they could sack me tomorrow

**Jobs and Bodies**

and find someone to replace me … It just made me feel my manager just did not care … They were phoning and doing welfare checks with their patients every day, but they did not do welfare checks with their own staff.[94]

Significantly, it was a fellow union shop steward who befriended Michelle and regularly gave her a 'welfare call' every week: 'She made sure I was ok, but my manager didn't.' Michelle's is just one voice, but it speaks volumes about the profound impact of the latest wave of infection to hit the workplace and the insidious legacy of long Covid (persisting symptoms for months, even years, including chronic fatigue), now estimated by the ONS to affect upwards of 2 million people in the UK. This has led to calls from within the NHS to declare long Covid a recognized disability and an occupational disease for NHS staff, including by Dr Alison Twycross.[95] It is hard to argue against the logic of such claims, given the evidence.

# CHAPTER 7
## PUSHING BACK: HEALTH AND SAFETY ACTIVISM AND ENVIRONMENTALISM

Karen Bell has recently made the point that we still know very little about working-class environmentalism.[1] This chapter makes a contribution to this neglected area. It examines occupational health and safety as industrial relations and advocacy issues in post-war Britain in what was a fiercely contested terrain between capital and labour. The subject is examined where possible through personal memoirs, especially through the lens of oral history interview material. Recent scholars of social movements have argued the case for the inclusion of oral history in the research mix for this subject area:

> In social movement studies, the relative scarcity of systematic collections of documents or reliable databases gives in-depth interviews even more importance … Qualitative interviews … have been preferred especially where the researcher is aiming to make a detailed description, attention is paid to the process, and interest taken in the interpretations interviewees give of the process itself. In social movement studies, in-depth interviews have provided information on (and from) rank-and-file activists, on which few alternative sources are available, and have been of fundamental importance for the study of motives, beliefs, and attitudes, as well as the identities and emotions of movement activists.[2]

The chapter is divided into two sections. The first section critically examines the historic role of the trade unions in occupational health and safety activism – engaging with the ongoing debates in the literature over the issue of how effective they were in preventing harm and protecting workers' bodies. The argument that medical science, management *and* the unions neglected health and safety issues pertinent to women will be critically engaged with here.[3] In part this was a product of male domination of positions of power in management and in the unions and misogynist reluctance (historically) to recognize women as anything but primary homemakers. That said, trade unions and trade unionists adopted a range of positions on health and safety (evident, for example, on asbestos) and their policies changed over time, becoming more progressive, influenced by feminist ideas, especially evident from the 1970s. Unions evolved to become key interlocutors performing a remarkably effective and progressive job in shielding workers' bodies from the worst excesses of competitive capitalism and negotiating compensation schemes for injured and ill workers. Workers own accounts testify to this and speak to the texture of feeling around union activism. They are drawn upon extensively in this section.

## Jobs and Bodies

The second section of this chapter analyses the emergence and work of the other arm of the injured and disabled workers' movement – the civil activism and community victims' advocacy groups, such as the local asbestos groups, formed from the mid-1970s. These community campaigns and action groups were led by dedicated and often outspoken individuals, including female pioneers in the safety, occupational and environmental health movement such as Lillian Bilocca, Nancy Tait and Phyllis Craig. They played a vitally important role in safety campaigns, victim's rights and compensation struggles. We will reconstruct here, through personal testimonies and other sources, the discourses around and role played by the community occupational health movement, which grew to become a key element of working-class environmentalism. As trade union membership and power waned from the 1970s on, these civil community-based groups became more influential in campaigning for victim's rights.

## Contested bodies: Activism in the workplace

The occupational health and safety literature has shown how medical recognition of occupational disorders, and the regulation of occupational health and safety, has in the past been the product of a complex interplay of actors and forces; the state, economy and politics, medical knowledge, public opinion and the media, employers and management, workers and their trade unions.[4] Influencing the discourse has been an ongoing struggle between capital and labour, where workers and the trade union movement played a key part. Trade unions campaigned to protect workers' bodies from damage inflicted by their work; both traumatic, as with 'accidents', and chronic, as with exposure to unhealthy and toxic work environments and labour processes. Sometimes they acted independently and sometimes in collaboration with other actors (such as politicians and sympathetic doctors and scientific researchers), forming alliances to best protect and advance the health of their members and, more widely, to set standards, and shape the regulatory regime to improve compensation and prevention of the harms workers were subject to.

For much of the nineteenth century, British employers regarded the organization of work as their sole prerogative. Workers bodies were widely considered as employers' property to do with virtually as employers wished. It was only at the very end of the eighteenth century, in 1799, that serfdom in mining was finally abolished. Apart from some notable exceptions, trade unions lacked the power and presence to have much if any significant impact on OHS before at least the middle of the nineteenth century. The main drivers of reforms of the first half of the nineteenth century – like the *Factory Act* (1833) and *Mines Act* (1842) – therefore, were not the unions but social reformers, medical/ health research and public opinion. An important influence was media exposés of mine disasters and factory accidents, playing on the patriarchal order of the day and the immorality of child labour and, albeit to a lesser extent, female employment. The patriarchal Victorian State stepped in initially to offer protection for these 'vulnerable' categories of workers, rather than wholesale protection for the labour force.

At the beginning of the twentieth century, still only around one in ten British workers were members of trade unions.[5] Hence union activity around the body at work in the Victorian era was frequently located within and a part of progressive alliances such as the anti-sweating leagues of the 1880s and 1890s, working with the support of sympathetic social reformers, politicians, factory and mines inspectors, doctors, physicians and religious groups.[6] The coal miners were perhaps the only real exception to this, with powerful enough unions to exert significant influence over the OHS discourse, shape the industry's safety regime and affect policy, notably from the last quarter of the nineteenth century.

Some historians have argued that historically trade unions neglected occupational health and safety – or at least that they prioritized wages, job security and compensation over preventing harm and protecting workers' bodies.[7] The Friendly Society 'insurance' functions of many craft and mining unions in the nineteenth and early twentieth centuries provided some financial cover if a worker was disabled by an injury on the job, or otherwise incapacitated. But this was reactive, rather than proactive. By not prioritizing prevention or providing an effective counterweight to the forces of capital, these historians argue, corporate exploitation and health and safety crime were enabled to persist. So much more could have been done, it is suggested, earlier and more aggressively by the unions had they chosen to do so. Health historian Paul Weindling declared that 'trade unions have often made pay a priority, and neglected health issues.'[8] In a study in 1960, John Williams criticized the trade unions in Britain for lacking a clear accident prevention policy, declaring: 'Within what limits can the community tolerate the introduction of safety standards by negotiation in slow motion.'[9] Whilst noting the importance of trade union activities on compensation, the Factory and Mines Acts in the twentieth century and the campaign to get joint safety committees, Williams criticized what he saw as 'a narrow approach' which did not focus on prevention.[10] Graham Wilson also asserted in 1985: 'Health and safety at work have mattered comparatively little to unions in Britain, as in the USA … Only a minority of union officers and officials have shown passionate concern for safety and health at work.'[11] Other studies developed this theme of union failure in relation to workers' bodies. William Kenefick has argued that before the Second World War, Glasgow (Scotland) dockers were more likely to strike for a wage premium ('dirty' or 'danger' money) than to down tools refusing to handle toxic products. He argued: 'for the dockers, trade unionism was more closely linked to gaining preference in employment, and to protecting jobs from outsiders, than concerns over safety.'[12]

There are also fragments of oral evidence that corroborate such a negative view of trade union inaction. For example, a Scottish occupational health consultant Robin Howie commented in 2001:

There are unions which are the exception to the rule, but in my own experience trade unions have not been as concerned about things like health and safety as they are about the fact the job is still there and what the wage rates are … the unions should have been going for better conditions … for better safety in the workplace and they chose not to … I blame the trade unions to a large extent … During the 1970s we had a series of wage freezes, that's when the unions should have been going for better conditions. They couldn't go for money, they could have gone for better conditions, for better safety in the workplace and they chose not to.[13]

Similarly, Scottish coal miner (and communist) Alec Mills declared in an interview in June 2000: 'Angry. Angry … We never went on strike for masks. But we should have went on strike for masks. A lot of men would be alive today if they had been provided with masks.'[14] Mills narrative represents a 'rank and filist' and leftist critique of the lack of radical militancy on the body at work and is referring to the lack of personal protection equipment amid the epidemic of dust-related respiratory disease and disability that decimated coal-mining communities in the UK. Following a court ruling in 1998 and the prescription of bronchitis and emphysema as occupational diseases for miners, over half a million claims were made for compensation for varying degrees of disability.[15] Other eye-witnesses reflected on the historic neglect of the unions of mental health issues. The president of the National Union of Mineworkers (NUM) – Nicky Wilson – lamented in a witness seminar in 2014 that whilst the miners' unions had played a key role relating to safety and physical ill-health, historically they had neglected the psychological impacts of injury, death and disability which he equated with forms of post-traumatic stress disorder.[16]

Environmental health activist Alan Dalton claimed that, right up to the mid-1970s, the trade unions were unable to provide significant information to the government on the incidence of the diseases associated with asbestos. This was compared to extensive union medical records in the United States, used to such good effect by the epidemiologist Irvine Selikoff.[17] Dalton also argued that the unions prioritized compensation struggles over prevention. Dangers were accepted and extra wage payments negotiated by some unions. Such 'danger money' deals were struck by unions with employers and employers' associations, thus effectively making the unions complicit in fatalities and injuries on the job.[18] Furthermore, Dalton claimed, where there were individual rank-and-file activists trying to do something they were invariably opposed and sometimes even obstructed by the union hierarchy, as for example with asbestos.[19] Dalton's negative view of the trade union hierarchy on asbestos has largely been confirmed by subsequent academic research. Geoffrey Tweedale's brilliant exposé of the corporate negligence of the premier British asbestos multi-national company Turner and Newall (using their own internal documents) depicts the trade unions as virtually invisible and having failed as a countervailing force to c1970. Hence, he asserts as regards asbestos: 'trade unions had little impact before the 1970s.'[20] Nick Wikeley, working through Trades Union Congress (TUC) papers, argued in a similar vein that UK unions played no significant role in shaping the pioneering Asbestos Industry (Asbestosis) Scheme 1931, nor in reforming and widening the coverage of such legislation up to the 1970s.[21]

Implicated in this alleged negligence were the peak organizations at the head of the union movement in Britain – the TUC and the Scottish Trades Union Congress (STUC). Robert Murray (TUC Medical Adviser, 1962–74) had impeccable prior credentials as an

International Labour Organisation (ILO) expert and UK Medical Inspector of Factories. However, he was at best extremely conservative in his views on asbestos in the 1960s and early 1970s. In 1967, he undermined the position of striking London dockers (on asbestos) by reporting 'no unacceptable risk at present exists', and subsequently supported the building of a new asbestos factory in Ireland and compromised the position of unions in the United States on the occupational cancer risk.[22] He went on to defend the use of asbestos, to argue that it was a waste of taxpayers' money to strip asbestos from buildings and schools and to act as a supportive witness for the UK asbestos multinational Turner and Newall.[23] His views influenced trade union policy in the UK in a critical period when the hazards of asbestos were becoming more widely known. Under his watch the unions continued to fail to initiate a comprehensive medical study of asbestos-related disease.

In Scotland the unions largely mirrored this neglect of asbestos as an OHS issue until the 1970s.[24] This emerged as a recurring critique within the thirty or so interviews we conducted for our Scottish asbestos study, *Lethal Work* (2000). For example, a Scottish asbestos insulation lagger recalled:

> Anytime you had a dispute or anything I found that if you tried to call them [TGWU officials] out they wouldnae come. So, what was going on was eh, just basically the guys on the job had to work it out for themselves whether they were going to do it or whether they wernae going to do it, you know. But, union help? Very disappointed with it.[25]

Similarly, a heating engineer who was a member of the Heating Ventilation and Air Conditioning Workers' Union recalled that his small union did not have the strength to do much to improve worker health and safety in this period:

> To my knowledge there has only been one strike in the heating trade, and they couldnae afford … They termed it a catch strike … They only could take out so many firms or so many jobs. Say for talking sake there was eh, say six jobs involved in heating in the town. Well, they'd take three of thae jobs out and the rest had to put a levy in to keep their wages up. The union hadnae enough money and the backing to support a full strike, you know, an all-out strike. So we had to work it on catch strikes, you know. And it only lasted, to my memory, I think it was three weeks, then we couldnae afford it after that. Packed it in. So the strike was just a no-go area.[26]

This testimony speaks to the realities of disempowerment in a fragmented trade dominated by small sub-contracting insulation firms and the constraints on strike activity in this context. Another Clydeside asbestos lagger commented that health and safety disputes when they did arise could be settled by wage concessions or the agreement to pay extra bonuses as an incentive:

> It always seemed to be that you wanted a bit of extra cash and better conditions. But they sometimes gave you the extra cash and the conditions were back-heeled

'cause they didnae want to know about them ... That was a lever used by the trade unions to get extra cash. Instead of pushing for better safety conditions ... At that time everybody knew asbestos caused all kinds of illnesses.[27]

Here we see reference to the use of health and safety as a bargaining tool in informal trade-offs where risk would be absorbed in return for financial compensation. Ryan Arthur has recently argued that up to the 1950s trade union involvement in OHS was 'weakened' by their commitment to a policy of prioritizing compensation and 'danger money' agreements over preventative measures.[28] 'Danger money' or 'dirt money' collective agreements were negotiated by some unions, allowing extra wage payments to do degrees of dangerous and unhealthy work. They were condoned by the workmen affected to varying degrees. And trade unionists could find themselves struggling against tradition and customary practice. A concerned Safety Officer in Scott Lithgows shipyard on the Clyde reflected in 1977: 'Somehow we have to persuade people to take a safe attitude to their work. It is easier said than done ... in a traditional industry like shipbuilding where *men are set in their ways*.'[29] The question and the response from Ayrshire miner Alec Mills in an interview in 2000 are also revealing:

> AMcI: *Why do you think there wasn't a strike on that issue [referring to masks and dust]?*
> AM: Well, the men as I say, if they had all been like myself, and had refused to work when they were firing shots on the return side. But the men weren't all built the same. They weren't all built the same.[30]

A persuasive critique of the record of trade unions on OHS has also been articulated by feminist historians and commentators. As Karen Messing has eloquently argued, work and OHS are deeply gendered. [31] The sorts of hazards and problems women have faced in the workplace have been neglected, with the unions failing historically to challenge official data collection that underrepresents actual female experience of accidents and chronic disease. 'People', Messing has asserted, 'just do not think of women's jobs in connection with occupational health.'[32] Before the 1970s unions in the UK tended to reflect the prevailing ideologies of gender difference and inequality, supporting, in the nineteenth and early twentieth centuries, the *Factory Acts*, *Mines Acts* and other legislation that excluded and subordinated women workers.[33] As Williams has argued this 'has privileged the families of working-class men at the expense of working women'.[34]

Implicit and at times explicit gender segregation was premised on acceptance by the unions of the prevailing discourse of masculinity and femininity – ideas around who should legitimately be in full-time paid employment (male workers as breadwinners) and who should be homemakers (married women). As referred to earlier, what was created was a 'dangerous work taboo' whereby women were largely excluded from the most visible areas of work deemed to affect adversely their functions as mothers (or potential mothers), such as underground mining, construction, night work or working with lead.[35] Whilst ostensibly protecting women from risk and harm, this practice ghettoized working women into other more precarious and poorly paid work, such as domestic service, clothing sweatshops, low-paid homework and monotonous machine-minding (as in textile factories) and assembly line work. Such work had less exposure to acute accident risk than the heavy industries, but more exposure to chronic long-term health problems that were less visible.[36] Amongst the serious gender-related problems were repetitive strain injuries (RSIs) like telegraphist's cramp, musculo skeletal problems like housemaid's knee and fatigue.[37] On top of this, as previously discussed, was the dual burden of paid work and unpaid domestic duties that women shouldered.

The male-dominated, and male-work oriented, British trade union movement largely neglected female-related OHS issues and not just through gender-exclusionary and discriminatory policies like failure to oppose the legal and societal marriage bar, or to promote equal pay. Unions also failed to recruit women pro-actively and they operated male-preference policies in relation to committee, executive and leadership positions.[38] Women's voices were thus muted within the labour movement and they struggled to influence the prevailing OHS discourse before the 1970s. Consequently, the OHS problems and needs of women workers remained largely overlooked. Furthermore, denied access to apprenticeships in skilled and well-paid rewarding work where men predominated, women were also denied the opportunity to enjoy enriching and dignified work that had positive implications for health and well-being.

The unions have thus been regarded as having somewhat failed their members. The case has been made that historically unions did not devote enough resources to prevention and campaigning on health. Also that they discriminated against women workers by failing for a long period – at least up to the 1970s – to develop policies on OHS that specifically addressed issues affecting women workers, including the dual burden of unpaid domestic labour combined with paid work.

These are important points and help to put the role of the unions in perspective. That said, the evidence overwhelmingly supports the view that the trade unions made key interventions in OHS and played a pivotal role in protecting workers' bodies, especially post-Second World War. Through their activism, working conditions were improved immeasurably. Quinlan, Bohle and Lamm have identified a set of 'priorities and strategic preferences of unions' in relation to health and safety at work.[39] The activities and effectiveness of trade unions increased up to the heyday of trade unionism in the 1970s, and indeed beyond. This was attested to by many workers in their interviews and personal accounts and, as we might expect, by the majority of trade union activist interviews. A dominant mode of narration here was to depict the trade unions as the pivotal interlocutors, at a range of levels, throwing a protective shield effectively around workers' bodies at the point of production.

Campaigning on health and safety at work by unions was widespread and has long historical roots in some industries. A key point here is that occupational health and safety was framed early on in the nineteenth century in a statutory setting with 'preventative' legislation (Factory Acts; Mines Acts), and, importantly, with the passage of 'no fault' Workmen's Compensation legislation from the 1890s. Strategically, trade union activity

## Jobs and Bodies

became focussed on this level – campaigning and lobbying to extend statutory protection and legal rights, with its responsibilities expanding as time went on – for example with the appointment of the first TUC Medical Advisers, Thomas Legge from 1931, followed by Hyacinth Morgan.[40]

Strikes against increased workloads (e.g. at Singer, Clydebank in 1911), the anti-Bedaux strikes in the 1920s and 1930s and the 'more looms' strikes of the early 1930s, were directed explicitly against work intensification and resultant stress placed on workers bodies, evident in fatigue and overstrain. The sustained campaigns and strike action to reduce working hours and increase holidays with pay might also be seen in this light. They were articulated within a discourse that incorporated the alienation of bodies under closer supervision and surveillance (including medical monitoring), the need for time for the body to recuperate, the concept of fatigue and the idea of some defined leisure time necessary for recovery, for mental as well as physical health. Hence the unions played a key role in the halving of average annual working hours over the course of the twentieth century. The trade unions were also central to campaigns against unhealthy and unsafe work conditions, from the National Federation of Women Workers campaigning on lead poisoning, to the coal mining union's challenge to orthodox medical discourses on dust disease in the 1930s, which led to the scheduling of coal workers' pneumoconiosis in 1942. Moreover, as we've noted previously, the Trades Union Congress (TUC) and Scottish Trades Union Congress campaigns on tuberculosis (as part of a wider medical-political 'progressive alliance') resulted ultimately in it being officially recognized as an occupational disease (in 1951).[41] Strikes, however, rarely, if at all, featured in these campaigns.

The Fabian socialist writers Beatrice and Sidney Webb identified the unions in the cotton textile industry as amongst the most active on OHS before the First World War.[42] The British cotton textile unions spearheaded several occupational health campaigns.[43] Fatigue and overstrain, for example, lay behind concerted trade union attempts to control working hours. Cotton textile unions played a prominent part in the shorter working hours campaigns of the nineteenth and early twentieth centuries and women textile factory workers such as the weavers benefitted as well as the men. The work of Bowden and Tweedale on byssinosis ('brown lung') and very recently Greenlees on the clean air movement in the United States and English textile factories also show the contribution of textile trade unions in reforming the factory system.[44] Other work has identified the agency of women workers, such as Bartrip's evaluation of the Women's Trade Union League which campaigned aggressively on lead poisoning from the 1880s to 1914, forcing reforms whilst retaining a commitment to a non-exclusionary employment strategy.[45] This jarred, however, with the position adopted by the male-dominated trade union movement who remained largely committed to prioritizing OHS issues that affected men. In the case of byssinosis, for example, the Cardroom Workers' Union endorsed the original compensation agreement that only applied to male and not female workers.[46]

Still, much depended on the power and strength of the trade unions at a local and national level. In the British coalfields miners organized powerful local and regional

## Pushing Back

unions in the second half of the nineteenth century and these became amalgamated into an effective force with the formation of the Miners' Federation of Great Britain (MFGB) in 1888. In the early 1890s around 60 per cent of all coal miners (and there were around a million) were trade union members, rising in 1920 to around 90 per cent, making it by far the largest and amongst the most powerful of all Britain's trade unions.[47] It was also amongst the most militant. As we've seen, mining was a notoriously dangerous industry to work in, with astronomically high injury and death rates. Here disability was normalized, as we argued in Chapter 4.[48] In the interwar years, around half of all workmen's compensation claims in the UK were made by coal miners.

Not surprisingly, miners' unions campaigned long and hard on occupational health and safety issues.[49] According to the Webbs, the miners' unions played a key role in campaigning for improved mines legislation from the 1860s to 1910.[50] Three of the seven founding objectives of the MFGB (the 'Fed') laid down in 1889 dealt with safety. A key focus was to improve health and safety through campaigning to extend and improve the mines and workmen's compensation statutes.[51] The power of the 'Fed', recognized by the owners for national collective bargaining, provided the impetus to make real changes. For example, three MFGB officials were appointed to the nine-person strong Royal Commission on Mines which sat from 1906 to 1911. The 1911 *Mines Act* provided the most extensive matrix of support for British miners to date, including the right to appoint workmen's inspectors (effectively trade union health and safety officers) to inspect sites where accidents had occurred. By 1914 a minimum wage (by coalfield area agreement) and an eight-hour day were achieved (uniquely amongst British workers at this time). Both were important in maintaining a healthier work-life balance, with the minimum wage acting to take some pressure off miners to take risks to make a decent income. Concurrently, the miners' unions and their political representatives in parliament spearheaded the campaign to get decent levels of financial compensation for miners and their families affected by injuries, deaths and disease in the pits. Key victories here were the passage of the *Employers' Liability Act* in 1880 (after over fifteen years of pressure from the miners unions and the TUC) and the first *Workmen's Compensation Act (WCA)* in 1897. The WCA finally gave workers and widows some 'no fault' financial compensation for death and disability in pit accidents.[52]

It was to be some time, however, before miners' industrial diseases were to be added to the list of diseases that could attract compensation under the Act. Crucially silicosis was not included on the list until 1918. Coal workers' pneumoconiosis was not officially recognized until 1942. This, too, came after long and persistent campaigning by the miners' trade unions, led by the South Wales Miners' Federation (SWMF). The SWMF played a key role between the wars in challenging the prevailing medical orthodoxy. This was fixated on silica as the injurious agent and even held that coal dust was benign, indeed protected miners' lungs against contracting tuberculosis. One of the SWMF's tactics was to initiate medical surveys amongst its members. Another was to support wider initiatives. In the 1940s and 1950s, this included community-wide pneumoconiosis X-ray campaigns and pit-level monitoring research. The Pneumoconiosis Fieldwork

## Jobs and Bodies

Research campaigns in twenty-five selected pits ran over more than two decades.[53] At the national level union policy was enshrined in the Miner's Charter drawn up by the newly created National Union of Mineworkers in December 1945. Four of the twelve clauses of the Charter dealt with occupational safety and health issues, with a renewed emphasis on prevention, medical exams, health promotion and acute occupational disease.[54]

Whilst the unions were joined by radical politicians, philanthropists, progressive doctors and Members of Parliament, including the miner MPs like Alex MacDonald, Thomas Burt and Keir Hardie, the miners themselves and their unions were pivotal interlocutors in protecting miners' health. As David Lyddon has persuasively argued, the mining unions were 'the single most important force for regulation and improvement'.[55] Quinlan, Bohle and Lamm endorse this view of the vanguard role of mining in many countries, which was shared in places by the waterfront unions.[56] Where mining unions were less effective – for example in the United States – coal workers' pneumoconiosis was regulated much later (1969) than it was in Britain (1943).[57]

Job security and wages were perceived by workers in all but the most dangerous trades to be the crucial elements in maintaining health and well-being for themselves and their families. Unions had to appeal to what their members wanted. Workers were long acculturated into work regimes that impacted negatively on their bodies, in which high accident, injury and disability rates prevailed. Furthermore in an era when ill health and low life expectancy were the norm from other rampant infectious diseases (such as tuberculosis), chronic ill-health caused by work-acquired disease (such as pneumoconiosis) was a distant concern, a long-term risk that might be tolerated. The relative invisibility of chronic occupational health issues delayed attention from unions in the most dangerous industries fixated on the carnage of occupational injuries and mortality. To some extent risks at work were compensated with a higher wage premium, the 'danger money' referred to earlier. In this context – perhaps right up to the creation of a comprehensive Welfare State in the 1940s – it was quite rational for many trade unions to prioritize wages and financial compensation over campaigns on occupational health and safety. Mobilizing support for chronic health issues that affected workers in varied ways to different degrees was intrinsically difficult as opposed to campaigns against wage cuts or for wage rises which affected most if not all workers.

For the miners' unions, though, protecting members' bodies was a key priority. They were also amongst those who were most willing to initiate 'wildcat' strike action at pit level, or even seam level strikes or 'walk-outs' to protect their members' bodies. We still know little about such subterranean activism on OHS. What is evident is that miners downed tools and walked out if safety was compromised or environmental conditions were deemed too risky and hazardous to health. These protests were limited, however, to seam or pit level strikes. They could occur at even the most inauspicious times and places – as with the 1932 'dust strike' at the Fife Coal Company's Mary Pit. Here in a modern anthracite colliery (a 'welfarist' company with a relatively good safety policy) employing 1,300 men new coal-cutting technology threw up large clouds of dust at the coalface. In response, the men affected walked out on strike in spite of unprecedented high levels of regional unemployment in the Fife coalfield at this high point of the interwar Depression. In an interview one of the 1932 strike participants recalled:

> Ye couldnae see one another … It wis bad. It wis bad. You couldnae see if the coal came over on the loaders … And, ah mean, the dust wis so bad you couldnae get it oot your eyes. We used tae pit margarine roond oor eyes, ye ken. The best thing ye could do wis if ye fell asleep, ye ken. Once ye wakened up and it wisnae sae bad. The coal dust used tae form in your eyes here. It wis bad, it really wis bad.[58]

Interestingly, in this case this miner – John Taylor – commented that direct action may not have been the best tactic to address the issue, reflecting: 'But, ah mean, it wis a wrong fight, ye ken. It could have been negotiated, ah think, better than what we did – what the older boys did'.[59] Welsh miners, in a coalfield where pneumoconiosis was particularly prevalent, recalled similar 'dust strikes': 'One or two boys would go on strike as it were. They wouldn't touch the coal because it was too dusty, and the whole face stopped.'[60] Another said: 'Well very often we'd come up the road [strike]. Very often I had to phone Tom and they'd come up the road because of the dust. They got more educated towards the end like. Years ago the colliers just got on with it.'[61] Nati Thomas suggested in this last comment that the risk acceptance threshold and strike propensity on health issues differed markedly across generations and over time in mining whilst some coalfields were more militant than others. Older workers were socialized into living with poor environmental conditions underground. As an alternative to striking there was the work to rule option, as Scots miner Tommy Coulter explained:

> By that time the dust suppression awareness was there and, see prior to that if we knew, we knew the rules but if when we operated the rules we didnae get any dough [money]. But when the management were acting the goat we responded wi' a go slow or a cacanny. What they call in factories, work to rule and it just didn't go.[62]

Capacities, political cultures and the will to resist varied considerably across the coalfields and even from pit to pit – as the work of Roy Church and Quentin Outram has shown.[63] Whereas Scottish and Welsh miners might initiate direct action on health and safety issues, those in the Midlands were as likely to tolerate unhealthy work environments. Work-health cultures varied widely across different places, as this following dialogue between two Scottish miners and interviewer, Neil Rafeek reveals:

> GB: I think it's fair to say this. In Scotland, we had a different approach from the NUM to safety and health and the rest of it. See down South, down South, [gasp], unbelievable … Much worse. I mean there were men cutting without water … I worked in Stoke–on–Trent, it was bloody awful … the men were on their own and men are very fearless on their own. Me, I worked in a stone mine with the blast borers for the drills – no water. Mining with dust often with a

## Jobs and Bodies

> low boring machine – 'Keep going Jock, you know, come on, come on keep going Jock', shocking stuff. Through a middle cut machine, no water. You imagine a machine up there [motioned to head height] throwing all the dust out.
>
> NR: Just what you said there about keeping on working, why was that part of the culture do you think?
>
> GB: It was just the lack of good trade union, how things developed.
>
> DC: I would say money at the end of the day.
>
> GB: There was money but there was also a bad culture. In Stoke–on–Trent, the men werenae, *they were not union conscious.* I remember working on a road, went out on strike one day, see when the place turned – other men doing the job for us [*laughs*] … that wouldn't happen in Scotland but it happened in Stoke on Trent and elsewhere in England. Different approach to trade unionism. That applies to Yorkshire too apparently, they're not as clever as they thought they were. They're very clever in Scotland and I think also in South Wales to some extent, from what I know of it, union conscious, safety conscious, dust conscious – really, really conscious. So that difference applied.[64]

Whilst this story-telling might have exaggerated somewhat the differences between Scots and English miners, the narratives of George Bolton and Derek Carruthers on health and safety do resonate with what we know about deep differences between work and political cultures across coalfields in the UK. Scots were amongst those more likely to resort to the strike weapon to defend workplace environmental standards. Workplace and community solidarity in Scotland underpinned such action, in contrast to elsewhere (e.g. the English Midlands coalfield).

Oral testimony is insightful at many levels but not least in demonstrating that when and where trade unions were powerful – as in post-Second World War coal mining in Scotland and Wales – they were capable of initiating and supporting health and safety strikes, albeit at the local level. This despite miners being inured to high levels of danger and working in an environment where manliness was equated with risk acceptance. Over time, the risk threshold shifted and workers and their unions became less willing to accept that high levels of death and disability were an intrinsic part of the work.

This move to embrace a more health and safety conscious culture was evident, to give another example, in the oil industry, though not before a major disaster. The oil industry was omitted from the provisions of the *Health and Safety at Work Act* 1974 and a 'gung-ho' anti-union productionist culture by management led directly to disaster in 1988 when 167 oil workers lost their lives in the Piper Alpha rig explosion.[65] The Piper Alpha disaster mobilized workers to refocus on directly protecting bodies. As Gregor Gall has noted there were nineteen successful brief rolling strikes and sit-ins organized in the North Sea oilfield by the new industrial union – the Offshore Industry Liaison Committee (OILC created 1988) after the explosion, including a major strike involving around 4,000 workers on the first anniversary of Piper Alpha. Industrial action continued into 1990. The disaster was an epiphany and clearly the new union was more actively safety-conscious than the unions that previously dominated the industry. 'Piper fundamentally changed the consciousness of workers', Gall has asserted, 'not only had "enough become enough" but readiness to confront the employers with widespread strike action emerged'.[66] The wonderful *Oil Lives* oral history project, led by Terry Brotherstone and Hugo Manson provides multiple accounts of the Piper disaster and the ways that the tragedy energized the unions, providing leverage to mobilize OHS campaigns in its aftermath.[67] That said, the transition was not a straightforward one and the work of Beck, Foster, Ryggvik and Woolfson has shown how contested this was and how oil companies mobilized to resist union campaigning to secure a more robust safety regime on the rigs.[68] Indeed the fatalities and accidents data actually indicate 'a qualitative deterioration of safety conditions in 1985/6 which continued through Piper Alpha (1988), and into the nineties'.[69] Oral testimonies collected by Beck, Foster, Ryggvik and Woolfson in the 1990s relate a systematic process of managerial pressure even *after* the disaster to work unsafely, prioritizing production targets, and to incentivize the under-reporting of incidents, including 'Lost Time Injuries'.[70]

Over time, the union movement in Britain came to campaign persistently and more aggressively on OHS at work *in tandem* with other issues, including wages, shifting their focus to more directly embrace chronic disease as well as acute safety issues. Trade unions aimed to protect and advance the interests of workers and OHS was central to this in union thinking and action at a number of levels, especially where unions had numerical strength and capacity. With perhaps a little exaggeration, the Webbs asserted in 1894: 'In the trade union world of today, there is no subject on which workmen of all shades of opinion, and all varieties of occupation, are so unanimous, *and so ready to take combined action*, as the prevention of accidents and the provision of healthy workplaces.'[71] A wide body of literature documents trade union challenges to prevailing discourses that blamed workers for the damage wrought to their health and shows union efforts to safeguard and promote the health and well-being of their members and other workers. OHS discourse was framed in the nineteenth-century statutory regime of preventative legislation and later, importantly, of 'no fault' workmen's compensation legislation from the 1890s. Strategically, as noted, trade union activity became focussed on the national level. With the formation of the TUC, in 1867, campaigning and lobbying were to extend statutory protection and legal rights rather than take direct action in the form of strikes. Responsibilities expanded in the twentieth century. Activity on OHS had considerable success, for example, in achieving shorter working hours, progressively extending factory and mines Acts, in new regulations governing the 'dangerous trades' and in the clear establishment of the right to workmen's compensation for 'accidents' in 1897. From 1906, this extended to a widening range of occupational diseases. And key unions, such as those in coal mining and iron and steel, widened their welfare provision to include assisted convalescence and rehabilitation for injured and exhausted members. In mining, union provision extended to nineteen convalescent homes around the country and several rehabilitation centres. Health education and promotion, as Long has shown in a beautifully crafted monograph, were also a key part of TUC policy.[72] That said, gaps in legislative provision, neglect of women workers and evasion of regulation continued. Still, the union movement had achieved much with a logical

## Jobs and Bodies

deployment of resources to improving working conditions and OHS standards across the board, via lobbying for improved legislation, which benefitted unionists and non-members alike. Other scholarship has challenged the notion that unions prioritized financial compensation over prevention.[73] There was a clear preventative element to the pursuit of workmen's compensation, when hitting the employers in the pocket forced them (sometimes under pressure from their insurers) to correct dangerous working conditions. That said, some more unscrupulous employers took the hit and reckoned that the profits they could get from ignoring health and safety measures outweighed the insurance premiums. This was a key factor, Ryan Arthur has argued, in the trade union movement in the UK shifting policy in the 1950s and moving towards the promotion of union safety representatives and safety committees across industry and a more aggressive focus on preventative measures.[74]

Where mobilization occurred against asbestos it began with strongly unionized clusters, such as the Glasgow laggers' (pipe coverers and insulation workers) branch of the TGWU in the 1950s and 1960s, the London dockers in 1965 and building workers on well-unionized sites in the later 1960s and 1970s.[75] Union responses to asbestos reflected different problems and a different context. Coal mining disasters were in the public eye in a way that asbestos was not (at least until the media exposes of the 1980s). It was easier to mobilize public support for effective statutory reform when acute injury and mortality was tangible and visible, as in mining communities, and the toll could be counted, as with the claims under the WCA. Occupational disease was frequently invisible, slowly encroaching upon and damaging tissue, organs and bones by stealth. In contrast to coal mining, the asbestos issue was spread across a disparate group of industries – textiles, construction, shipbuilding, the docks – where unions were more divided making it harder to mobilize opposition. Added to this was a significant pro-asbestos lobby within some UK trade unions fearful of the impact a ban on asbestos would have on jobs, fears exacerbated by the deep recession from the late 1970s.[76]

The story of asbestos illustrates a wider point about the spectrum of responses and positions on OHS across a heterogeneous, voluntary union movement where tensions existed between jobs, wages and health. Many workmen feared medical inspection and exposure of problems in their workplaces that might provoke regulation that could jeopardize jobs. Sensitivities here could filter through to influence trade union policies. Identifiably macho work cultures in industries like construction, steel, mining and shipbuilding constituted a drag anchor, despite union efforts on the job to change work-health cultures. Moreover, unions in sectors of the economy where dangers and chronic ill-health were evidently more of a problem (like coal mining) were perhaps inevitably going to be more pro-active than where workplaces were seemingly more benign – such as offices and shops – where risks to health and impacts on the body were far less visible. Agriculture would be a case in point where trade unionism failed to gain a foothold and OHS hardly featured in union campaigns. Before the Second World War, union membership in agriculture and forestry in the UK hovered persistently below 10 per cent and barely touched a quarter of the workforce even in the post-Second World War heyday of trade unionism.[77] This left a legacy. It is perhaps no coincidence that by the early twenty-first century, agriculture and forestry had risen to be one of the most hazardous of all sectors globally.[78]

The economic and political milieu also affected the capacities of trade unions to mobilize on OHS. The 1930s were a period of retrenchment for the unions and deteriorating OHS standards in many of the failing heavy industries across the developed Western economies. The worst coal mining disaster between the wars in the UK at the Gresford Pit in North Wales in 1934 was attributed to managerial negligence, enabled to a degree by the erosion of a union presence in the district. Less than 30 per cent of the 266 men killed were paid up union members.[79] Then the outbreak of war in 1939 empowered labour, providing an environment in which trade union initiatives on OHS flourished.[80] We see this, for example, in the proliferation of joint production committees on which union officials made the case for OHS as a wartime 'efficiency' measure. During the war some unions, such as the Foundry Workers' Union, initiated important campaigns to tackle long-standing issues around health and safety, including the scourge of silicosis in the industry.[81] However, what does not appear to have happened is any significant strike action to protect workers' bodies. Scottish docker and union activist Tom Murray scathingly criticized the unwillingness of the TGWU to support strike action to protect dockers exposed to dangerous chemicals at Leith docks in 1941–2.[82] In wartime strikes were technically illegal, under Order 1305, but that did not stop them happening and with some frequency, especially in the mines and shipyards.[83] Strikes pivoted around challenges to skilled status with 'dilution' and pay differentials and injustices, as with the 1943 equal pay strike led by Agnes Maclean at Rolls Royce in Hillington, Glasgow.[84] Despite relatively high levels of strike activity compared to the 1930s, few wartime Reserved Occupation workers interviewed for a recent AHRC oral history research project could recall any strikes, never mind ones that were linked to health and safety.[85] Fairly typical was this response in an interview from Scottish railwayman William Mcnaul: 'Q. Was there any trade union action during the war, or strikes? A. No. No, nothing like that. Wasn't allowed … No, no, no you daren't do anything like that.'[86] The erasure in oral testimonies regarding strikes in wartime might be connected to a sense on the part of such wartime home front narrators that striking was subversive to the national war effort. This clashed with the ways they were composing their memories (and sense of self) in the light of efforts to present a narrative that emphasized their contribution to war in a similar way to combatants: that is to place themselves within wartime hierarchies of masculinities that were headed by hegemonic military masculinity associated with armed service.

After the war, trade unions enjoyed a 'Golden Age' as part of the fabric of British society. From the 1940s to the 1970s they came to exert much more influence over OHS. The same can be said for Australia, New Zealand and most countries across Western Europe, especially Scandinavia where unions perhaps exerted most influence shaping the 'social protection regime'.[87] In the UK, union membership and density rose from a nadir of less than 5 million members and a quarter of the workforce in 1930 to a peak of 13 million members and over 50 per cent in the late 1970s. Campaigning for statutory reform continued, and was a key element of the post-war Labour government's Welfare

## Jobs and Bodies

State in the workplace. Workmen's compensation law was overhauled and replaced with the more generous *Industrial Injuries Act* in 1947. There followed the recognition of tuberculosis (TB) as an occupational disease in 1951, after a long campaign spearheaded by the TUC's Medical Adviser, and in 1961 the passage of a new more comprehensive *Factories Act*.[88] The scheduling of TB was significant because it signalled a campaign that was directed primarily at the female workforce, nurses and health workers. In addition there was a vigorous campaign by the union movement – ultimately unsuccessful – to integrate an occupational health service within the fledgling National Health Service (NHS).[89] And the TUCs commitment to expanding OHS research and providing a scientific research service for its members is also evident in the creation of the TUC Centenary Institute of Occupational Health (1968) at the London School of Health and Tropical Medicine. Its Director, Richard Schilling, described this as a 'controversial enterprise partly financed by the trade unions'.[90]

The TUC also campaigned to extend union safety representatives and committees across all sectors of industry and widen health and safety legislation to cover all workers. The nationalization of a swathe of heavy industries – a long-term aim of the trade union movement spearheaded by the miners – resulted directly in improved OHS standards, most evidently, perhaps, in coal mining, steel and transport. Union action thus contributed to saving countless lives and cutting the grim toll of workplace injuries and disabilities. Occupational 'accident' deaths, as a proportion of workers employed, dropped markedly from the 1940s to the 1970s.[91]

And by the 1960s and 1970s, we see growing evidence of strike activity on health and safety issues. This was in part a product of a more health-oriented society as the environmental movement gathered momentum and in part a consequence of the shifting balance of power and assertiveness of trade unions. As plant-level bargaining proliferated, health and safety became greater priorities for the growing numbers of shop stewards who worked in industry – as the Donovan Commission in 1968 reported. As Philip Beaumont has shown, union pressure led to the establishment of joint health and safety committees across many industries in the 1960s and these played a significant role in raising occupational health and safety standards.[92] Precursors flourished briefly during the Second World War when the Joint Production Committees frequently embraced health and safety functions. By the 1970s these joint health and safety committees were shored up by an extension of such provision in the Health and Safety at Work Act 1974 and the Safety Representatives and Safety Committee Regulations in 1977. This increased focus on the reform of statutory provision for health and safety in the 1970s appears to have been paralleled by a surge in direct action. Beaumont surveyed 225 trade union health and safety officers across different industries in Glasgow in 1979 and around 20 per cent reported they had witnessed industrial action on health and safety in the previous year.[93]

Working with asbestos provides a good example of this process unfolding, with growing levels of resistance to the idea of an 'acceptable level of risk'. A traditional macho, wage maximization culture clashed with other ideas around protecting the body, health as capital and more collectivist approaches. And local activists and shop stewards emerged who were critical of national union leaderships and the STUC/TUC for what they perceived as a failure to support local health and safety disputes by making them official and providing strike pay. Rank-and-file activity spurned the constraints of official trade union policy and cultural indifference on the job and mobilized to expose the high death and disability toll of industrial work and to protect the body at work utilizing a range of tactics, including direct strike action. Examples would be local activists such as Hugh Cairney and John Todd and the campaigns of the local Glasgow branch of the insulation workers (laggers) affiliated to the TGWU (local 7/162) from the 1940s to the 1970s on asbestos. In two oral interviews in 1999 and in 2005 former local 7/162 branch secretary Hugh Cairney reflected on how the Glasgow asbestos laggers got organized by the mid-1950s and, with 100 per cent membership and a closed shop, initiated a series of health and conditions strikes to raise environmental standards. They initially faced employer intransigence, typical of the more entrenched managerial authoritarianism and residual anti-unionism that characterized Clydeside. As Cairney recalled: 'When I first started the bosses didnae want to know anything aboot us or talk to us.'[94] Another TGWU activist recalled how the Glasgow laggers' branch had to fight even for basic amenities and PPE:

> There were no overalls. No boots. And you were swallowing it [asbestos] all the time, and so was all the people that were working near you. But they had a hut where they made [asbestos] mats only in it. Nae extractor fan or nothing ... At one time we didnae have any huts. We had to sit between decks on the ships. We had to go and fight for tae get a hut. You know, an ordinary hut. And in that hut was a' the material. And you were taking your tea during the meal breaks, and a' that material. And every part of the material had asbestos in it, a percentage.[95]

Cairney stressed how the main 'fighting strength' of the trade union was at local branch level:

> Well, if you're talking about the unions. I always think the union is a mythical body. This branch done a lot. We happened to belong to a trade union. We fought ... I mean, we walked the streets for twenty-six weeks to get conditions. We were the ones that forced them to give us tables and chairs to sit down to have a meal with. Made them give us a changing room to hang our clothes up.[96]

When asked 'Was it hard bringing in health and safety into the job?' Cairney replied: 'It was at the start, yes. We always nearly had to hit the gates [strike] to get any health and safety, not noo we dae, but then, aye'. Cairney spoke eloquently in the language of solidarity and social justice about protecting his members' bodies:

> When we came, when we took action it was every lagger. We didnae just say we worked for a firm called Millers, we had a dispute in Grangemouth with Millers, we called oot everybody *that worked in Millers*, didn't matter whether they were in Grangemouth whether they were working in Saltcoats or – you hit the company,

## Jobs and Bodies

right? Everybody. So companies had to come doon and talk to you. I mean we werenae actually bully boys, we just wanted what we thought we were entitled to. We're entitled to be able to wash our hands, we're entitled to take overalls *that are covered with asbestos off* and go and sit doon, have something to eat without wearing these dirty boiler suits. So we brought they things in. In Grangemouth noo everybody has changing rooms noo and that. So we caused an awful lot of it and it was all through health and safety.[97]

At another point in the interview he returned to the issue of human rights and 'entitlement':

I mean we went on to a job, if the toilets were frozen, that was it. You'd give them until ten o'clock, if they werenae unblocked and cleaned oot, oot the gate and away. And see when we come back the next day? They were fixed but we wouldnae start work until we were paid for that day, things like that. We were quite right. I mean if somebody's got to go to the toilet you're entitled to go to the toilet and it's their job to maintain it and make sure the toilets were clean and working and that.[98]

Cairney's narrative is interesting at a number of levels, apart from what he reveals about rank-and-file activism, including strikes, on health and safety issues. This is an archetypal emotive activist narrative, transposing the heroic role of the union branch in the struggle to protect bodies against the 'villains' – both complicit (the employers and managers) and implicit (the union hierarchy in the TGWU). Later the Glasgow TGWU 7/162 branch supported an unofficial month-long strike at Newalls Insulation in 1966 for masks, protective clothing and medical exams.[99] The TGWU and STUC offered no support and the STUC eventually banned local activist John Todd from its Health and Safety training schools because of his outspoken criticism of TGWU inaction on asbestos. Other unofficial action followed, as with London dockers blacking asbestos handling in 1967 and building workers' strikes against asbestos and hazardous asbestos substitutes in the 1970s (e.g. there was a two-week strike at the Barbican building site in London in 1976 which succeeded in getting asbestos banned on the site; and another strike at the Isle of Grain power station for nine months in 1976 against the use of glass fibre). This 'prairie fire' of health strikes spread to the oil refineries, including Grangemouth, in the later 1970s.

The 1970s appear to be a watershed with a cluster of significant occupational health and safety strikes. In relation to asbestos in Scotland, the Glasgow laggers branch of the TGWU led the way, with a series of strikes which achieved reforms in health and safety, craft status and wage rates which English areas were struggling to achieve parity with in the 1970s.[100] Here were ripples of a long tradition of rank-and-file radicalism on 'Red Clydeside' which undoubtedly shaped this more assertive phase of direct action on health and safety. This was also a quite unique mobilization which drew strength from the close kinship and ethnic links of Irish Catholics amongst the asbestos lagging workers in Glasgow. Several activists in the 7/162 Glasgow branch (together with others

**Figure 7.1** Protest lobby at the TUC 1976 (Brighton) by workers sacked from the Isle of Grain Power Station site (by contractor Babcock and Wilcox) for refusing to work with asbestos without protective clothing.
Courtesy of TUC Library Collections at London Metropolitan University, see www.unionhistory.info

including ex-joiners who worked on the asbestos-riddled high-rise flats) went on to form the community advocacy and pressure group Clydeside Action on Asbestos (CAA) which we'll reflect on more in the next section in this chapter.

Where trade union levels were relatively high and labour markets buoyant in 'dangerous trades', there was a pattern of 'wildcat' strikes and walkouts on occupational health issues at a local level in the 1960s and 1970s. Thus, on closer scrutiny it was not that workers failed to go out on strike on health and safety issues, rather that these strikes were short and often unofficial, hence less visible, slipping under the radar. Oral interviews reveal this hidden world of subterranean conflict and resistance around the body and its exploitation at the point of production. Witness, for example, the testimony of Scottish shipbuilding worker John Keggie recalling the 1960s and 1970s:

> By and large most o' the disputes in Robb's [shipyard] were about health and safety issues. They were not really about arguments about money or wages, terms and conditions. They were about health and safety issues, where management under pressure to complete orders would try and put people into environments that were unsafe. And the workers would refuse and the management would then suspend an individual and one individual bein' suspended … Ah mean, ah remember once

## Jobs and Bodies

three – maself and two others – were asked tae go intae a tank that was unsafe and didn't have ventilation. We refused and were suspended. The entire shipyard workforce walked out and a thirteen-week dispute took place.[101]

This strike was followed by a long ban on overtime because, as Keggie recalled: 'management insisted that when we went back we had tae go back intae that unsafe environment.' This 'insider' witness testimony may be interpreted as directly contradicting the narratives and interpretations of some 'outsider' academics, professionals and the 'official' strike statistics where health and safety do not feature. However, both have meaning and credibility in that one was recounting workplace struggle, agency and activism and the other a relative failure of trade union bureaucracies to support such radicalism and direct action. That is not to say the trade union hierarchy was indifferent, rather that tactics diverged. At the national union level and at the STUC and TUC, campaigns were predominantly directed towards influencing policy and legislation, as the work of Vicky Long has shown.[102] And the union hierarchy in the post-war era tended to frown on unofficial 'wildcat' strike action. The injured and diseased workers' movement was multi-layered, with action at the local and the national, political level, demonstrating that workers and their unions were also agents in this process at the point of production and not just passive victims. At the workplace and local level, workers and their unions mobilized and deployed the strike weapon and other forms of direct action to protect their bodies.

Shop stewards proliferated in the UK workplace in the 1950s, 60s and 70s. As Quinlan, Bohle and Lamm argued, in this period OHS was increasingly being bargained over, with union intervention at a number of levels including crucially in the workplace, at the point of production.[103] Bradley has discussed this in relation to the steel industry in the UK arguing this marked a transition from a more individualist approach by the trade unions on OHS (characterized by 'assisted convalescence') towards a more openly collectivist and more proactively preventionist approach.[104] In the UK numbers of shop stewards rose from 90,000 in 1961 to 250,000 by 1980.[105] These union activists provided another layer of protection for workers' bodies at the point of production. They came to play a key role in OHS in the workplace, identifying issues and representing workers, acting as unofficial 'welfare' consultants, challenging managerial power and entrenched macho work-health cultures, thus raising OHS standards across the board. One vulnerable immigrant worker when asked in 1980 why he had joined a union put it this way: 'What the management would like to do to the workers is prevented by the unions, so we are protected.'[106] In workers' eyes, unionization provided protection, a buffer from what one worker at the Ford factory at Halewood, Liverpool described (referring to the 1960s) as 'push, push, push all the time here' and another 'the iron fist' of management.[107] Without the union 'the worker would be in a hell of a position … the place would be in a terrible state' he continued. A female London railway worker argued this was about personal protection:

> But everybody joined the union and it wasn't because they felt they had to, it was just that the reps came round and everybody just felt it would be a sensible thing

to do. To look after themselves – so I didn't know anyone who didn't join the union … I joined the NUR: the National Union of Railwaymen.[108]

Another Ford car factory worker made a similar case: 'I have been in a union since 1960 when I was on the docks. You need a union for your own protection. To protect your *rights*. A firm like this would have you working like horses without the union'.[109] And a former company manager recalled in an interview in 2005:

Particularly from 1945 onwards, if an operative found himself exposed to something that he considered dangerous he would take it up with his union shop steward who would then take it up with the management who had to have a proper look at it. I think the unions were very active and effective in promoting health and safety.[110]

Eddie Pymm, shop steward on the safety committee at the Chatham Dockyard in the 1970s and early 1980s, reflected on his experience campaigning to improve the standards of the health physics monitors who were employed to measure radiation exposure:

We had complained and complained several times about conditions, the lack of cover by the Health Physics people. You know, the monitoring it was, well it was a disgrace really and some people, you know, you'd have a dosimeter on to measure the amount of radiation, some people would take it off, you'd put the coveralls on before you went in the reactor compartment or contaminated areas and they'd leave their pencil [dosimeter] behind because if it got to a certain figure that's it there was a cut off, you don't take any more …[111]

Reporting an incident to the shop steward thus became a very real threat to management in the post-war decade. David Walker has made the point that negotiating 'danger money' was a pragmatic response by union officials, not a 'sell out'. In the real world where workers could be replaced and had to make a living to support their families and pay their bills it was better tactically to squeeze managers for more pay to compensate somewhat for the additional risks taken, rather than walking off the job. Then the additional cost of 'danger' and 'dirt' money might act as a lever to improve conditions. Doug May, involved in negotiations for his union at ICI, commented:

We knew the risks attached to the job and we knew that we had to wear safety equipment and all the rest of it … I knew that the conditions were not really right to work in, the supervisor knew that they were not really right to work in, the manager didn't want to be present [in the negotiations], and I thought, well if the guys are happy enough to do it but they wanted extra payments for it … so you would have a situation where you'd say 'OK eight for four' so in actual fact they'd probably get eight hours pay for two and a half hours work.[112]

## Jobs and Bodies

In the Chatham Dockyards there were 'obnoxious conditions' rates and later 'Environmental Allowances' that could double earnings for certain jobs (such as working in radiation risk areas on nuclear submarines).[113]

Trade union activism culminated in the wholesale overhaul of the OHS regulatory system with the Health and Safety at Work Act of 1974 bringing an additional eight million workers into the orbit of regulation, including in agriculture, schools and hospitals. Related legislation followed in 1977 when the Safety Representatives and Safety Committee Regulations forced employers to establish safety committees and safety representatives with full powers to inspect. At the centre of this was the idea that employers had a 'duty of care' and needed to initiate risk assessments to determine if changes in work affected OHS. The new legislation in turn ushered in an era of unprecedented training of trade union health and safety representatives, cascading down knowledge and expertise to the shop floor and assisting further positive changes in OHS in industry. 80,000 people were trained in the ten day TUC health and safety training courses over 1974–82. Lyddon has argued that 'this mass provision of training, more than anything, was probably responsible for the distinct culture shift on health and safety, within many workplaces, that occurred from the late 1970s'.[114]

A surge in union involvement in OHS from the 1970s is evident across most developed countries, the UK included.[115] And many non-industrial unions (UNISON is one that stands out here), as well as the TUC played important roles, as we've seen, in representing individual members in compensation claims and influencing the discourse on the stress epidemic in the workplace (see Chapter 5). Over time OHS has become a much more central priority of most of the major unions in Britain – with workloads and stress predominating as campaigning issues. Our own Universities and Colleges Union (UCU) would be a good example. Indicative here is the fact that in 2022 (as I write) the RCN brought its union members out on strike for the first time in its history because of workload-related stress and grievances over wages. This heightened sensitivity towards the body at work is also evident at grass-roots level. Michelle McBride became a UNISON health and safety officer in Glasgow in 2017 after being made a shop steward a couple of years earlier. In a recent interview she expressed an acute sense of the danger points in the places she worked (from 1999) and how the local union representative played a key welfare role for union members.[116] Amongst the incidents which motivated her were the near fatal electrocution of her younger brother from a live electric rail track, and her own painful lived experience of stress and breakdown caused by an abusive and bullying manager.

Trade unionists, however, could pay a very heavy price for their occupational health activism. Quinlan, Bohle and Lamm identify one of the core union policies on OHS as being to protect OHS activists from victimization.[117] In some sectors in the UK, including in the North Sea oilfields and the construction industry, union health and safety officers could find themselves quietly sacked, victimized, blacklisted and denied work in a scandalous misuse of power by industry, supported by right-wing social movement organizations.[118] In an account that drew heavily on oral interviews, Smith has shown the blacklisting of OHS activists in the English construction industry

200

to have been widespread in the second half of the twentieth century, and a recent Scottish Affairs Committee enquiry in 2015 has shown this also to have been the case in Scotland.[119] Construction had one of the highest accident rates of all industries in the second half of the twentieth century and disproportionately high occupational cancer rates (associated with asbestos), as well as other hazards, such as vibration white finger and dermatitis.[120] Trade union health and safety officers pushed back against this and could find themselves sacked and victimized as a consequence. This happened, for example, to a construction worker (Francis) who after raising safety concerns on the Terminal 5 construction job at Heathrow in the 1990s, recalled a: 'tap on the shoulder and off I was – dismissed'[121]. Another construction worker asserted: 'if you bring up health and safety, I am afraid your days are numbered'. He refused to enter ducts with asbestos lining, then was threatened with being sacked, recalling that his manager had commented: 'I've worked with it all my life and it hasn't done me any harm up till now'.[122] In some cases in construction, as George Fuller testified, health and safety representatives were violently assaulted, and had to use false names, insurance numbers and addresses to secure work.[123]

Blacklisting for health and safety activities also affected workers employed on the oil and gas rigs in the North Sea. James Fowler, an electrician nightshift safety representative for the Electrical and Plumbing Industries Union, found himself in trouble after campaigning on occupational health issues on the Piper Bravo oil platform in 1991 (a sister platform to the Piper Alpha rig where the disaster occurred in 1988). After witnessing a death on site, a helicopter crash (killing eleven workmen) and being told by management that three deaths per year was an acceptable level he reflected: 'it dawned on me then, this isn't right, these men have died just going to work'.[124] Fowler reported a regime of fear amongst fellow rig workers: 'I could see the fear on their faces ... no one else was raising their head above the parapet'. Fowler fought with management over safety measures and workers being pushed to cut corners, including joining with all the rigs' safety representatives in handing in their resignation. He found himself blacklisted as a consequence. On the rigs the expression 'NRB', 'not required back' was well known.[125] Employer culpability in such illegal blacklisting was proven in a series of court cases in the 2010s supported by the unions in the construction industry (led by UNITE) which resulted in over £10m awarded in compensation for loss of earnings. The main organizations proven to be running these vetting and blacklisting agencies for big business were the Economic League (1919–93) and subsequently the construction industry dominated Consulting Association (1993–2009).[126]

Activist interventions and trade union campaigns on OHS made a real difference to OHS standards and work-health cultures. Whilst the UK data remain challenging to interpret, some accounts suggested that in non-unionized workplaces workers were around 50 per cent more likely to be killed in a workplace accident as in a unionized workplace.[127] *Hazards* magazine estimated that 2.5 million serious injuries had been saved over the first twenty years of the workplace safety officers appointed under the 1977 legislation, claiming 'workplaces with a full union safety structure are twice as safe as those without.'[128] Another study of thirty-one industrialized countries concluded that 'union density is the most important external determinant of workplace psychosocial safety climate, health and GDP.'[129] Recent ILO data also support this conclusion. Globally, where there are strong independent trade unions, fatality rates on the job tend to be considerably lower than where union densities are low or no independent trade union exists (as, for example, in China). The United States, for example, with only 10 per cent of its workers in trade unions, had an occupational accident fatality rate (per 100,000 workers) in 2018 almost three times higher than the Scandinavian countries, where unionization rates average over 60 per cent.[130] There is also a strong correlation between unionization rates and countries ratifying ILO conventions on health and safety.[131] Trade unions have clearly made a real difference, as the ILO argued in 2002:

> Since their very inception, trade unions have seen the improvement of working conditions as one of their top priorities. And indeed, progress in that field, including a clear decrease in work-related accidents in the industrialized world, the improvement of work methods and recognition of the human factor in industries over the last century, owes a lot to efforts by organized labour.[132]

Whilst the day-to-day welfare work of the well-trained union health and safety representatives made a difference in the workplace[133], trade union activities on occupational health also contributed to wider public health campaigns and working-class environmentalism, a fact often overlooked in the OHS literature.[134] Quinlan, Bohle and Lamm have made the point that unions were frequently involved in alliances and collaborations in public health and community-based campaigns.[135] As scholars have shown for the United States, and Karen Bell for the UK, there was a cross-fertilization between occupational and environmental health, that was evident, for example, in campaigning on issues like pneumoconiosis, byssinosis, lead and asbestos, and recent union promotion of sustainable development.[136] Another example would be the unions successful boycotting of nuclear waste dumping at sea in 1983. Such dumping had happened since 1949. After pressure from Greenpeace the National Union of Seamen blacked such dumping, supported by other unions (including the TGWU and the NUR) who refused to transport nuclear waste overland to the ports.[137] We need more research to deepen our understanding of the role of the trade unions in such campaigns and to determine their relationships with the wider public health, community and environmental movements, such as the pioneering UK Occupational and Environmental Diseases Association (OEDA), established in 1979.[138]

Trade unions then were a product of their times – inclusive, sectional and capable of absorbing prevailing attitudes as well as radically challenging the status quo as transformative agents in struggles around the body at work. The evidence suggests a more positive evaluation of their role in OHS is warranted. There were synergistic links between compensation and prevention in trade union policy in Britain.[139] A range of positions existed within a heterogeneous trade union movement and union action ebbed and flowed, influenced by fluctuating labour markets and political context. Considered in

**Figure 7.2** International Workers' Memorial Day Poster, 2020, courtesy of *Hazards* magazine, www.hazards.org.

international perspective and against the typology of union functions on OHS developed by Quinlan, Bohle and Lamm, the historical record of UK trade unions is a positive and proactive one protecting the body at work, at many levels – national, sectoral and in the workplace. In this respect, the UK sits somewhere between the Nordic countries and the significantly less well unionized southern European countries (such as Spain and Italy) and the United States.

## Jobs and Bodies

### *Victims' groups and community activism*

Trade unions were not alone in advocating and campaigning for those harmed by their work. Other civil and community groups were active too, independent of the unions and sometimes acting in unison with them. Civil protest and voluntary social movement organizations played an important role in social justice and environmental activism, representing and supporting victims and their families with a range of services, whilst campaigning for better compensation and improvements in work conditions, safety measures, welfare services and the law. Whilst there was some overlap, union activities tended to focus on those still in employment and OHS on the job. Whereas the community OHS movement primarily represented the interests of those outside employment, usually the 'walking wounded' who were injured, sick, unemployed, redundant, retired or disabled and their families and dependents who were directly or indirectly impacted by occupational injury, harm or chronic disease.

In coal mining, the Coal Industry Social Welfare Organisation (CISWO) played an important role in supporting the disabled and the families of those miners killed on the job. Formed in 1952, CISWO pioneered social work, got involved in rehabilitation services and convalescence for miners and their families and a range of other 'medico-social services'. In the 1950s mining in the UK had one of the most developed rehabilitation services in the world and CISWO played an important role in this. The activities of CISWO widened in the 1960s and 1970s into addressing mental health issues with 'therapeutic listening' (an early form of 'reminiscence therapy'), funding 'recuperative holidays' and provision of practical help in areas such as housing and mobility. This included assistance with portable oxygen equipment to pneumoconiotics at a time when such was not available through the NHS to these groups.[140] CISWO worked closely with the NUM, who was represented directly on the CISWO board. Undoubtedly, the pioneering work of CISWO contributed to mitigating some of the social isolation that characterized the experience of disabled people in post-war mining communities. That said, of all trade unions the NUM were also most directly involved in the post-employment health and welfare of ex-miners. Indeed this became the primary role of the NUM under Nicky Wilson from the late twentieth century across the coalfields as deep mining disappeared.[141]

Lillian Bilocca and the 1968 campaign to improve safety aboard fishing trawlers provide a different example of community mobilization to protect bodies at work and those damaged by their employment. Fishing was a more deadly industry than even coal mining after the Second World War (see Chapter 1). Within a month in 1968 three Hull-based trawlers sank with the total loss of fifty-eight lives (there was only one survivor). In response, Lillian Bilocca – who worked in a Hull fish gutting and preparation factory – organized the Hull fishermen's wives in a campaign to improve safety aboard the vessels. Three other wives were prominent in the action that ensued, Christine Jensen, Mary Denness and Yvonne Blenkinsop, which included organizing local meetings, protest marches and the collection of 10,000 signatures calling for legislative reform, presented by the media-dubbed 'headscarf revolutionaries' to the

Pushing Back

**Figure 7.3** Lilian Bilocca (right of policeman) leading a protest march in Hull, 2 February 1968. Courtesy of Mirrorpix/Getty Images.

Harold Wilson-led Labour government in London. The campaigners also drew up a long list of demands for eighty-eight improved safety measures on board the trawlers.

The campaign was widely supported by wives and mothers in Hull (one meeting was reported to have had over 500 present) but met with recalcitrant opposition from the trawler owners and some hostility within traditional elements of the fishing community amongst some of the fishermen. One of the female leaders was punched in the face during one of the demonstrations and Lilian Bilocca faced death threats and was blacklisted from working on the docks. Trade unionism in the industry had proven notoriously difficult to sustain but the TGWU was involved and supportive. The disaster and the civil action by Lilian Bilocca and the wives achieved in weeks what the unions had been campaigning on for years. The reforms, enshrined in a new Shipping Act, included vessel safety checks before leaving harbour and compulsory employment of a radio operator aboard at all times.[142] Thousands of lives of fishermen were saved by the civil action of Lilian Bilocca and her fellow activists in 1968.

Jan O'Malley and her work in London provide a different example of the convergence of community activism with occupational health and safety. Jan was a housing activist in London in the late 1960s and 70s, involved in a grass roots organization, the Notting Hill People's Association, campaigning to improve conditions for working-class tenants. In 1974, through her contacts with local tenants and the housing struggle she heard stories of the exploitation of female workers in the local Fidelity Radio factory, where some

## Jobs and Bodies

450 were employed. Amongst the health and safety issues were blocked fire escapes, poor ventilation and heating, a bonus wage system that was difficult to comprehend and which incentivized overwork, and compulsory overtime of up to 14 hours a week: 'They were exhausted' Jan recalled, from all this and 'the frenetic pace of the production line.' And the workforce were not unionized. Jan brought all her experience of housing activism to support the Fidelity workers, recalling:

> We wrote a story in *People's News*. We sold it outside the factory for a penny. People were quite surprised that anybody knew what went on inside. We contacted the AUEW [the Amalgamated Union of Engineering Workers] official and started having factory gate meetings at lunch time. We got up to 100 people coming. And then we had separate meetings in local halls before the evening shift started ... In April/May [1974], after we had had some meetings we built up the membership, the AUEW official asked/approached management for recognition of the union. He raised some of the issues like getting the fire escapes unblocked and getting fans and ventilators installed. We publicised in the local press, not just *People's News*, the bad conditions in which they were working. We got reporters down and that kind of contributed a bit of pressure, before we had any union there, to get marginal improvements. So it gave the workers inside some sense that things could change.[143]

Here we see again the intertwining of community activism with trade union support evident in mining communities and in the social movement in Hull. The mobilizing experience in Notting Hill fed into Jan's philosophy that industrial and community action should be integrated, something she went on to strongly advocate in her book, *The Politics of Community Action* (1977). She commented:

> Giving them [the workers] weapons, levers and supporting them in using them. It's the same process. It's solidarity in action. You don't have to be in there to do it. You can share concern about the issues, give energy to try to change them and if they accept that help – it's just the same thing isn't it? ... Community struggles on their own can never win. Industrial struggles are stronger if they have community support.[144]

A broader occupational health movement emerged in the UK from the 1970s with the mobilization of victims, family members and a wide range of advocates, professionals (such as lawyers and doctors) and supporters who campaigned for more effective prevention measures, fairer compensation, welfare reforms and better treatment and palliative care. Wives and ex-industrial workers played key roles in this movement. This paralleled the emergence of such groups and a more distinctive industrial injury and disease movement across other countries, including the United States, Canada and Europe.[145] In a recent interview, Phyllis Craig, welfare officer for the asbestos pressure group Clydeside Action on Asbestos, formed in 1983, observed that those with or experiencing mesothelioma 'are *consumed* with anger'.[146] A burning sense of injustice and rage drew many into activism and advocacy, though individuals and communities responded to the unfolding asbestos tragedy in a range of ways.

The first known asbestos victims' advocacy group in the world was established in London in 1978 by Nancy Tait (1920–2009).[147] Her husband Bill had died of mesothelioma in 1968 and Nancy fought a long four-year battle to get his death established as caused by occupational exposure, against the opposition of his employers and the ambivalence of government.[148] She went on to help other asbestos victims and families, to write

**Figure 7.4** SPAID poster, late 1980s.
Courtesy of University of Strathclyde Archives and Special Collections (where the SPAID/OEDA Archive is located).

## Jobs and Bodies

a booklet, *Asbestos Kills* (1976), before establishing the Society for the Prevention of Asbestosis and Industrial Diseases (SPAID) in 1978.

SPAID initiated medical enquiries into mesothelioma that exposed the fallacies prevailing in the late 1970s, effectively challenging the claims of the industry that low exposure levels, white asbestos and asbestos cement were all benign. SPAID was also instrumental in campaigning to get the ineffective diagnosis by optical microscope examination used by the state Social Security department (to determine degrees of respiratory impairment and hence compensation levels) changed to electron microscopy in the mid-1980s. SPAID acquired its own such microscope to assist victims in their compensation struggles. Tait was a tireless advocate for ARD victims' rights. Her organization supported the compensation claims of thousands of ARD victims, and, until her death in 2009, she remained one of the UK's most outspoken campaigners against the asbestos industry lobby.[149] Perhaps above all else, as the historian of SPAID/OEDA argued, Tait and the organization was responsible for widening the discourse on asbestos from a workplace to an environmental hazard, a move epitomized in the retitling of the organization in 1996 to the Occupational and Environmental Diseases Association. In the process they developed a closer relationship and alliance with the UK trade union movement from the mid-1990s (from when the TUC directly encouraged its member unions to affiliate to OEDA) and with the wider environmental health movement, with close links being developed between SPAID/OEDA and the Green Party from the 1990s.[150]

As McDougall has shown, SPAID/OEDA was predominantly a middle-class campaigning group based in London. In the UK, other city-wide and regional victims' support groups soon emerged, initially focusing on asbestos in Hull and Glasgow, followed by Clydebank, Merseyside and Manchester. The roots of these were more clearly working class, with unemployed and sick ex-trade union activists being at the forefront of the local mobilization of victims' groups.[151] With funding support, sometimes from local councils (as in Glasgow), these groups went on to rent premises and employ professional welfare officers to represent the interests of those diagnosed with ARDs. Formed in the mid-1970s following the HSWA 1974, the *Hazards* magazine, representing union health and safety officers and led by editor Rory O'Neill, also played an important role in publicizing issues, campaigning and advocating (e.g. assisting the creation of the Merseyside asbestos group in 1993).

Clydeside Action on Asbestos (CAA), formed in 1983, was created by a group of volunteer ARD sufferers who had previously worked in the shipyards, on construction sites and in asbestos factories around the city. John Todd, who experienced the trauma of several members of his family, including his father, being killed by ARDs, was a rank-and-file OHS activist from the 1960s and one of those responsible for the creation of CAA.[152] Another was Robert Crockett (who became the first CAA chairman), who had worked as a joiner on the Red Road Flats and died of mesothelioma soon after. One of the founder members, William Harkness, had, for twelve years, been refused any state compensation benefits for his advanced asbestosis. He epitomized the

**Figure 7.5** Newspaper clipping of Nancy Tait, Director of SPAID.
Courtesy of University of Strathclyde Archives and Special Collections.

mutual help ethos of the OHS workers' movement in the UK in the 1980s and 1990s. In 1988, he commented:

> I am half dead. I can't walk anywhere. I have to get taxis all the time and I have a machine at home I have to use every day to help me breathe. Clyde Action on Asbestos have been a great help to me over the years and I am determined to be part of the group and help others in the same condition caused by that filth.[153]

Like SPAID, CAA campaigned for change, liaising with supportive politicians, legal experts, doctors and medical professionals and providing support for victims at a number of levels, most notably relating to guiding them through the bureaucratic quagmire of applying for compensation. CAA opened premises in central Glasgow in 1988, creating

## Jobs and Bodies

**Figure 7.6** Phyllis Craig, Manager and Senior Welfare Rights Officer, Action on Asbestos (formerly Clydeside Action on Asbestos).
Courtesy of Phyllis Craig.

a walk-in self-help centre for ARD victims and their families. From 1995 they were (and continue to be) ably led by their inspirational and indefatigable Welfare Rights Officer, Phyllis Craig.[154]

Sandra Samuel, whose father died with mesothelioma, recalled:

Clydeside Action on Asbestos has been excellent … You can 'phone up and you are maybe just a wee bit unsure have I done this right and I found them very responsive and encouraging, saying you must make a claim, reminding me that someone's negligence caused my father's death. I wasn't aware that all these years ago they knew the dangers. I didn't realise there was blame to apportion, unless it was perhaps ignorance in the 1940s. I know now but then I didn't … I found them really down to earth. They put it into layman's terms and don't try to baffle you and don't make you feel greedy. By the time Dad got his money he was dead. They said it was fine and he got £9000 and they said it was for your Mum.[155]

Janet Ross, whose husband had mesothelioma, emphasized the supportive role of CAA at a critical time:

> Clydeside Action were extremely helpful and they were the ones that pointed out what we should do and how to do it. They helped with paperwork, benefits and financial aid. They made it clear what we were entitled to. They took it on board to send the package of paperwork for Ian to fill in. They took a lot off our shoulders, they were very good and it helped to speak to someone who know all about what we were going through. They were very supportive, kind, and helpful. I can't fault them.[156]

Some activists channelled their energies into improving medical provision and treatment. Despite being on oxygen 24 hours a day and largely house-bound (with asbestosis, pleural thickening, pleural plaques and COPD) Ian McConaghy led a crusade to create a 'Centre of Excellence' for asbestos-related diseases in a West Central Scotland hospital.[157] This to address the continuing issues with misdiagnosis and late diagnosis of mesothelioma, and the limited range of treatment.

Other victims were active in establishing and supporting the local groups. Like Nancy Tait, Vera Rigby's husband Barrie died of mesothelioma. Vera became involved as a founder member of the Barrow Asbestos Group (Cumbria), led by local GP and hospice manager Helen Clayson and a solicitor. The law firms that were involved in the compensation cases, like Pickerings and Thompsons, played an important role, and Vera stressed what a key part her solicitor played in putting her at ease about making a claim and taking her patiently through the process. Initially, widows were the focus of the Barrow support group, but it expanded to include patients and helping families with compensation claims. A big part of the campaigning, as elsewhere, was on defending and improving victim's rights to compensation. And the annual Mesothelioma Action Day (usually in the first week in July every year) was an important campaigning event in the calendar. When Vera moved to Manchester she continued her active role, switching to the Manchester Asbestos Group (with Tony Whitson and others). One of the things Vera did, inspired by asbestos activist Michael Lees whose wife died of mesothelioma after exposure as a teacher, was to go into her granddaughters' schools and ask directly what their asbestos policy was.[158]

Barbara Eason similarly became an activist in Manchester after her husband was diagnosed with mesothelioma. She recalled: 'I feel as though I'm doing it for Mike, trying to help people who are, you know, people which are still coming across asbestos'. On Tony Whitson's initiative Barbara became involved in the widow's group that also involved Vera. She reflected on some of the work they did:

> So a few of us went, been going ever since. And the campaigns we've done. 2006 we stood outside the House of Lords. My mother-in-law used to come then, you know. Stood outside the House of Lords. It was a case, I can't remember the case now, it was a compensation case, and it was coming before the House of

## Jobs and Bodies

Lords. And we stood with banners outside the House of Lords! Then we went again. And then – oh I don't know we've done all sorts. I'll tell you what we did last year, stood outside the ... Russian Embassy. Because they're the biggest exporters them ...[159]

Like Vera, Barbara acted as a community environmental monitor – a kind of asbestos sniffer – checking on potential exposure points with asbestos in local buildings around the community. Once, she recalled, she enquired at the local hospital and sometime later spotted an asbestos removal van arriving to strip out asbestos from the X-ray department. Barbara admitted her surveillance involved having the binoculars out to keep track of what was happening!

The mobilizing capacity of injury, harm, exploitation and a burning sense of social injustice have been evident across the globe, reflected in the creation of OHS victims' pressure groups across all continents, including at least thirty-five ARD victims groups.[160] The story of the Jonckheere family in Belgium provides a good example of this process at work. The family, as we have seen, had a tradition of working for the multinational Eternit asbestos cement factory in the small town of Kapelle-op-den-Bos in Flanders. Several members of the family died of mesothelioma across at least two generations.[161] In 1999 Francoise Jonckheere Francoise, was diagnosed with mesothelioma due to environmental exposure in the area around the Eternit factory.[162] Gardens in the vicinity of the plant were covered in white dust. She insisted that her five sons be examined, and it was found that they all had asbestos contamination in their lungs. Eternit offered the standard sum of 42,000 euros as compensation, with the proviso that this entailed no admission of blame and that acceptance of the money gave the company immunity from further damages claims. Francoise refused and subsequently became an asbestos campaigner and activist, and a cause célèbre, receiving much media attention in Belgium. Before she died in 2000 (aged sixty-five) she was influential in the formation of the Belgian asbestos victims group (Association Belge des Victimes de l'Amiante [ABEVA]). This advocacy and campaigning work have been continued by Francoise's son, Eric Jonckheere, who has been president of ABEVA since 2007. 'We started to take the side of the victims', Eric commented. 'We were aware we could be next [...] These days I cannot answer: will I be the next? Will my brothers be the next?'[163] This alludes to the uncertainty and apprehension hanging over the heads of those who worked with asbestos. To date, two of Eric's brothers have also died of mesothelioma: Pierre Paul (aged forty-three) in May 2003 and Stéphane (aged forty-four) in January 2009. Both had young families.

Eric Jonckheere's activist interview testimony and his family experience raise many issues. One that stands out is the power and control that Eternit exercised over the community, where, for decades, its reassuring pronouncements and paternalist strategy of ad hoc compensation (combined with control over the local labour market) ensured virtual silence on the economic violence it was perpetrating. The Jonckheeres were for some time the only family who stood up against Eternit: 'No-one was talking in the village; nobody was raising awareness ... or challenging the pro-asbestos lobby, very

## Pushing Back

influential in Belgium … You were bound to keep quiet,' Eric noted, 'they were able to silence the people.'[164] Another theme evident here is that of agency – how the family's devastating experience marked the transition from deference and denial to organizing and mobilizing a diseased workers' movement.

Our book, *Lethal Work* and the oral testimonies that inform it entered the public domain in 2000. These have subsequently become part of the body of knowledge and, in turn, have had some influence in shaping ideas and deepening our understanding of the managerial practice and work cultures that underpinned economic violence relating to asbestos. The research thus played a small part in influencing policy and practice, as has other work of academic activists from a range of disciplines, such as Alan Dalton, Rory O'Neill, Tommy Gorman, Nick Wikeley and Geoff Tweedale. Asbestos researcher and campaigner Jock McCulloch paid the ultimate price, losing his life to mesothelioma from contact with the carcinogenic mineral, most likely on his research fieldwork in South Africa. The oral histories of witnesses and victims provide an alternative discourse, and frequently a critical one, in which what Michael Bloor describes as the 'bump of irreverence' is much in evidence.[165] These often powerful and frequently moving narratives (with the interpretation that developed around them) challenged medical orthodoxies and official explanations and placed everyday personal experience at centre stage. Through them the personal becomes political.

Some politicians (like the Clydebank Member of the Scottish Parliament Des McNulty) attested to the influence of our book *Lethal Work*, which added a little weight to the campaign for more extensive compensation for ARDs in Scotland, including for pleural plaques, which CAA spearheaded. Plaques are evidence of asbestos in the lungs, though the scarring may not necessarily lead to cancer. At the time of writing, *Lethal Work* continues to be featured on the CAA website, and an article written by the authors has had a permanent presence on the International Ban Asbestos Secretariat (IBAS) website since 2002.[166] The IBAS coordinator, Laurie Kazan-Allen, has attested to the importance of *Lethal Work* in shaping her ideas, as have other asbestos researchers, medics and campaigners (e.g. Dr Helen Clayson, cited previously). Upon Kazan-Allen's request, my colleague Ronnie Johnston and I assisted with providing witness testimony in compensation litigation, locating two oral history interviewees who worked on the *Queen Mary* refit in Southampton in 1946–7 and similar jobs around that time. Sam Irvine and Hugh Cairney were flown to San Francisco (at the lawyer's expense), where they gave oral evidence in a mesothelioma damages case (March 2001) that resulted in a $1 million settlement.[167] Unfortunately, the plaintiff, Tom Wilmot, never regained consciousness and died before hearing the outcome of the litigation. Oral history can thus contribute to disease movement mobilizations and compensation struggles – not least as such witness testimony is an established part of evidence accumulation in damages litigation to corroborate product placement (in the Thomas Wilmot case, this was established by asbestos sacks and packages stamped with manufacturers' logos). Other researchers (such as Geoff Tweedale and Nick Wikeley) have played a more direct role, providing expert evidence in litigation cases in support of victims seeking compensation.

## Jobs and Bodies

Whilst neoliberal economics and the return to mass unemployment across developed Western economies from the 1980s onwards undoubtedly operated as degenerative forces with a negative impact on the body at work, in some places a cluster of countervailing forces strengthening the occupational health movement. Castleman and Tweedale have pointed to the importance of empathetic and supportive journalism, both in print and film/TV. They provide the examples of Laurie Flynn and his 'World in Action' documentaries and the pivotal Yorkshire TV production of *Alice: A Fight for Life* (a powerful two-hour documentary which traced a mesothelioma victim Alice Jefferson's story from her death bed, screened in 1982).[168] The latter – based on a SPAID compensation case – had an immediate impact on UK health and safety regulation. The rise of the Greens and environmental politics from the 1990s, fuelled by the climate crisis, also had a synergistic impact. As Sellers has demonstrated for the United States, in the UK many occupational health activists became interested in and engaged in environmental politics. Individual occupational health activists like David Gee of the GMB, Alan Dalton of the TGWU and Owen Tudor, senior policy officer at the TUC in the 1990s (and later with the ILO) epitomized this transition to environmentalism.[169] A significant marker of this was the movement of SPAID into environmental issues, indicated by its name change in 1996 to the Occupational and Environmental Diseases Association (OEDA). Tactical alliances also proved effective. One of the best known recent examples is the formation of the Asbestos Victims Support Group Forum UK who fought a protracted three-year battle ending in 2022 to hold Cape Asbestos to account for a 'cover up'. The sequestered Cape documents (from litigation brought against Cape by insurers) showed the extent to which the company were aware of the health risks of asbestos in the 1950s and 1960s and did little or nothing about it. Indeed, they withheld data that was unfavourable and gave false assurances denying the toxicity of the product through to the 1970s.[170]

Over time, the occupational health and safety movement became accepted; more mainstream and morphed to embrace mental health issues at work, campaigning on stress and workloads, for example through Work*stress*: the UK National Work Stress Network (NWSN). NWSN was formed in the mid-1990s, following the formation of a European Work Stress network.[171] Its aims are to campaign, educate, advocate and support victims of work-induced stress and to work in conjunction with trade unions and the *Hazards* campaign group to these ends. These developments were connected to a wider public awareness of health, stress and depression, and consciousness of the damage being wrought by industry and fossil fuel dependency. Such efforts were complemented and supported by grassroots initiatives in working-class communities up and down the country. For example, local action groups struggling against toxic pollution, as in Rutherglen, Glasgow where toxic and carcinogenic chemicals (including chromium IV) which had affected workers on the job continued to contaminate the local environment for decades after the factory closure. That the unions and the occupational health movement were effective as a countervailing force is without doubt, as numerous personal testimonies evidence and the data on health, mortality and unionization show. Concurrently, underlying forces, nonetheless, served to undermine the capacity to resist and mediate this assault on the body, notably the political attack on labour and trade union rights from the 1980s, the shift towards individualism and deregulation, the collapse in trade union membership and Britain's withdrawal from the European Union, which threatened the removal of the protective matrix of European labour regulations. That said, activism and civil disobedience have continued at many levels. A recent example would be Extinction Rebellion where the fact that asbestos has been banned has been cited (in 2019) as a precedent for the banning of all plastics.

The transition in public consciousness towards awareness of the damage work could do to health and towards environmentalism was uneven however. Scotland, for example, had a more distinctively proletarian and leftist culture, exhibited in the strength of the Labour Party vote in that country in contrast to much of England. The formation of a new devolved Scottish Parliament in 1999 and the dominance of a left-oriented Scottish Nationalist Party proved to be more sympathetic to the plight of ARD and industrial disease victims. The growing influence of European Union Directives on employment rights, including health and safety also had an impact. In contrast to elsewhere, in Scotland these prevailing circumstances and mobilization capacities helped to neuter some of the worst excesses of economic violence and environmental negligence, at least by the early twenty-first century. Amongst the outcomes are that civil law damages tend to be higher in Scotland than in England, and, over the past decade (in the 2010s), the Scottish Parliament has passed compensation legislation that covers pleural plaques, giving Scotland one of the most progressive welfare regimes in the world (at least with regard to ARDs). However, this is no reason to be sanguine. Whilst this may have somewhat eased the economic burden of ARDs in Scotland, relatively little has, or can, be done to reverse or relieve the pain, the suffering, and the utter devastation caused by the economic violence associated with the asbestos epidemic in the UK and elsewhere. The same could be said about respiratory disability and mortality in coal mining communities. The harm is irrevocable; the damage has been done.

## Conclusion

Occupational health and safety was a fiercely contested terrain, with trade unions, workers, families and communities pushing back against economic violence and environmental negligence and injustice. In the UK, the well-established and powerful trade union movement played a pivotal role in pushing back against business interests and protecting workers, campaigning to reduce risks, dangers and toxicity on the job, to improve workers' compensation and reduce workloads. A wider social movement also emerged beyond the trade unions (and often working with them) with OHS activism in the form of community campaigns and groups which represented the victims of unsafe and unhealthy working practices. The wider occupational health and safety movement drew upon the collective resources of their communities – their trade unions, civil action and their voluntary victims' advocacy groups, and medical experts, lawyers and politicians that supported their cause. And women were prominent in this social

## Jobs and Bodies

movement, including such figures as Lilian Bilocca in Hull, Jan O'Malley and Nancy Tait in London and Phyllis Craig in Glasgow, to name just a few. And the civil movement adapted to the transition in risk and changing nature of harms, morphing from a focus on accidents, trauma and disasters, towards chronic industrial disease (such as asbestos and pneumoconiosis) and then to the mental health crisis at work associated with the neo-liberal economy. Along the way the unions adapted, influenced by the feminist movement and environmentalism and transitioning to represent the interests of women workers more centrally and effectively. Concurrently, the industrial wing of the labour movement fought a rearguard battle against industrial closures and job losses. This did create some tension between the sometimes conflicting agendas of jobs and bodies, evident, for example in some transient union support for asbestos and for nuclear energy to retain jobs. Redundancy and unemployment did have significant negative impacts on physical and mental health, so the trade-off that sometimes happened here is perfectly understandable. Union policies did adapt to be more gender aware, supporting just transitions, retraining programmes and a strong welfare state support network to protect the health and welfare of those displaced by deindustrialization. And the evidence, surveyed above, strongly supports the argument that the unions and the environmental health movement were effective in protecting bodies at work and supporting the victims of industrialization and deindustrialization. A unionized workplace was a safer and healthier workplace.

That said, there were concomitant processes which were compromising the *capacity* to mobilise, repel and mediate threats to the body, health and well-being. Union membership fell back sharply with the neo-liberal political attack on workers' rights from the 1980s, mass unemployment, deregulation of the market and privatization, whilst exit from the European Union jeopardised the protective matrix of European labour regulations. With a more 'flexible' labour market, job insecurity has deepened and become endemic over the past two decades – with precarity increasing by something like 50 per cent since 2005 measured by a basket of indicators, according to one recent study.[172] Covid-19 came to us in this context, and again the trade unions have proven to be an important countervailing force campaigning for workers' rights and protecting workers bodies against the resurgence of infection risk on the job – as well as addressing the broader ramifications of the sharp shift towards home-working. One pivotal challenge for the trade unions and the OHS movement moving forward will be how they can adapt and build on this and feed off the public consciousness of the need for a better work-life balance (evidenced in the marked voluntary drift towards early retirement and 'opting out') and the importance of health and well-being together with sustainable development. Perhaps here in a refocus on jobs, bodies and the environment trade unions can find a path back to popularity and to levels of power and influence they exercised in the past, enabling even more effective prosecution of their historic and much-needed role as guardians of workers' health and well-being. This is more vital than ever in the fast-changing, viciously exploitative, increasingly insecure and precarious workplaces of modern Britain.

# CONCLUSION

Work in the UK interacted with and impacted upon the body in complex ways which changed significantly over time as the economy morphed from industrial to post-industrial. Power, social class, gender and race are amongst the factors that intersect to shape embodied outcomes. As we have seen, workers' bodies have their past inscribed upon them, some in more evident ways than others. That said, the risk of traumatic injury and toxic exposure (e.g. to asbestos and carcinogenic chemicals) has declined dramatically in the UK, as has the incidence of many chronically disabling and fatal industrial diseases, such as pneumoconiosis. Work-health cultures have changed too, and health and safety regulatory regimes at work are much more robust today than they were in c.1950. Still, new occupational hazards, ailments and diseases have replaced old, declining ones, with RSIs, MSDs and the modern-day stress at work epidemic associated with intensifying workloads, exacerbated recently by Covid-19. Moreover, to some degree the risks have been shunted in the globalized economy from relatively well-regulated and unionized countries like the UK to developing countries, like India, where workers continue to suffer obscene levels of occupational ill health, injury and mortality.

This book provides a social and cultural history of health and safety at work since the Second World War through the lens of workers themselves, with heavy dependence upon workers' own voices, stories and narratives and ways of telling in autobiographical personal accounts, including *Mass Observation* respondents and oral history interviews. It traverses the 'blue-collar' post-war industrial workplace that dominated the economy until the 1970s, through to the modern workplace of non-manual service sector and creative work. We explore work and the body through industrialization and deindustrialization, to the modern-day issues of chronic stress at work and infection as occupational diseases, culminating with Covid-19. I hope the book has offered some useful reflections on the ways that workers have narrated their accident and occupational disease and sickness stories. Such personal testimonies and oral histories, I would argue, provide us with privileged insights, giving us the capability of standing on the shoulders of those who directly witnessed or experienced industrial work and its myriad hazards and risks. I hope this has been sustained through subsequent chapters with the personal accounts of those who experienced the modern workplace in the office, the classroom and the NHS. We see the workplace environment through their eyes, giving us a unique lens into the impact, good and bad, that employment had upon workers' bodies. Work could be a joy, conferring a deep sense of achievement and satisfaction, and it could be health-enhancing and

## Jobs and Bodies

positive for well-being, including experiencing low levels of stress. But work could also be a blight, harming and even destroying minds and bodies. And there were many hues of grey in between. For many, losing industrial work was devastating; for others a relief. Extremes of 'ruination' narratives as well as 'escape' or 'liberation' narratives are evident in the oral history testimonies of displaced, redundant workers experiencing plant closures, with degrees of adaptation between.

And the oral testimonies show work was a sensory experience; industrial work was smelt, heard and seen, the labour process taxed muscles and nerves, and the cold, heat, dust and fumes felt through the skin or inhaled into the body. We learn something of the texture of feelings from these often intimate personal reminiscences. This gets us beyond the numbers – the statistics of accidents, injuries, stress-incidents, disabilities and deaths on the job – to a deeper sense of what it actually felt like and how workers themselves thought, voiced and articulated their lived experience and feelings. And how folk navigated and mediated, as best they could, the mutating range of risks and dangers inherent in the modern workplace, from the mid-twentieth-century industrial era to the present contemporary economy. A spectrum of feelings and emotions is evident from the oral interview testimonies, from pride, pleasure and joy, through embarrassment, shame, pain, exhaustion, anguish, sorrow and anger.

Employer and managerial abuse of power played a key role, as we've seen, in the economic violence that blighted industrial communities causing untold pain and suffering from workplace injuries and chronic occupational diseases as profit and production took priority over health and safety. This is clearly and unequivocally evident in our case studies of coal mining respiratory disability and asbestos-related disease, whilst evident elsewhere, for example in the oil industry, chemicals and coastal fishing. Other labour processes and workplaces were certainly more benign. Unpacking this, there appear from the stories to be a range of managerial health and safety regimes, from the compassionate welfarist through to the blatantly inhumane.

Workers pushed back against this and played a part in shaping their working lives, though clearly some had greater capacities to do this than others. The oral testimonies depict workers as not just victims but agents in this process, capable through personal and collective choices (albeit constrained and prescribed) and mobilizations of making a difference. We are told in many work story accounts of acculturation to risk and danger; of ingrained gender roles, of socialization and the use of banter and black humour to mediate and humanize an otherwise brutal working world. We also hear of a damaging workplace culture, where wage and production incentives (such as piecework payments and bonuses) encouraged overworking and where, in some traditional workplaces, behaving like 'real men' necessitated taking risks or eschewing protective clothing. To not conform in the shipyards, steel works or coal mines risked being labelled as effeminate. But we are also told of politicization, mobilization and activism. Clearly trade unions and the wider occupational health and safety movement – including the community-based victims' pressure groups – played significant roles in shielding workers bodies from harm and, when they were struck down, fighting for decent compensation for victims and their families.

Conclusion

Female industrial workers also, however, took risks on the job and faced a wide range of hazards and dangers in the context of a heavily gendered labour market post-1945, where a dangerous work taboo doggedly persisted. Some women's wartime work-health stories are told and reviewed here and an attempt has been made to bring into the analysis a range of female work-health narratives from the post-war era. The importance of the 'double-burden' is again reiterated here, not least as a primary cause of fatigue, stress and breakdown for women, particularly, perhaps where married women were employed in paid work as the 'dual earner' family became more common from the 1960s. And this cause of exhaustion was even more evident in single parent families. And we've also explored the neglected area of women as carers for the victims of accidents, disabling injuries and occupational disease – as evoked, for example, in the oral testimonies of the women with husbands with mesothelioma in the Greater Manchester area. Coping strategies, the oral evidence suggests, ranged widely. Working-class communities also rallied around to provide support that mediated, to a degree, the impacts of toxic workplaces. This is most evident, perhaps in the case of coal-mining communities which were historically conditioned to dealing with death and disability on a monumental scale. And we need to be more sensitive to how occupational health has been and continues to be gendered. It is hoped this book has contributed a little to redressing the serious neglect in research on the health and safety at work experience of women. That research needs to continue for sure and the conversation deepen around the gendered nature of risk and danger on the job.

Hopefully this book will contribute to an ongoing conversation about the role of oral history as a methodology for workplace environment and health and safety history. I believe there is much potential in this approach for expanding and deepening the history of working-class environmentalism. And I hope the book invites reflective dialogue on the importance of a healthy work-life balance, contributing to ongoing critical discussions on the modern-day workplace and the impact of excessive workloads. We need to weigh the positive benefits of 'good' work upon the body against the negative impacts of excessive workloads and productivity surveillance which have led to the current chronic stress at work epidemic in 'burn-out' Britain.

It seems to me that the lessons of the past demand closer attention be paid to the adverse toll occupations have upon our bodies. We need to be more cognizant of how industrial work has left a long and deep legacy of ill-health blighting working-class communities to this day. This embodied legacy of industrialization is sedimented beneath the deleterious mental health impacts of plant closures, losing work and redundancy associated with the accelerated deindustrialization that the UK has undergone since c.1980. Job-induced mental ill health, stress and infection (Covid) need to be more widely recognized as occupational diseases. Many occupations appear today to be near breaking point, with unsustainable workloads. Unhealthy and insecure casual and precarious work is growing exponentially. The concept of 'burn-out' Britain has much credence. This book advocates the need for policies to support transition to a more healthy work-life balance, and tackle the stress epidemic, including the current experimentation with the four-day week, the 'right to disconnect' from information technology (as in France, Ireland and Ontario,

219

## Jobs and Bodies

for example) and more genuine flexible working patterns that suit workers' needs and lifestyles.[1] The aim moving forward surely has to be learning the lessons of the past, recognizing the toll that work has had and can have upon the body and putting health, well-being and people's personal preferences before profit and production.

I have argued the case here that the trade unions in Britain, as elsewhere, have been pivotal sentinels playing a key role in protecting workers, developing and shaping the OHS discourse and improving OHS standards. They provided mutual insurance, bargained collectively with employers on OHS and advocated for effective social protective legislation, educated members on public and occupational health, and supported and extended workers' claims for financial compensation. The unions also played an important role in shifting the OHS discourse from victim-blaming that placed primary culpability upon the behaviour of the individual worker, to identification of structural factors around power, control, competition, profit and new managerial production regimes. The interests of trade unions on OHS progressively deepened, with the 1970s marking a watershed in trade union mobilizing on OHS issues. Initially narrowly focused on the interests of male workers and on safety (acute issues), the movement morphed into a more inclusive strategy in the twentieth century recognizing chronic occupational health issues and incorporating female workers and acknowledging the 'dual burden' of unpaid and paid work so central to the OHS experience of women. Here we see the unions shifting from their earlier historic function as agents representing vested and sectional interests to embracing a broader function as a transformative social movement. The oral testimonies of workers and worker-activists attest to this. In this movement, workers' bodies became part of the struggle for social justice. The unions transitioned towards the modern discourse of shared responsibility and the employers having a 'duty of care'. Gains made in the past were and remain fragile, however, and have been undermined by the collapse in trade union membership and power across high-income economies since the 1970s, associated with deindustrialization, neo-liberal politics and globalization.

The subject demands more attention from researchers. We need to know more, for example, about the part played in the workplace by shop stewards and health and safety representatives and committees in changing work-health cultures, challenging the dual degenerative influences of a productionist and a macho work culture. Questions remain about how trade unions related to and developed alliances with other progressive forces, such as victims' pressure groups, community health and environmental campaigns and politicians (locally and nationally). We also need to understand better how tensions played out between jobs and health, why and how a spectrum of positions existed across different trade unions – craft; industrial; service sector; professional and creative; breakaways – and between the rank and file and union leaderships. Working-class environmentalism expressed through the labour movement merits more attention.

The oral history and other evidence reviewed here clearly indicates that trade unions did clearly make a big difference – and continue to do so. Unions have been resilient and are now much more engaged and invested in OHS than they once were. That said, their capacity to resist and to mediate wider forces has been critically undermined now (2023) that less than a quarter of the UK workforce are union members (down from over 50 per cent), and collective bargaining has dissipated with a return to individual contracts as the norm. These are developments that have occurred to varying degrees across most high-income nations globally. Occupational health and safety standards are being challenged in the process. Physical acute injury and disability are still visible and continue to blight traditional working-class communities, as does chronic disease (including vulnerability to Covid-19) and deteriorating psycho-social health. Tackling health inequalities and ensuring just transitions for deindustrialized and deindustrializing communities remain vital. The current mental health crisis at work, exacerbated by Covid-19, demonstrates how trade union vigilance and action to protect workers is as relevant today as it was a century ago. That is if the impact of work-related harm, sickness and injury is not to be just as devastating in the future as was the impact of industrialization. Workers oral history testimonies bear witness to this. They narrate the myriad ways that work interacts with the body and how this felt and was experienced. Through this lens we get to understand better the prevailing and mutating work-health cultures and the centrality of the trade unions as guardians of workers' health and well-being. We need to acknowledge that a strong trade union movement operating in an economy and society with a robust legal and regulatory framework is essential to protect workers' bodies and maintain civilized health and safety standards on the job.

# NOTES

## Chapter 1

1.  Alan Napier, interviewed by Neil Rafeek, Scottish Oral History Centre Archive (hereafter referred to as SOHC), 017/C43, 31 March 2004.

2.  This builds on a recurring conversation in my work, raised, for example in relation to the wider meanings of work in my book: Arthur McIvor, *Working Lives* (Basingstoke: Palgrave, 2013).

3.  Michelle Winslow and Graham Smith, 'Ethical Challenges in the Oral History of Medicine', in D.A. Ritchie (ed.), *The Oxford Handbook of Oral History* (Oxford: Oxford University Press, 2011), 372–92, here 372.

4.  Joanna Bornat, 'A Second Take: Revisiting Interviews with a Different Purpose', *Oral History* 31, 1 (Spring 2003): 47–53.

5.  For recent examples see Steven High, *One Job Town: Work, Belonging, and Betrayal in Northern Ontario* (Toronto: University of Toronto Press, 2018); Lachlan MacKinnon, *Closing Sysco: Industrial Decline in Atlantic Canada's Steel City* (Toronto: University of Toronto Press, 2020); Robert Storey, 'Beyond the Body Count? Injured Workers in the Aftermath of Deindustrialization', in S. High, L. MacKinnon, and A. Perchard (eds), *The Deindustrialized World: Confronting Ruination in Postindustrial Places* (Vancouver: University of British Columbia Press, 2017), 46–67.

6.  For the best introduction to these conversations in oral history see Lynn Abrams, *Oral History Theory* (London: Routledge, 2010; 2nd ed., 2016). The second edition includes a new chapter on 'trauma and ethics'. See also Paul Thompson with Joanna Bornat, *The Voice of the Past*, 4th ed. (Oxford: Oxford University Press, 2017).

7.  Anna Green has argued this case persuasively. See Anna Green, 'Individual Remembering and "Collective Memory": Theoretical Presuppositions and Contemporary Debates', *Oral History* 32, 2 (2004): 35–44.

8.  Paul Thompson, *The Edwardians* (London: HarperCollins, 1977); Elizabeth Roberts, *A Woman's Place: An Oral History of Working Class Women 1890–1940* (Oxford: Basil Blackwell, 1984).

9.  Linda McCray Beier, *For Their Own Good: The Transformation of English Working Class Health Culture, 1880–1970* (Ohio: Ohio State University Press, 2008).

10. Joanna Bornat, Rob Perks, Paul Thompson, and Jan Walmsley (eds), *Oral History, Health and Welfare* (London: Routledge, 1999).

11. Claudia Malacrida, 'Contested Memories: Efforts of the Powerful to Silence Former Inmates Histories of Life in an Institution for "Mental Defectives"', in K.R. Llewellyn, A. Freund, and N. Reilly (eds), *The Canadian Oral History Reader* (Montreal: McGill-Queens University Press, 2015), 318–34, here 322.

12. E.K. Tsui and A. Starecheski, 'Uses of Oral History and Digital Storytelling in Public Health Research and Practice', *Public Health* 154 (2018): 24–30, here 24.

## Notes

13. McCray Beier, *For Their Own Good*, 9.

14. Jocelyn Cornwall, *Hard Earned Lives: Accounts of Health and Illness from East London* (London: Tavistock, 1990); Ann Oakley, *The Captured Womb: A History of the Medical Care of Pregnant Women* (Oxford: Blackwell, 1984); Jan Walmsley and D. Atkinson, 'Oral History and the History of Learning Disability', in Joanna Bornat, Robert Perks, Paul Thompson and Jan Walmsley (eds), *Oral History, Health and Welfare* (London: Routledge, 2000), 181–204.

15. Alison Haggett, *Desperate Housewives: Neuroses and the Domestic Environment 1945–1970* (Abingdon: Routledge, 2012).

16. For a recent example see Paul Almond and Mike Esbester, *Health and Safety in Contemporary Britain: Society, Legitimacy and Change since 1960* (London: Palgrave Macmillan, 2019).

17. See, for example, Peter Bartrip, *The Way from Dusty Death* (London: Athlone Press, 2001); Geoff Tweedale, *Magic Mineral to Killer Dust* (Oxford: Oxford University Press, 2001); Jock McCulloch and Geoff Tweedale, *Defending the Indefensible: The Global Asbestos Industry and Its Fight for Survival* (Oxford: Oxford University Press, 2008).

18. Michael Bloor, 'No Longer Dying for a Living', *Sociology* 36, 1 (2002): 89–105; Andrew Perchard, *Aluminiumville* (Lancaster: Crucible Books, 2012); David Walker, '"Danger Was Something You Were Brought up wi": Workers' Narratives on Occupational Health and Safety in the Workplace', *Scottish Labour History* 46 (2011): 54–70; Arthur McIvor and Ronald Johnston, *Miners' Lung: A History of Dust Disease in British Coal Mining* (Aldershot: Ashgate, 2007); Ben Rogaly, *Stories from a Migrant City: Living and Working Together in the Shadow of Brexit* (Manchester: Manchester University Press, 2020); William Burns, 'We Just Thought We Were Superhuman: An Oral History of Noise and Piecework in Paisley's Thread Mills, *Labour History* 119 (2020): 173–96; High, *One Job Town*; Storey, 'Beyond the Body Count'; Alessandro Portelli, *They Say in Harlan County: An Oral History* (New York: Oxford University Press, 2010); Suroopa Mukherjee, *Surviving Bhopal* (New York: Palgrave, 2010); Almond and Esbester, *Health and Safety*.

19. See, for example, Luisa Passerini, *Fascism in Popular Memory* (Cambridge: Cambridge University Press, 1987); Alessandro Portelli, *The Death of Luigi Trastulli and Other Stories: Form and Meaning in Oral History* (Albany: SUNY Press, 1991).

20. Classic studies of the 'cultural circuit' include those of Graham Dawson, *Soldier Heroes. British Adventure, Empire and the Imagining of Masculinities* (London: Routledge, 1994); Alistair Thomson, *Anzac Memories: Living with the Legend* (Oxford: Oxford University Press, 1994); Penny Summerfield, *Reconstructing Women's Wartime Lives: Discourse and Subjectivity in Oral Histories of the Second World War* (Manchester: Manchester University Press, 1998).

21. See references in footnote 18 above, and also Christine Walley, *Exit Zero: Family and Class in Post-Industrial Chicago* (Chicago: Chicago University Press, 2013); Tim Strangleman, *Voices of Guinness* (Oxford: Oxford University Press, 2019); L. Feltrin, Alice Mah, and D. Brown, 'Noxious Deindustrialization: Experiences of Precarity and Pollution in Scotland's Petrochemical Capital', *Environment and Planning: Politics and Space* (2022), https://doi.org/10.1177/23996544211056328.

22. Vicky Long, '"A Satisfactory Job Is the Best Psychotherapist": Employment and Mental Health, 1939–60', in Pamela Dale and Joseph Melling (eds), *Mental Illness and Learning Disability since 1850* (Abingdon: Routledge, 2006); Angela Turner, 'From Institutions to Community Care? Learning Disability in Glasgow from c1945' (PhD thesis, University of Strathclyde, 2010). See also the disability and industrial society website: https://www.dis-ind-soc.org.uk/en/index.htm.

## Notes

23. George Orwell, *The Road to Wigan Pier* (London: Victor Gollancz Left Book Club, 1937).

24. Trevor Blackwell and Jeremy Seabrook, *Talking Work: An Oral History* (London: Faber and Faber, 1996), 32.

25. Tracey Carpenter, interviewed by David Welsh, 17 February 2011, for the TUC Britain at Work project. Accessed at http://www.unionhistory.info/britainatwork/display.php.

26. Portelli, *They Say in Harlan County*, 139.

27. Vicky Long, *The Rise and Fall of the Healthy Factory: The Politics of Industrial Health in Britain, 1914–60* (Basingstoke: Ashgate, 2011).

28. Drs J.A. Ryle and W.T. Russell cited in Mel Bartley, 'Coronary Heart Disease', in Paul Weindling (ed.), *The Social History of Occupational Health* (London: Croom Helm, 1985), 137.

29. Duncan Gallie (ed.), *Employment in Britain* (Oxford: Wiley-Blackwell, 1988), 308.

30. Melanie Bunting, *Willing Slaves: How the Overwork Culture Is Ruining Our Lives* (London: HarperCollins, 2004).

31. Carol Wolkowitz, *Bodies at Work* (London: Sage, 2006), 16.

32. For a full discussion see Juliette Pattinson, Arthur McIvor, and Linsey Robb, *Men in Reserve: British Civilian Masculinities in the Second World War* (Manchester: Manchester University Press, 2017), Chapters 4 and 5.

33. See Peter Bartrip, *Workmen's Compensation in Twentieth Century Britain: Law, History and Social Policy* (Aldershot: Gower Publishing, 1987).

34. McIvor and Johnston, *Miners' Lung*, 100–5.

35. J.L. Williams, *Accidents and Ill-Health at Work* (London: Staples Press, 1960), 383–4.

36. *Annual Report of the Factory Inspectorate* for 1950, 40–1.

37. See Long, *The Rise and Fall of the Healthy Factory*, for a discussion of the campaigning of the TUC.

38. Arthur McIvor, *A History of Work in Britain, 1880–1950* (Basingstoke: Palgrave, 2001), 132; Gallie, *Employment in Britain*, 302–3. We have no fully reliable figures for non-fatal injuries because of serious under-reporting.

39. Emma Newlands, *Civilians into Soldiers: The British Male Military Body in the Second World War* (Manchester: Manchester University Press, 2014).

40. *Registrar Generals Decennial Supplement on Occupational Mortality*, England and Wales, 1951, Pt 2, Vol 1, HMSO, 1958, 145–9.

41. Martin, cited in R. Fraser (ed.), *Work 2: Twenty Personal Accounts* (Harmondsworth: Penguin, 1969), 82.

42. Martin, cited in Fraser, *Work 2*, 86.

43. Kevin Topham, interviewed 18 October 2000; Lives in the Oil Industry Archive, British Library Sound Archive, F10593/A.

44. Ralph Glasser, *Growing Up in the Gorbals* (London: Pan, 1987), 5.

45. Dorothy Radwanski, interviewed by Neil Rafeek (nd, but *c.* 2001–2), SOHC 018/B6.

46. Ian Kellie, interviewed by Neil Rafeek, 5 December 2001, SOHC 018/B1.

47. Perchard, *Aluminiumville*.

48. *Glasgow Herald*, 31 January 1968.

49. Cited in Fraser, *Work 2*, 95.

## Notes

50. Source: *Annual Report of the Factory Inspectorate*, 1950, 37; see McIvor, *Working Lives*, 169.

51. Ronald Johnston and Arthur McIvor, *Lethal Work* (East Linton: Tuckwell Press, 2000), 58; Theo Nichols, *The Sociology of Industrial Injury* (London: Mansell Publishing, 1997); Theo Nichols, 'Death and Injury at Work: A Sociological Approach', in Norma Daykin and Lesley Doyal (eds), *Health and Work: Critical Perspectives* (Basingstoke: Palgrave Macmillan, 1999), 97–100; A.M. Robinson and C. Smallman, 'The Contemporary British Workplace: A Safer and Healthier Place?' *Work Employment Society* 20 (2006): 87–107.

52. *Annual Report of the Factory Inspectorate*, 1950, 59.

53. Dr Barnett Stross, Labour MP and radiologist; *Hansard*, 30 July 1958, 1540–1.

54. David Walker, 'Occupational Health and Safety in the British Chemical Industry, 1914–1974' (PhD thesis, University of Strathclyde, 2007).

55. Williams, *Accidents and Ill-Health*, 401–6.

56. Donald Hunter, *Health in Industry* (Harmondsworth: Penguin, 1959), 20.

57. E. Hammond, *An Analysis of Regional Economic and Social Statistics* (London: Her Majesty's Stationery Office, 1968), tables 5.2., 3–5.

58. Health and Safety Executive (HSE), *British Partnership in Health and Safety*, 2006.

59. *Scott Lithgow House Magazine*, Summer 1977, cited in Martin Bellamy, *The Shipbuilders* (Edinburgh: Berlinn, 2001), 74.

60. Annie Phizacklea, 'Gender, Racism and Occupational Segregation', in Sylvia Walby (ed.), *Gender Segregation at Work* (Milton Keynes: Open University Press, 1988); Annie Phizacklea and Robert Miles, *Labour and Racism* (London: Routledge and Kegan Paul, 1980); and see 'the colour bar', Chapter 4 in McIvor, *Working Lives*.

61. At 85 per cent greater than the average SMR from lung cancer: *Registrar Generals Report*, 1951, 144.

62. *Annual Report of the Factory Inspectorate*, for 1950, 47–50; 63.

63. Ibid. Appendix II, 'All Reported Accidents, 1950'.

64. Cited in Blackwell and Seabrook, *Talking Work*, 145.

65. David Marshall, interviewed by Ronnie Johnston, 29 June 2000 (SOHC 017/C7).

66. Bert Smith, interviewed by Ronnie Johnston, 5 July 2000 (SOHC 017/C14) – and see McIvor and Johnston, *Miners' Lung* for a full discussion.

67. SOHC Asbestos Interview A26 (anonymous), conducted in 1999 by Ronnie Johnston and Arthur McIvor (SOHC 016/A26).

68. Ibid.

69. SOHC Asbestos Interview A9 (anonymous) conducted 1 February 1999 by Ronnie Johnston (SOHC 016/A9).

70. Portelli, *They Say in Harlan County*, 143.

71. Scott McCabe, interviewed by Arthur McIvor, 24 March 2022 (SOHC Archive; currently uncatalogued).

72. Karen Messing, *One Eyed Science: Occupational Health and Women Workers* (Philadelphia: Temple University Press, 1998), xviii. See also Karen Messing, *Bent Out of Shape: Shame, Solidarity and Women's Bodies at Work* (Toronto: Between the Lines, 2021).

73. Messing, *One Eyed Science*, 12.

74. Ibid., 13–15.

## Notes

75. For a UK perspective on this, see Sylvia Walby, *Patriarchy at Work: Patriarchal and Capitalist Relations in Employment* (Minneapolis: University of Minnesota Press, 1986); McIvor, *A History of Work*, 174–84.

76. Claire Williams, 'Women and Occupational Health and Safety: From Narratives of Danger to Invisibility', *Labour History* 73 (November 1997): 30–52, here 31.

77. The persistence of this 'macho' dangerous work taboo is discussed in Ronnie Johnston and Arthur McIvor, 'Dangerous Work, Hard Men and Broken Bodies: Masculinity in the Clydeside Heavy Industries', *Labour History Review* 69, 2 (August 2004): 135–53.

78. Williams, 'Women and Occupational Health', 45.

79. Ibid., 46–8.

80. For a fuller discussion, see McIvor, *A History of Work*, 193–5.

81. See Geoff Tweedale and P. Hansen, 'Protecting the Workers: The Medical Board and the Asbestos Industry, 1930s–1960s', *Medical History* 42 (1998): 439–57.

82. As in the infamous tragic case of Charlie Coyle in 1955–6; see Johnston and McIvor, *Lethal Work*, 7–8.

83. Alan Dembe, *Occupation and Disease* (New Haven: Yale University Press, 1996); and for sex workers see G. Scambler and A. Scambler, 'Health and Work in the Sex Industry', in Norma Daykin and Lesley Doyal (eds), *Health and Work: Critical Perspectives* (Basingstoke: Macmillan Press, 1999), 71–85.

84. See for example The British Safety Council, *Common Causes of Factory Accidents, c.1970* (pamphlet in the Royal Society for the Prevention of Accidents Archive; undated); Nichols, 'Death and Injury at Work', 86–90.

85. P.I. Powell, M. Hale, J. Martin, and M. Simon, *200 Accidents: A Shop Floor Study of Their Causes* (London: National Institute of Industrial Psychology, 1971).

86. Nichols, 'Death and Injury at Work', 90; See also Vincent Navarro and D. Berman (eds), *Health and Work under Capitalism: An International Perspective* (Farmington, NY: Routledge, 1983) and Hugh Beynon and Ray Hudson, *The Shadow of the Mine* (London: Verso, 2021).

87. See, for example, Joseph Melling, 'The Risks of Working and the Risks of Not Working: Trade Unions, Employers and Responses to the Risk of Occupational Illness in British Industry, c1890–1940s', *ESRC Centre for Analysis of Risk and Regulation Discussion Paper* 12 (2003): 14–34; Ronald Johnston and Arthur McIvor, 'Marginalising the Body at Work? Employers' Occupational Health Strategies and Occupational Medicine in Scotland *c.1930–1974*', *Social History of Medicine* 21, 1 (2008): 127–44.

88. Ibid., 136.

89. *Report of Her Majesty's Inspector of Mines, Scottish Division*, for 1953, 5.

90. *Report of Her Majesty's Inspector of Mines, Scottish Division*, for 1949, 36; 1952, 5.

91. Abe Moffat, *My Life with the Miners* (London: Lawrence and Wishart, 1965), 239.

92. John McKean, interviewed by Ronnie Johnston, 29 June 2000 (SOHC Interview 017/C10).

93. Nichols, *The Sociology of Industrial Injury*.

94. See Mathias Beck, John Foster, and Charles Woolfson, *Paying for the Piper: Capital and Labour in Britain's Offshore Oil Industry* (London: Mansell, 1996); Terry Brotherstone and Hugo Manson, 'North Sea Oil, Its Narratives and Its History', *Northern Scotland* 27 (2007): 15–41.

95. Scott McCabe, interviewed by Arthur McIvor, 24 March 2022 (SOHC Archive; currently uncatalogued).

# Notes

96. Williams, *Accidents at Work*, 440–1; the role of trade unions and voluntary organizations in OHS is explored in more depth in the last chapter of this book.

97. Williams, *Accidents at Work*, 5; Helen Jones, 'An Inspector Calls' in Weindling, *The Social History of Occupational Health*.

98. Williams, *Accidents at Work*, 5.

99. Long, *The Rise and Fall of the Healthy Factory*.

100. Williams, *Accidents at Work*, 413.

101. Walker, 'Occupational Health and Safety' (PhD), 141.

102. See Tweedale, *Magic Mineral to Killer Dust*, 174–5.

103. http://www.hse.gov.uk/statistics/history/fatal.htm.

104. Phil Taylor and L. Connelly, 'Before the Disaster: Health, Safety and Working Conditions at a Plastics Factory', *Work, Employment & Society* 23, 1 (2009): 160–8.

105. For a wider discussion, based on a wide range of sources, including forty oral interviews with regulators, safety professionals, policy-makers, employers and six trade union leaders working in OHS see Almond and Esbester, *Health and Safety*.

106. HSWA, Section 2(1); see D. Eva and R. Oswald, *Health and Safety at Work* (London: Pan, 1981), 43.

107. Ibid., 43–4.

108. Beck, Foster, and Woolfson, *Paying for the Piper*, 56–63.

109. Eva and Oswald, *Health and Safety*, 56. No employers were jailed under the HSWA before the 1990s.

110. SOHC Asbestos Interview A6 (anonymous) conducted in 1999 by Ronnie Johnston (SOHC 016/A6).

111. Alan Dalton, *Safety, Health and Environmental Hazards at the Workplace* (London: Cassell, 1998); Charles Woolfson and Mathias Beck, *Corporate Social Responsibility Failures in the Oil Industry* (New York: Amityville, 2005); and see the Corporate Crime & Governance website: http://www.gla.ac.uk/faculties/socialsciences/corpcrime/links.htm.

112. Almond and Esbester, *Health and Safety*, 194.

113. http://www.hse.gov.uk/statistics/european/fatal.htm; McIvor, *Working Lives*, 183.

114. HSE Consultation Document, 1998, 4. And see Almond and Esbester, *Health and Safety*.

115. Andrew Watterson, 'Why We Still Have "Old" Epidemics and "Endemics" in Occupational Health: Policy and Practice Failures and Some Possible Solutions', in Daykin and Doyal, *Health and Work*, 107–26, here 107.

116. Ibid.

117. Mukherjee, *Surviving Bhopal*; see also Paul Shrivastava, *Bhopal, Anatomy of a Crisis* (London: Chapman Publishing, 1992).

118. Randy Hodson, *Dignity at Work* (Cambridge: Cambridge University Press, 2001), 117.

119. K. Geiser, 'Health Hazards in the Microelectronics Industry', *International Journal of Health Services* 16, 1 (1986): 105–20.

120. Williams, *Accidents at Work*, 33.

121. See, for example, Ann Borsay, *Disability and Social Policy in Britain since 1750: A History of Exclusion* (Basingstoke: Palgrave, 2005).

227

## Notes

122. A stand-out exception addressing this is the disability and industrial society project. See David M. Turner and Daniel Blackie, *Disability in the Industrial Revolution: Physical Impairment in British Coalmining, 1780–1880* (Manchester: Manchester University Press, 2018); Kirsti Bohata, Alexandra Jones, Mike Mantin, and Steven Thompson, *Disability in Industrial Britain: A Cultural and Literary History of Impairment in the Coal Industry* (Manchester: Manchester University Press, 2020).

123. For a recent study, see Beynon and Hudson, *The Shadow of the Mine*.

124. See Robinson and Smallman, 'The Contemporary British Workplace', 87–107.

## Chapter 2

1. John Allan, interviewed by Linsey Robb, 7 November 2011 (SOHC Archive 50/09).

2. Fred and Doreen Hibbs, interviewed by Dave Welsh and Rima Joebear, 6 July 2010. Trades Union Congress, Britain at Work Oral History Project. Accessed at http://www.unionhistory.info/britainatwork/display.php.

3. Strangleman, *Voices of Guinness*, 83.

4. For example see Bornat, Perks, Thompson, and Walmsley (eds), *Oral History, Health and Welfare*; McCray Beier, *For Their Own Good*.

5. See High, *One Job Town*.

6. See Walker, 'Danger Was Something You Were Brought up wi', 46, 54–70.

7. BBC People's War Archive: Kathy Hind (Lincoln area), Article ID: A4625165, contributed on 30 July 2005.

8. Willie Dewar, interviewed by Arthur McIvor, 9 December 2008 (SOHC Archive 50/04).

9. Effie Anderson, interviewed by Ian MacDougall, 28 November 1996, SWPHT collection (SOHC Archive).

10. Thomas McMurdo, interviewed by Ronnie Johnston, 11 July 2000 (SOHC 017/C20).

11. Tommy Coulter, interviewed by Neil Rafeek and Hilary Young, 12 January 2005 (SOHC 017/C21).

12. Steven High, *One Job Town*, 102; see also Alessandro Portelli, *They Say in Harlan County: An Oral History* (Oxford: Oxford University Press, 2010).

13. John Foley, interviewed by David Bradley, 28 April 2010 (SOHC Archive).

14. Mr Sloan, interviewed 14 May 1991, Motherwell Heritage Centre, Interview T089.

15. SOHC Asbestos Interview A19 (anonymous) conducted 1 February 1999 by Ronnie Johnston (SOHC 016/A19).

16. See Johnston and McIvor, *Lethal Work*, 63–111; Walker, 2011, 63.

17. See Emma Copestake's PhD, 'Laughing through the Pain? Occupational Wellbeing on the Waterfront in Liverpool c.1964–1998' (University of Liverpool, 2022).

18. Walker, 'Danger Was Something', 62–3.

19. John Hopkins, interviewed by Alison Clague, 10 January 2007 for Warwickshire County Council's project Working Lives: Memories of Work and Industry in Nuneaton and Bedworth. Accessed at https://library.warwickshire.gov.uk/iguana/www.main.cls?surl=workinglives.

# Notes

20. Emma Taaffe, 'We Suffered in Silence': Health and Safety at Chatham Dockyard, 1945 to 1984. Evaluating the causes and management of occupational hazards, relating especially to asbestos, ionising radiation and masculinity (PhD thesis, University of Hull, 2013), 199–200.

21. Walker, 'Danger Was Something', 63.

22. Ibid., 63–4.

23. Vera Rigby, interviewed by Nigel Ingham, 13 October 2014 (Manchester Asbestos Group Collection, SOHC Archive).

24. See, for example, William Burns, 'We Just Thought We Were Superhuman: An Oral History of Noise and Piecework in Paisley's Thread Mills', *Labour History* 119 (2020): 173–96.

25. Rob Nixon, *Slow Violence and the Environmentalism of the Poor* (Cambridge, MA: Harvard University Press, 2013).

26. Husband Mike Eason's testimony read by Barbara Eason interviewed by Nigel Ingham, 27 October 2014 (Manchester Asbestos Group, SOHC).

27. Anonymous, interviewed by Arthur McIvor, 1 June 1999, (SOHC 016/A26).

28. Michele Abendstern, Christine Hallett, and Lesley Wade, 'Flouting the Law: Women and the Hazards of Cleaning Moving Machinery in the Cotton Industry, 1930–1970', *Oral History* 33, 2 (2005): 69–78.

29. SOHC Asbestos Interview A19 (anonymous) 1 February 1999 by Ronnie Johnston (SOHC 016/A19).

30. Clyde Shipbuilding Association, *Minutes*, 20 December 1967 (TD 241/12/1136).

31. SOHC Asbestos Interviews A5 and A11 (anonymous) by Ronnie Johnston (SOHC 016/A5; 016/A11).

32. SOHC Asbestos Interview A5 (anonymous) by Ronnie Johnston (SOHC 016/A5).

33. SOHC Asbestos Interviews A4 (anonymous) by Ronnie Johnston (SOHC 016/A4).

34. Lauren Ross, interviewed by Nigel Ingham, 15 October 2014 (Manchester Asbestos Group, SOHC).

35. Peter Lancaster, interviewed by Nigel Ingham, 26 January 2015 (Manchester Asbestos Group, SOHC).

36. Ibid.

37. SOHC Asbestos Interview A16 (anonymous) by Ronnie Johnston (SOHC 016/A16).

38. SOHC Asbestos Interviews A22 (anonymous) by Ronnie Johnston (SOHC 016/A22).

39. Taaffe, 'We Suffered in Silence', 271–2.

40. K. Paap, *Working Construction: Why White Working-Class Men Put Themselves – and the Labor Movement – in Harm's Way* (Ithaca: Cornell University Press, 2006). See also D. Iacuone, '"Real Men Are Tough Guys": Hegemonic Masculinity and Safety in the Construction Industry', *The Journal of Men's Studies* 13, 2 (2005).

41. Taaffe, 'We Suffered in Silence', 122–3.

42. Ibid., 123.

43. Named after Soviet worker Alexey Stakhanov, a Stakhanovite was an exceptionally hard-working person, zealously exceeding production targets.

44. Interviewed by Ronnie Johnston, 1 February 1999, SOHC 016/A9.

45. Portelli, *They Say in Harlan County*, 139, 143.

# Notes

46. Cited in David Allen and Laurie Kazan-Allen, *India's Asbestos Time Bomb* (International Ban Asbestos Secretariat, online publication, 2008), 34. Accessed at http://ibasecretariat.org/india_asb_time_bomb.pdf.

47. Allen and Kazan-Allen, *India's Asbestos Time Bomb*, 7. Indian casual workers were also not given the regular medical check-ups that permanent workers received.

48. Interviewed by Ronnie Johnston, 3 February 1999, SOHC 016/A18.

49. Richard Fitzpatrick, interviewed by David Walker, 13 August 2004 (SOHC Archive).

50. SOHC Asbestos Interviews A23 (anonymous) by Ronnie Johnston and Arthur McIvor, 1 December 1999 (SOHC 016/A23).

51. Jock McCulloch and Geoff Tweedale, *Defending the Indefensible: The Global Asbestos Industry and Its Fight for Survival* (Oxford: Oxford University Press, 2008) 118.

52. Jenny Constant, born Malvern 1946, interviewed 10 July, 13 August, 2 September 2013. British Library Sound Archive, Pioneering Women Collection, Shelf mark: C1379/98.

53. Walker, 'Danger Was Something', 66.

54. Peter Dawson, interviewed by Emma Taaffe, in Taaffe, 'We Suffered in Silence', 126.

55. Walker, 'Danger Was Something', 65.

56. Ibid.

57. Peter Lancaster, interviewed by Nigel Ingham, 26 January 2015 (Manchester Asbestos Group, SOHC).

58. SOHC Asbestos Interview A19 (anonymous) by Ronnie Johnston (SOHC 016/A19).

59. Phyllis Craig, interviewed by Arthur McIvor, 28 January 2013 (SOHC Archive 016/35).

60. Nicky Wilson, 'Witness Seminar', chaired by Arthur McIvor, 28 April 2014 (SOHC Archive).

61. Raymond Williams, *Marxism and Literature* (Oxford: Oxford University Press, 1977). John Kirk and Tim Strangleman are amongst those who apply these ideas. See John Kirk, 'Coming to the End of the Line? Identity, Work and Structures of Feeling', *Oral History* 36, 2 (2008); Strangleman, *Voices of Guinness*, 103.

62. Catherine Kohler Riessman, *Narrative Analysis* (Newbury Park, CA: Sage Publications, 1993).

63. Juliette Pattinson, Arthur McIvor, and Linsey Robb, *Men in Reserve: British Civilian Masculinities in the Second World War* (Manchester: Manchester University Press, 2017).

64. Fred Clark, interviewed for the TUC 'Workers' War' project in 2005, http://www.unionhistory.info/workerswar/voices.php.

65. Derek Sims, interviewed by Linsey Robb, 20 February 2013 (SOHC 050/012).

66. D.C.M. Howe, interviewed by the Imperial War Museum, 1 May 1990 (IWM SA 12882).

67. Richard Fitzpatrick, interviewed by David Walker, 13 August 2004 (SOHC).

68. William Ryder, interviewed by the Imperial War Museum, 10 September 1999 (IWM SA 19662).

69. Willie Dewar, interviewed by Arthur McIvor, 9 December 2008 (SOHC 050/04).

70. Thomas Stewart, interviewed 10 June 1996, *2000 Glasgow Lives Project*, Glasgow Museums.

71. Robert W. Connell, *The Men and the Boys* (Cambridge: Polity Press, 2000).

72. Joe Kenyon, *A Passion for Justice* (Nottingham: Trent Editions, 2003).

73. Wight, *Workers Not Wasters*.

# Notes

74. Alison Chand, 'Same Interviewee, Different Interviewer: Researching Intersubjectivity in Studies of the Reserved Occupations in the Second World War', *The Oral History Review*, 48, 1, 2021, 3–19. https://doi.org/10.1080/00940798.2021.1879600. And see the author (Chand) interview at https://oralhistoryreview.org/ohr-authors/author-interview-alison-chand/.

75. Stewart McIntosh, interviewed by Neil Rafeek, 6 June 2003 (SOHC Archive).

76. Ronald Johnston and Arthur McIvor, 'Marginalising the Body at Work? Employers' Occupational Health Strategies and Occupational Medicine in Scotland c.1930–1974', *Social History of Medicine* 21, 1 (2008): 127–44.

77. Taaffe, 'We Suffered in Silence', 295. In support of this, Taaffe cites Hugh Beynon's classic study, *Working for Ford* (London: Allen Lane, 1973).

78. *Glasgow Herald*, 24 February 1967.

79. Clyde Shipbuilding Association, *Minutes*, 20 December 1967.

80. SOHC Asbestos Interview A14 (anonymous) by Ronnie Johnston (SOHC 016/A14).

81. Michael King, interviewed by Nigel Ingham, 7 January 2015 (SOHC Archive).

82. See Ronald Johnston and Arthur McIvor, *Lethal Work: A History of the Asbestos Tragedy in Scotland* (East Linton: Tuckwell Press, 2000), 152–8.

83. Eric Jonkheere, interviewed by Arthur McIvor, 21 February 2013 (SOHC Archive).

84. See Jessica van Horssen, *A Town Called Asbestos: Environmental Contamination, Health, and Resilience in a Resource Community* (Vancouver: University of British Columbia Press, 2016).

85. Lesley Doyal, *What Makes Women Sick* (Basingstoke: Macmillan, 1995), 153–4.

86. Taaffe, 'We Suffered in Silence', 269.

87. Cited in Burns, 'We Just Thought We Were Superhuman', 176.

88. Janet Chapman, interviewed by Ian MacDougall, 2 July 1999, SWPHT Collection (SOHC Archive).

89. Doyal, *What Makes Women Sick*, 158.

90. Edna McDonald (nee Moon), born 1921, Workington, interviewed 6 December 1991. British Library Sound Archive, National Life Story Collection: Lives in Steel, Shelf mark: C532/041.

91. Ibid.

92. Ibid.

93. Ibid.

94. Betty Saffill (nee Tyson), born 1922, Workington, interviewed 7 December 1991, British Library Sound Archive, National Life Story Collection: Lives in Steel, Shelf mark: C532/043.

95. SOHC Asbestos Interview A22 (anonymous) by Ronnie Johnston (SOHC 016/A22). This female respondent was at the time of interview suffering from the ARD pleural thickening.

96. SOHC Asbestos Interview A23 (anonymous) by Ronnie Johnston (SOHC 016/A23).

97. SOHC Asbestos Interview A22 (anonymous) by Ronnie Johnston (SOHC 016/22).

98. *Evening Times*, 16 June 1993.

99. Mari A.Williams, *A Forgotten Army: Female Munitions Workers of South Wales, 1939–1945* (Cardiff: University of Wales Press, 2002).

100. Williams, *A Forgotten Army*, 84.

# Notes

101. Ibid.

102. Ibid., 84–5.

103. Ibid., 85.

104. Ibid., 88–9.

105. Mrs Maureen Holdsworth (Hapton, Nelson, Lancs), Article ID: A3956349, Contributed 26 April 2005 by Lancshomeguard. BBC People's War Archive. Accessed at https://www.bbc.co.uk/history/ww2peopleswar/.

106. See Penny Summerfield, *Reconstructing Women's Wartime Lives: Discourse and Subjectivity in Oral Histories of the Second World War* (Manchester: Manchester University Press, 1998) and Alison Chand, *Masculinities on Clydeside: Men in Reserved Occupations during the Second World War* (Edinburgh: Edinburgh University Press, 2016).

107. See Abendstern, Hallett, and Wade, 'Flouting the Law'.

108. Lucy Baker, born 1924, cited in Abendstern, Hallett, and Wade, 'Flouting the Law', 73.

109. Burns, 'We Just Thought We Were Superhuman', 173.

110. Ibid., 181.

111. Ibid., 181, 190.

112. Ibid., 194–5.

113. Vera Rigby, interviewed by Nigel Ingham, 13 October 2014 (SOHC Archive).

114. Tracy Carpenter, interviewed by David Welsh, 17 February 2011 for the TUC Britain at Work project. Accessed at http://www.unionhistory.info/britainatwork/resources/audio.php.

115. Pam Singer, interviewed by David Welsh and Rima Joebear, 17 June 2010. TUC Britain at Work Oral History Project. Accessed at http://www.unionhistory.info/britainatwork/display.php.

116. Cited in Taaffe, 'We Suffered in Silence', 177.

117. Interview with Sally Groves by David Welsh and Rima Joebear on 25 March 2013. TUC Britain at Work Oral History Project. Accessed at http://www.unionhistory.info/britainatwork/display.php.

118. Mary Spicer, interviewed by Alison Clague, 7 July 2006, for Warwickshire County Council's project Working Lives: Memories of Work and Industry in Nuneaton and Bedworth. Accessed at https://library.warwickshire.gov.uk/iguana/www.main.cls?surl=workinglives.

119. Joyce Igo, born Castletown, Sunderland, 1923, interviewed 23 October 1991, British Library Sound Archive, National Life Story Collection: Lives in Steel, Shelf mark: C532/023.

120. Ibid.

121. Ibid.

122. Sheila Emmanuel, interviewed by Myrna Shoa, 14 January 2011. TUC Britain at Work Oral History Project. Accessed at http://www.unionhistory.info/britainatwork/display.php.

123. Eileen Magee, interviewed by David Welsh and Rima Joebear on 31 May 2011. TUC Britain at Work Oral History Project. Accessed at http://www.unionhistory.info/britainatwork/display.php.

124. Joyce Igo, born Castletown, Sunderland, 1923, interviewed 23 October 1991, British Library Sound Archive, National Life Story Collection: Lives in Steel, Shelf mark: C532/023.

## Notes

125. SOHC Asbestos Interview A6 (anonymous) by Ronnie Johnston (SOHC 016/A6).

126. Lauren Ross, interviewed by Nigel Ingham, 15 October 2014 (Manchester Asbestos Group, SOHC).

127. Taaffe, 'We Suffered in Silence', 171–2.

128. High, *One Job Town*, 103.

129. Scott McCabe, interviewed by Arthur McIvor, 24 March 2022 (SOHC Archive).

130. Scott McCabe, interviewed by Arthur McIvor, 24 March 2022 (SOHC Archive). And on higher cancer and heart disease rates amongst firefighters, see *The Guardian*, 10 January 2023. Accessed at https://www.theguardian.com/uk-news/2023/jan/10/firefighters-cancer-toxic-chemicals-study?CMP=Share_iOSApp_Other.

## Chapter 3

1. Frederick Brady, interviewed by Virtue Jones, 1999, for the Millenium Memory Bank Observing the 1980s Project. BLSA, shelf mark C900/11057.

2. Wing-Chung Ho, *Occupational Health and Social Estrangement in China* (Manchester: Manchester University Press, 2017).

3. Bohata, Jones, Mantin, and Thompson, *Disability in Industrial Britain*; Turner and Blackie, *Disability in the Industrial Revolution*; Angela Turner and Arthur McIvor, '"Bottom Dog Men": Disability, Social Welfare and Advocacy in the Scottish Coalfields in the Interwar Years, 1918–1939' [open access], *Scottish Historical Review* 96, 2 (2017): 187–213.

4. Mildred Blaxter, *The Meaning of Disability* (London: Heinemann, 1976).

5. From the Mass Observation Archive, FR 1498, 'Blaina Report', 41–60, cited in Williams, *A Forgotten Army*, 96.

6. Ibid., 93.

7. Dr R.I. McCallum, 'Pneumoconiosis and the Coalfields of Durham and Northumberland', *Transactions of the Institute of Mining Engineers* 113 (1953–4): 105.

8. John Jones, interviewed by Susan Morrison, 15 September 2002, SOHC 017/C27. A 'hard-heading man' is one working on building tunnels and roadways underground.

9. Blaxter, *The Meaning of Disability*; See also Colin Barnes and Geoff Mercer, *Disability* (Cambridge: Polity Press, 2003), 63.

10. Tommy Coulter, interviewed by Neil Rafeek and Hilary Young (SOHC Archive) 017/C21.

11. William Dunsmore, interviewed by Ronald Johnston, 11 July 2000 (SOHC Archive) 017/C16.

12. Marshall Wylde, interviewed by Neil Rafeek, 10 March 2004 (SOHC 017/C35).

13. George Bolton, interviewed by Neil Rafeek and Hilary Young, 12 January 2005 (SOHC 017/C23).

14. David Carruthers, interviewed by Neil Rafeek and Hilary Young, 12 January 2005, (SOHC 017/C23); See also Harry Steel, interviewed by Ronnie Johnston, 29 June 2000 (SOHC 017/C9).

15. For more on CISWO, see Chapter 7.

16. David Guy, interviewed by Neil Rafeek, 8 March 2004 (SOHC 017/C44).

17. Cited in *Saga Magazine*, March 1998, at www.deadline.demon.co.uk/archive/saga/980301.htm.

233

# Notes

18. Moffat, *My Life with the Miners*, 232.

19. John McKean, interviewed by Ronnie Johnston, 29 June 2000, SOHC Interview 017/C10. Another interviewee commented that he was impotent as a result of his occupation – see SOHC Asbestos Interviews (anonymous), SOHC 016/A14.

20. Joanna Bourke, *Working Class Cultures* (London: Routledge, 1994), 132–3.

21. Billy Affleck, interviewed by Arthur McIvor and Ronald Johnston, 19 June 2000 (SOHC 017/C2).

22. Pat Ferguson, interviewed by Ronnie Johnston, 5 July 2000 (SOHC 017/C12).

23. Cited in *Saga Magazine*, March 1998, at www.deadline.demon.co.uk/archive/saga/980301.htm.

24. Bert Smith, interviewed by Ronnie Johnston, 5 July 2000, SOHC Interview 017/C14.

25. Frederick Hall, interviewed by Neil Rafeek, 29 March 2004, SOHC 017/C41.

26. George Burns, interviewed by Neil Rafeek, 28 April 2004, SOHC 017/C40.

27. Blaxter, *The Meaning of Disability*.

28. Anonymous (asbestos project), interviewed by Ronnie Johnston, 15 March 1999, SOHC 016/A13.

29. See Johnston and McIvor, *Lethal Work*, 177–208.

30. Barry Castleman and Geoffrey Tweedale, 'The Struggle for Compensation for Asbestos-Related Diseases and the Banning of Asbestos', in Christopher Sellers and Joseph Melling (eds), *Dangerous Trade: Histories of Industrial Hazard across a Globalising World* (Philadelphia: Temple, 2012), 181–94, here 187.

31. Janet Ross, interviewed by Graeme Naylor, 30 December 2003, (Inverclyde Oral History Project, SOHC 021/3).

32. Anonymous (asbestos project), interviewed by Ronnie Johnston (SOHC 016/A7).

33. Julie Blair, interviewed by Graeme Naylor, 21 October 2003 (Inverclyde Oral History Project, SOHC 021/1).

34. Ibid.

35. Wight, *Workers Not Wasters*.

36. Phyllis Craig, interviewed by Arthur McIvor, 28 January 2013 (SOHC 016/A35).

37. Margaret Poole, interviewed by Nigel Ingham, 21 January 2015, (Manchester Asbestos Victims Group Collection, SOHC Archive).

38. Vera Rigby, interviewed by Nigel Ingham, 13 October 2014 (Manchester Asbestos Victims Group Collection, SOHC Archive).

39. Helen Clayson, 'The Experience of Mesothelioma in Northern England' (MD thesis, University of Sheffield, 2007), 4, 30.

40. Ibid., 131–67.

41. Ibid., 30, 135–6, 252–3. A diagnosis of pleural plaques, or pleural thickening, provided evidence of asbestos exposure and was the cause of much 'anticipatory anxiety'. However, it was rare for compensation systems to provide any benefits for these conditions in their own right.

42. Cited in David Allen and Laurie Kazan-Allen, *India's Asbestos Time Bomb* (2008), 5. Accessed at http://ibasecretariat.org/india_asb_time_bomb.pdf.

43. Mrs. T, cited in Clayson, *Experience of Mesothelioma*, 149.

44. Mr. J, cited in Clayson, *Experience of Mesothelioma*, 149.

## Notes

45. Phyllis Craig, interviewed by Arthur McIvor, 28 January 2013 (SOHC 016/A35).

46. Tommy Gorman, 'Women and Asbestos', in Tommy Gorman (ed.), *Clydebank: Asbestos, the Unwanted Legacy* (Glasgow: Clydeside Press, 2000), 127–37.

47. Ibid., 131.

48. Ibid., 137.

49. Former and existing female teachers born between 1935 and 1974 have a 40 per cent higher risk of mesothelioma. See *The Observer*, 15 January 2023.

50. Kirk, 'Coming to the End of the Line?', 49, 51.

51. Clayson, *Experience of Mesothelioma*, 253.

52. Anonymous (asbestos project), interviewed by Ronnie Johnston, 22 March 1999 (SOHC 016/A20).

53. Mr. I, cited in Clayson, *Experience of Mesothelioma*, 140.

54. Anonymous (asbestos project), interviewed by Ronnie Johnston (SOHC 016/A12).

55. Anonymous (asbestos project), interviewed by Ronnie Johnston, 22 December 1998, SOHC 016/A2.

56. Tommy Nelson, interview on *Hidden Hazard, Forgotten Victims* (Clydeside Action on Asbestos video, 1995).

57. Anonymous (asbestos project), interviewed by Ronnie Johnston (SOHC 016/A9).

58. Anonymous (asbestos project), interviewed by Ronnie Johnston (SOHC 016/A20).

59. Anonymous (asbestos project), interviewed by Ronnie Johnston (SOHC 016/A12).

60. Anonymous (asbestos project), interviewed by Ronnie Johnston (SOHC 016/A13).

61. The Mesothelioma Action Group for wives of victims had been set up in 2005 by the Greater Manchester Asbestos Victims Support Group.

62. Margaret Poole, interviewed by Nigel Ingham, 21 January 2015 (Manchester Asbestos Group, SOHC).

63. Lauren Ross, interviewed by Nigel Ingham, 15 October 2014 (Manchester Asbestos Group, SOHC).

64. Ibid.

65. Ibid.

66. Mavis Tong, interviewed by Nigel Ingham, 6 February 2015 (Manchester Asbestos Group, SOHC).

67. Margaret Poole, interviewed by Nigel Ingham, 21 January 2015 (Manchester Asbestos Group, SOHC).

68. Barbara Eason, interviewed by Nigel Ingham, 27 October 2014.

69. Ibid.

70. Ibid.

71. Vera Rigby, interviewed by Nigel Ingham, 13 October 2014.

72. Margaret Poole, interviewed by Nigel Ingham, 21 January 2015.

73. Mavis Tong, interviewed by Nigel Ingham, 6 February 2015.

74. Lauren Ross, interviewed by Nigel Ingham, 15 October 2014.

75. Ibid.

76. Raymond and Mavis Nye, interviewed by Emma Taafe. See Taaffe, 'We Suffered in Silence', 172.

## Notes

77. Ross Raisin, *Waterline* (London: Penguin, 2011), 64–5.

78. Cited in Taaffe, 'We Suffered in Silence', 268.

79. See 'Red Dust' a documentary film by Ilona Kacieja (2013). https://www.imdb.com/title/tt3175650/.

80. For more on this see Arthur McIvor, 'Blighted City: Toxic Industrial Legacies, the Environment and Health in Deindustrializing Glasgow', in Liz Kryder-Reid and Sarah May (eds), *Toxic Heritage: Legacies, Futures, and Environmental Injustice* (forthcoming, London: Routledge, 2023).

81. Michael King, interviewed by Nigel Ingham, 7 January 2015 (Manchester Asbestos Group, SOHC).

82. Ibid.

83. *Asbestos Bulletin*, 15, 4, July–August 1974, 92.

84. H. Lewinsohn to J.K. Shepherd, Turners Asbestos Cement Co., 10 December 1968. I am grateful to Geoffrey Tweedale for this reference from the Chase Manhattan Archive.

85. Gorman, 'Women and Asbestos', 132–3.

86. Anonymous (asbestos project), interviewed by Ronnie Johnston (SOHC 016/A22).

87. Anonymous (asbestos project), interviewed by Ronnie Johnston (SOHC 016/A19).

88. See Tweedale, *Magic Mineral to Killer Dust*, 270–3 for more detail.

89. *The Scotsman*, 31 May 1986; *The Times Educational Supplement*, 20 November 1992.

90. *Evening Times*, 26 October 1987.

91. *The Scotsman*, 4 June 1980.

92. *Lennox Herald*, 20 December 1985.

93. *Glasgow Herald*, 8 March 1991; *Evening Times*, 12 March 1991; Clydebank Health Care Campaign, 'Case for a Public Enquiry', and 'Comments on an Asbestos Removal Scheme at Clydebank' (Clydebank Library, ref. 362.11 LC).

94. Alison Reid, Peter Franklin, Nola Olsen, Jan Sleith, Latha Samuel, Patrick Aboagye-Sarfo, Nicholas de Klerk, and A.W. (Bill) Musk, 'All-cause Mortality and Cancer Incidence among Adults Exposed to Blue Asbestos during Childhood', *American Journal of Industrial Medicine* (2013). https://www.academia.edu/25644855/All_cause_mortality_and_cancer_incidence_among_adults_exposed_to_blue_asbestos_during_childhood?auto=download&email_work_card=download-paper.

## Chapter 4

1. McIvor, *Working Lives*, 178–9 for a discussion of the data and trends in OHS since SWW.

2. See, for example, Steven High, Lachlan MacKinnon, and Andrew Perchard (eds), *The Deindustrialized World: Confronting Ruination in Post-Industrial Spaces* (Vancouver: University of British Columbia Press, 2017); High, *One Job Town*; Mackinnon, *Closing Sysco*; Jefferson Cowie and Joseph Heathcott (eds), *Beyond the Ruins: The Meanings of Deindustrialization* (Ithaca, NY: Cornell University Press, 2003); Steven High and David Lewis, *Corporate Wasteland: The Landscape and Memory of Deindustrialization* (Ithaca, NY: Cornell University Press, 2007); Tim Strangleman, *Work Identity at the End of the Line? Privatisation and Culture Change in the UK Rail Industry* (Basingstoke: Palgrave Macmillan,

# Notes

2004). For a discussion of the changing meaning of work and the loss of work in Britain, see McIvor, *Working Lives.*

3. Tim Strangleman, "'Smokestack Nostalgia,' "Ruin Porn" or Working Class Obituary: The Role and Meaning of Deindustrial Representation', *International Labor and Working-Class History* 84 (2013): 23–37.

4. David Walsh, Gerry McCartney, Chik Collins, Melanie Taulbut, and G. David Batty, 'History, Politics and Vulnerability: Explaining Excess Mortality in Scotland and Glasgow' (2016): 62. Accessed at https://www.gcph.co.uk/assets/0000/5988/Excess_mortality_final_report_with_appendices.pdf.

5. Edward Fieldhouse and Emma Hollywood, 'Life after Mining: Hidden Unemployment and Changing Patterns of Economic Activity amongst Miners in England and Wales, 1981–1991', *Work, Employment and Society* 13, 3 (1999): 487.

6. Respondent H1348, Mass Observation Project 1980–2009. Accessed at https://www.massobservationproject.amdigital.co.uk/Documents/Detail/h1328s-response-to-1997-summer-directive-part-1/9445556?item=9445558.

7. See, for example, Mel Bartley, *Authorities and Partisans: The Debate on Unemployment and Health* (Edinburgh: Edinburgh University Press, 1992), 57; McIvor, *Working Lives,* 240–69; Paul Bellaby and Felix Bellaby, 'Unemployment and Ill Health: Local Labour Markets and Ill Health in Britain, 1984–1991', *Work, Employment and Society* 13, 3 (1999): 461–82.

8. Bartley, *Authorities and Partisans,* 57.

9. Bellaby and Bellaby, 'Unemployment and Ill Health'. 463.

10. Mary Shaw, Daniel Dorling, David Gordon, and George Davey Smith, *The Widening Gap: Health Inequalities and Policy in Britain* (Bristol: Policy Press, 1999), 45; M.H. Brenner and A. Mooney, 'Unemployment and Health in the Context of Economic Change', *Social Science and Medicine* 17 (2003): 1125–38.

11. Bellaby and Bellaby, 'Unemployment and Ill Health', 464–5.

12. Shaw et al., *The Widening Gap* 47.

13. Ibid., 46, 49.

14. Ken Coates and Michael Barratt Brown, *Community under Attack: The Struggle for Survival in the Coalfield Communities of Britain* (Nottingham: Spokesman,1997), 47–9.

15. Cited in Ines Wichert, 'Job Insecurity and Work Intensification: The Effects on Health and Well-being', in Brendan Burchill, David Ladipo, and Frank Wilkinson (eds), *Job Insecurity and Work Intensification* (London: Routledge, 2002), 92–111, here 92.

16. See, for example, David Walsh, Martin Taulbut, and Phil Hanlon, *The Aftershock of Deindustrialization* (Glasgow: Glasgow Centre for Population Health, 2008); David Walsh, N. Bendel, R. Jones, and Phil Hanlon, 'It's Not "Just Deprivation": Why Do Equally Deprived UK Cities Experience Different Health Outcomes?' *Public Health* 124 (2010): 487–95.

17. Tim Strangleman and Tracey Warren, *Work and Society: Sociological Approaches, Themes and Methods* (Abingdon, UK: Routledge 2008), 256; Roderick Martin and Judith Wallace, *Working Women in Recession: Employment, Redundancy and Unemployment* (Oxford: Oxford University Press, 1984), 260–7; Bartley, *Authorities and Partisans.*

18. Strangleman and Warren, *Work and Society,* 256; Shaw et al., *The Widening Gap,* 45.

19. Respondent A12, Mass Observation Project 1981–2009. Accessed at https://www.massobservationproject.amdigital.co.uk/Documents/Detail/a12s-response-to-1983-summer-directive/2744412?item=2744421. *Mass Observation* was a social reporting investigation set up in the 1930s which gathered qualitative data from a panel of 'observers'

# Notes

throughout the country who responded in writing to 'directives' – questions set by the organization.

20. Glyn Lewis and Andy Sloggett, 'Suicide, Deprivation and Unemployment: Record Linkage Study', *British Medical Journal* 317 (7 November 1998): 1283.

21. Pearl L. Mok, Navneet Kapur, Kirsten Windfuhr, Alistair H. Leyland, Louis Appleby, Stephen Platt, and Roger T. Webb, 'Trends in National Suicide Rates for Scotland and for England & Wales, 1960–2008', *British Journal of Psychiatry* 200, 3 (2012): 245–51, here 246.

22. David Fryer, 'Psychological or Material Deprivation: Why Does Unemployment Have Mental Health Consequences', in Eithne McLaughlin (ed.), *Understanding Unemployment* (London: Routledge, 1992), 103–25, here 119.

23. Mel Bartley and Ian Plewis, 'Accumulated Labour Market Disadvantage and Limiting Long Term Illness', *International Journal of Epidemiology* 31 (2002): 336–41.

24. See Shaw et al., *Widening Gap*.

25. See Martin and Wallace, *Working Women in Recession*, 260–2, 286.

26. Ibid., 263–5.

27. Bellaby and Bellaby, 'Unemployment and Ill Health', 479.

28. Peter Warr, *Work, Unemployment and Mental Health* (Oxford: Clarendon Press, 1987).

29. *Mass Observation* respondent G1803. https://www.massobservationproject.amdigital.co.uk/Documents/Detail/g1803s-response-to-1998-autumn-directive-part-2/9854769.

30. Dave Waddington, Chas Critcher, Bella Dicks, and David Parry, *Out of the Ashes?: The Social Impact of Industrial Contraction and Regeneration on Britain's Mining Communities* (London: Routledge, 2001), 212–14; Tim Strangleman, 'Networks, Place and Identities in Post–Industrial Mining Communities', *International Journal of Urban and Regional Research* 25, 2 (2001): 259–60.

31. John Goodwin, *Men's Work and Male Lives: Men and Work in Britain* (Aldershot: Ashgate, 1999), 192.

32. Health and Safety Executive, *British Partnership in Health and Safety* (London: Health and Safety Executive, 2006).

33. Walsh, Taulbut, and Hanlon, *The Aftershock of Deindustrialization*, 118–23, 128–9.

34. Community Renewal, 'The Craigneuk Report' (June 2007): 2–4. Consulted at http://www.communityrenewal.org.uk/wp-content/uploads/2015/09/communityrenewal_craigneukreport_07.pdf.

35. David Webster, Judith Brown, Ewan B. Macdonald, and Ivan Turok, 'The Interaction of Health, Labour Market Conditions, and Long-Term Sickness Benefit Claims in a Post-Industrial City: A Glasgow Case Study', in Colin Lindsay and Donald Houston (eds), *Disability Benefits, Welfare Reform and Employment Policy* (Basingstoke: Palgrave Macmillan, 2013), 111–33.

36. See Shaw et al., *Widening Gap*, 46–9.

37. Waddington et al., *Out of the Ashes*, 85–7; Coates and Barratt Brown, *Community under Attack*, 47–9; Geoff Pearson, *The New Heroin Users* (Oxford: Blackwell, 1987).

38. Coalfield Regeneration Trust, *Report on Coalfield Area Deprivation in Scotland* (2013). Consulted at http://www.coalfields-regen.org.uk/wp-content/uploads/2013/06/Coalfields-Deprivation-in-Scotland2013.pdf.

39. Consulted at http://www.healthscotland.scot/health-inequalities/fundamental-causes/employment-inequality.

# Notes

40. Sam Purdie, 'The Scottish Miner', unpublished paper 2015.

41. 'Historical Picture Statistics in Great Britain, 2019: Trends in Work-Related Ill Health and Workplace Injury'. Health and Safety Executive. www.hse.gov.uk/statistics/history. Accessed July 2020.

42. 'Statistics on Safety and Health at Work' (Fatal Occupational Injuries per 100,000 Workers by Economic Activity: Annual). http://www.hse.gov.uk/statistics/history/fatal.htm; http://www.hse.gov.uk/statistics/european/fatal.htm.

43. Charles McLauchlan, interviewed by Thomas Collins, 11 October 2018.

44. Frederick Brady, interviewed by Virtue Jones, 1999, for the Millenium Memory Bank Observing the 1980s Project, BLSA, shelf mark C900/11057.

45. Email Davie Higgins to Sam Purdie, 27 October 2021 [permission granted for authors use].

46. Ilona Kacieja, 'Red Dust: The Craig Documentary Film Project' (Masters dissertation, Edinburgh College of Art, 2013), 17.

47. William Baker, interviewed by Alison Clague, 22 August 2006. Warwickshire County Council Working Lives: Memories of Work and Industry in Nuneaton and Bedworth. Accessed at https://library.warwickshire.gov.uk/iguana/www.main.cls?surl=workinglives.

48. Margaret Cullen, interviewed by Rebekah Russell, 8 October 2014 (SOHC uncatalogued).

49. Irene Dickson, interviewed by Helen Moore (SOHC volunteer), 18 June 2019 (SOHC).

50. Elizabeth Bryan, *Bathgate Once More: The Story of the BMC/Leyland Truck and Tractor Plant, 1961–86* (Edinburgh: Workers' Educational Association, 2012), 49. Jim was one of the fifty-nine oral interviews undertaken in this Heritage Lottery-funded community oral history project.

51. Ibid., 49.

52. Ross Raisin, *Waterline* (London: Penguin, 2011), 88–9.

53. Mhairi Mackenzie, Chik Collins, John Connolly, Mick Doyle, and Gerry McCartney, 'Working-class Discourses of Politics, Policy and Health: "I Don't Smoke; I Don't Drink. The Only Thing Wrong with Me Is My Health", *Policy & Politics* 45, 2 (2015): 8.

54. Ibid., 9.

55. Farquhar McLay (ed.), *Workers City: The Reckoning: Public Loss, Private Gain* (Glasgow: Clydeside Press, 1990), 10.

56. Valerie Walkerdine and Luis Jimenez, *Gender, Work and Community after Deindustrialization* (Basingstoke: Palgrave Macmillan, 2012).

57. Mackenzie et al., 'Working Class Discourses', 10.

58. George Montgomery, interviewed by Ian MacDougall, 13 June 1997 (SWPHT collection; SOHC Archive).

59. Colin Campbell, interviewed by Rory Stride, 16 October 2016 (SOHC).

60. John Keggie, interviewed by Ian MacDougall, 6 May 1997 (SWPHT collection; SOHC Archive).

61. Angela Coyle, *Redundant Women* (London: Women's Press, 1984).

62. For a discussion of this, see Ronald Johnston and Arthur McIvor, 'Dangerous Work, Hard Men and Broken Bodies: Masculinity in the Clydeside Heavy Industries, c1930–1970s', *Working Class Masculinities in Britain, 1850 to the Present* special issue, *Labour History Review* 69, 2 (2004): 135–52.

63. Cited in Wight, *Workers Not Wasters*, 102 f.

## Notes

64. Colin Quigley, interviewed by Rory Stride, 30 October 2016 (SOHC).

65. Betty Long, interviewed by Rebekah Russell, 1 October 2014 (SOHC).

66. Mackenzie et al., 'Working Class Discourses' 12.

67. John Potter (Rev.), interviewed by Susan Morrison, 29 January 2008 (SOHC). I am grateful to Dr Morrison for providing access to a transcript of this interview.

68. Danny Houston, interviewed by Rory Stride, 11 October 2016 (SOHC).

69. Gerry Slater, interviewed by Rory Stride, 30 August 2016 (SOHC).

70. Colin Campbell, interviewed by Rory Stride, 16 October 2016 (SOHC).

71. Andrew Perchard. '"Broken Men" and "Thatcher's Children": Memory and Legacy in Scotland's Coalfields', *International Labour and Working-Class History* 84 (2013b): 78–98, 80. https://doi.org/10.1017/S0147547913000252.

72. Cited in Jeremy Seabrook, *Unemployment* (London: Quartet, 1982), 123.

73. Clare Bambra, *Work, Worklessness and the Political Economy of Health* (Oxford: Oxford University Press, 2012), ix.

74. Colin Lindsay and Donald Houston, 'Fit for Purpose?' in Colin Lindsay and Donald Houston (eds), *Disability Benefits, Welfare Reform and Employment Policy* (Basingstoke: Palgrave Macmillan, 2013), 233–5.

75. R.M. Archibald, 'Coal Mining: Non-Respiratory Problems', in A. Ward Gardner (ed.), *Current Approaches to Occupational Health 2* (Bristol: John Wright, 1982), 31.

76. Nicky Wilson, oral evidence to a SOHC 'Witness Seminar', University of Strathclyde, 28 April 2014 (SOHC Archive).

77. Tracey Carpenter, interviewed by David Welsh, 17 February 2011. Trades Union Congress, Britain at Work Oral History Project. Accessed at http://www.unionhistory.info/britainatwork/display.php.

78. McIvor, *Working Lives*, 35.

79. Ann Borsay, *Disability and Social Policy in Britain since 1750: A History of Exclusion* (Basingstoke: Palgrave Macmillan, 2005), 136.

80. Ken Blakemore and Robert Drake, *Understanding Equal Opportunity Policies* (London: Harvester Wheatsheaf, 1996), 142.

81. These sixteen interviews on the Johnnie Walker factory closure, titled 'Stories from Kilmarnock' were undertaken by Diageo Archivist Joanne McKerchar and are deposited in the Diageo Archive in Menstrie. I am indebted to Joanne for permission to cite them.

82. *The Herald*, 8 March 2012.

83. Janice Withers, interviewed by Diageo Archivist Joanne McKerchar, 2011, for 'Johnnie Walker: Stories from Kilmarnock project (Diageo Archive, Menstrie).

84. Rhona Roberts, interviewed by Diageo Archivist Joanne McKerchar, 2011, for 'Johnnie Walker: Stories from Kilmarnock project (Diageo Archive, Menstrie).

85. Rory Stride, 'Women, Work and Deindustrialization: The Case of James Templeton and Company, Glasgow, c1960–1981', *Scottish Labour History* 54 (2019): 154–80.

86. Mrs Tysoe; cited in Seabrook, *Unemployment*, 209–12.

87. Douglas Stuart, *Young Mungo* (London: Pan Macmillan, 2022), 168–9.

88. 'Laura' (anonymized pseudonym), interviewed by Anni Donaldson, 23 September 2013. See also Annie Donaldson, 'An Oral History of Domestic Abuse in Scotland, 1945–92' (PhD thesis, University of Strathclyde, 2019), 157, 160.

## Notes

89. See Joshi Chitra, 'De-Industrialization" and the Crisis of Male Identities', *International Review of Social History* 47, Supplement 10 (2002): 159–75.

90. Nicky Wilson, 'SOHC Witness Seminar', chaired by Arthur McIvor, 28 April 2014 (SOHC Archive).

91. Steve Tombs, 'Industrial Injuries in British Manufacturing', *Sociological Review* 38, 2 (1990): 324–43. See also Steve Tombs and Dave Whyte, *Safety Crimes* (Devon: Willan Publishing, 2007); Theo Nichols, 'Death and Injury at Work: A Sociological Approach', in Norma Daykin and Lesley Doyal (eds), *Health and Work, Critical Perspectives* (Hampshire: Macmillan Press, 1999), 92.

92. Andrew M. Robinson and Clive Smallman, 'The Contemporary British Workplace: A Safer and Healthier Place', *Work, Employment and Society* 20 (2006): 87–107.

93. Colin Campbell, interviewed by Rory Stride, 16 October 2016 (SOHC).

94. Cited in Lisa M. Garnham, 'Public Health Implications of 4 Decades of Neoliberal Policy: A Qualitative Case Study from Post-industrial West Central Scotland', *Journal of Public Health* 39, 4 (2017): 1–10, here 7.

95. Cited in David Walker, 'Occupational Health and Safety in the British Chemical Industry, 1914–1974' (PhD thesis, University of Strathclyde, 2007).

96. Peter L. Schnall, Marnie Dobson, and Ellen Tosskam (eds), *Unhealthy Work: Causes, Consequences, Cures* (New York: Baywood, 2009).

97. Robinson and Smallman, 'The Contemporary British Workplace', 87–107.

98. See, for example, Andrew Brunton, interviewed by Ian MacDougall, 17 January 1997 (SWPHT: SOHC Archive).

99. See Ronald Johnston and Arthur McIvor, *Lethal Work* (East Linton: Tuckwell Press, 2000), 106–9; Arthur McIvor and Ronald Johnston, *Miners' Lung* (Aldershot: Ashgate, 2007), 237–72.

100. Cited in Kenneth Roy, *The Broken Journey* (Edinburgh: Berlinn, 2016), consulted online at https://books.google.co.uk/books?id=8589DQAAQBAJ&pg.

101. Cited in Herbert Gallery, *Coming to Coventry* (Coventry: Coventry Teaching PCT, 2006), 48.

102. Wichert, 'Job Insecurity and Work Intensification', 110 (emphasis added).

103. Andrew Perchard, *The Mine Management Professions in the Twentieth Century Scottish Coal Mining Industry* (Lampeter: Edwin Mellen Press, 2007). There were dissenters, and Perchard's work argues in a very nuanced way the complexity of managerial decision making in the industry.

104. Waddington et al., *Out of the Ashes,* 52.

105. Alec Mills, interviewed by Arthur McIvor and Ronnie Johnston, 19 June 2000 (SOHC 017/C1).

106. Waddington et al., *Out of the Ashes,* 130–1.

107. William Dunsmore, interview with Ronald Johnston, 11 July 2000 (SOHC 017/C16); and see McIvor and Johnston, *Miners' Lung,* 242–8.

108. John Orr, interview with Arthur McIvor and Ronald Johnston, 19 June 2000 (SOHC 017/C3).

109. Alec Mills, interviewed by Arthur McIvor and Ronnie Johnston, 19 June 2000 (SOHC 017/C1).

110. Bambra, *Work, Worklessness,* 54.

# Notes

111. Emma Wallis, *Industrial Relations in the Privatised Coal Industry* (Aldershot: Ashgate, 2000).

112. Mathias Beck and Andrew Watterson, 'Privatization and Multi-Fatality Disasters: A Causal Connection Exposing Both Worker and Citizen Health and Safety Failures in the UK?' *International Journal of Environmental Research and Public Health* 19 (2022), https://doi.org/10.3390/ijerph192013138.

113. Michael Quinlan, Claire Mayhew, and Philip Bohle, 'The Global Expansion of Precarious Employment, Work Disorganisation and Occupational Health: A Review of Recent Research', *International Journal of Health Services* 31, 2 (2001): 1–39.

114. Ibid., 1, 6.

115. Dana Loomis, David B. Richardson, J.F. Bena, and A.J. Bailer, 'Deindustrialization and the Long Term Decline in Fatal Occupational Injuries', *Occupational and Environmental Medicine* 61, 7 (2004): 616–21; Aleck S. Ostry, M. Barroetavena, R. Hershler, Shona Kelly et al., 'Effect of De-industrialisation on Working Conditions and Self-Reported Health in a Sample of Manufacturing Workers', *Epidemiology and Community Health* 56 (2002): 506–9.

116. Deborah Orr, *Motherwell: A Girlhood* (London: Weidenfeld and Nicholson, 2020), 273.

117. Jim McCaig, interview with Gillian Wylie, 16 October 2013 (SOHC 054/1).

118. Tommy Brennan cited in journalist Steven Moss article, 'Life after Steel', *The Guardian*, 15 February 2001, consulted at https://www.theguardian.com/g2/story/0,3604,438063,00.html.

119. McLay, *Workers City*, 7.

120. Ibid., 10.

121. Danny Houston, interviewed by Rory Stride, 11 October 2016 (SOHC).

122. James Ferns, 'Workers' Identities in Transition: Deindustrialization and Scottish Steelworkers', *Journal of Working-Class Studies* 4, 2 (2019). And see James Ferns forthcoming PhD, University of Strathclyde.

123. Interview BA036, by Emily Grabham, *Balancing Precarious Work and Care*, 2018, http://doi.org/10.5255/UKDA-SN-853015.

124. David Hall, *Working Lives* (London: Bantam Press, 2012), 460.

125. David Graham, interviewed by Ian MacDougall, 30 October 1999 (SWPHT: SOHC Archive), 117.

126. James Dempsey, interviewed by Ian MacDougall, 22 April 1998 (SWPHT: SOHC Archive), 178.

127. Joe Bokas, interviewed by Ian MacDougall, 16 September 1999 (SWPHT: SOHC Archive), 101–2.

128. James Bush, interviewed by Ian MacDougall, 9 June 1997 (SWPHT: SOHC Archive), 61–2.

129. Kacieja, 'Red Dust: The Craig Documentary Film' *Project*, 26.

130. On this see James Ferns, 'Workers' Identities in Transition'.

131. Walley, *Exit Zero*, 162.

## Chapter 5

1. HSE, Annual Statistics, *Work-Related Stress, Anxiety or Depression Statistics in Great Britain, 2020* (20 November 2020), 4. Accessed at https://www.hse.gov.uk/statistics/causdis/stress.pdf.

# Notes

2. Jill Kirby, *Feeling the Strain: A Cultural History of Stress in Twentieth Century Britain* (Manchester: Manchester University Press, 2019); Mark Jackson, *The Age of Stress: Science and the Search for Stability* (Oxford: Oxford University Press, 2013); Mark Jackson (ed.), *Stress in Post-War Britain, 1945–85* (London: Pickering and Chatto, 2015); Joseph Melling, 'Labouring Stress: Scientific Research, Trade Unions and Perceptions of Workplace Stress in Mid-Twentieth Century Britain', in Mark Jackson (ed.), *Stress in Post-War Britain*; Haggett, *Desperate Housewives*; Ali Haggett, *A History of Male Psychological Disorders in Britain, 1945–1970* (Basingstoke: Palgrave Macmillan, 2015); Anna K. Schaffner, *Exhaustion: A History* (New York: Columbia University Press, 2016).

3. See Horace Middleton Vernon, *Health in Relation to Occupation* (Oxford: Oxford University Press, 1939), 297–307, here 300.

4. Ibid., 326–7.

5. Kirby, *Feeling the Strain*, 217 and 174–5 for a discussion of the role of newspapers in this.

6. HSE, 'Work-Related Stress', 6.

7. Haggett, *A History of Male Psychological Disorders*, 147–51.

8. Paul Bellaby, *Sick from Work: The Body in Employment* (Aldershot: Ashgate 1999), 89.

9. Michelle McBride, interviewed by Arthur McIvor, 18 March 2022 (SOHC Archive).

10. Haggett, *A History of Male Psychological Disorders*, 145. See also Anne Case and Alistair Deaton, *Deaths of Despair* (Princeton: Princeton University Press, 2020).

11. Matt Cook, 'AIDS, Mass Observation, and the Fate of the Permissive Turn', *Journal of the History of Sexuality* 26, 2 (2017): 239–72, here 248. https://www.jstor.org/stable/44862383. Accessed 2 February 2022.

12. Willie Dewar, interviewed by Arthur McIvor, 9 December 2008 (SOHC 050/04/07).

13. Wolkowitz, *Bodies at Work*, 1–2. Noon and Blyton have also argued that work stress is particularly associated with the growth of 'emotion work' and point to a series of studies that mostly support this view. See Mike Noon and Paul Blyton, *The Realities of Work* (Basingstoke: Palgrave Macmillan, 2002), 194–5.

14. Doyal, *What Makes Women Sick*, 166–7.

15. Ibid., 167–74.

16. Ibid.; Daykin and Doyal (eds), *Health and Work*, 1–2; Soraya Seedat and Marta Rondon, 'Women's Wellbeing and the Burden of Unpaid Work', *British Medical Journal* 374 (2021): 1–3. https://doi.org/10.1136/bmj.n1972n.

17. For an extended discussion, see Haggett, *Desperate Housewives*.

18. Health and Safety Executive, 'HSG 218 – Tackling Work Related Stress: A Managers' Guide to Improving and Maintaining Employee Health and Wellbeing' (Sudbery: HMSO 2001),130. Accessed at https://www.thenbs.com/PublicationIndex/documents/details?Pub=HSE&DocID=265718.

19. https://www.hse.gov.uk/statistics/causdis/stress.pdf.

20. Wolkowitz, *Bodies at Work*, 115; Kirby, *Feeling the Strain*, 192–3.

21. Respondent H2825, Mass Observation Project 1981–2009. https://www.massobservationproject.amdigital.co.uk/Documents/Detail/h2825s-response-to-1998-autumn-directive-part-2/9854897?item=9854898.

22. Dalton, *Safety, Health and Environmental Hazards at the Workplace*, 136–7; David Wainwright and Michael Calnan, *Work Stress: The Making of a Modern Epidemic* (Buckingham: Open University Press, 2002), 3–4.

## Notes

23. Health and Safety Executive, *The Stress and Health at Work Study* (London: HMSO, 1998).

24. Dalton, *Safety, Health and Environmental Hazards,* 144.

25. Kirby, *Feeling the Strain*, 197.

26. NHS Staff Survey of 2020, consulted at https://www.nhsconfed.org/publications/nhs-staff-survey-2020.

27. Dalton, *Safety, Health and Environmental Hazards,* 135.

28. Wainwright and Calnan, *Work Stress*, 1–2.

29. Phil Taylor, Gareth Mulvey, Jeff Hyman, and Peter Bain, 'Work Organisation, Control and the Experience of Work in Call Centres', *Work, Employment & Society* 16, 1 (2002): 133–50; Phil Taylor, Chris Baldry, Peter Bain, and Vaughn Ellis, '"A Unique Working Environment": Health, Sickness and Absence Management in UK Call Centres', *Work, Employment & Society* 17, 3 (2003): 435–58.

30. Wolkowitz, *Bodies at Work*, 105–6.

31. Seedat and Rondon, 'Women's Wellbeing'.

32. Dalton, *Safety, Health and Environmental Hazards,* 135; Wainwright and Calnan, *Work Stress*, 12–13.

33. http://www.telegraph.co.uk/health/healthnews/7991620/Stress-increases-risk-of-death-five-fold.html.

34. Christian Wolmar, *Broken Rails: How Privatisation Wrecked Britain's Railways* (London: Aurum Press, 2001).

35. Tim Strangleman, 'Nostalgia for Nationalisation – the Politics of Privatisation', *Sociological Research Online* 7, 1 (2002). http://www.socresonline.org.uk/7/1/strangleman.html; Strangleman, *Work Identity at the End of the Line?*.

36. Wainwright and Calnan, *Work Stress*, 6.

37. Hunter, *Health in Industry*, 60–1. See also Joseph Melling, 'Making Sense of Workplace Fear: The Role of Physicians, Psychiatrists, and Labor in Reforming Occupational Strain in Industrial Britain, c 1850–1970', in David Cantor and Edmund Ramsden (eds), *Stress, Shock and Adaptation in the Twentieth Century* (Rochester, NY: University of Rochester Press, 2014).

38. Wainwright and Calnan, *Work Stress*, 28, 32.

39. Ibid., 29.

40. *The Observer*, 1 January 2023 (*The New Review*, 23).

41. Wainwright and Calnan, *Work Stress*, 196.

42. Wolkowitz, *Bodies at Work*, 117.

43. HSE, 'Work-Related Stress', 4; Sharon Bolton and Carol Boyd, 'Trolley Dolly or Skilled Emotion Manager? Moving on From Hochschild's Managed Heart', *Work, Employment and Society* 17, 2 (2003): 289–308; Carol Boyd, 'Customer Violence and Employee Health and Safety', *Work, Employment and Society* 16, 1 (2002): 151–69.

44. Oliver James, *Affluenza* (London: Vermilion, 2007). For a wider discussion see Haggett, *Desperate Housewives* and Kirby, *Feeling the Strain*, 173.

45. See, for example, Bunting, *Willing Slaves*.

46. https://www.capital-ges.com/right-to-disconnect-legislation-in-europe/#:~:text=France%20was%20the%20first%20European,from%20technology%20after%20working%20hours. France, Italy, Belgium, Spain and Ontario, Canada are amongst those who have introduced such legislation.

# Notes

47. Kirby, *Feeling the Strain*, 216 and see Kirby, *Troubled by Life: The Experience of Stress in Twentieth-century Britain* (DPhil thesis, University of Sussex, 2014), 78. Available and consulted online via Sussex Research Online: http://sro.sussex.ac.uk/.

48. Kirby, *Feeling the Strain*, 180, citing Peter Allen, 10 November 1998, Millennium Memory Bank Collection, British Library, C900/07016 © BBC.

49. Kirby, *Feeling the Strain*, 183–6.

50. Tracey Carpenter, interviewed by David Welsh, 17 February 2011, for the TUC Britain at Work project. Accessed at http://www.unionhistory.info/britainatwork/display.php.

51. Claire Langhamer, 'Feeling, Women and Work in the Long 1950s', *Women's History Review* 26, 1 (2017): 77–92, here 8–9. Consulted at Sussex Research Online: http://sro.sussex.ac.uk/id/eprint/59365/.

52. Ibid.

53. Ibid., 9.

54. K2721. Mass Observation Project 1981–2009. https://www.massobservationproject.amdigital.co.uk/Documents/Detail/k2721s-response-to-1998-autumn-directive-part-2/9854935?item=9854936. For this chapter I searched through the 123 responses that mentioned stress to the MO 1998 Part 2 directive 'Staying Well and Everyday Life'.

55. W571. Mass Observation Project 1981–2009. https://www.massobservationproject.amdigital.co.uk/Documents/Detail/w571s-response-to-1998-autumn-directive-part-2/9855326?item=9855327.

56. See Kirby, *Feeling the Strain*, 175–7, 201–2 for a discussion of prescription drugs for stress.

57. Kamaldeep Bhui, Sokratis Dinos, Magdalena Galant-Miecznikowska, Bertine de Jongh, and Stephen Stansfeld, 'Perceptions of Work Stress Causes and Effective Interventions in Employees Working in Public, Private and Non-governmental Organisations: A Qualitative Study', *British Journal of Psychology Bulletin* 40, 6 (2016). https://www.ncbi.nlm.nih.gov/pmc/articles/PMC5353523/

58. Ibid.

59. Karen Levy, interviewed for *The Observer*, New Review, 18–19, 22 January 2023. See also Karen Levy, *Data Driven: Truckers, Technology and the New Workplace Surveillance* (Princeton: Princeton University Press, 2022).

60. Tracey Carpenter, interviewed by David Welsh, 17 February 2011, for the TUC Britain at Work project. Accessed at http://www.unionhistory.info/britainatwork/display.php.

61. Ibid.

62. Ibid.

63. Taylor, Mulvey, Hyman, and Bain, 'Work Organisation, Control and the Experience of Work in Call Centres'; Taylor, Baldry, Bain, and Ellis, 'A Unique Working Environment'.

64. Interview R-BA024-LEEDS-CARE-C-E, 15 October 2015. Emily Katharine Grabham, *Balancing Precarious Work and Care: Interviews with Women Workers 2015–2017*. 2018. [Data Collection]. Colchester: UK Data Archive. 10.5255/UKDA-SN-853015. Accessed at https://reshare.ukdataservice.ac.uk/853015/.

65. Catherine McBean, interviewed by David Walker, 21 February 2011, Scottish Oral History Centre/Glasgow Museums, Glasgow Working Lives Project. Catherine left the call centre in 1998.

66. *Hazards Magazine*, 155, July–September 2021. https://www.hazards.org/gallery/suicidal.htm.

## Notes

67. G2640. Mass Observation Project 1981–2009: response to 1998 Autumn directive part 2. Accessed at https://www.massobservationproject.amdigital.co.uk/Documents/Detail/g2640s-response-to-1998-autumn-directive-part-2/9854795?item=9854796.

68. H1806. Mass Observation Project 1981–2009. https://www.massobservationproject.amdigital.co.uk/Documents/Detail/h1806s-response-to-1992-spring-directive-part-2/8777746?item=8777754.

69. W633. Mass Observation Project 1981–2009. https://www.massobservationproject.amdigital.co.uk/Documents/Detail/w633s-response-to-1998-autumn-directive-part-2/9855343?item=9855347.

70. Deborah Collins, journalist (born 1957) interviewed by Jim Ludlam in 2019 (no date). Trades Union Congress, Britain at Work Oral History Project. Accessed at http://www.unionhistory.info/britainatwork/display.php.

71. D1602. Mass Observation Project 1981–2009. https://www.massobservationproject.amdigital.co.uk/Documents/Detail/c2834s-response-to-1998-autumn-directive-part-2/9854660?item=9854661.

72. Ian Millar, interview with Rachel Meach, 21 September 2017 (Scottish Oral History Centre Archive). I am indebted to Rachel for alerting me to this story and permission to use this extract. See Rachel Meach, 'A Spoonful of Sugar: Dietary Advice and Diabetes in Britain and the United States, 1945–2015' (PhD thesis, University of Strathclyde, 2022).

73. Ibid.

74. Kirby, *Feeling the Strain*, 189.

75. Ibid., 190.

76. Rogaly, *Stories from a Migrant City*.

77. Ibid., 92–7.

78. Ibid., 93.

79. Ibid., 93.

80. Ibid., 188.

81. Jessica Bruder, *Nomadland: Surviving America in the Twenty-First Century* (London: Swift Press, 2017), 98–101.

82. Ibid., 99, 101.

83. Kirby, *Feeling the Strain*, 192–3. Head teachers were amongst those particularly susceptible to work-related stress illness.

84. Kate Rawnsley was interviewed by Rory O'Neill, editor of *Hazards* Magazine, and the case extensively reported in *Hazards,* 140, 2017. This section relies heavily on this account.

85. Ibid.

86. R2247. Mass Observation Project 1981–2009: response to 1998 Autumn directive part 2. https://www.massobservationproject.amdigital.co.uk/Documents/Detail/r2247s-response-to-1998-autumn-directive-part-2/9855127?item=9855132.

87. Michelle McBride, interviewed by Arthur McIvor, 18 March 2022 (SOHC Archive).

88. Ibid.

89. Ibid.

90. https://www.theguardian.com/world/2011/aug/04/chilean-miners-financial-psychological-problems.

91. Scott McCabe, interviewed by Arthur McIvor, 24 March 2022 (SOHC Archive).

# Notes

92. Ibid.

93. Ibid.

94. T2150. Mass Observation Project. https://www.massobservationproject.amdigital.co.uk/Documents/Detail/t2150s-response-to-1998-autumn-directive-part-2/9855312.

95. Scott McCabe, interviewed by Arthur McIvor, 24 March 2022 (SOHC Archive).

96. Kirby, *Feeling the Strain*, 194–6.

97. Michelle McBride, interview by Arthur McIvor, 18 March 2022 (SOHC Archive).

98. A1706. Mass Observation Project 1981–2009: response to 1998 Autumn directive part 2. Accessed at https://www.massobservationproject.amdigital.co.uk/Documents/Detail/a1706s-response-to-1998-autumn-directive-part-2/9854450.

99. Ibid. C2579. https://www.massobservationproject.amdigital.co.uk/Documents/Detail/c2579s-response-to-1998-autumn-directive-part-2/9854628?item=9854630.

100. Ibid. A2801. https://www.massobservationproject.amdigital.co.uk/Documents/Detail/a2801s-response-to-1998-autumn-directive-part-2/9854461.

101. Ibid. B2197. https://www.massobservationproject.amdigital.co.uk/Documents/Detail/b2197s-response-to-1998-autumn-directive-part-2/9854531?item=9854534.

102. Ibid. C1786. https://www.massobservationproject.amdigital.co.uk/Documents/Detail/c1786s-response-to-1998-autumn-directive-part-2/9854608?item=9854614.

103. Ibid. C2834. https://www.massobservationproject.amdigital.co.uk/Documents/Detail/c2834s-response-to-1998-autumn-directive-part-2/9854660?item=9854661.

104. Ibid. L1691. https://www.massobservationproject.amdigital.co.uk/Documents/Detail/l1691s-response-to-1998-autumn-directive-part-2/9854950?item=9854951.

105. Ibid. D156. https://www.massobservationproject.amdigital.co.uk/Documents/Detail/d156s-response-to-1998-autumn-directive-part-2/9854665?item=9854667.

106. Emily Grabham, *Balancing Precarious Work and Care: Interviews with Women Workers 2015–2017*. 2018. [Data Collection]. Colchester: UK Data Archive. 10.5255/UKDA-SN-853015. Accessed at https://reshare.ukdataservice.ac.uk/853015/.

107. Interview BA041, E. Grabham, *Balancing Precarious Work and Care*, 2018, http://doi.org/10.5255/UKDA-SN-853015.

108. Ibid.

109. Ibid.

110. Ibid.

111. Interview BA063, E. Grabham, *Balancing Precarious Work and Care*, 2018, http://doi.org/10.5255/UKDA-SN-853015.

112. Ibid.

113. Ibid.

114. Ibid.

115. Ibid.

116. Ibid.

117. Avril Brunton, interviewed by David Welsh, 15 August 2011, for the TUC Britain at Work project. Accessed at http://www.unionhistory.info/britainatwork/display.php.

118. Anne Bromwich, interviewed by David Welsh, 17 March 2011, for the TUC Britain at Work project. Accessed at http://www.unionhistory.info/britainatwork/display.php. It was noted that the union (the NUT) was subsequently 'smashed' at Holland Park School.

# Notes

119. Christine Rowe, interviewed by David Welsh, 1 February 2011. Accessed at http://www.unionhistory.info/britainatwork/display.php.

120. Interview BA015, E. Grabham, *Balancing Precarious Work and Care*, 2018, http://doi.org/10.5255/UKDA-SN-853015.

121. 'My husband worked so hard ... there was no sign he'd do anything like this ... but then he killed himself'. Accessed at https://www.walesonline.co.uk/news/wales-news/my-husband-worked-hard-no-15866821. See also: https://www.bbc.co.uk/news/uk-wales-47296631

122. Interview BA048, Grabham, *Balancing Precarious Work and Care*, http://doi.org/10.5255/UKDA-SN-853015.

123. Ibid.

124. See interview BA047, Grabham, *Balancing Precarious Work and Care*, http://doi.org/10.5255/UKDA-SN-853015.

125. Interview BA015; BA023, Grabham, *Balancing Precarious Work and Care*, http://doi.org/10.5255/UKDA-SN-853015.

126. Interview BA024; BA038, Grabham, *Balancing Precarious Work and Care*, http://doi.org/10.5255/UKDA-SN-853015.

127. Interview BA028, Grabham, *Balancing precarious work and care*, http://doi.org/10.5255/UKDA-SN-853015.

128. Ibid.

129. Interview BA030, Grabham, *Balancing precarious work and care*, http://doi.org/10.5255/UKDA-SN-853015.

130. Interview BA029, Grabham, *Balancing precarious work and care*, http://doi.org/10.5255/UKDA-SN-853015.

131. Interview BA063, Grabham, *Balancing precarious work and care*, http://doi.org/10.5255/UKDA-SN-853015.

132. Seedat and Rondon, 'Women's Wellbeing and the Burden of Unpaid Work', 3.

133. Ibid., 2–3.

## Chapter 6

1. See Johnston and McIvor, 'Marginalising the Body at Work'.

2. Hunter, *Health in Industry*, 222.

3. Tim Carter and Joseph Melling, 'Trade, Spores and the Culture of Disease: Attempts to Regulate Anthrax in Britain and Its International Trade, 1875–1930', in Christopher Sellers and Joseph Melling (eds), *Dangerous Trade: Histories of Industrial Hazard across a Globalising World* (Philadelphia: Temple University Press, 2012), 65–6, 69–70.

4. Ibid., 70.

5. Ibid.

6. Arthur McIvor, 'Germs at Work: Establishing Tuberculosis as an Occupational Disease in Britain, c1900–1951', *Social History of Medicine* 25, 4 (2012): 812–29; Laura Newman, *Germs in the English Workplace, c1880–1945* (Abingdon: Routledge, 2021), 213; Janet Greenlees, *When the Air Became Important* (New Brunswick: Rutgers University Press, 2019).

7. Greenlees, *When the Air Became Important*, 68.

248

## Notes

8.  See Newman, *Germs in the English Workplace.*

9.  See McIvor, 'Germs at work'.

10. Scambler and Scambler, 'Health and Work in the Sex Industry', 71–85, here 71.

11. Tamsin Wilton, 'Selling Sex, Giving Care: The Construction of AIDS as a Workplace Hazard', in Daykin and Doyal, *Health and Work,* 180.

12. Scambler and Scambler, 'Health and Work', 80.

13. https://www.iqsolutions.com/section/ideas/sex-workers-and-stis-ignored-epidemic.

14. H.A. Waldron, 'Antibody Response to Hepatitis B Vaccination', *British Journal of Industrial Medicine* 47 (1990): 354–5.

15. https://www.hse.gov.uk/biosafety/blood-borne-viruses/risk-healthcare-workers.htm.

16. https://www.telegraph.co.uk/global-health/science-and-disease/wearing-face-mask-not-new-backlash-against-say-historians/.

17. https://www.manchestereveningnews.co.uk/news/greater-manchester-news/gallery/smog-manchester-london-sheffield-1950s-8873555.

18. See https://www.statnews.com/2016/09/28/2016-flu-season-shots-science/.

19. https://apimagesblog.com/historical/2020/3/12/influenza-pandemics-throughout-history. And see the Getty and Alamy photo archives for recorded evidence of this.

20. https://www.theguardian.com/world/2020/oct/01/flu-vaccine-for-hospitals-epidemic-1957.

21. Mark Honigsbaum, 'The Art of Medicine: Revisiting the 1957 and 1968 Influenza Epidemics', *The Lancet* 395 (2020): 1826. https://doi.org/10.1016/S0140-6736 (20)31201-0; www.thelancet.com.

22. https://www.bbc.co.uk/news/av/uk-scotland-60293190.

23. Ibid.

24. R.A. Watt, 'HIV, Discrimination, Unfair Dismissal and Pressure to Dismiss', *Industrial Law Journal* 21, 4 (1992): 280–92.

25. Dai Harris and Richard Haigh (eds) for the Terence Higgins Trust, *AIDS; a Guide to the Law* (London: Tavistock/Routledge, 1990).

26. Watt, 'HIV, Discrimination', 288.

27. Ibid., 292.

28. Cook, 'AIDS, Mass Observation, and the Fate of the Permissive Turn', here 270. https://www.jstor.org/stable/44862383. Accessed 2 February 2022.

29. Janet Weston and Virginia Berridge, 'AIDS Inside and Out: HIV/AIDS and Penal Policy in Ireland and England & Wales in the 1980s and 1990s', *Social History of Medicine* 33, 1 (2020): 247–67, https://doi.org/10.1093/shm/hky090.

30. Virginia Berridge, *Aids in the UK: The Making of Policy* (Oxford: Oxford University Press, 1996), 60.

31. Ibid., 56–7.

32. Mirium Mutambudzi, Claire Niedzwiedz, Ewan B. Macdonald et al., 'Occupation and Risk of Severe COVID-19: Prospective Cohort Study of 120 075 UK Biobank Participants', *Occupational and Environmental Medicine* 78 (2021): 314.

33. https://content.tfl.gov.uk/phase-2-assessment-of-london-bus-driver-mortality-from-covid-19.pdf, 26–7.

34. *The Observer*, 13 December 2020, 1.

# Notes

35. See Roopa Farooki, *Everything Is True: A Junior Doctor's Story of Life, Death and Grief in a Time of Pandemic* (London: Bloomsbury, 2022).

36. *The Observer*, 13 February 2022, 40; Tom Templeton, *34 Patients* (Dublin: Michael Joseph / Penguin Random House, 2021).

37. https://theconversation.com/healthcare-workers-and-coronavirus-behind-the-stiff-upper-lip-we-are-highly-vulnerable-133864. Accessed 8 April 2020. And around 20,000 older retired nurses were also drawn back into employment during the crisis as a result of emergency appeals.

38. https://theconversation-com.cdn.ampproject.org/c/s/theconversation.com/amp/nurses-are-on-the-coronavirus-frontline-so-why-are-they-being-left-out-of-the-response-143658. Accessed 11 September 2020.

39. For an insightful recent study of this process in the United States see Gabriel Winant, *The Next Shift: The Fall of Industry and the Rise of Healthcare in Rust Belt America* (Cambridge, MA: Harvard University Press, 2021).

40. https://theconversation-com.cdn.ampproject.org/c/s/theconversation.com/amp/nurses-are-on-the-coronavirus-frontline-so-why-are-they-being-left-out-of-the-response-143658. Accessed 11 September 2020. Health workers from a Black, Asian or minority ethnic background were found to be five times more likely to test positive for Covid-19 than white people who did not work in healthcare.

41. Ibid.

42. 'Covid Voices: A Moment in Time' film aired 23/4 March 2022. Part of the NHS Voices from Covid-19 Project: Manchester University. https://www.nhs70.org.uk/story/nhs-voices-covid-19.

43. Templeton, *34 Patients*, 6.

44. *The Guardian*, 23 September 2020, 19.

45. *The Observer*, 24 January 2021, *New Review* Magazine, 16–17. See also Rachel Clarke, *Breathtaking: Inside the NHS in a Time of Pandemic* (London: Little Brown, 2020).

46. https://theconversation.com/healthcare-workers-and-coronavirus-behind-the-stiff-upper-lip-we-are-highly-vulnerable-133864. Accessed 8 April 2020.

47. E.W. (pseudonym), interviewed by Alison Chand, 10 June 2020 (SOHC Archive). I am grateful to Alison for supplying this reference and permission to cite it.

48. Hazel Gibson, interviewed by Alison Chand, 20 May 2020. I am grateful to Alison for supplying this reference and permission to cite it.

49. https://theconversation.com/healthcare-workers-and-coronavirus-behind-the-stiff-upper-lip-we-are-highly-vulnerable-133864. Accessed 8 April 2020.

50. *The Observer*, 13 December 2020, 10.

51. *The Observer*, 27 February 2022, 26.

52. Ibid. The respondent requested anonymity.

53. *The Observer*, 13 December 2020, 10.

54. *The Observer*, 28 March 2021, 8. The report was by Dr Adrian James, President of the Royal College of Psychiatrists.

55. Louise Poplar (pseudonym), interviewed by Alison Chand, 15 May 2020 for the NHS at 70 Project. Voices of Our National Health Service collection at the British Library Sound Archive (Shelfmark C1887). See the project website for more information: https://www.nhs70.org.uk/.

# Notes

56. Ibid.

57. Ibid.

58. https://www.bmj.com/content/374/bmj.n2060.

59. Hannah Cardona, born 1987, team leader in learning support, interviewed by Alison Chand, 11 June 2020.

60. Chris Naylor, born 1983, teacher, interviewed by Alison Chand, 19 May 2020.

61. Debbie Taylor, born 1979, teacher, interviewed by Alison Chand, 26 May 2020; see also Scott McCabe, interviewed by Arthur McIvor, 24 March 2022 (SOHC Archive) on these developments at Glasgow College where he was an educator.

62. Gender Equality and Diversity Inclusion Committee (Daniella Sime), *The Impact of Covid-19 on Colleagues in HaSS: Survey Results* (University of Strathclyde, August 2020), 3.

63. *The Observer*, 31 January 2021, 13.

64. *The Observer*, 28 March 2021, 8.

65. https://www.london.gov.uk/questions/2020/1725.

66. https://content.tfl.gov.uk/phase-2-assessment-of-london-bus-driver-mortality-from-covid-19.pdf. Ninety-one per cent of all employed bus drivers were male. And see responses to Lord Mayor's Questions eg https://www.london.gov.uk/questions/2020/1725.

67. https://www.bbc.co.uk/programmes/m001009z.

68. Ibid.

69. *The Observer*, 14 February 2021, 12.

70. Ibid.

71. *The Observer*, 28 March 2021, 8.

72. *The Observer*, 17 January 2021, 1; 13.

73. https://edm.parliament.uk/early-day-motion/57194/professor-philip-taylors-report-on-the-effect-of-covid19-on-callcentre-workers.

74. *The Observer*, 17 January 2021, 7.

75. *The Observer*, 28 March 2021, 8.

76. https://www.walesonline.co.uk/news/local-news/dvla-staff-swansea-scared-go-19691094.

77. *The Observer*, 24 January 2021, 1; *The Observer*, 31 January 2021, 8; *The Observer*, 28 March 2021, 8. By summer 2021 the numbers were up to 643 Covid-19 cases at the DVLA.

78. https://www.theguardian.com/world/2021/jan/23/minister-faces-fury-over-mass-covid-outbreak-at-top-government-agency.

79. https://www.ier.org.uk/news/dvla-head-misleads-mps-over-coronavirus-outbreak/.

80. Cited in *The Observer*, 24 January 2021, 9. Over 2,800 DVLA workers responded to Taylor's questionnaire enquiry.

81. Transport Committee Oral evidence: *Work of the DVLA*, HC 567. July 2021, 14.

82. *The Observer*, 28 March 2021, 8.

83. Transport Committee Oral evidence: *Work of the DVLA*, HC 567. July 2021.

84. Ibid., 3–4.

85. Ibid. Chief Executive Julie Lennard's evidence, 22–4.

86. Ibid., 42.

## Notes

87. https://www.itv.com/news/wales/2021-03-03/lack-of-safe-distancing-at-dvla-a-national-scandal-as-investigation-reveals-staff-were-not-sat-two-metres-apart.

88. Michelle McBride, interviewed by Arthur McIvor, 18 March 2022 (SOHC Archive).

89. Adam Kay, *This Is Going to Hurt: Secret Diaries of a Junior Doctor* (London: Picador, 2017).

90. Gender Equality and Diversity Inclusion Committee, 3.

91. Baowen Xue and Anne McMunn, 'Gender Differences in Unpaid Care Work and Psychological Distress in the UK Covid-19 Lockdown', *PLoS One* 16 (2021): doi:10.1371/journal.pone.0247959; Soraya Seedat and Marta Rondon, 'Women's Wellbeing and the Burden of Unpaid Work', *British Medical Journal*, 31 August 2021; doi: 10.1136/bmj.n1972.

92. Gender Equality and Diversity Inclusion Committee, 30.

93. Michelle McBride, interviewed by Arthur McIvor, 18 March 2022 (SOHC Archive).

94. Ibid.

95. https://nursingnotes.co.uk/news/clinical/long-covid-should-be-recognised-as-a-disability-as-patients-and-staff-struggle-to-recover/.

## Chapter 7

1. Karen Bell, *Working-Class Environmentalism* (London: Palgrave Macmillan, 2020).

2. Donatella Della Porta, *Methodological Practices in Social Movement Research* (Oxford: Oxford University Press, 2014). https://oxford-universitypressscholarship-com.proxy.lib.strath.ac.uk/view/10.1093/acprof:oso/9780198719571.001.0001/acprof-9780198719571-chapter-1. Accessed 30 August 2021.

3. On the neglect of women in health and safety see Messing, *One Eyed Science*.

4. Dembe, *Occupation and Disease*; and see the historiography section of McIvor and Johnston, '*Miners' Lung*, 14–23.

5. McIvor, *A History of Work in Britain*, 201.

6. Michael Quinlan, Philip Bohle, and Felicity Lamm, *Managing Occupational Health and Safety: A Multidisciplinary Approach* (South Yarra: Palgrave Macmillan, 3rd ed., 2010), 486.

7. See Phil B. Beaumont, *Safety at Work and the Unions* (Beckenham: Croom Helm, 1983), 42; Mass Observation, *People in Production* (Harmondsworth: Penguin, 1942), 203.

8. Paul Weindling, 'Linking Self-Help and Medical Science', in P. Weindling (ed.), *The Social History of Occupational Health* (London: Croom Helm, 1985), 10.

9. Williams, *Accidents and Ill Health at Work*, 341.

10. Ibid., 343–4.

11. Graham Wilson, *The Politics of Safety and Health* (Oxford: Oxford University Press, 1985), 114.

12. William Kenefick, *Rebellious and Contrary: The Glasgow Dockers, 1853–1932* (East Linton: Tuckwell Press, 2000), 150–1.

13. Robin Howie, interviewed by Neil Rafeek, 20 September 2001 (SOHC 017/C45).

14. Alec Mills, interviewed by Arthur McIvor, 19 June 2000 (SOHC 017/C1).

15. See McIvor and Johnston, *Miners' Lung*, 180–1.

# Notes

16. Nicky Wilson contribution to the Mining Disability Witness Seminar, University of Strathclyde, 28 April 2014 (SOHC).

17. Alan Dalton, *Asbestos Killer Dust* (London: British Society for Social Responsibility in Science Publications, 1979), 79–80.

18. Ibid., 85.

19. Ibid., 86.

20. Tweedale, *Magic Mineral to Killer Dust*, 169.

21. Nick Wikeley, 'Asbestos and Cancer: An Early Warning to the British TUC', *American Journal of Industrial Medicine* 22 (1992): 449–54.

22. Dalton, *Asbestos Killer Dust*, 90–1.

23. Tweedale, *Magic Mineral*, 248–9; Dalton, *Asbestos Killer Dust*, 90–1.

24. For a wider discussion, see Ronald Johnston and Arthur McIvor, *Lethal Work* (East Linton: Tuckwell Press, 2000), 30–62.

25. Interview (anonymous), Glasgow insulation engineer born 1943 with Ronald Johnston, 15 March 1999 (SOHC 016/A16).

26. Interview (anonymous), heating engineer born 1940 with Ronald Johnston, 22 December 1998 (SOHC 016/A6).

27. Interview (anonymous), Clydeside insulation engineer born 1930 with Ronald Johnston, 26 January 1999 (SOHC 016/A14).

28. Ryan Arthur, 'The Capture, Release and Recapture of Occupational Health and Safety' (PhD thesis, University of Reading, 2018), 139.

29. J.P.K. Garthwaite, Safety Officer, Scott Lithgows, cited in Bellamy, *The Shipbuilders*, 74.

30. Alec Mills, interviewed by Arthur McIvor and Ronnie Johnston, 19 June, 2000 (SOHC 017/C1).

31. Messing, *One-Eyed Science*, xviii.

32. Ibid., 12.

33. For a UK perspective on this, see Sylvia Walby, *Patriarchy at Work: Patriarchal and Capitalist Relations in Employment* (Minneapolis: University of Minnesota Press, 1986); McIvor, *A History of Work*, 174–84.

34. Williams, 'Women and Occupational Health and Safety', 31.

35. The prevalence of this 'macho' dangerous work taboo is discussed in Johnston and McIvor, 'Dangerous Work, Hard Men and Broken Bodies'.

36. Williams, 'Women and Occupational Health', 45.

37. Ibid., 46–8.

38. For a fuller discussion, see McIvor, *A History of Work*, 193–5.

39. Quinlan, Bohle, and Lamm, *Managing Occupational Health and Safety,* 486.

40. See Long, *The Rise and Fall of the Healthy Factory*.

41. See Arthur McIvor, 'Germs at Work: Establishing Tuberculosis as an Occupational Disease in Britain, c1900–1951', *Social History of Medicine*, 25 (2012), 812–29.

42. Sidney Webb and Beatrice Webb, *Industrial Democracy* (London: Longmans, 1897; 1902 ed.), 364.

43. Arthur McIvor, 'Health and Safety in the Cotton Industry', *Manchester Region History Review* 9 (1995): 50–7.

# Notes

44. Sue Bowden and Geoff Tweedale, 'Mondays without Dread: The Trade Union Response to Byssinosis in the Lancashire Cotton Industry in the Twentieth Century', *Social History of Medicine* 16, 1 (2003): 79–95; Greenlees, *When the Air Became Important*.

45. Peter Bartrip, '"Petticoat Pestering": The Women's Trade Union League and Lead Poisoning in the Staffordshire Potteries, 1890–1914', *Historical Studies in Industrial Relations* 2 (1996): 3–26.

46. Bowden and Tweedale, 'Mondays without Dread'.

47. Robert Page Arnot, *The Miners: A History of the Miners' Federation of Great Britain from 1910 Onwards* (London: George Allen and Unwin, 1953), 545.

48. Turner and Blackie, *Disability in the Industrial Revolution*.

49. McIvor and Johnston, *Miners' Lung*, 185–233; Dave Lyddon, 'Trade Unions and the History of Health and Safety in Britain', *Historical Studies in Industrial Relations* 35 (2014): 157–79. Lyddon's important paper focuses on coal mining in an extended review of McIvor and Johnston, *Miners' Lung* and Catherine Mills, *Regulating Health and Safety in the British Mining Industries, 1800–1914* (Farnham: Ashgate, 2010).

50. Webb and Webb, *Industrial Democracy*, 364.

51. Lyddon, 'Trade Unions', 161.

52. Ibid., 157–79 for a detailed discussion of these developments.

53. For a fuller discussion of the trade union campaigns on dust disease in coal mining, see McIvor and Johnston, *Miners' Lung*, 185–236.

54. Ibid., 200–1.

55. Lyddon, 'Trade Unions', 179.

56. Quinlan, Bohle, and Lamm, *Managing Occupational Health and Safety*, 495.

57. McIvor and Johnston, *Miners' Lung*, 230–3.

58. John Taylor, interviewed by Ian MacDougall, 16 May 1997 (SWPHT Collection; SOHC Archive).

59. Ibid.

60. John Jones, born 1934, interviewed by Susan Morrison, 15 September 2002, (SOHC 017/C27).

61. Colin (Nati) Thomas, born 1940, interviewed by Arthur McIvor and Ronnie Johnston, 12 May 2004 (SOHC 017/C26).

62. Tommy Coulter, born 1928, interviewed by Neil Rafeek and Hilary Young, 12 January 2005 (SOHC 017/C21).

63. See Roy Church and Quentin Outram, *Strikes and Solidarity: Coalfield Conflict in Britain, 1889–1996* (Cambridge: Cambridge University Press, 1998); Keith Gildart and Andrew Perchard's AHRC research project: 'On Behalf of the People: Work, Community and Class in the British Coal Industry 1947–1994'. Accessed at https://www.coalandcommunity.org.uk/about.

64. George Bolton and David Carruthers, both born 1934, interviewed by Neil Rafeek and Hilary Young, 12 January 2005 (SOHC 017/C23).

65. Beck, Foster, and Woolfson, *Paying for the Piper*.

66. Gregor Gall, 'Union Organising in the Offshore Oil and Gas Industry', *Scottish Labour History* 41 (2006): 58. See also Charles Woolfson, John Foster, and Matthias Beck, *Paying for the Piper: Capital and Labour in Britain's Offshore Oil Industry* (London: Mansell, 1996).

## Notes

67. See Terry Brotherstone and Hugo Manson, 'Voices of Piper Alpha: Enduring Injury in Private Memory, Oral Representation and Labour History', *Scottish Labour History* 46 (2011): 71–85. And see the *Oil Lives* oral history project, archived at the British Library Sound Archive.

68. See Mathias Beck, John Foster, Helge Ryggvik, Charles Woolfson, *Piper Alpha Ten Years After* (Glasgow: University of Glasgow, 1998).

69. Ibid., 29.

70. Ibid., 40–2.

71. Webb and Webb, *Industrial Democracy*, 357. Emphasis added.

72. Long, *The Rise and Fall of the Healthy Factory*, 85–129.

73. Mark Bufton and Joe Melling, 'Coming Up for Air: Experts, Employers and Workers in Campaigns to Compensate Silicosis Sufferers in Britain, 1918–1939', *Social History of Medicine* 18 (2005): 85.

74. Arthur, 'The Capture, Release and Recapture of Occupational Health and Safety', 140–4.

75. Dalton, *Asbestos Killer Dust*, 98–101; Johnston and McIvor, *Lethal Work*, 158–72.

76. Helen Chappell, 'Fighting Each Other over Asbestos', *New Society*, 29 September 1983, 471–3.

77. McIvor, *A History of Work*, 202.

78. ILO, *Safety and Health in Agriculture* (Geneva: ILO, 2011), 5.

79. Robert Page Arnot, *The Miners in Crisis and War* (London: George Allen and Unwin, 1961), 139.

80. Pattinson, McIvor, and Robb, *Men in Reserve*, 168–80, 191–231; Ronald Johnston and Arthur McIvor, 'The War at Work: Occupational Health and Safety in Scottish Industry, 1939–1945', *Journal of Scottish Historical Studies* 2 (2005): 113–36.

81. Hubert J. Fyrth and Henry Collins, *The Foundry Workers* (Manchester: Amalgamated Union of Foundry Workers, 1959), 223–4, 292–8.

82. Tom Murray's interview testimony in Ian MacDougall (ed.), *Voices from Work and Home* (Edinburgh, 2000), 287.

83. See Keith Gildart, 'Coal Strikes on the Home Front: Miners' Militancy and Socialist Politics in the Second World War', *Twentieth Century British History* 20 (2009): 121–51.

84. Peter Bain, '"Is you is or is you ain't my baby": Women's Pay and the Clydeside Strikes of 1943', *Scottish Labour History* 30 (1995): 35–60.

85. See Pattinson, McIvor, and Robb, *Men in Reserve*; Alison Chand, *Masculinities on Clydeside: Men in Reserved Occupations during the Second World War* (Edinburgh: Edinburgh University Press, 2016).

86. William Mcnaul, interviewed by Linsey Robb, 27 March 2013 (SOHC Archive).

87. Quinlan, Bohle and Lamm, *Managing Occupational Health and Safety*, 492.

88. See McIvor, 'Germs at Work'.

89. Long, *The Rise and Fall of the Healthy Factory*, 156–86.

90. Richard Schilling, *A Challenging Life: Sixty Years in Occupational Health* (London: Canning Press, 1998), 160.

91. Health and Safety Executive, 'Historical Picture Statistics in Great Britain, 2019: Trends in Work-Related Ill Health and Workplace Injury'. www.hse.gov.uk/statistics/history. Accessed July 2020.

92. Beaumont, *Safety at Work*, 59–60.

## Notes

93. Ibid., 101–2.

94. Hugh Cairney, insulation worker born 1934 interviewed by Neil Rafeek, 26 March 2005 (SOHC 016/35).

95. Interview (anonymous), Glasgow insulation engineer born 1918 by Arthur McIvor and Ronald Johnston, 1 December 1999 (SOHC 016/A23).

96. Hugh Cairney, interviewed by Arthur McIvor and Ronald Johnston, 1 December 1999 (SOHC 016/A22).

97. Hugh Cairney, interviewed by Neil Rafeek, 26 March 2005 (SOHC 016/A35).

98. Ibid.

99. Dalton, *Asbestos: Killer Dust*, 99.

100. Hugh Cairney, interviewed by Neil Rafeek, 26 March 2005 (SOHC 016/A35).

101. John Keggie, interviewed by Ian MacDougall, 6 May 1997 (SWPHT collection; SOHC Archive).

102. Long, *The Rise and Fall of the Healthy Factory*.

103. Quinlan, Bohle, and Lamm, *Managing Occupational Health and Safety*, 489–91.

104. David Bradley, 'Occupational Health and Safety in the Scottish Steel Industry, c.1930–1988: The Road to "Its Own Wee Empire"' (PhD thesis, Glasgow Caledonian University, 2012), 185–94.

105. Alan Booth and Joseph Melling, 'Workplace Cultures and Business Performance', in Joseph Melling and Alan Booth (ed.), *Managing the Modern Workplace* (Aldershot: Ashgate, 2008), 9.

106. Phizacklea and Miles, *Labour and Racism*, 102–3.

107. Beynon, *Working for Ford*, 191–3.

108. Tracey Carpenter, interviewed by David Welsh, 17 February 2011. Trades Union Congress, Britain at Work Oral History Project. Accessed at http://www.unionhistory.info/britainatwork/display.php.

109. Beynon, *Working for Ford*, 199.

110. Brian Watson, interviewed by David Walker, 8 October 2005 (SOHC 022).

111. Cited in Taafe, 'We Suffered in Silence', 250.

112. Doug May, cited in Walker, 'Danger Was Something You Were Brought up Wi', 59.

113. Taaffe, 'We Suffered in Silence', 123; 140.

114. Dave Lyddon, 'Health and Safety', Britain at Work, London Metropolitan University. http://www.unionhistory.info/britainatwork/narrativedisplay.php?type=healthandsafety. Accessed July 2020.

115. Quinlan, Bohle, and Lamm, *Managing Occupational Health and Safety*, 485–500.

116. Michelle McBride, interview with Arthur McIvor, 18 March 2022 (SOHC Archive).

117. Quinlan, Bohle, and Lamm, *Managing Occupational Health and Safety*, 485.

118. See the wonderful documentary, *Solidarity*. Director Lucy Parker (London: City Projects, 2019). http://www.solidarityfilm.com/. Accessed July 2020; Chappell, 'Fighting Each Other', 472–3; House of Commons Scottish Affairs Committee, *Blacklisting in Employment: Final Report Seventh Report of Session 2014–15*, HC 272, 18 March 2015 (London: The Stationery Office) https://www.parliament.uk/blacklisting-in-employment. Accessed July 2020. For a discussion of the origins of such blacklisting see Arthur McIvor, 'A Crusade for Capitalism: The Economic League, 1919–39', *Journal of Contemporary History*, 1988, 23, 4, 631–55; Arthur McIvor, 'Political Blacklisting and Anti-Socialist Activity between the Wars', *Society for the Study of Labour History Bulletin* 54, 1 (1988): 18–26.

# Notes

119. See Dave Smith and Phil Chamberlain, *Blacklisted: The War between Big Business and Union Activists* (Oxford: New Internationalist Publications Ltd, 2015); Jack Huey, '"Being Blacked": A History of Blacklisting in the Construction Industry' (BA History dissertation, University of Strathclyde, 2019).

120. Smith and Chamberlain, *Blacklisted*, 70. Construction accounted for 27 per cent of all accident fatalities and 10 per cent of all major industries, whilst it only employed around 5 per cent of the labour force.

121. House of Commons Scottish Affairs Committee (SAC), *Blacklisting in Employment Oral and Written Evidence*. 30. Heathrow airport Terminal 5 was started in 1993 and construction finished in 2008.

122. SAC, *Blacklisting in Employment Oral and Written Evidence*, 33. See also SAC, Written Evidence. Accessed at https://publications.parliament.uk/pa/cm201213/cmselect/cmscotaf/writev/blacklisting/blacklisting.pdf.

123. SAC, Written Evidence, 53–4.

124. James Fowler (Liverpool), interviewed by Jack Huey, 15 November 2018 (SOHC).

125. SAC, Written Evidence, 7.

126. See the SAC written and oral evidence.

127. Barry Reilly, Pierella Paci, and Peter Holl, 'Unions, Safety Committees and Workplace Injuries', *British Journal of Industrial Relations* 33, 2 (1995): 275–88; Theo Nichols, David Walters, and Ali Tasiran, 'Trade Unions, Institutional Mediation and Industrial Safety', *Journal of Industrial Relations* 49, 2 (April 2007): 211–25. See also Trades Union Congress, *The Union Effect: How Unions Make a Difference on Health and Safety* (London: TUC, 2015). https://www.tuc.ordg.uk/research-analysis/reports/union-effect. Accessed July 2020.

128. *Hazards*, 64 (October–December 1998). See also Rory O'Neill, 'When It Comes to Health and Safety Your Life Should Be in Union Hands', in ILO, *Health and Safety at Work: A Trade Union Priority*, Labour Education Series, 126 (Geneva: ILO, 2002), 13–18.

129. Maureen Dollard and Daniel Neser, 'Worker Health Is Good for the Economy', *Social Science and Medicine* 92 (2013): 114–23. See also ILO, *Health and Safety at Work*, and Quinlan, Boyle, and Lamm, *Managing Occupational Health and Safety*, 488–9.

130. Comparing 'Statistics on Union Membership', ILOSTAT, International Labour Organisation. https://ilostat.ilo.org/topics/union-membership/. Accessed July 2020; with 'Statistics on Safety and Health at Work' (Fatal Occupational Injuries per 100,000 Workers by Economic Activity: Annual), ILOSTAT, International Labour Organisation. https://ilostat.ilo.org/topics/safety-and-health-at-work/. Accessed July 2020.

131. ILO, *Health and Safety at Work*, 5.

132. Ibid.

133. Michelle McBride, interview with Arthur McIvor, 18 March 2022 (SOHC Archive).

134. I've made this case elsewhere in relation to TB. See McIvor, 'Germs at Work'.

135. Quinlan, Bohle, and Lamm, *Managing Occupational Health and Safety*, 487.

136. Chris Sellers, *Hazards of the Job: From Industrial Science to Environmental Health Science* (Chapel Hill: University of North Carolina Press, 1997); David Rosner and Gerald Markowitz, *Deadly Dust* (Princeton: Princeton University Press, 1994); Gerald Markowitz and David Rosner, *Lead Wars* (Berkeley: University of California Press, 2013); Bell, *Working Class Environmentalism*.

137. Kim Hunter, 'When Workers Fight for Our Environment', *International Socialism*, 168 (October 2020). Accessed at http://isj.org.uk/workers-fight-for-environment/#footnote-10080-40.

# Notes

138. The full archive of this organization can be consulted at the University of Strathclyde Archives and Special Collections. Its role in the environmental health movement merits closer analysis.

139. Long, *The Rise and Fall of the Healthy Factory*, 128–9, 211–12.

140. Coal Industry Social Welfare Organisation, *Annual Reports* for 1953, 1954, 1955, 1957, 1964, 1973, 1976, 1978. Consulted at the South Wales Coalfield Collection, University of Swansea.

141. The last deep pit (Longannet) in Scotland closed in 2002; in Wales (Tower) in 2008; and in England (Kellingley) in 2015. The NUM continues in existence representing ex-miners and their communities.

142. For the full story see Brian W. Lavery, *The Headscarf Revolutionaries: Lillian Bilocca and the Hull Triple-Trawler Disaster* (London: Barbican Press, 2015). There has also been a play and a BBC documentary (https://www.bbc.co.uk/programmes/b09r8jvr) made of the disaster, and Bilocca is memorialized in a wall mural in the dock community in Hull and, recently, by a street being named after her and a plaque outside the house she lived in. See https://www.bbc.co.uk/news/uk-england-humber-35735318. And also Tom White, 'Radical Object'. Accessed at https://www.historyworkshop.org.uk/radical-objects-hulls-headscarf-revolutionaries-mural/.

143. Jan O'Malley, interviewed by Dave Welsh on 18 August 2011. Trades Union Congress, Britain at Work Oral History Project. Accessed at http://www.unionhistory.info/britainatwork/display.php.

144. Ibid.

145. Barry Castleman and Geoff Tweedale, 'Turning the Tide: The Struggle for Asbestos-Related Diseases and the Banning of Asbestos', in Chris Sellars and Joseph Melling (eds) *Dangerous Trade* (Philadelphia: Temple University Press, 2012); Robert Storey, 'Pessimism of the Intellect, Optimism of the Will: Engaging with the "Testimony" of Injured Workers', in Steven High (ed.), *Beyond Testimony and Trauma: Oral History in the Aftermath of Mass Violence* (Vancouver: University of British Columbia Press, 2015); Storey, 'Beyond the Body Count? Injured Workers in the Aftermath of Deindustrialization', 46–67.

146. Phyllis Craig, interviewed by Arthur McIvor, 28 January 2013 (SOHC 016/A35). Narrator's emphasis.

147. This was the Society for the Prevention of Asbestosis and Industrial Diseases (in 1996, renamed Occupational and Environmental Diseases Association). See W. McDougall, 'Pressure Group Influence and Occupational Health, SPAID/OEDA, 1978–2008' (PhD thesis, Glasgow Caledonian University, 2013). Nancy Tait was later awarded an MBE for her charitable work with asbestos victims.

148. Castleman and Tweedale, 'Turning the Tide', 187.

149. She died in February 2009 aged eighty-nine the year after OEDA was disbanded. See https://www.britishasbestosnewsletter.org/ban74.htm and https://www.theguardian.com/society/2009/feb/23/nancy-tait.

150. McDougall, 'Pressure Group Influence', 198–206.

151. Ibid., 125.

152. Castleman and Tweedale, 'Turning the Tide', 189.

153. Cited in *The Scotsman*, 15 January 1988, 6.

154. Like Nancy Tait, Phyllis Craig was awarded an MBE for her services to asbestos victims.

155. Sandra Samuel, interviewed by Graeme Naylor, 21 October 2003 (SOHC 21/4).

### Notes

156. Janet Ross, interviewed by Graeme Naylor, 30 December 2003 (SOHC 21/3).

157. Ian McConaghy, born 1946, interviewed by Arthur McIvor, 13 June 2018 (SOHC). Ian continues to lead this campaign at the time of writing.

158. Vera Rigby, interviewed by Nigel Ingham, 13 October 2014 (SOHC).

159. Barbara Eason, interviewed by Nigel Ingham, 27 October 2014 (SOHC).

160. Castleman and Tweedale, 'Turning the Tide', 188.

161. Eric Jonckheere, interviewed by Arthur McIvor, 21 February 2013 (SOHC 016/A36). Significantly, the same Eternit company doctor, Dr. Lepoutre, also later died of mesothelioma. See Salvator Y. Nay, 'Asbestos in Belgium: Use and Abuse', *International Journal of Occupational and Environmental Health* 9 (2003): 287–93.

162. This was one of many such environmental, family, or 'bystander' fatalities from asbestos. Fibres were transferred into the home on workers' overalls and dispersed widely on air currents from work sites and waste dumps.

163. Jonckheere interview (SOHC 16/A36).

164. Ibid. For a parallel in which a single company controlled the community through paternalist policies with a wide range of impacts on workers bodies, see Perchard, *Aluminiumville*.

165. See Bloor, 'No Longer Dying'.

166. See Ronnie Johnston and Arthur McIvor, 'Oral Histories of the Asbestos Tragedy in Scotland,' http://ibasecretariat.org/search_item.php?l0=5+25+51&l1=94+10+36&f=eas_rj_am_scotland.php.

167. The full story is told in Ronnie Johnston and Arthur McIvor, 'Oral History in Asbestos Investigations', in George A. Peters and Barbara J. Peters (eds), *The Asbestos Legacy: The Sourcebook on Asbestos Diseases* (San Francisco: LexisNexis, 2001), 23, 3–35.

168. Castleman and Tweedale, 'Turning the Tide', 191. Laurie Flynn's papers are deposited in the University of Strathclyde Archives and Special Collections, along with some of Alan Dalton's.

169. McDougall, 'Pressure Group Influence', 198–200.

170. *The Guardian*, 20 March 2022. Accessed at https://www.theguardian.com/uk-news/2022/mar/20/uk-asbestos-maker-withheld-information-on-material-risks-court-papers-show.

171. http://www.workstress.net/uknwsns-origins.

172. Dalia Gebrial and Paddy Bettington, 'The Insecure Economy: Measuring and Understanding the Contemporary Labour Market' for *Autonomy* and the *Centre for Labour and Social Studies*. http://classonline.org.uk/pubs/item/the-insecure-economy-measuring-and-understanding-the-contemporary-labour-ma. See also *The Observer*, 1 May 2022, 41.

## Conclusion

1. As I write (January 2023), the first local council (South Cambridgeshire) and the largest ever pilot scheme trialling a four-day working week is underway in the UK, involving 3300 workers across seventy firms. See Richard Godwin's article in *The Observer Magazine*, 22 January 2023.

# BIBLIOGRAPHY

## Oral History Interviews

### British Library Sound Archive (BLSA)

Frederick Brady interviewed by Virtue Jones, 1999, for the Millennium Memory Bank Observing the 1980s Project, BLSA Shelf mark C900/11057.

Jenny Constant, born Malvern 1946, interviewed 10 July, 13 August, 2 September 2013, Pioneering Women Collection, BLSA Shelf mark: C1379/98.

Joyce Igo, born Castletown, Sunderland, 1923, interviewed 23 October 1991, National Life Story Collection: Lives in Steel, BLSA Shelf mark: C532/023.

Edna McDonald (nee Moon), born Workington 1921, interviewed 6 December 1991, National Life Story Collection: Lives in Steel, BLSA Shelf mark: C532/041.

Louise Poplar (pseudonym), interviewed (by Alison Chand), 15 May 2020, Voices of Our National Health Service (NHS at 70) collection, BLSA Shelf mark C1887.

Betty Saffill (nee Tyson), born Workington 1922, interviewed 7 December 1991, National Life Story Collection: Lives in Steel, BLSA Shelf mark: C532/043.

Kevin Topham, interviewed 18 October 2000; Lives in the Oil Industry Project (Terry Brotherstone and Hugo Manson), BLSA Shelf mark: F10593/A.

### Trades Union Congress, Britain at Work Oral History Project

Accessed at http://www.unionhistory.info/britainatwork/display.php.

Anne Bromwich, interviewed by David Welsh, 17 March 2011.

Avril Brunton, interviewed by David Welsh, 15 August 2011.

Tracey Carpenter, interviewed by David Welsh, 17 February 2011.

Deborah Collins, interviewed by Jim Ludlam in 2019 (no date).

Sheila Emmanuel, interviewed by Myrna Shoa, 14 January 2011.

Sally Groves, interviewed by David Welsh and Rima Joebear on 25 March 2013.

Fred and Doreen Hibbs, interviewed by Dave Welsh and Rima Joebear, 6 July 2010.

Eileen Magee, interviewed by David Welsh and Rima Joebear on 31 May 2011.

Jan O'Malley, interviewed by Dave Welsh on 18 August 2011.

Christine Rowe, interviewed by David Welsh, 1 February 2011.

Pam Singer, interviewed by David Welsh and Rima Joebear, 17 June 2010.

### UK Data Archive (interviews)

Grabham, Emily Katharine, *Balancing Precarious Work and Care: Interviews with Women Workers 2015–2017*. 2018. [Data Collection]. Colchester: UK Data Archive. 10.5255/UKDA-SN-853015. Accessed at https://reshare.ukdataservice.ac.uk/853015/.

Interview BA015, http://doi.org/10.5255/UKDA-SN-853015.

Interview BA024, http://doi.org/10.5255/UKDA-SN-853015.

Interview BA028, http://doi.org/10.5255/UKDA-SN-853015.

# Bibliography

Interview BA029, http://doi.org/10.5255/UKDA-SN-853015.
Interview BA030, http://doi.org/10.5255/UKDA-SN-853015.
Interview BA036, http://doi.org/10.5255/UKDA-SN-853015.
Interview BA038, http://doi.org/10.5255/UKDA-SN-853015.
Interview BA041, http://doi.org/10.5255/UKDA-SN-853015.
Interview BA047, http://doi.org/10.5255/UKDA-SN-853015.
Interview BA048, http://doi.org/10.5255/UKDA-SN-853015.
Interview BA063, http://doi.org/10.5255/UKDA-SN-853015.

## Scottish Oral History Centre (SOHC) Archive, University of Strathclyde

These interviews can be accessed either via the University of Strathclyde Archives and Special
    Collections at http://atom.lib.strath.ac.uk/sohc-archive or via the SOHC at https://www.
    strath.ac.uk/humanities/schoolofhumanities/history/scottishoralhistorycentre/.
Billy Affleck, interviewed by Arthur McIvor and Ronald Johnston, 19 June 2000 (SOHC 017/C2).
John Allan, interviewed by Linsey Robb, 7 November 2011 (SOHC 50/09).
Asbestos Interviews (anonymous), SOHC 016/A4, A5, A6, A7, A9, A11, A12, A13, A14, A16,
    A18, A19, A20, A22, A23, A26, conducted in 1998–9 by Ronnie Johnston and Arthur McIvor.
Julie Blair, interviewed by Graeme Naylor, 21 October 2003 (Inverclyde Oral History Project,
    SOHC 21/1).
George Bolton, interviewed by Neil Rafeek and Hilary Young, 12 January 2005 (SOHC 017/C23).
George Burns, interviewed by Neil Rafeek, 28 April 2004 (SOHC 017/C40).
Hugh Cairney, interviewed by Arthur McIvor and Ronald Johnston, 1 December 1999 (SOHC
    016/A22).
Hugh Cairney, interviewed by Neil Rafeek, 26 March 2005 (SOHC 016/35).
Colin Campbell, interviewed by Rory Stride, 16 October 2016 (SOHC).
Hannah Cardona, interviewed by Alison Chand, 11 June 2020 (SOHC). 'Rainbows in the
    Windows': An Oral History of Young Families in Britain during the Covid-19 Pandemic'
    project.
David Carruthers, interviewed by Neil Rafeek and Hilary Young, 12 January 2005 (SOHC 017/
    C23).
Tommy Coulter, interviewed by Neil Rafeek and Hilary Young, 12 January 2005 (SOHC 017/
    C21).
Phyllis Craig, interviewed by Arthur McIvor, 28 January 2013 (SOHC 016/35).
Margaret Cullen, interviewed by Rebekah Russell, 8 October 2014 (SOHC).
Willie Dewar, interviewed by Arthur McIvor, 9 December 2008 (SOHC 50/04).
Irene Dickson, interviewed by Helen Moore, 18 June 2019 (SOHC).
William Dunsmore, interviewed by Ronald Johnston, 11 July 2000 (SOHC 017/C16).
Barbara Eason, interviewed by Nigel Ingham, 27 October 2014 (Manchester Asbestos Group
    hereafter MAG Archive, SOHC).
Pat Ferguson, interviewed by Ronnie Johnston, 5 July 2000 (SOHC 017/C12).
Richard Fitzpatrick, interviewed by David Walker, 13 August 2004 (SOHC).
John Foley, interviewed by David Bradley, 28 April 2010 (SOHC).
James Fowler, interviewed by Jack Huey, 15 November 2018 (SOHC).
Hazel Gibson, interviewed by Alison Chand, 20 May 2020 (SOHC). 'Rainbows in the Windows'
    project.
David Guy, interviewed by Neil Rafeek, 8 March 2004 (SOHC 017/C44).
Frederick Hall, interviewed by Neil Rafeek, 29 March 2004 (SOHC 017/C41).
Danny Houston, interviewed by Rory Stride, 11 October 2016 (SOHC).
Robin Howie, interviewed by Neil Rafeek, 20 September 2001 (SOHC 017/C45).

## Bibliography

Eric Jonckheere, interviewed by Arthur McIvor, 21 February 2013 (SOHC 016/A36).

John Jones, interviewed by Sue Morrison, 15 September 2002 (SOHC 017/C27).

Ian Kellie, interviewed by Neil Rafeek, c.2002–3 (SOHC 018/B1).

Michael King, interviewed by Nigel Ingham, 7 January 2015 (MAG Archive, SOHC).

Peter Lancaster, interviewed by Nigel Ingham, 26 Jan 2015 (MAG Archive, SOHC).

'Laura' (pseudonym), interviewed by Anni Donaldson, 23 September 2013 (SOHC).

Betty Long, interviewed by Rebekah Russell, 1 October 2014 (SOHC).

David Marshall, interviewed by Ronnie Johnston, 29 June 2000 (SOHC 017/C7).

Catherine McBean, interviewed by David Walker, 21 February 2011, Glasgow Working Lives Project, Glasgow Museums/SOHC).

Michelle McBride, interviewed by Arthur McIvor, 18 March 2022 (SOHC).

Scott McCabe, interviewed by Arthur McIvor, 24 March 2022 (SOHC).

Jim McCaig, interviewed by Gillian Wylie, 16 October 2013 (SOHC 054/1).

Ian McConaghy, interviewed by Arthur McIvor, 13 June 2018 (SOHC).

Stewart McIntosh, interviewed by Neil Rafeek, 9 June 2003 (SOHC).

John McKean, interviewed by Ronnie Johnston, 29 June 2000 (SOHC 017/C10).

Charles McLauchlan, interviewed by Thomas Collins, 11 October 2018 (SOHC).

Thomas McMurdo, interviewed by Ronnie Johnston, 11 July 2000 (SOHC 017/C20).

William Mcnaul, interviewed by Linsey Robb, 27 March 2013 (SOHC 050/22).

Doug May, interviewed by David Walker, 5 September 2005 (SOHC/022).

Ian Millar, interviewed by Rachel Meach, 21 September 2017 (SOHC).

Alec Mills, interviewed by Arthur McIvor and Ronnie Johnston, 19 June 2000 (SOHC 017/C1).

Alan Napier, interviewed by Neil Rafeek, 31 March 2004 (SOHC 017/C43).

Chris Naylor, interviewed by Alison Chand, 19 May 2020 (SOHC). 'Rainbows in the Windows' project.

John Orr, interviewed by Arthur McIvor and Ronald Johnston, 19 June 2000 (SOHC 017/C3).

Margaret Poole, interviewed by Nigel Ingham, 21 January 2015 (MAG Archive, SOHC).

John Potter (Rev.), interviewed by Susan Morrison, 29 January 2008 (SOHC).

Colin Quigley, interviewed by Rory Stride, 30 October 2016 (SOHC).

Dorothy Radwanski, interviewed by Neil Rafeek, c.2002–3 (SOHC 018/B6).

Vera Rigby, interviewed by Nigel Ingham, 13 October 2014 (MAG Archive, SOHC).

Janet Ross, interviewed by Graeme Naylor, 30 December 2003, Inverclyde Oral History Project (SOHC 21/3).

Lauren Ross, interviewed by Nigel Ingham, 15 October 2014 (MAG Archive, SOHC).

Sandra Samuel, interviewed by Graeme Naylor, 21 October 2003 (SOHC 21/4).

Derek Sims, interviewed by Linsey Robb, 20 February 2013 (SOHC 050/012).

Gerry Slater, interviewed by Rory Stride, 30 August 2016 (SOHC).

Bert Smith, interviewed by Ronnie Johnston, 5 July 2000 (SOHC 017/C14).

Harry Steel, interviewed by Ronnie Johnston, 29 June 2000 (SOHC 017/C9).

Debbie Taylor, interviewed by Alison Chand 26 May 2020 (SOHC). 'Rainbows in the Windows' project.

Colin (Nati) Thomas, interviewed by Arthur McIvor and Ronnie Johnston, 12 May 2004 (SOHC 017/C26).

Mavis Tong, interviewed by Nigel Ingham, 6 February 2015 (MAG Archive, SOHC).

E.W. (pseudonym), interviewed by Alison Chand, 10 June 2020 (SOHC). 'Rainbows in the Windows' project.

Brian Watson, interviewed by David Walker, 8 October 2005 (SOHC 022).

Nicky Wilson, SOHC Witness Seminar, chaired by Arthur McIvor, 28 April 2014 (SOHC).

Marshall Wylde, interviewed by Neil Rafeek, 10 March 2004 (SOHC 017/C35).

# Bibliography

## Scottish Working People's History Trust (SWPHT) Interviews (SOHC Archive)

Effie Anderson, interviewed by Ian MacDougall, 28 November 1996.
Joe Bokas, interviewed by Ian MacDougall, 16 September 1999.
Andrew Brunton, interviewed by Ian MacDougall, 17 January 1997.
James Bush, interviewed by Ian MacDougall, 9 June 1997.
Janet Chapman, interviewed by Ian MacDougall, 2 July 1999.
James Dempsey, interviewed by Ian MacDougall, 22 April 1998.
David Graham, interviewed by Ian MacDougall, 30 October 1999.
John Keggie, interviewed by Ian MacDougall, 6 May 1997.
George Montgomery, interviewed by Ian MacDougall, 13 June 1997.
John Taylor, interviewed by Ian MacDougall, 16 May 1997.

## Warwickshire County Council

**Working Lives: Memories of Work and Industry in Nuneaton and Bedworth.**
Fifty-six interviews conducted 2005–8. Accessed at https://library.warwickshire.gov.uk/iguana/
www.main.cls?surl=workinglives.
William Baker, interviewed by Alison Clague, 22 August 2006.
John Hopkins, interviewed by Alison Clague, 10 January 2007.
Mary Spicer, interviewed by Alison Clague, 7 July 2006.

## Other oral history interviews/archives

Fred Clark, interviewed for the TUC 'Workers' War' project in 2005, http://www.unionhistory.
info/workerswar/voices.php.
D.C.M. Howe, interviewed by the Imperial War Museum, 1 May 1990 (IWM SA 12882).
Rhona Roberts, interviewed by Diageo Archivist Joanne McKerchar, 2011, for 'Johnnie Walker:
Stories from Kilmarnock' project (Diageo Archive, Menstrie).
William Ryder, interviewed by the Imperial War Museum, 10 September 1999 (IWM SA 19662).
Mr Sloan, interview T089, 14 May 1991, Motherwell Heritage Centre.
Thomas Stewart, interviewed 10 June 1996, *2000 Glasgow Lives Project,* Glasgow Museums.
Dr Thomas interview, Audio/374; South Wales Coal Collection, University of Swansea.
Janice Withers, interviewed by Diageo Archivist Joanne McKerchar, 2011, for 'Johnnie Walker:
Stories from Kilmarnock' project (Diageo Archive, Menstrie).

## Mass Observation Archive (online)

A12, accessed at https://www.massobservationproject.amdigital.co.uk/Documents/Detail/a12s-
response-to-1983-summer-directive/2744412?item=2744421.
H1348, accessed at https://www.massobservationproject.amdigital.co.uk/Documents/Detail/
h1328s-response-to-1997-summer-directive-part-1/9445556?item=9445558.
G1803, accessed at https://www.massobservationproject.amdigital.co.uk/Documents/Detail/
g1803s-response-to-1998-autumn-directive-part-2/9854769.
H2825, accessed at https://www.massobservationproject.amdigital.co.uk/Documents/Detail/
h2825s-response-to-1998-autumn-directive-part-2/9854897?item=9854898.

**Bibliography**

K2721, accessed at https://www.massobservationproject.amdigital.co.uk/Documents/Detail/k2721s-response-to-1998-autumn-directive-part-2/9854935?item=9854936.

W571, accessed at https://www.massobservationproject.amdigital.co.uk/Documents/Detail/w571s-response-to-1998-autumn-directive-part-2/9855326?item=9855327.

G2640, accessed at https://www.massobservationproject.amdigital.co.uk/Documents/Detail/g2640s-response-to-1998-autumn-directive-part-2/9854795?item=9854796.

H1806, accessed at https://www.massobservationproject.amdigital.co.uk/Documents/Detail/h1806s-response-to-1992-spring-directive-part-2/8777746?item=8777754.

W633, accessed at https://www.massobservationproject.amdigital.co.uk/Documents/Detail/w633s-response-to-1998-autumn-directive-part-2/9855343?item=9855347.

D1602, accessed at https://www.massobservationproject.amdigital.co.uk/Documents/Detail/c2834s-response-to-1998-autumn-directive-part-2/9854660?item=9854661.

R2247, accessed at https://www.massobservationproject.amdigital.co.uk/Documents/Detail/r2247s-response-to-1998-autumn-directive-part-2/9855127?item=9855132.

T2150, accessed at https://www.massobservationproject.amdigital.co.uk/Documents/Detail/t2150s-response-to-1998-autumn-directive-part-2/9855312.

A1706, accessed at https://www.massobservationproject.amdigital.co.uk/Documents/Detail/a1706s-response-to-1998-autumn-directive-part-2/9854450.

C2579, accessed at https://www.massobservationproject.amdigital.co.uk/Documents/Detail/c2579s-response-to-1998-autumn-directive-part-2/9854628?item=9854630.

A2801, accessed at https://www.massobservationproject.amdigital.co.uk/Documents/Detail/a2801s-response-to-1998-autumn-directive-part-2/9854461.

B2197, accessed at https://www.massobservationproject.amdigital.co.uk/Documents/Detail/b2197s-response-to-1998-autumn-directive-part-2/9854531?item=9854534.

C1786, accessed at https://www.massobservationproject.amdigital.co.uk/Documents/Detail/c1786s-response-to-1998-autumn-directive-part-2/9854608?item=9854614.

C2834, accessed at https://www.massobservationproject.amdigital.co.uk/Documents/Detail/c2834s-response-to-1998-autumn-directive-part-2/9854660?item=9854661.

L1691, accessed at https://www.massobservationproject.amdigital.co.uk/Documents/Detail/l1691s-response-to-1998-autumn-directive-part-2/9854950?item=9854951.

D156, accessed at https://www.massobservationproject.amdigital.co.uk/Documents/Detail/d156s-response-to-1998-autumn-directive-part-2/9854665?item=9854667.

## *Newspapers*

*Evening Times*, 26 October 1987.

*Evening Times*, 12 March 1991.

*Evening Times*, 16 June 1993.

*Glasgow Herald*, 24 February 1967.

*Glasgow Herald*, 31 January 1968.

*Glasgow Herald*, 8 March 1991.

*The Guardian*, 15 February 2001 (Steven Moss article, 'Life after Steel'). Accessed at https://www.theguardian.com/g2/story/0,3604,438063,00.html.

*The Guardian*, 23 September 2020.

*The Guardian*, 20 March 2022. Accessed at https://www.theguardian.com/uk-news/2022/mar/20/uk-asbestos-maker-withheld-information-on-material-risks-court-papers-show.

*The Guardian,* 10 January 2023. Accessed at https://www.theguardian.com/uk-news/2023/jan/10/firefighters-cancer-toxic-chemicals-study?CMP=Share_iOSApp_Other.

*Hazards Magazine*, 64 (October–December 1998).

*Hazards Magazine*, 140 (October–December 2017).

*Hazards Magazine*, 155 (July–September 2021).
*The Herald*, 8 March 2012.
*Lennox Herald*, 20 December 1985.
*The Observer*, 13 December 2020.
*The Observer*, 17 January 2021.
*The Observer*, 24 January 2021.
*The Observer*, 31 January 2021.
*The Observer*, 14 February 2021.
*The Observer*, 28 March 2021.
*The Observer*, 13 February 2022.
*The Observer*, 27 February 2022.
*The Observer*, 1 May 2022.
*The Observer*, 1 January 2023 (*The New Review*).
*The Scotsman*, 4 June 1980.
*The Scotsman*, 31 May 1986.
*The Scotsman*, 15 January 1988.
*The Times Educational Supplement*, 20 November 1992.

### Health and Safety Executive/Factory/Mines Inspectorate

*Annual Report of the Chief Inspector of Factories*, for 1950.
*Report of HM Inspector of Mines, Scottish Division*, for 1949.
*Report of HM Inspector of Mines, Scottish Division*, for 1952.
*Report of HM Inspector of Mines, Scottish Division*, for 1953.
HSE, *The Stress and Health at Work Study* (London, 1998).
HSE Consultation Document, 1998.
HSE, *British Partnership in Health and Safety* (London, 2006).
Health and Safety Executive, 'Annual Statistics, Work-related stress, anxiety or depression statistics in Great Britain, 2020' (20 November 2020). Accessed at https://www.hse.gov.uk/statistics/causdis/stress.pdf.
HSE, 'HSG 218 – Tackling Work Related Stress: A Managers' Guide to Improving and Maintaining Employee Health and Wellbeing' (Sudbury: HMSO 2001). Accessed at https://www.thenbs.com/PublicationIndex/documents/details?Pub=HSE&DocID=265718.
Health and Safety Executive, 'Historical Picture Statistics in Great Britain, 2019: Trends in Work-Related Ill Health and Workplace Injury'. Accessed at www.hse.gov.uk/statistics/history.
http://www.hse.gov.uk/statistics/history/fatal.htm.
http://www.hse.gov.uk/statistics/european/fatal.htm.
https://www.hse.gov.uk/statistics/causdis/stress.pdf.
https://www.hse.gov.uk/biosafety/blood-borne-viruses/risk-healthcare-workers.htm.

### Other Primary Sources

*Alice: Fight for Life*, documentary (Yorkshire Television, 1982).
*Asbestos Bulletin*, 15, 4, July–August 1974.
BBC People's War Archive: Kathy Hind (Lincoln area), Article ID: A4625165, contributed 30 July 2005: https://www.bbc.co.uk/history/ww2peopleswar/.
BBC People's War Archive: Mrs Maureen Holdsworth (Hapton, Nelson), Article ID: A3956349, contributed 26 April 2005 by Lancshomeguard. BBC People's War Archive: https://www.bbc.co.uk/history/ww2peopleswar/.

**Bibliography**

The British Safety Council, *Common Causes of Factory Accidents*, *c.*1970 (pamphlet in the Royal Society for the Prevention of Accidents Archive).

Clyde Shipbuilding Association, *Minutes*, 20 December 1967 (TD 241/12/1136).

Clydebank Health Care Campaign, 'Case for a Public Enquiry' (Clydebank Library, ref. 362.11 LC).

Clydebank Health Care Campaign, 'Comments on an Asbestos Removal Scheme at Clydebank' (Clydebank Library, ref. 362.11 LC).

Clydeside Action on Asbestos, *Hidden Hazard, Forgotten Victims* (video, 1995).

Coal Industry Social Welfare Organisation, *Annual Reports*, for 1953, 1954, 1955, 1957, 1964, 1973, 1976, 1978. Consulted at the South Wales Coalfield Collection, University of Swansea.

'Covid Voices: A Moment in Time' film aired 23/4 March 2022. Part of the NHS Voices from Covid-19 Project: Manchester University. https://www.nhs70.org.uk/story/nhs-voices-covid-19

Ronald Fraser (ed.), *Work 2: Twenty Personal Accounts* (Harmondsworth: Penguin, 1969).

Gender Equality and Diversity Inclusion Committee, Humanities and Social Sciences, University of Strathclyde (Prof Daniela Sime & GEDI Committee members), *The Impact of COVID-19 Lockdown on Colleagues in HaSS: Survey Results*, August 2020.

*Hansard*, 30 July 1958, 1540–1.

House of Commons Scottish Affairs Committee, *Blacklisting in Employment: Final Report Seventh Report of Session 2014–15*, HC 272, 18 March 2015 (London: The Stationery Office). https://www.parliament.uk/blacklisting-in-employment. Accessed July 2020.

House of Commons Scottish Affairs Committee, *Blacklisting in Employment Oral and Written Evidence*. https://www.parliament.uk/blacklisting-in-employment.

House of Commons Scottish Affairs Committee, *Blacklisting in Employment Written Evidence*. https://publications.parliament.uk/pa/cm201213/cmselect/cmscotaf/writev/blacklisting/blacklisting.pdf.

Ilona Kacieja, 'Red Dust' a documentary film (2013). https://www.imdb.com/title/tt3175650/.

ILOSTAT, International Labour Organisation, 'Statistics on Safety and Health at Work' (Fatal Occupational Injuries per 100,000 Workers by Economic Activity: Annual), ILOSTAT. Accessed at https://ilostat.ilo.org/topics/safety-and-health-at-work/.

ILOSTAT, International Labour Organisation, 'Statistics on Union Membership'. Accessed at https://ilostat.ilo.org/topics/union-membership/.

Lucy Parker (director), documentary, *Solidarity* (London: City Projects, 2019). http://www.solidarityfilm.com/. Accessed July 2020.

*Registrar Generals Decennial Supplement on Occupational Mortality*, England and Wales, 1951, 2,1 (London: HMSO, 1958).

*Saga Magazine*, March 1998, www.deadline.demon.co.uk/archive/saga/980301.htm.

Transport Committee Oral Evidence, *Work of the Driving Vehicle Licensing Agency*, HC 567. July 2021.

## *Websites*

*Other than those cited above:*

Coalfield Regeneration Trust, *Report on Coalfield Area Deprivation in Scotland* (2013), 7, 14. http://www.coalfields-regen.org.uk/wp-content/uploads/2013/06/Coalfields-Deprivation-in-Scotland2013.pdf.

Community Renewal, 'The Craigneuk Report', June 2007. http://www.communityrenewal.org.uk/wp-content/uploads/2015/09/communityrenewal_craigneukreport_07.pdf.

Corporate Crime & Governance website: http://www.gla.ac.uk/faculties/socialsciences/corpcrime/links.htm.

## Bibliography

Dave Lyddon, 'Health and Safety', Britain at Work, London Metropolitan University. http://www.unionhistory.info/britainatwork/narrativedisplay.php?type=healthandsafety. Accessed July 2020.

Disability and Industrial Society: https://www.dis-ind-soc.org.uk/en/index.htm.

NHS Scotland, http://www.healthscotland.scot/health-inequalities/fundamental-causes/employment-inequality.

NHS Staff Survey of 2020. https://www.nhsconfed.org/publications/nhs-staff-survey-2020.

NHS Voices from Covid-19 Project: Manchester University. https://www.nhs70.org.uk/story/nhs-voices-covid-19.

Ronnie Johnston and Arthur McIvor, 'Oral Histories of the Asbestos Tragedy in Scotland', http://ibasecretariat.org/search_item.php?l0=5±25±51&l1=94±10±36&f=eas_rj_am_scotland.php.

Tom White, 'Radical Object'. Accessed at https://www.historyworkshop.org.uk/radical-objects-hulls-headscarf-revolutionaries-mural/.

http://www.telegraph.co.uk/health/healthnews/7991620/Stress-increases-risk-of-death-five-fold.html.

https://www.theguardian.com/world/2011/aug/04/chilean-miners-financial-psychological-problems.

https://www.walesonline.co.uk/news/wales-news/my-husband-worked-hard-no-15866821

https://www.bbc.co.uk/news/uk-wales-47296631.

https://www.iqsolutions.com/section/ideas/sex-workers-and-stis-ignored-epidemic.

https://www.telegraph.co.uk/global-health/science-and-disease/wearing-face-mask-not-new-backlash-against-say-historians/.

https://www.manchestereveningnews.co.uk/news/greater-manchester-news/gallery/smog-manchester-london-sheffield-1950s-8873555.

https://www.statnews.com/2016/09/28/2016-flu-season-shots-science/.

https://apimagesblog.com/historical/2020/3/12/influenza-pandemics-throughout-history.

https://www.theguardian.com/world/2020/oct/01/flu-vaccine-for-hospitals-epidemic-1957

https://www.bbc.co.uk/news/av/uk-scotland-60293190.

https://www.bmj.com/company/newsroom/healthcare-workers-7-times-as-likely-to-have-severe-covid-19-as-other-workers/.

https://content.tfl.gov.uk/phase-2-assessment-of-london-bus-driver-mortality-from-covid-19.pdf.

https://theconversation.com/healthcare-workers-and-coronavirus-behind-the-stiff-upper-lip-we-are-highly-vulnerable-133864.

https://theconversation-com.cdn.ampproject.org/c/s/theconversation.com/amp/nurses-are-on-the-coronavirus-frontline-so-why-are-they-being-left-out-of-the-response-143658.

https://www.london.gov.uk/questions/2020/1725.

https://content.tfl.gov.uk/phase-2-assessment-of-london-bus-driver-mortality-from-covid-19.pdf.

https://www.bbc.co.uk/programmes/m001009z.

https://www.bbc.co.uk/news/uk-england-humber-35735318.

https://edm.parliament.uk/early-day-motion/57194/professor-philip-taylors-report-on-the-effect-of-covid19-on-callcentre-workers.

https://www.walesonline.co.uk/news/local-news/dvla-staff-swansea-scared-go-19691094

https://www.theguardian.com/world/2021/jan/23/minister-faces-fury-over-mass-covid-outbreak-at-top-government-agency.

https://www.ier.org.uk/news/dvla-head-misleads-mps-over-coronavirus-outbreak/.

https://www.itv.com/news/wales/2021-03-03/lack-of-safe-distancing-at-dvla-a-national-scandal-as-investigation-reveals-staff-were-not-sat-two-metres-apart.

## Bibliography

https://nursingnotes.co.uk/news/clinical/long-covid-should-be-recognised-as-a-disability-as-patients-and-staff-struggle-to-recover/.
http://www.workstress.net/uknwsns-origins.

### Secondary Sources (books, chapters, articles, theses)

Abendstern, Michele, Christine Hallett, and Lesley Wade. 'Flouting the Law: Women and the Hazards of Cleaning Moving Machinery in the Cotton Industry, 1930–1970', *Oral History*, 33, 2 (2005): 69–78.

Abrams, Lynn. *Oral History Theory* (London: Routledge, 2010; 2nd ed., 2016).

Allen, David and Laurie Kazan-Allen. *India's Asbestos Time Bomb* (International Ban Asbestos Secretariat, online publication, 2008). Accessed at http://ibasecretariat.org/india_asb_time_bomb.pdf.

Almond, Paul and Mike Esbester. *Health and Safety in Contemporary Britain: Society, Legitimacy and Change since 1960* (London: Palgrave Macmillan, 2019).

Archibald, R.M. 'Coal Mining: Non-Respiratory Problems', in A. Ward Gardner (ed.), *Current Approaches to Occupational Health 2* (Bristol: John Wright, 1982): 30–61.

Arnot, Robert Page. *The Miners: A History of the Miners' Federation of Great Britain from 1910 Onwards* (London: George Allen and Unwin, 1953).

Arnot, Robert Page. *The Miners in Crisis and War* (London: George Allen and Unwin, 1961).

Arthur, Ryan. 'The Capture, Release and Recapture of Occupational Health and Safety' (PhD thesis, University of Reading, 2018).

Bain, Peter. '"Is you is or is you ain't my baby": Women's Pay and the Clydeside Strikes of 1943', *Scottish Labour History*, 30 (1995): 35–60.

Bambra, Clare. *Work, Worklessness and the Political Economy of Health* (Oxford: Oxford University Press, 2012).

Barnes, Colin and Geoff Mercer. *Disability* (Cambridge: Polity Press, 2003).

Bartley, Mel. 'Coronary Heart Disease', in Paul Weindling (ed.), *The Social History of Occupational Health* (London: Croom Helm, 1985): 137–156.

Bartley, Mel. *Authorities and Partisans: The Debate on Unemployment and Health* (Edinburgh: Edinburgh University Press, 1992).

Bartley, Mel and Ian Plewis. 'Accumulated Labour Market Disadvantage and Limiting Long Term Illness', *International Journal of Epidemiology*, 31 (2002): 336–41.

Bartrip, Peter. *Workmen's Compensation in Twentieth Century Britain: Law, History and Social Policy* (Aldershot: Gower, 1987).

Bartrip, Peter. '"Petticoat Pestering": The Women's Trade Union League and Lead Poisoning in the Staffordshire Potteries, 1890–1914', *Historical Studies in Industrial Relations*, 2 (September 1996): 3–26.

Bartrip, Peter. *The Way from Dusty Death: Turner and Newall and the Regulation of the British Asbestos Industry 1890s–1970* (London: Athlone Press, 2001).

Beaumont, Phil B. *Safety at Work and the Unions* (Beckenham: Croom Helm, 1983).

Beck, Mathias and Andrew Watterson. 'Privatization and Multi-Fatality Disasters: A Causal Connection Exposing Both Worker and Citizen Health and Safety Failures in the UK?' *International Journal of Environmental Research and Public Health* 19 (2022), https://doi.org/10.3390/ijerph192013138.

Beck, Mathias, John Foster, and Charles Woolfson. *Paying for the Piper: Capital and Labour in Britain's Offshore Oil Industry* (London: Mansell, 1996).

Beck, Mathias, John Foster, Helge Ryggvik, and Charles Woolfson. *Piper Alpha Ten Years After* (Glasgow: University of Glasgow, 1998).

Bell, Karen. *Working-Class Environmentalism* (London: Palgrave Macmillan, 2020).

## Bibliography

Bellaby, Paul. *Sick from Work: The Body in Employment* (Aldershot: Ashgate, 1999).

Bellaby, Paul and Felix Bellaby. 'Unemployment and Ill Health: Local Labour Markets and Ill Health in Britain, 1984–1991', *Work, Employment and Society*, 13, 3 (1999): 461–82.

Bellamy, Martin. *The Shipbuilders* (Edinburgh: Berlinn, 2001).

Berridge, Virginia. *Aids in the UK: The Making of Policy* (Oxford: Oxford University Press, 1996).

Beynon, Hugh. *Working for Ford* (London: Allen Lane, 1973).

Beynon, Hugh and Ray Hudson. *The Shadow of the Mine* (London: Verso, 2021).

Bhui, Kamaldeep, Sokratis Dinos, Magdalena Galant-Miecznikowska, Bertine de Jongh, and Stephen Stansfeld. 'Perceptions of Work Stress Causes and Effective Interventions in Employees Working in Public, Private and Non-governmental Organisations: A Qualitative Study', *British Journal of Psychology Bulletin* 40, 6 (December 2016): 318–25. Accessed at https://www.ncbi.nlm.nih.gov/pmc/articles/PMC5353523/.

Blakemore, Ken and Robert Drake. *Understanding Equal Opportunity Policies* (London: Harvester Wheatsheaf, 1996).

Blackwell, Trevor and Jeremy Seabrook. *Talking Work: An Oral History* (London: Faber and Faber, 1996).

Blaxter, Mildred. *The Meaning of Disability* (London: Heinemann, 1976).

Bloor, Michael. 'No Longer Dying for a Living', *Sociology*, 36, 1 (2002): 89–105.

Bohata, Kirsti, Alexandra Jones, Mike Mantin, and Steven Thompson. *Disability in Industrial Britain: A Cultural and Literary History of Impairment in the Coal Industry* (Manchester: Manchester University Press, 2020).

Bolton, Sharon and Carol Boyd. 'Trolley Dolly or Skilled Emotion Manager? Moving on From Hochschild's Managed Heart', *Work, Employment & Society*, 17, 2 (2003): 289–308.

Booth, Alan and Joseph Melling. 'Workplace Cultures and Business Performance', in Joseph Melling and Alan Booth (eds), *Managing the Modern Workplace* (Aldershot: Ashgate, 2008): 1–26.

Bornat, Joanna. 'A Second Take: Revisiting Interviews with a Different Purpose', *Oral History*, 31, 1 (Spring 2003): 47–53.

Bornat, Joanna, Rob Perks, Paul Thompson, and Jan Walmsley (eds), *Oral History, Health and Welfare*, London: Routledge, 1999).

Borsay, Ann. *Disability and Social Policy in Britain since 1750: A History of Exclusion* (Basingstoke: Palgrave 2005).

Bourke, Joanna. *Working Class Cultures in Britain, 1890–1960* (London: Routledge, 1993).

Bowden, Sue and Geoff Tweedale. 'Mondays without Dread: The Trade Union Response to Byssinosis in the Lancashire Cotton Industry in the Twentieth Century', *Social History of Medicine*, 16, 1 (2003): 79–95.

Boyd, Carol. 'Customer Violence and Employee Health and Safety', *Work, Employment and Society*, 16, 1 (2002): 151–69.

Bradley, David. 'Occupational Health and Safety in the Scottish Steel Industry, c.1930–1988: The Road to "Its Own Wee Empire"' (PhD thesis, Caledonian University, 2012).

Brenner, M.H. and A. Mooney. 'Unemployment and Health in the Context of Economic Change', *Social Science and Medicine*, 17 (2003): 1125–38.

Brotherstone, Terry and Hugo Manson. 'North Sea Oil, Its Narratives and Its History', *Northern Scotland*, 27 (2007): 15–41.

Brotherstone, Terry and Hugo Manson. 'Voices of Piper Alpha: Enduring Injury in Private Memory, Oral Representation and Labour History', *Scottish Labour History*, 46, 2011: 71–85.

Bruder, Jessica. *Nomadland: Surviving America in the Twenty-First Century* (London: Swift Press, 2017).

Bryan, Elizabeth. *Bathgate Once More: The Story of the BMC/Leyland Truck and Tractor Plant, 1961–86* (Edinburgh: Workers' Educational Association, 2012).

# Bibliography

Bufton, Mark and Joe Melling. 'Coming Up for Air: Experts, Employers and Workers in Campaigns to Compensate Silicosis Sufferers in Britain, 1918–1939', *Social History of Medicine*, 18 (2005): 63–86.

Bunting, Madeleine. *Willing Slaves: How the Overwork Culture Is Ruining Our Lives* (London: HarperCollins, 2004).

Burns, William. 'We Just Thought We Were Superhuman: An Oral History of Noise and Piecework in Paisley's Thread Mills', *Labour History*, 119 (2020): 173–96.

Carter, Tim and Joseph Melling. 'Trade, Spores and the Culture of Disease: Attempts to Regulate Anthrax in Britain and Its International Trade, 1875–1930', in Christopher Sellers and Joseph Melling (eds), *Dangerous Trade: Histories of Industrial Hazard across a Globalising World* (Philadelphia: Temple University Press, 2012), 60–72.

Case, Anne and Angus Deaton. *Deaths of Despair* (Princeton: Princeton University Press, 2020).

Castleman, Barry and Geoffrey Tweedale. 'Turning the Tide: The Struggle for Compensation for Asbestos-Related Diseases and the Banning of Asbestos', in Christopher Sellers and Joseph Melling (eds), *Dangerous Trade: Histories of Industrial Hazard across a Globalising World* (Philadelphia: Temple, 2012), 181–94.

Chand, Alison. *Masculinities on Clydeside: Men in Reserved Occupations during the Second World War* (Edinburgh: Edinburgh University Press, 2016).

Chand, Alison. 'Same Interviewee, Different Interviewer: Researching Intersubjectivity in Studies of the Reserved Occupations in the Second World War', *The Oral History Review*, 48, 1 (2021): 3–19. https://doi.org/10.1080/00940798.2021.1879600

Chappell, Helen. 'Fighting Each Other over Asbestos', *New Society*, 29 September 1983, 471–3.

Church, Roy and Quentin Outram. *Strikes and Solidarity: Coalfield Conflict in Britain, 1889–1996* (Cambridge: Cambridge University Press, 1998).

Clarke, Rachel. *Breathtaking: Inside the NHS in a Time of Pandemic* (London: Little Brown, 2020).

Clayson, Helen. 'The Experience of Mesothelioma in Northern England' (MD thesis, University of Sheffield, 2007).

Coates, Ken and Michael Barratt Brown. *Community under Attack: The Struggle for Survival in the Coalfield Communities of Britain* (Nottingham: Spokesman, 1997).

Connell, Robert W. *The Men and the Boys* (Cambridge: Polity Press, 2000).

Cook, Matthew. 'AIDS, Mass Observation, and the Fate of the Permissive Turn', *Journal of the History of Sexuality*, 26, 2 (2017): 239–72.

Copestake, Emma. 'Laughing through the Pain? Occupational Wellbeing on the Waterfront in Liverpool c.1964–1998' (PhD thesis, University of Liverpool, 2022).

Cowie, Jefferson and Joseph Heathcott (eds), *Beyond the Ruins: The Meanings of Deindustrialization* (Ithaca, NY: Cornell University Press, 2003).

Coyle, Angela. *Redundant Women* (London: Women's Press, 1984).

Cornwell, Jocelyn. *Hard Earned Lives: Accounts of Health and Illness from East London* (London: Tavistock, 1990).

Dalton, Alan. *Asbestos Killer Dust* (London: British Society for Social Responsibility in Science Publications, 1979).

Dalton, Alan. *Safety, Health and Environmental Hazards at the Workplace* (London: Cassell, 1998).

Dawson, Graham. *Soldier Heroes. British Adventure, Empire and the Imagining of Masculinities* (London: Routledge, 1994).

Daykin, Norma and Lesley Doyal (eds.), *Health and Work, Critical Perspectives* (Basingstoke: Macmillan, 1999).

Della Porta, Donatella. *Methodological Practices in Social Movement Research* (Oxford: Oxford University Press, 2014).

Dembe, Alan. *Occupation and Disease: How Social Factors Affect the Conception of Work-Related Disorders* (New Haven, CT: Yale University Press, 1996).

## Bibliography

Dollard, Maureen and Daniel Neser. 'Worker Health Is Good for the Economy', *Social Science and Medicine* 92 (September 2013), 114–23.

Donaldson, Annie. *An Oral History of Domestic Abuse in Scotland, 1945–92* (PhD thesis, University of Strathclyde, 2019).

Doyal, Lesley. *What Makes Women Sick* (Houndmills: Macmillan, 1995).

Eva, D. and R. Oswald, *Health and Safety at Work* (London: Pan Books, 1981).

Farooki, Roopa. *Everything Is True: A Junior Doctor's Story of Life, Death and Grief in a Time of Pandemic* (London: Bloomsbury, 2022).

Feltrin, Lorenzo, Alice Mah, and David Brown. 'Noxious Deindustrialization: Experiences of Precarity and Pollution in Scotland's Petrochemical Capital', *Environment and Planning C: Politics and Space*, 40, 4 (2022): 950–69.

Ferns, James. 'Workers' Identities in Transition: Deindustrialisation and Scottish Steelworkers', *Journal of Working-Class Studies*, 4, 2 (2019): 55–78.

Fieldhouse, Edward and Emma Hollywood. 'Life after Mining: Hidden Unemployment and Changing Patterns of Economic Activity amongst Miners in England and Wales, 1981–1991', *Work, Employment and Society*, 13, 3 (1999): 483–502.

Fryer, David. 'Psychological or Material Deprivation: Why Does Unemployment Have Mental Health Consequences', in Eithne McLaughlin (ed.), *Understanding Unemployment* (London: Routledge, 1992), 103–25.

Fyrth, Hubert and Henry Collins. *The Foundry Workers* (Manchester: Amalgamated Union of Foundry Workers, 1959).

Gall, Gregor. 'Union Organising in the Offshore Oil and Gas Industry', *Scottish Labour History*, 41 (2006): 51–69.

Gallie, Duncan (ed.), *Employment in Britain* (Oxford: Blackwell, 1988).

Gebrial, Dalia and Paddy Bettington. 'The Insecure Economy: Measuring and Understanding the Contemporary Labour Market', policy paper for *Autonomy* and *The Centre for Labour and Social Studies* (March 2022): consulted at http://classonline.org.uk/pubs/item/the-insecure-economy-measuring-and-understanding-the-contemporary-labour-ma.

Geiser, Kenneth. 'Health Hazards in the Microelectronics Industry', *International Journal of Health Services*, 16, 1 (1986): 105–20.

Gildart, Keith. 'Coal Strikes on the Home Front: Miners' Militancy and Socialist Politics in the Second World War', *Twentieth Century British History*, 20 (2009): 121–51.

Glasser, Ralph. *Growing Up in the Gorbals* (London: Pan Books, 1987).

Goodwin, John. *Men's Work and Male Lives: Men and Work in Britain* (Aldershot: Ashgate, 1999).

Gorman, Tommy. 'Women and Asbestos', in Tommy Gorman (ed.), *Clydebank: Asbestos, the Unwanted Legacy* (Glasgow: Clydeside Press, 2000), 127–37.

Green, Anna. 'Individual Remembering and "collective memory": Theoretical Presuppositions and Contemporary Debates', *Oral History*, 32, 2 (2004): 35–44.

Greenlees, Janet. *When the Air Became Important* (New Brunswick: Rutgers University Press, 2019).

Haggett, Ali. *Desperate Housewives: Neuroses and the Domestic Environment 1945–1970* (Abingdon: Routledge, 2012).

Haggett, Ali. *A History of Male Psychological Disorders in Britain, 1945–1970* (Basingstoke: Palgrave Macmillan, 2015).

Hall, David. *Working Lives* (London: Bantam Press, 2012).

Hammond, E. *An Analysis of Regional Economic and Social Statistics* (Durham: University of Durham, Rowntree Research Unit, 1968).

Harris, Dai and Richard Haigh (eds) for the Terence Higgins Trust, *AIDS; a Guide to the Law* (London: Tavistock/Routledge, 1990).

Harrison, Barbara. *Not Only the Dangerous Trades: Women's Work and Health in Britain, 1880–1914* (London: Routledge, 1996).

## Bibliography

High, Steven. *Industrial Sunset: The Making of North America's Rust Belt, 1969–1984* (Toronto: University of Toronto Press, 2003).

High, Steven. *One Job Town: Work, Belonging, and Betrayal in Northern Ontario* (Toronto: University of Toronto Press, 2018).

High, Steven and David Lewis. *Corporate Wasteland: The Landscape and Memory of Deindustrialisation* (Ithaca, NY: Cornell University Press, 2007).

High, Steven, Lachlan MacKinnon, and Andrew Perchard (eds), *The Deindustrialized World: Confronting Ruination in Post-Industrial Spaces* (Vancouver: University of British Columbia Press, 2017).

Ho, Wing-Chung. *Occupational Health and Social Estrangement in China* (Manchester: Manchester University Press, 2017).

Hodson, Randy. *Dignity at Work* (Cambridge: Cambridge University Press, 2001).

Honigsbaum, Mark. 'The Art of Medicine: Revisiting the 1957 and 1968 Influenza Epidemics', *The Lancet*, 395 (2020): 1824–1826. https://doi.org/10.1016/ S0140-6736(20)31201-0; www.thelancet.com.

Hunter, Donald. *Health in Industry* (Harmondsworth: Penguin, 1959).

Hunter, Kim. 'When Workers Fight for Our Environment', *International Socialism*, 168 (October 2020). Accessed at http://isj.org.uk/workers-fight-for-environment/#footnote-10080-40.

Huey, Jack. '"Being Blacked": A History of Blacklisting in the Construction Industry' (BA History dissertation, University of Strathclyde, 2019).

Iacuone, David. '"Real Men Are Tough Guys": Hegemonic Masculinity and Safety in the Construction Industry', *The Journal of Men's Studies*, 13, 2 (2005): 75–88.

ILO. *Health and Safety at Work: A Trade Union Priority*, Labour Education Series, 126 (Geneva: ILO, 2002).

ILO. *Safety and Health in Agriculture* (Geneva: ILO, 2011).

Jackson, Mark. *The Age of Stress: Science and the Search for Stability* (Oxford: Oxford University Press, 2013).

Jackson, Mark (ed.). *Stress in Post-War Britain, 1945–85* (London: Pickering and Chatto, 2015).

James, Oliver. *Affluenza* (London: Vermilion, 2007).

Johnston, Ronald and Arthur McIvor. *Lethal Work: A History of the Asbestos Tragedy in Scotland* (East Linton: Tuckwell Press, 2000).

Johnston, Ronald and Arthur McIvor. 'Oral History in Asbestos Investigations', in George A. Peters and Barbara J. Peters (eds), *The Asbestos Legacy: The Sourcebook on Asbestos Diseases*, 23 (San Francisco: LexisNexis, 2001): 3–35.

Johnston, Ronald and Arthur McIvor. 'Dangerous Work, Hard Men and Broken Bodies: Masculinity in the Clydeside Heavy Industries', *Labour History Review*, 69, 2 (2004): 135–53.

Johnston, Ronald and Arthur McIvor. 'The War at Work: Occupational Health and Safety in Scottish Industry, 1939–1945', *Journal of Scottish Historical Studies*, 2 (2005): 113–36.

Johnston, Ronald and Arthur McIvor. 'Marginalising the Body at Work? Employers' Occupational Health Strategies and Occupational Medicine in Scotland c. 1930–1974', *Social History of Medicine*, 21, 1 (2008): 127–44.

Joshi, Chitra. 'De-industrialization" and the Crisis of Male Identities', *International Review of Social History*, 47, Supplement 10 (2002): 159–75.

Jones, Helen. 'An Inspector Calls', in Paul Weindling (ed.), *The Social History of Occupational Health* (London: Croom Helm, 1985).

Kacieja, Ilona. *Red Dust: The Craig Documentary Film Project* (Masters dissertation, Edinburgh College of Art, 2013).

Kay, Adam. *This Is Going to Hurt: Secret Diaries of a Junior Doctor* (London: Picador, 2017).

Kenefick, William. *Rebellious and Contrary: The Glasgow Dockers, 1853–1932* (East Linton: Tuckwell Press, 2000).

# Bibliography

Kenyon, Joe. *A Passion for Justice* (Nottingham: Trent Editions, 2003).

Kirby, Jill. 'Troubled by Life: The Experience of Stress in Twentieth-century Britain' (Univ Sussex DPhil, 2014). Consulted online via Sussex Research Online: http://sro.sussex.ac.uk/.

Kirby, Jill. *Feeling the Strain: A Cultural History of Stress in Twentieth Century Britain* (Manchester: Manchester University Press, 2019).

Kirk, John. 'Coming to the End of the Line? Identity, Work and Structures of Feeling', *Oral History*, 36, 2 (2008): 44–53.

Langhamer, Claire. 'Feeling, Women and Work in the Long 1950s', *Women's History Review*, 26, 1 (2017): 77–92. Consulted at Sussex Research Online: http://sro.sussex.ac.uk/id/eprint/59365/.

Lavery, Brian W. *The Headscarf Revolutionaries: Lillian Bilocca and the Hull Triple-Trawler Disaster* (London: Barbican Press, 2015).

Levy, Karen. *Data Driven: Truckers, Technology and the New Workplace Surveillance* (Princeton: Princeton Press, 2022).

Lewis, Glynn and Andy Sloggett. 'Suicide, Deprivation and Unemployment: Record Linkage Study', *British Medical Journal*, 317 (7 November 1998): 26–29.

Lindsay, Colin and Donald Houston (eds), *Disability Benefits, Welfare Reform and Employment Policy* (Basingstoke: Palgrave Macmillan, 2013).

Long, Vicky. '"A Satisfactory Job Is the Best Psychotherapist": Employment and Mental Health, 1939–60', in Pamela Dale and Joseph Melling (eds), *Mental Illness and Learning Disability since 1850* (Abingdon: Routledge, 2006).

Long, Vicky. *The Rise and Fall of the Healthy Factory: The Politics of Industrial Health in Britain, 1914–60* (Basingstoke: Macmillan, 2011).

Loomis, Dana, David B. Richardson, James Bena, and John Bailer. 'Deindustrialisation and the Long Term Decline in Fatal Occupational Injuries', *Occupational and Environmental Medicine*, 61, 7 (2004): 616–21.

Lyddon, Dave. 'Trade Unions and the History of Health and Safety in British Mining', *Historical Studies in Industrial Relations*, 35 (2014): 157–79.

MacDougall, Ian (ed.), *Voices from Work and Home* (Edinburgh: Mercat Press, 2000).

Mackenzie, Mhairi, Chik Collins, John Connolly, Mick Doyle, and Gerry McCartney. 'Working-class Discourses of Politics, Policy and Health: "I Don't Smoke; I Don't Drink. The Only Thing Wrong with Me Is My Health."' *Policy & Politics*, 45, 2 (2015): 231–49.

MacKinnon, Lachlan. *Closing Sysco: Industrial Decline in Atlantic Canada's Steel City* (Toronto: University of Toronto Press, 2020).

Malacrida, Claudia. 'Contested Memories: Efforts of the Powerful to Silence Former Inmates Histories of Life in an Institution for "Mental Defectives"', in Kristina Llewellyn, Alexander Freund and Nolan Reilly (eds), *The Canadian Oral History Reader* (Montreal: McGill-Queens University Press, 2015), 318–34.

Markowitz, Gerald and David Rosner. *Lead Wars* (Berkeley: University of California Press, 2013).

Mass Observation, *People in Production* (Harmondsworth: Penguin, 1942).

McCray Beier, Linda. *For Their Own Good: The Transformation of English Working Class Health Culture, 1880–1970* (Ohio: Ohio State University Press, 2008).

McCulloch, Jock and Geoff Tweedale. *Defending the Indefensible: The Global Asbestos Industry and Its Fight for Survival* (Oxford: Oxford University Press, 2008).

McDougall, William. 'Pressure Group Influence and Occupational Health, SPAID/OEDA, 1978–2008' (PhD thesis, Glasgow Caledonian University, 2013).

McIvor, Arthur. *A History of Work in Britain, 1880–1950* (Basingstoke: Palgrave, 2001).

McIvor, Arthur. 'Germs at Work: Establishing Tuberculosis as an Occupational Disease in Britain, c1900–1951', *Social History of Medicine*, 25, 4 (2012): 812–29.

McIvor, Arthur. *Working Lives: Work in Britain since 1945* (Basingstoke: Palgrave, 2013).

# Bibliography

McIvor, Arthur. 'Toxic City: Industrial Residues, the Body and Community Activism as Heritage Practice in Glasgow', in Liz Kryder-Reid and Sarah May (eds), *Toxic Heritage: Legacies, Futures, and Environmental Injustice* (Abington: Routledge, 2023).

McIvor, Arthur and Ronald Johnston. *Miners' Lung: A History of Dust Disease in British Coal Mining* (Aldershot: Ashgate, 2007).

McKessock, Brenda. *Mesothelioma: The Story of an Illness* (Argyll: Argyll Publishing, 1995).

McLay, Farquhar (ed.), *Workers City: The Reckoning: Public Loss, Private Gain* (Glasgow: Clydeside Press, 1990).

Melling, Joseph. 'The Risks of Working and the Risks of Not Working: Trade Unions, Employers and Responses to the Risk of Occupational Illness in British Industry, c1890–1940s', *ESRC Centre for Analysis of Risk and Regulation Discussion Paper*, 12 (2003).

Melling, Joseph. 'Making Sense of Workplace Fear: The Role of Physicians, Psychiatrists, and Labor in Reforming Occupational Strain in Industrial Britain, c 1850–1970', in David Cantor and Edmund Ramsden (eds), *Stress, Shock and Adaptation in the Twentieth Century* (Rochester, NY: University of Rochester Press, 2014).

Melling, Joseph. 'Labouring Stress: Scientific Research, Trade Unions and Perceptions of Workplace Stress in Mid-Twentieth Century Britain', in Mark Jackson (ed.), *Stress in Post-War Britain, 1945–85* (London: Pickering and Chatto, 2015).

Messing, Karen. *One Eyed Science: Occupational Health and Women Workers* (Philadelphia: Temple University Press, 1998).

Messing, Karen. *Bent Out of Shape: Shame, Solidarity and Women's Bodies at Work* (Toronto: Between the Lines, 2021).

Moffat, Abe. *My Life with the Miners* (London: Lawrence and Wishart, 1965).

Mok, Pearl L., Navneet Kapur, Kirsten Windfuhr, Alistair H. Leyland, Louis Appleby, Stephen Platt, and Roger T. Webb. 'Trends in National Suicide Rates for Scotland and for England & Wales, 1960–2008', *British Journal of Psychiatry*, 200, 3 (2012): 245–51.

Mukherjee, Suroopa. *Surviving Bhopal* (New York: Palgrave, 2010).

Mutambudzi, Mirium Claire Niedzwiedz, Ewan B. Macdonald et al. 'Occupation and Risk of Severe COVID-19: Prospective Cohort Study of 120,075 UK Biobank Participants', *Occupational and Environmental Medicine*, 78 (2021): 307–14.

Navarro, Vincent and David Berman (eds), *Health and Safety under Capitalism: An International Perspective* (Farmington, NY: Routledge, 1983).

Nay, Salvator Y. 'Asbestos in Belgium: Use and Abuse', *International Journal of Occupational and Environmental Health*, 9 (2003): 287–93.

Newman, Laura. *Germs in the English Workplace, c1880–1945* (Abingdon: Routledge, 2021).

Newlands, Emma. *Civilians into Soldiers: The British Male Military Body in the Second World War* (Manchester: Manchester University Press, 2014).

Nichols, Theo. *The Sociology of Industrial Injury* (London: Mansell, 1997).

Nichols, Theo. 'Death and Injury at Work: A Sociological Approach', in Norma Daykin and Lesley Doyal (eds), *Health and Work, Critical Perspectives* (Hampshire: Macmillan Press, 1999).

Nichols, Theo, David Walters, and Ali Tasiran. 'Trade Unions, Institutional Mediation and Industrial Safety', *Journal of Industrial Relations*, 49, 2 (April 2007): 211–25.

Nixon, Rob. *Slow Violence and the Environmentalism of the Poor* (Cambridge, MA: Harvard University Press, 2013).

Noon, Mike and Paul Blyton. *The Realities of Work* (Basingstoke: Palgrave Macmillan, 2002).

Oakley, Ann. *The Captured Womb: A History of the Medical Care of Pregnant Women* (Oxford: Blackwell, 1984).

O'Neill, Rory. 'When It Comes to Health and Safety Your Life Should Be in Union Hands', in *Health and Safety at Work: A Trade Union Priority*, Labour Education Series, 126 (Geneva: ILO, 2002), 13–18.

## Bibliography

Orr, Deborah. *Motherwell: A Girlhood* (London: Weidenfeld and Nicholson, 2020).

Orwell, George. *The Road to Wigan Pier* (London: Victor Gollancz, 1937).

Ostry, Aleck S, M. Barroetavena, R. Hershler, Shona Kelly et al. 'Effect of De-industrialisation on Working Conditions and Self-Reported Health in a Sample of Manufacturing Workers', *Epidemiology and Community Health*, 56 (2002): 506–9.

Paap, Kris. *Working Construction: Why White Working-Class Men Put Themselves – and the Labor Movement–in Harm's Way* (Ithaca: Cornell University Press, 2006).

Passerini, Luisa. *Fascism in Popular Memory* (Cambridge: Cambridge University Press, 1987).

Pattinson, Juliette, Arthur McIvor, and Linsey Robb. *Men in Reserve: British Civilian Masculinities in the Second World War* (Manchester: Manchester University Press, 2017).

Mok, Pearl L., Navneet Kapur, Kirsten Windfuhr, Alistair H. Leyland, Louis Appleby, Stephen Platt, and Roger T. Webb. 'Trends in National Suicide Rates for Scotland and for England & Wales, 1960–2008', *British Journal of Psychiatry*, 200, 3 (2012): 245–51.

Pearson, Geoff. *The New Heroin Users* (Oxford: Blackwell, 1987).

Perchard, Andrew. *The Mine Management Professions in the Twentieth Century Scottish Coal Mining Industry* (Lampeter: Edwin Mellen Press, 2007).

Perchard, Andrew. *Aluminiumville* (Lancaster: Crucible Books, 2012).

Perchard, Andrew. '"Broken Men" and "Thatcher's Children": Memory and Legacy in Scotland's Coalfields', *International Labour and Working-Class History*, 84 (2013): 78–98. https://doi.org/10.1017/S0147547913000252.

Phizacklea, Annie. 'Gender, Racism and Occupational Segregation', in Sylvia Walby (ed.), *Gender Segregation at Work* (Milton Keynes: Open University Press, 1988).

Phizacklea, Annie and Robert Miles. *Labour and Racism* (London: Routledge and Kegan Paul, 1980).

Portelli, Alessandro. *The Death of Luigi Trastulli and Other Stories: Form and Meaning in Oral History* (Albany: SUNY Press, 1991).

Portelli, Alessandro. *They Say in Harlan County: An Oral History* (New York: Oxford University Press, 2010).

Powell, P.I., M. Hale, J. Martin, and M. Simon. *200 Accidents: A Shop Floor Study of Their Causes* (London: National Institute of Industrial Psychology, 1971).

Purdie, Sam. 'The Scottish Miner' (unpublished paper 2015 gifted from Sam Purdie to Arthur McIvor).

Quinlan, Michael, Claire Mayhew, and Philip Bohle. 'The Global Expansion of Precarious Employment, Work Disorganisation and Occupational Health: A Review of Recent Research', *International Journal of Health Services*, 31, 2 (2001): 1–39.

Quinlan, Michael, Philip Bohle, and Felicity Lamm. *Managing Occupational Health and Safety* (Melbourne: Palgrave Macmillan, 2010).

Reilly, Barry, Pierella Paci, and Peter Holl. 'Unions, Safety Committees and Workplace Injuries', *British Journal of Industrial Relations*, 33, 2 (1995): 275–88.

Riessman, Catherine Kohler. *Narrative Analysis* (Newbury Park, CA: Sage Publications, 1993).

Roberts, Elizabeth. *A Woman's Place: An Oral History of Working Class Women 1890–1940* (Oxford: Basil Blackwell, 1984).

Robinson, Andrew and Clive Smallman. 'The Contemporary British Workplace: A Safer and Healthier Place?', *Work Employment Society*, 2006, 20 (2006): 87–107.

Rogaly, Ben. *Stories from a Migrant City: Living and Working Together in the Shadow of Brexit* (Manchester: Manchester University Press, 2020).

Rosner, David and Gerald Markowitz. *Deadly Dust* (Princeton: Princeton University Press, 1994).

Roy, Kenneth. *The Broken Journey* (Edinburgh: Berlinn, 2016), consulted online at https://books.google.co.uk/books?id=8589DQAAQBAJ&pg.

Reid, Alison, Peter Franklin, Nola Olsen, Jan Sleith, Latha Samuel, Patrick Aboagye-Sarfo, Nicholas de Klerk, and A.W. (Bill) Musk. 'All-cause Mortality and Cancer Incidence

## Bibliography

among Adults Exposed to Blue Asbestos during Childhood', *American Journal of Industrial Medicine*, 2013, Accessed at https://www.academia.edu/25644855/All_cause_mortality_and_cancer_incidence_among_adults_exposed_to_blue_asbestos_during_childhood?auto=download&email_work_card=download-paper.

Scambler, Graham and Annette Scambler. 'Health and Work in the Sex Industry', in Norma Daykin and Lesley Doyal (eds), *Health and Work: Critical Perspectives* (Basingstoke: Macmillan, 1999), 71–85.

Schaffner, Anna K. *Exhaustion: A History* (New York: Columbia University Press, 2016).

Schilling, Richard. *A Challenging Life: Sixty Years in Occupational Health* (London: Canning Press, 1998).

Schnall, Peter L., Marnie Dobson, and Ellen Tosskam (eds), *Unhealthy Work: Causes, Consequences, Cures* (New York: Baywood, 2009).

Seabrook, Jeremy. *Unemployment* (London: Quartet, 1982).

Sellers, Chris. *Hazards of the Job: From Industrial Science to Environmental Health Science* (Chapel Hill: University of North Carolina Press, 1997).

Seedat, Soraya and Marta Rondon. 'Women's Wellbeing and the Burden of Unpaid Work', *British Medical Journal*, (2021): 374 https://doi.org/10.1136/bmj.n1972n (published 31 August 2021), 1–3.

Shaw, Mary, Daniel Dorling, David Gordon, and George Davey Smith. *The Widening Gap: Health Inequalities and Policy in Britain* (Bristol: Policy Press, 1999).

Shrivastava, Paul. *Bhopal, Anatomy of a Crisis* (London: Chapman Publishing,1992).

Smith, Dave and Phil Chamberlain. *Blacklisted: The War between Big Business and Union Activists* (Oxford: New Internationalist Publications Ltd, 2015).

Stuart, Douglas. *Young Mungo* (London: Pan Macmillan, 2022).

Storey, Robert. 'Pessimism of the Intellect, Optimism of the Will: Engaging with the "Testimony" of Injured Workers', in Steven High (ed.), *Beyond Testimony and Trauma: Oral History in the Aftermath of Mass Violence* (Vancouver: University of British Columbia Press, 2015).

Storey, Robert. 'Beyond the Body Count? Injured Workers in the Aftermath of Deindustrialization', in Steven High, Lachlan MacKinnon, and Andrew Perchard (eds), *The Deindustrialized World: Confronting Ruination in Postindustrial Places* (Vancouver: University of British Columbia Press, 2017), 46–67.

Strangleman, Tim. 'Networks, Place and Identities in Post–Industrial Mining Communities', *International Journal of Urban and Regional Research*, 25, 2 (2001): 253–67.

Strangleman, Tim. 'Nostalgia for Nationalisation–the Politics of Privatisation', *Sociological Research Online*, 7, 1 (2002). http://www.socresonline.org.uk/7/1/strangleman.html.

Strangleman, Tim. *Work Identity at the End of the Line? Privatisation and Culture Change in the UK Rail Industry* (Basingstoke: Palgrave Macmillan, 2004).

Strangleman, Tim. '"Smokestack Nostalgia", "Ruin Porn" or Working Class Obituary: The Role and Meaning of Deindustrial Representation', *International Labor and Working-Class History*, 84 (2013): 23–37.

Strangleman, Tim. *Voices of Guinness* (Oxford: Oxford University Press, 2019).

Strangleman, Tim and Tracey Warren. *Work and Society: Sociological Approaches, Themes and Methods* (Abingdon: Routledge, 2008).

Stride, Rory. 'Proud to Be a Clyde Shipbuilder. "Clyde Built": The Changing Work Identity of Govan's Shipbuilders, c.1960–Present' (History Undergraduate Dissertation, University of Strathclyde, 2017).

Stride, Rory. 'Women, Work and Deindustrialisation: The Case of James Templeton and Company, Glasgow, c 1960–1981', *Scottish Labour History*, 54 (2019): 154–80.

Summerfield, Penny. *Reconstructing Women's Wartime Lives: Discourse and Subjectivity in Oral Histories of the Second World War* (Manchester: Manchester University Press, 1998).

# Bibliography

Summerfield, Penny. *Histories of the Self: Personal Narratives and Historical Practice* (London: Routledge, 2019).

Taaffe, Emma. '"We Suffered in Silence": Health and Safety at Chatham Dockyard, 1945 to 1984. Evaluating the Causes and Management of Occupational Hazards, Relating Especially to Asbestos, Ionising Radiation and Masculinity' (PhD thesis, University of Hull, 2013).

Taylor, Phil, Gareth Mulvey, Jeff Hyman, and Peter Bain. 'Work Organisation, Control and the Experience of Work in Call Centres', *Work, Employment & Society*, 16, 1 (2002): 133–50.

Taylor, Phil, Chris Baldry, Peter Bain, and Vaughn Ellis. '"A Unique Working Environment": Health, Sickness and Absence Management in UK Call Centres', *Work, Employment & Society*, 17, 3 (2003): 435–58.

Taylor, Phil and Laurence Connelly. 'Before the Disaster: Health, Safety and Working Conditions at a Plastics Factory', *Work, Employment & Society*, 23, 1 (2009): 160–8.

Templeton, Tom. *34 Patients* (London: Michael Joseph, 2022).

Thompson, Paul. *The Edwardians* (London: HarperCollins, 1977).

Thompson, Paul with Joanna Bornat. *The Voice of the Past* (4th ed., Oxford: Oxford University Press, 2017).

Thomson, Alistair. *Anzac Memories: Living with the Legend* (Oxford: Oxford University Press, 1994).

Tombs, Steve. 'Industrial Injuries in British Manufacturing', *Sociological Review*, 38, 2 (1990): 324–43.

Tombs, Steve and Dave Whyte. *Safety Crimes* (Devon: Willan Publishing, 2007).

Trades Union Congress. *The Union Effect: How Unions Make a Difference on Health and Safety* (London: TUC, 2015). https://www.tuc.org.uk/research-analysis/reports/union-effect. Accessed July 2020.

Tsui, E.K. and A. Starecheski. 'Uses of Oral History and Digital Storytelling in Public Health Research and Practice', *Public Health*, 154 (2018): 24–30.

Turner, Angela. 'From Institutions to Community Care? Learning Disability in Glasgow from c1945' (PhD thesis, University of Strathclyde, 2010).

Turner, Angela and Arthur McIvor. '"Bottom Dog Men": Disability, Social Welfare and Advocacy in the Scottish Coalfields in the Interwar Years, 1918–1939', *Scottish Historical Review*, 96, 2 (2017): 187–213.

Turner, David and Daniel Blackie. *Disability in the Industrial Revolution: Physical Impairment in British Coalmining, 1780–1880* (Manchester: Manchester University Press, 2018).

Tweedale, Geoff. *Magic Mineral to Killer Dust* (Oxford: Oxford University Press, 2001).

Tweedale, Geoff and Peter Hansen. 'Protecting the Workers: The Medical Board and the Asbestos Industry, 1930s-1960s', *Medical History*, 42 (1998): 439–57.

van Horssen, Jessica. *A Town Called Asbestos: Environmental Contamination, Health, and Resilience in a Resource Community* (Vancouver: University of British Columbia Press, 2016).

Vernon, Horace Middleton. *Health in Relation to Occupation* (Oxford: Oxford University Press, 1939).

Waddington, Dave, Chas Critcher, Bella Dicks, and David Parry. *Out of the Ashes?: The Social Impact of Industrial Contraction and Regeneration on Britain's Mining Communities* (London: Routledge, 2001).

Wainwright, David and Michael Calnan. *Work Stress: The Making of a Modern Epidemic* (Buckingham: Open University Press, 2002).

Walby, Sylvia. *Patriarchy at Work: Patriarchal and Capitalist Relations in Employment* (Minneapolis: University of Minnesota Press, 1986).

Walker, David. 'Occupational Health and Safety in the British Chemical Industry, 1914–1974' (PhD thesis, University of Strathclyde, 2007).

Walker, David. '"Danger Was Something You Were Brought up wi"": Workers' Narratives on Occupational Health and Safety in the Workplace', *Scottish Labour History*, 46 (2011): 54–70.

## Bibliography

Walkerdine, Valerie and Luis Jimenez. *Gender, Work and Community after Deindustrialisation* (Basingstoke: Palgrave Macmillan, 2012).

Walley, Christine. *Exit Zero: Family and Class in Post-Industrial Chicago* (Chicago: Chicago University Press, 2013).

Wallis, Emma. *Industrial Relations in the Privatised Coal Industry* (Aldershot: Ashgate, 2000).

Walmsley, Jan and Dorothy Atkinson. 'Oral History and the History of Learning Disability', in Jan Bornat, Rob Perks, Paul Thompson, and Jan Walmsley (eds), *Oral History, Health and Welfare* (London: Routledge, 1999), 181–204.

Walsh, David, Martin Taulbut, and Phil Hanlon. *The Aftershock of Deindustrialization* (Glasgow: Glasgow Centre for Population Health, 2008).

Walsh, David, Neil Bendel, R. Jones, and Phil Hanlon. 'It's Not "Just Deprivation": Why Do Equally Deprived UK Cities Experience Different Health Outcomes?' *Public Health,* 124 (2010): 487–95.

Walsh, David, Gerry McCartney, Chik Collins, G. Melanie Taulbut, and David Batty. 'History, Politics and Vulnerability: Explaining Excess Mortality in Scotland and Glasgow' (Glasgow: Glasgow Centre for Population Health, 2016).

Warr, Peter. *Work, Unemployment and Mental Health* (Oxford: Clarendon Press, 1987).

Watt, R.A. 'HIV, Discrimination, Unfair Dismissal and Pressure to Dismiss', *Industrial Law Journal,* 21, 4 (1992): 280–92.

Watterson, Andrew. 'Why We Still Have "Old" Epidemics and "Endemics" in Occupational Health: Policy and Practice Failures and Some Possible Solutions', in Norma Daykin and Lesley Doyal (eds), *Health and Work: Critical Perspectives* (Basingstoke: Macmillan, 1999), 107–26.

Webb, Sidney and Beatrice Webb. *Industrial Democracy*, 2nd ed. (London: Longmans, 1902).

Webster, David, Judith Brown, Ewan B. Macdonald, and Ivan Turok. 'The Interaction of Health, Labour Market Conditions, and Long-Term Sickness Benefit Claims in a Post-Industrial City: A Glasgow Case Study', in Colin Lindsay and Donald Houston (eds), *Disability Benefits, Welfare Reform and Employment Policy* (Basingstoke: Palgrave Macmillan, 2013), 111–33.

Weindling, Paul. 'Linking Self-Help and Medical Science', in Paul Weindling (ed.), *The Social History of Occupational Health* (London: Croom Helm, 1985).

Weston, Janet and Virginia Berridge. 'AIDS Inside and Out: HIV/AIDS and Penal Policy in Ireland and England & Wales in the 1980s and 1990s', *Social History of Medicine*, 33, 1 (2020): 247–67.

Wichert, Ines. 'Job Insecurity and Work Intensification: The Effects on Health and Well-being', in Brendan Burchill, David Ladipo, and Frank Wilkinson (eds), *Job Insecurity and Work Intensification* (London: Routledge, 2002).

Wight, Daniel. *Workers Not Wasters* (Edinburgh: Edinburgh University Press, 1993).

Wikeley, Nick. 'Asbestos and Cancer: An Early Warning to the British TUC', *American Journal of Industrial Medicine,* 22 (1992): 449–54.

Williams, Claire. 'Women and Occupational Health and Safety: From Narratives of Danger to Invisibility', *Labour History,* 73 (1997): 30–52.

Williams, John L. *Accidents and Ill-Health at Work* (London: Staples Press, 1960).

Williams, Mari. *A Forgotten Army: Female Munitions Workers of South Wales, 1939–1945* (Cardiff: University of Wales Press, 2002).

Wilson, Graham. *The Politics of Safety and Health* (Oxford: Oxford University Press, 1985).

Wilton, Tamsin. 'Selling Sex, Giving Care: The Construction of AIDS as a Workplace Hazard', in Norma Daykin and Lesley Doyal (eds), *Health and Work: Critical Perspectives* (Basingstoke: Palgrave Macmillan, 1999), 180–97.

Winant, Gabriel. *The Next Shift: The Fall of Industry and the Rise of Healthcare in Rust Belt America* (Cambridge, MA: Harvard University Press, 2021).

## Bibliography

Winslow, Michelle and Graham Smith. 'Ethical Challenges in the Oral History of Medicine', in Don A. Ritchie (ed.), *The Oxford Handbook of Oral History* (Oxford: Oxford University Press, 2011), 372–92.

Wolkowitz, Carol. *Bodies at Work* (London: Sage, 2006).

Wolmar, Christian. *Broken Rails: How Privatisation Wrecked Britain's Railways* (London: Aurum Press, 2001).

Woolfson, Charles and Mathias Beck. *Corporate Social Responsibility Failures in the Oil Industry* (London: Routledge, 2005).

Xue, Baowen and Anne McMunn. 'Gender Differences in Unpaid Care Work and Psychological Distress in the UK Covid-19 Lockdown', *PLoS One* 16 (2021): e0247959. doi:10.1371/journal.pone.0247959.

# INDEX

Abrams, Lynn, *Oral History Theory* 9
accidents, work-related 3, 6, 14, 16, 24–5, 60, 62, 70, 81, 101, 122, 129, 146, 180, 184, 219
    fatal (death rate from) 18–19, 31, 42, 44, 71, 146, 191, 194, 201–2 (*See also* mortality, occupational)
    narratives (*See* work-life stories)
Acquired Immune Deficiency Syndrome (AIDS) 24, 130, 157, 162, 165–6, 176
Action on Asbestos group (*See* Clydeside Action on Asbestos)
activism 51, 55, 74, 78, 84, 100, 179–203
    activist narratives 3, 39, 88, 127, 182, 195–6
    victims' groups and 204–15
advocacy 78, 84, 100, 147, 179–80, 197, 207, 212, 215
agriculture 26, 28, 192–3, 200
Agriculture (Safety, Health and Welfare Provision) Act 1956 26
alcohol/alcoholism 104, 106–7, 113, 130, 132, 150, 168
*Alice: Fight for Life* documentary 53, 89, 214
aluminium industry 16
Amazon warehouse 143–4
*American Rust* TV drama 132
anthrax 3, 157–8, 160, 176
anti-Bedaux strikes 186 (*See also* strikes)
antibiotics 61, 158, 160
anticipatory anxiety 88, 234 n.41
antiseptics 158
anxiety 87–8, 92, 94, 104, 129–32, 135–48, 152, 156, 165, 168, 172–3, 175–6
apprentices/apprenticeships 2, 23, 32, 53, 70, 185
asbestos, hazards of 4, 27, 34, 43–8, 53–5, 60–1, 73, 121, 183, 192, 195–6, 202, 207, 211–12, 215–16
    company's risk denial of 60–1
    contamination 212
        environmental pollution 96–9
        by washing work clothes 73–4, 89, 95
    female (wartime) workers 65–6, 70, 88–9
    secondary/bystander exposure to 98, 259 n.162
    worker's awareness of 48–9
Asbestos Industry (Asbestosis) Scheme 1931 182
Asbestosis Research Council 27
Asbestos Regulations (1969) 29, 32
asbestos-related diseases (ARD) 3–4, 7, 13, 19, 32,

43, 45, 55, 65, 77–8, 99, 132, 144, 182–3, 208–9, 212–13, 215, 218
    asbestosis 17, 24, 45, 50, 60, 86, 208, 211 (*See also* pneumoconiosis)
    cancer 31–2, 45, 86, 88, 201
    caring for sick/injured 91–6
    for coal miners 84–91
    mesothelioma (*See* mesothelioma)
Asbestos Victims Support Group Forum UK 214
asthma, occupational 16, 90
Asylum Workers' Union 161
Atlas Glass Works (Lancashire), woman operator in 8
authoritarianism 25, 195

Barrow Asbestos Group (Cumbria) 211
Bartley, Mel 103, 105
Barton Power Station, Lancashire 46
BBC People's War Archive 68
Beaumont, Philip 194
Beier, Lucinda McCray, *For Their Own Good: The Transformation of English Working Class Health Culture, 1880–1970* 6
Belgian asbestos victims group (Association Belge des Victimes de l'Amiante, ABEVA) 212
Bellaby, Felix 130
Bevin, Ernest 13, 129
Bhopal disaster (1984) 7, 9, 32 (*See also* Flixborough disaster; Hull trawler disaster; Piper Alpha disaster)
Bilocca, Lillian 180, 204–5, 216
Birmingham Battery and Metal Company 5
Black and minority ethic (BME) groups 167, 173
black box monitoring unit 139
black lung disease 7, 42 (*See also* pneumoconiosis)
Blaxter, Mildred 77, 81, 84
Bloor, Michael 8, 213
blue-collar workers 1, 27, 37–8, 105, 111, 135, 167, 217
Blyton, Paul, *The Realities of Work* 243 n.13
BMC Leyland factory 111–12
Bohle, Philip 185, 188, 198, 200, 202–3
bonus system 12, 44, 47, 143, 153, 183, 206, 218 (*See also* incentives; piecework payments; wage payment systems)
Bornat, Joanna 4, 7
Bridgend Royal Ordnance Factory, ROF (the suicide club) 67, 79

## Index

British Leyland 2
British Library Sound Archive 4, 77, 136
British Medical Association 17
British Oxygen Steel (BOS) plant 73
British Rail, privatization of 134, 138–9
British Trades Union Congress Archive 4
bronchitis 24, 31, 73, 77, 83–4, 125, 132, 182
Bruder, Jessica, *Nomadland* 143–4
building workers 31, 67, 192, 196
bullying, workplace 12, 134, 145, 147, 151–2, 154, 196, 200
Burns, William 9, 68–9
bus drivers and conductors 129, 161, 173–4
byssinosis (brown lung) 17, 62, 69, 186, 202

Cairney, Hugh 195–6, 213
call centres (workers) 4, 131, 135, 139–40, 157, 174
Calnan, Michael 134–5
cancer 16–17, 50, 60–1, 75, 99, 183
    asbestos-related 31–2, 45, 86, 88, 201
    bladder cancer 17, 24
    breast cancer 21
    lung cancer 19, 85 (*See also* mesothelioma)
Cape Asbestos, London 61, 96–7, 214
carcinogens/carcinogenic 16, 31–4, 61–2, 73–4, 105, 126, 134, 213–14, 217
Cardowan pit, Ayrshire 116
Cardroom Workers' Union 186
car industry 2–3, 44, 71, 161, 199
Carpenter, Tracey 10, 69, 116, 136, 138
Castleman, Barry 85, 214
casual worker 50–1, 230 n.47
causal pathways 24, 127, 157
Centenary Institute of Occupational Health 194
Central Council for Health Education 63
Chatham Dockyards 45, 49–50, 53, 60, 70, 95, 199–200
chemicals, toxic 3, 16–17, 19, 28–9, 31–4, 37, 44, 46–9, 52–4, 62, 75, 96, 193, 214, 217–18
chemotherapy 92–3
chronic arthritis 150
chronic fatigue syndrome 149
chronic occupation-related diseases 11, 13, 16, 21–3, 31, 34, 54, 77, 81, 88, 100, 122, 129, 135, 137–8, 140, 142–3, 188, 191–2, 217, 220
chrysotile (white asbestos) 32, 60–1
CISWO Paraplegic Centre, Pontefract, Yorkshire 82, 204
class 9, 14, 19, 102, 104, 119, 133, 217
Clayson, Helen 88–9, 211, 213
clooties (cloth bandages) 158–9
closures of factories/mines 47, 82, 101–3, 106, 108–14, 116–17, 120–3, 124–7, 214, 216–17, 219 (*See also* redundancy)

Clydebank Asbestos Group, Clydebank 91
*Clyde Film,* Cranhill Arts documentary 106
Clyde Shipbuilders' Association survey 25
Clydeside Action on Asbestos (CAA) 33, 55, 86, 197, 206, 213
    volunteer ARD sufferers group 208–11
coalfields 17, 55, 77–8, 85, 104, 107, 116, 122, 186–90, 204
Coal Industry Social Welfare Organisation (CISWO) 82, 84, 204
coal miners/mining 3, 9, 11, 13–14, 17, 20, 25–6, 34, 40–3, 47, 49, 50, 54–5, 62, 67, 72–3, 77–9, 99, 103, 106, 108, 114, 122, 125, 181, 186–8, 191–3, 215, 219 (*See also* mines/mining)
    contraction of 102–7
    flu vaccines for 164
    living with death/occupational disability 78–84, 99–100
    oral testimonies of ex-coal miners (and family) 81–96, 99–100, 113
    women in 62
    workmen's safety committees 26
collective bargaining 123, 187, 221
colliery (*See* coal miners/mining)
common cold 157, 166
community activism 3
    victims' groups and 204–15
community mobilization 78, 204
company doctors 18, 60–1, 259 n.161
compensation system, financial 7, 16, 19, 20–1, 23–4, 27, 33, 45–6, 52, 55–6, 78, 81, 85, 89, 94, 98, 101, 121, 132–4, 144, 147, 160, 162, 165, 179–81, 184, 186–7, 191–2, 200–1, 208, 212–13, 215, 218, 220
Constant, Jenny 53
Construction Regulations (1966) 29
construction workers/industry 14, 19, 22, 43, 50, 165, 200–1
Consulting Association (1993–2009) 201
contagion 23, 158, 161, 163, 165–6, 176
contract workers 50, 133, 154
convalescence 78, 81, 191, 198, 204
corporate capitalism 34, 39, 132
corporate crime/criminals (killing) 7, 26, 29, 30–1
cotton mills (workers) 69, 103, 161
Covid-19 (coronavirus) in workplace 1, 3, 7, 12, 24, 34, 146, 156–8, 164–76, 216–17
    childcare during lockdowns 168–9
    death rate 166, 170, 172–3, 175
    and education sector 172–3, 177
    healthcare workers, challenges of 167–72
    impact of 176–8
    social distancing 174–5
    transport workers 173–6

281

# Index

Craig, Phyllis 55, 86–8, 180, 206, 210, 216, 258 n.154
crocidolite (blue asbestos) 89
cultural circuit 5, 9, 53, 56, 58

Dale Committee (1951) 17–18
Dalton, Alan 133, 182, 213–14
Dangerous Pathogens Advisory Group 162
dangerous trades 19, 188, 191, 197
dehumanization 11, 135, 139, 151, 153, 155
deindustrialization 2–3, 6, 10, 41, 47, 100, 127, 135, 143, 167, 216–17, 219–20 (*See also* industrialization)
  adaptation and escape narratives 123–6
  downsizing and rundowns 120–3
  ill-health impacts of job loss 102–7
  scrap heap stories 108–19
Department of Health and Social Security (DHSS) 89, 98
dependency 33, 77–9, 113, 126, 214
depression 10, 12, 91, 104–6, 113, 132, 135–47, 154, 156, 168, 214
deprivation/poverty 2, 11, 23–4, 50, 78, 85, 104–8, 157, 167
deregulation 30, 32, 121, 123, 135, 147, 215–16
dermatitis 17–18, 201
deterioration 13, 99, 105, 107, 112, 122–3, 126–7, 142, 191
diabetes 135, 142, 167
dirty/danger money 181–2, 184, 188, 199
disability/disabling injuries 3, 6, 8, 10–11, 14, 16, 19–20, 31–4, 37, 43, 46, 55, 68, 74–5, 77–8, 78–84, 182, 99, 101–3, 115–16, 187, 221
Disabled Persons (Employment) Act 116
disasters, occupational (*See* Bhopal disaster; Flixborough disaster; Hull trawler disaster; Piper Alpha disaster)
discrimination 19, 62, 89, 115–16, 124, 165
disempowerment 66, 103, 120, 122, 143–4, 155, 174, 183
docks/dockers 2, 19–20, 43, 45, 53–4, 61, 181, 183, 192–3, 196
domestic violence 118–19, 177
Donovan Commission (1968) 194
Driving Vehicle Licencing Agency (DVLA) offices, Swansea 166, 175–6
drug abuse 106–7, 113, 130, 132, 160

Eason, Barbara 92, 211–12
Economic League (1919–93) 201
economic restructuring 27–33, 101–2, 155
economic violence 7, 9, 37, 42–56, 74, 85, 99, 115, 126, 212–13, 215, 218
education reforms of Thatcher 153–4

Electrical and Plumbing Industries Union 201
Electrical Trade Union 47
electronics sector 32, 62, 122
emasculation 81, 84, 86, 89, 99, 113, 118, 124, 136 (*See also* masculinity)
embodied legacies of industrialization 1, 4, 77, 219
emotional distress 134, 137 (*See also* stress and burn-out at work)
emotional labour 131, 135
emphysema 16, 24, 83–4, 132, 182
Employers' Liability Act (1880) 187
employment protection legislation (1978) 165
employment rights tribunal 151, 165
English Collective of Prostitutes 162–3
Environmental Allowances 200
environmentalism 3–4, 179–80, 202, 214–16, 219–20 (*See also* pollution, environmental)
*Erin Brockovitch* film 96
Eternit asbestos factory 61, 212
ethnicity 19, 34, 157, 168, 196, 250 n.40
Europe 12, 49, 96, 106, 168, 193, 206
European Union (EU) 31, 107, 215–16
  European Union Directives 29–30, 147, 215
European Work Stress network 214
Extinction Rebellion 215

Factory Acts 7, 21, 29, 47, 180, 184–5, 191, 194
Factory Inspectorate (FI) 16, 18–19
Factory Inspectors Reports 134
fatalism 39, 52, 66, 88
fatigue 3, 12–14, 22, 57, 105, 129, 131, 149, 156, 165, 178, 185–6, 219 (*See also* stress and burn-out at work)
feminine/femininity 7, 21, 67, 74, 88, 117, 184
Fidelity Radio factory 205–6
Fife Coal Company 188–9
Fire Brigades' Union (FBU) 146
firefighters/firefighting 21, 75, 146–7, 233 n.130
  'the cuddle club' 146
first aid systems 158
First World War 13, 159
fishing/fishermen 14, 28, 204–5, 218
Fitzpatrick, Richard 52, 57
Fletcher, Charles 80
flexible working policies 103, 152, 154, 216, 220
Flixborough disaster (1974) 28 (*See also* Bhopal disaster; Hull trawler disaster; Piper Alpha disaster)
flu (*See* influenza)
Flynn, Laurie, 'World in Action' documentaries 214
Fordism/Fordist 11, 34, 47, 121, 135
forestry 14, 192–3
Foundry Workers' Union 193
full-time employment 18, 25, 99, 103, 184

# Index

gay plague 165
gender 7, 9, 19–23, 34, 40, 50, 62, 67, 74, 78, 85,
129–30, 133, 138, 177, 185, 217, 219
    gender-based violence 118–19, 177
    sexual division of labour (gender segregation)
7, 19, 21, 61, 65, 89, 117, 184
    and stress 148–55
Glasgow Centre for Population Health 106
Glasgow Social and Public Health Sciences Unit
166
Glasser, Ralph, *Growing Up in the Gorbals* 16
globalization 129, 133, 135, 220
Golden Age of work (1945–75) 2, 39–40, 102, 134,
193
Gorman, Tommy 89, 213
Govan Kvaerner shipyard 18, 113–115, 120
Grabham, Emily 140, 150
    *Balancing precarious work and care: Interviews*
*with women workers 2015–2017* 131
Greater Manchester Asbestos Victims Support
Group 91
Greenlees, Janet 161, 186
Guy, David 82

Haggett, Ali 129–30
    on neurotic housewives 7
Harland & Woolf shipyard, Glasgow 114
Harrison, Barbara, *Not Only the Dangerous Trades*
22
headscarf revolutionaries (protest march)
204–5
Health and Safety at Work Act, HSWA (1974) 27,
29–31, 56, 107, 190, 194, 200, 208
Health and Safety Executive (HSE) 3, 28–9, 32, 120,
129–30, 132, 135, 174, 176
    Scottish anomaly 18, 106
Health and Safety (First Aid) Regulations (1981)
158
healthcare workers, challenges for 166–71
health-enhancing work narratives 38–41, 74,
127
health inequalities 19, 99, 104, 115, 167, 221
healthy factory 14, 26
healthy worker effect 103, 105
Heating Ventilation and Air Conditioning Workers'
Union 183
hegemonic 6, 50, 59, 75, 81, 127, 193
hepatitis 162
herring gutters, Great Yarmouth 158–9
High, Steven, *One Job Town: Work, Belonging, and*
*Betrayal in Northern Ontario* 42, 74
HIV (*See* Acquired Immune Deficiency Syndrome
(AIDS))
home front 13, 67, 129, 131, 157, 193
Ho, Wing-Chung 77, 84

Hull trawler disaster (1968) 15, 28, 204 (*See also*
Bhopal disaster; Flixborough disaster;
Piper Alpha disaster)
headscarf revolutionaries (protest march) 204–5
Hunter, Donald 18, 134, 159

immigrant workers 28, 51, 133, 198
Imperial Chemicals (ICI) plant, Dumfries 121, 199
incentives 25, 43, 49–50, 68, 134, 143, 183, 206,
218 (*See also* bonus system; piecework
payments; wage payment systems)
industrial disease epidemics (*See specific diseases*)
Industrial Diseases Advisory Committee 23
Industrial Health Advisory Committee 18
Industrial Health Research Board (Industrial
Fatigue Research Board) 129
Industrial Injuries Act (1947) 194
Industrial Injury Advisory Committee 27
industrialization 6, 115, 131, 217, 219, 221 (*See also*
deindustrialization)
Industrial Medical Officers (IMO) 25
industrial work/workers 37–8, 40, 42, 44–7, 52–4,
56, 61–75, 77, 99, 102–3, 102–3, 108,
115, 126, 195, 217–19
infection, risks of 1, 3, 44, 157–8 (*See also* Acquired
Immune Deficiency Syndrome;
anthrax; Covid-19; sexually transmitted
infections)
    Covid-19 in workplace 166–76
    germs in workplace (infected workers) 158–66
    and vaccination 163–4
influenza 157, 163–5
    vaccination 163–4
Ingham, Nigel 91
inhalation of dust 13, 16–17, 19, 23, 31, 34, 44, 52,
122, 161 (*See also* asbestosis; byssinosis;
pneumoconiosis; silicosis)
inoculation 27, 163–4
insomnia 104, 141, 144, 168
insurance companies 24, 144
International Asbestos Memorial, Clydebank
90–1
International Ban Asbestos Secretariat (IBAS) 213
International Business Machines Co. (IBM) 32
International Labour Organisation (ILO) 13–14,
26, 202
International Workers' Memorial Day Poster (2020)
203
Isle of Grain power station, strike at (1976) 196–7

job insecurity 32, 34, 43, 47, 133–4, 143, 216
    adaptation and escape narratives 123–6
    downsizing and rundowns 120–3
    ill-health impacts of job loss 102–7
    scrap heap stories 108–19

# Index

Johnnie Walker Kilmarnock plant 116–17
Johnston, Ronald (Ronnie), *Lethal Work* 53, 85–6, 88, 183, 213
Joint Production Committees 162, 193–4
Jonckheere, Eric 212–13

Kacieja, Ilona, 'Red Dust' 96
Kazan-Allen, Laurie 213
    *India's Asbestos Time Bomb* 230 n.47
Kellie, Ian 16
Killoch Colliery, Ayrshire 109
Kirby, Diane 136, 142, 147
Kirby, Jill 129

labour market 3, 19, 21, 26, 38, 62, 102, 104–5, 116, 147–8, 151, 155, 197, 202, 212, 216, 219
labour movement 13, 21, 23, 26, 185, 216, 220
Lamm, Felicity 185, 188, 198, 200, 202–3
Lavery, Brian W., *The Headscarf Revolutionaries: Lillian Bilocca and the Hull Triple-Trawler Disaster* 258 n.142
lead poisoning 132, 186
legislation, health and safety 21, 26, 29–30, 56, 61–2, 89, 121, 135, 182, 184, 187, 191–2, 194, 198, 200–1, 215, 220 (*See also specific Acts*)
Levy, Karen 138
liberation narratives 127, 218
libido, diminution of 83
life expectancy 2, 50, 75, 104, 130, 188
limiting long-term illness 104, 107
litigation 56, 213–14
lived experience 2, 4, 6, 8, 12, 38, 53, 62–74, 77, 102, 108, 126–7, 200, 218 (*See also* oral testimonies; work-life stories)
Lloyds Bank PLC (Lloyds Trustee Savings Bank) 147
locomotive industry 4, 10, 16, 40, 54, 58
London Playboy Club 163–4
Long, Vicky 26, 198
Lothian Health Board 164
Lyddon, David 188, 200

Macmillan nurses 94 (*See also* nurses, occupational)
Malacrida, Claudia, on disability 6
Management of Health and Safety Regulations (1992) 30
Manchester Asbestos Group 211
manual (labouring) workers 2–3, 11, 14, 19, 21, 33, 38, 50, 58–9, 79, 126, 137, 158 (*See also* non-manual workers)
marginalization 27, 33, 77, 79, 116
Marinite 60

Martin, Peter 105
    on fishermen 14–15
masculinity (macho) 19–21, 25–6, 32, 39, 50–1, 53, 67, 74–5, 84, 86, 90, 106, 112–13, 117, 130, 184, 192–4, 226 n.77 (*See also* emasculation)
Mass Observation (MO) Archive 1, 130–1, 136–7, 137–8, 141, 145, 148–9, 155–6, 165, 217
McBride, Michelle 145, 147, 177, 200
McCulloch, Jock 213
    *Defending the Indefensible* 32, 53
McDonald, Andy 174
MacDougall, Ian 62
MacDougall, William 208
McGeown, Patrick, *Heat the Furnace Seven Times Over* 16
McKessock, Brenda, *Mesothelioma: The Story of an Illness* 89
medicine 4, 34, 89, 105
    medical knowledge 12–13, 18, 23–4, 27, 44, 61, 180
    medical schemes/coverage 11, 13
    medicine services at workplaces 18, 25, 60–1, 259 n.161
memory(ies), workers' (*See* oral testimonies; work-life stories)
mental (ill-)health 3, 10–12, 32, 39–40, 71, 78, 85–7, 129–30, 136, 143, 146–8, 154, 168, 219, 221 (*See also* stress and burn-out at work)
    impacts of job loss 102–7, 113, 122
    isolation 131–2
Merseyside asbestos group 106, 113, 208
mesothelioma 6, 19, 31–2, 45–6, 48, 53, 61, 73, 85–99, 206–8, 210–12, 214, 219 (*See also* cancer)
Mesothelioma Action Day 211
Messing, Karen 21, 61, 184
microbiological hazards 162
microelectronics workers 62
migrant workers 115, 121, 143
Miners' Federation of Great Britain (MFGB) 187
Mines Acts 21, 55, 180, 184–5, 187, 191
Mines and Quarries Acts (1954) 29
Mines Inspectorate (MI) for Scottish Division 25–6
Mines Medical Service 13
mines/mining 14, 20, 22–3, 26, 28, 38, 40, 42, 47 (*See also* coal miners/mining)
misdiagnosis of disease 61, 93, 211
misogyny 51, 75, 179
Moffat, Abe 25, 83
monitoring and surveillance systems in workplace 134, 138–40, 143, 150, 152–3, 219
moral economy 42, 55, 74
morphine 92

284

# Index

mortality, occupational 11, 13–14, 17–19, 27–8, 31–2, 34, 42, 61, 94, 104, 106, 159, 187, 192, 215–17
 from Covid-19 166, 170, 172–3, 175
 of female workers 21
 of fishermen 14, 28
 from influenza 165
 living with occupational disability 78–84
 premature death 11, 38, 75, 84–5, 99–101, 104, 107, 115, 126–7
 suicides/suicide rates 105, 113, 115, 130, 136, 140, 146, 154, 168
Mukherjee, Suroopa, *Surviving Bhopal* 9
musculoskeletal disorders (MSD) 31, 34, 42, 68, 132, 185, 217
mutual support system 2, 81, 117
myalgic encephalomyelitis (ME) 149

National Coal Board (NCB) 25, 55, 79, 115, 122
National Dock Labour Board 45, 60
National Federation of Women Workers 186
National Health Service (NHS) 3–4, 6, 12, 17, 26–7, 34, 38, 101, 107, 131–2, 144, 153, 166–7, 173–4, 176, 194, 204, 217
 NHS Staff Survey (2020) 133
National Insurance (Industrial Injuries) Act (1946) 13, 23, 33, 161–2
nationalization 13, 55, 101, 115, 194
National Union of Mineworkers (NUM) 122, 188, 204
National Union of Railwaymen (NUR) 199, 202
National Union of Vehicle Builders 2
National Work Stress Network (NWSN) 147, 214
neo-liberal 3, 102, 121, 135, 214, 216, 220
neurosis/nervous breakdown 57, 129, 134, 146, 155
Newman, Laura 161–2
 everyday germ practices 162
Nixon, Rob, slow violence 46
non-fatal injury rate 14, 19, 28, 224 n.38
non-manual workers 11, 14, 19, 28, 34, 38, 217 (*See also* manual (labouring) workers)
non-unionism/non-unionized 122, 174, 201
Noon, Mike, *The Realities of Work* 243 n.13
North British Locomotive Works, Glasgow 16, 18, 40
North Sea oil and gas industry 15, 26, 29–30, 32, 121
Notting Hill People's Association 205
Nuclear Installations Act (1965) 29
nurses, occupational 16, 18, 23, 25, 78, 94, 131, 161, 164
 BME nursing and care staff 167, 173
 during Covid-19, challenges 167–72
 gay nurses with AIDS 165
 Macmillan nurses 94

Oakley, Ann 7, 131
obesity 104, 107, 113, 135, 167
Occupational and Environmental Diseases Association (OEDA) 202, 208, 214
Occupational Census (1931) 102–3
occupational diseases 13, 16–19, 23–4, 27, 31, 33–4, 62, 71, 77–8, 89, 132, 157, 160–2, 191–2, 194, 201, 219 (*See also specific diseases*)
occupational health and safety (OHS) 3–4, 13–14, 18–19, 23–6, 34, 37, 44–5, 56, 61–2, 68, 74, 100, 106–7, 110, 122–3, 131–2, 147, 179–80, 214, 216, 218, 220–1 (*See also* public health)
 activism 179–203
 blacklisting agencies 200–1
 campaigns 3, 23–4, 26, 89, 96, 100, 134–5, 147, 161–3, 165, 180–1, 185–8, 191–5, 198, 201–2, 204–6, 208–9, 211–16, 220
 and economic restructuring 27–33
 enquiries 7, 17–18, 32
 health and safety poster 63
 oral history of 6–10
 in post-war Britain 10–12
 protective clothing (*See* Personal Protective Equipment; protective clothing at workplace)
 and public health 27 (*See also* public health)
 shared responsibility (employers and employees) 29–30, 220
 trade union's neglect of female-related 23, 184–5
Occupational Health Service 17, 26–7, 194
occupational injury 3, 6–7, 9, 11, 13–14, 16, 18–19, 21, 24–5, 27–8, 32–4, 37, 42–4, 46, 78, 89, 91, 99, 101, 204, 221 (*See also* accidents, work-related)
 eye injuries 16, 18
 mortality from (*See* mortality, occupational)
 repetitive strain injuries 2, 18, 22, 31–2, 34, 131–2, 185, 217
 worker burnt in explosion 5
Office for National Statistics (ONS) 166, 178
Offshore Industry Liaison Committee (OILC) 190
*Oil Lives* oral history project 191
O'Malley, Jan 205–6, 216
O'Neill, Rory 147, 208, 213
open-cast mining 61, 103, 107–8, 125 (*See also* quarries)
oral history approach 1, 3–6, 50, 53, 213, 219
 of occupational health and safety 6–10
 scholarship 9–10, 33–4
oral testimonies 4, 6, 9, 32, 35, 38, 42, 47, 51–3, 61–71, 77, 79, 83–5, 91, 191, 213, 216–17 (*See also* work-life stories)

**285**

# Index

on bullying and harassment 134, 144–5, 150–2, 154–5, 200
of call centre workers 139–40
on Covid-19 166–78
on educational reforms 153–4
of electricians 45, 85, 91, 109–10
by (ex-)coal miners (and family) 81–96, 99–100, 113, 188–90
by ex-steelworkers 112, 124
of firefighters 75, 146
of forewoman at Bridgend ROF 79
of metal workers 37, 50, 71, 110
of migrant workers 121, 143
on negative view of trade union 181–4, 190, 195–6, 199
of nursery school teacher 149–50
of police officer 142
of retail sector workers 150–3, 155
of school secretary 149
scrap heap stories 3, 108–19
of shipbuilding workers 37, 114, 124, 197–8
on stress and burn-out at work 136–47
on strikes 193
of women's pressure on paid work 148–9
Orwell, George, on Wigan miners 10
Osborn Hadfields Steel Founders, Sheffield 44
overstrain 3, 13, 129, 143, 186
overwork (workload) 12, 19, 21, 25, 27, 32, 34, 44, 53, 131, 135, 151, 154–5, 165, 172, 177, 186, 200, 206, 219 (*See also* working hours)

paid work 1–2, 7, 22–3, 38, 40, 62, 103, 115, 133, 135, 137, 148, 156, 185, 219 (*See also* unpaid household work)
double burden of 7, 62, 71, 137, 148–55, 185, 219
Paisley mills, Scotland 68–9, 103
panopticon 12, 140
paranoia 79, 157, 165, 176
paraplegics 82
Park Royal Guinness factory, London 37
part-time works 25, 86, 137, 148, 153, 169
Passerini, Luisa 9
patriarchy/patriarchal 19, 21, 23, 40, 50, 180, 205
Perchard, Andrew 16, 115, 122
Personal Protective Equipment (PPE) 34, 37, 163, 165, 169, 171–2, 174, 195
lack of PPE 164, 167, 173, 182
for female wartime workers 66–7, 70–2
worker's demand for (strike) 196–7
phosphorus poisoning 67
piecework payments 19, 41, 47, 50, 68–70, 218 (*See also* bonus system; incentives; wage payment systems)

Piper Alpha disaster (1988) 15–16, 28, 30, 121, 146, 190–1 (*See also* Bhopal disaster; Flixborough disaster; Hull trawler disaster)
Piper Bravo oil platform 201
pleural plaques 88, 91, 211, 213, 215, 234 n.41
Plewis, Ian 105
pneumoconiosis 6–7, 13, 17, 23, 27, 31, 79–80, 83, 99, 122, 125–6, 132, 137, 186–8, 202, 204, 216–17
Pneumoconiosis Fieldwork Research campaigns 187–8
Pneumoconiosis Medical Panels 24
pneumonia 157
pollution, environmental 34, 46, 96–9
Portelli, Alessandro 9, 11, 21, 42, 50
post-industrial economy 101, 107, 127, 129, 150
post-traumatic stress disorder (PTSD) 78, 85–6, 146, 168–70, 182
post-war Britain 2, 42, 47, 179
health and safety in 10–12, 78
structural/regulatory flaws at workplace 12, 26
power relations 6, 11–12, 26, 43, 102
pride and identity of workers 2–3, 39–41, 69, 71, 81, 84, 101, 108, 110–12, 218
Prison Officers' Association 165
privatization 70, 121–3, 133–4, 138
productionist work culture 47, 75
production regimes 11, 30, 121, 220
profit maximization 47, 50
Prohibition and Improvement Notices 29
Prophit study (1935–44) 161
PROSPECT union 135
protective clothing at workplace 19, 58, 160, 163 (*See also* Personal Protective Equipment (PPE))
risks for workers not using 20, 37, 66–7
psychological disorders 129–30, 133
psychoneurosis 129
psychosomatic headaches 149
Public and Commercial Services' Union (PCS) 175
public-facing workers 131, 161, 166, 173, 176
public health 7, 17, 23–4, 27, 157, 161, 175, 202 (*See also* occupational health and safety (OHS))
pulmonary TB 161
Purdie, Sam 107

quarries 43–4 (*See also* open-cast mining)
Quinlan, Michael 185, 188, 198, 200, 202–3

race/racism 9, 19, 34, 72, 143, 152, 157, 167, 173, 217
racial capitalism 143

# Index

radiation, exposure to 32, 45, 49–50, 54, 61, 95, 199–200
radiotherapy 92
Radwanski, Dorothy 16
Raisin, Ross, *Waterline* 95, 106, 112
rank-and-file activism 179, 182, 195–6, 208
Ravenscraig Steelworks, Lanarkshire 43, 96, 106, 110, 123–4, 126
recession, economic 30, 32, 115, 120, 135, 192
Red Clydeside 106, 196
redundancy 2, 7, 11, 41, 103, 106–20, 123–5, 216, 218–19 (*See also* closures of factories/mines)
*Registrar Generals Decennial Supplement on Occupational Mortality* 14, 19
regulatory system/regimes 9, 12, 14, 20, 23, 26–7, 29–32, 34, 47–8, 55–6, 74, 180, 217
rehabilitation 6, 10, 33, 55, 78, 81, 146, 177, 191, 204
repetitive strain injuries (RSIs) 2, 18, 22, 31–2, 34, 131–2, 185, 217
Reporting of Injuries, Diseases and Dangerous Occurrences Regulations 30
Reserved Occupation workers 58, 193
resilience 57, 78, 134, 147, 220
respiratory illness/damage 17–20, 24, 37, 55, 62, 69, 83, 86, 160–1, 166, 182, 215, 218
Rigby, Vera 45, 69, 87, 93–4, 100, 211–12
right to disconnect 135, 219
Robb, Jephson 91
Robens Report (1972) 25
Roberts, Elizabeth 6
Rogaly, Ben 143
Rolls Royce factory, Hillington 103, 193
Royal College of Nursing (RCN) 167, 169
Royal Commission on Mines 187
ruination narratives 124, 218

Safety Representatives and Safety Committee Regulations (1977) 194, 200
Scandinavia 27, 107, 193, 202
Scotland 18, 85, 97, 99, 103, 105–7, 110, 119, 124, 160–1, 164, 174, 181, 183, 190, 196, 201, 211, 213, 215
Scottish Affairs Committee 201
Scottish Oral History Centre (SOHC) 4, 91
Scottish Trades Union Congress (STUC) 147, 182, 186, 194, 196, 198
scrap heap stories, unemployment and health 3, 108–19, 126
Second World War 1–2, 12–13, 29, 37–8, 62, 79, 89, 101, 131, 157, 160–2, 194, 217
self-employed workers 2, 30–1, 132, 158
sepsis (blood poisoning)/septic infections 158
service-based economy 103, 126

severe acute respiratory syndrome (SARS) 166, 168
sex (industry) work/workers 24, 162–3
sexually transmitted infections (STIs) 24, 162, 165 (*See also* Acquired Immune Deficiency Syndrome (AIDS))
shell filling factories 64, 67
shift-working 2, 68, 70, 120, 137, 143, 148, 168, 175 (*See also* overwork)
shipbuilders/shipbuilding 14, 18–20, 37, 43, 67, 77, 85, 88, 90, 106, 114, 124, 184, 192, 197
shipyards/shipyard worker 3–4, 16, 19, 25, 37, 42–3, 49, 55–6, 60–1, 75, 77, 90, 113–14, 184, 193, 208, 218
sick building syndrome 131
sickness, occupational 77–8, 81, 83, 99, 101, 103–5, 107, 115, 129, 217, 221
silicosis 16–17, 20, 23, 125, 157, 187, 193
silico-tuberculosis 79, 161
Smith, Graham 4
smog masks 163
smoke/smoking 10, 24, 31, 78, 81, 86, 104, 106–7, 132
smokestack nostalgia 39, 102
social exclusion 11, 33, 77, 79, 84, 99, 116
socialization 11, 19, 74, 218
social justice 195, 204, 220
social medicine movement 13
social movement 179, 200, 204, 206, 215, 220
social relations 25, 101, 111, 114, 117, 126
social workers 23, 78, 94, 126, 133, 153, 157, 166, 176, 204
Society for the Prevention of Asbestosis and Industrial Diseases (SPAID) 207–9, 214
South Wales 13, 17–18, 67, 78, 112, 118, 122
South Wales Miners' Federation (SWMF) 187
Stakhanovite (Alexey Stakhanov) 50, 229 n.43
standardized mortality rate (SMR) for accidental deaths 14, 19, 31
Standard Triumph car factory 2
Staying Well and Everyday Life directive 130, 148–9
steel works/workers 10, 13–14, 16, 19–20, 40, 42–3, 62–5, 71, 75, 77–8, 96, 106, 112
female workers 62–6
oral narrative by ex-steelworker 124
Steinberg and Sons gown factory, Hawthorn 41
Stewart, Douglas
*Shuggie Bain* 106
*Young Mungo* 106
St Johns Ambulance voluntary service 158
Stockline plastics factory explosion, Glasgow 28
storytelling 5–6, 9, 38, 40, 42, 55, 59, 71, 74, 190 (*See also* work-life stories)
Strangleman, Tim, *Voices of Guinness* 37

# Index

stress and burn-out at work 3–4, 6–7, 12, 14, 24, 31–2, 34, 62, 85–8, 91, 129–30, 165, 200, 217, 219 (*See also* chronic occupation-related diseases; fatigue)
    body and mind at work (stressful workplace) 131–5
    during Covid-19 pandemic 167–76
    and gender (double burden of paid work) 148–55, 219
    monitoring and surveillance systems 138–40
    personal accounts of 136–47
*Stress and Health at Work Study* (SHAW), *The* 132
stress management industry 147
strikes 26, 55, 70, 101, 120, 122, 132, 134, 144, 165, 175–7, 181–4, 186, 188–91, 193–8, 200
submarines 61, 70
Summerfield, Penny 56, 65, 67
sunrise industries 13, 18, 38, 122
survey(s), industrial health 18, 62, 98–9, 131, 169, 173–5, 177, 187, 194
    Clyde Shipbuilders' Association 25
    of National Institute of Industrial Psychology 25
    NHS Staff Survey (2020) 133
sustainable development 202, 216

Taafe, Emma 45, 50, 53, 61, 70, 73
    'We suffered in silence' 229 n.20
Tait, Nancy 180, 207, 209, 216, 258 n.147
    *Asbestos Kills* 208
talking therapy 146
Taylorism 121
technologies/technological innovations 12, 20, 25, 29–30, 70, 132, 139, 141, 143, 152, 173, 188, 219
textile factory (workers) 4, 16, 19–20, 40–1, 46, 62, 68–9, 75, 87, 106, 161, 185–6, 192
    unhygienic practice (shuttle-kissing) in 161
Thatcherism 32, 102, 116, 121, 125, 165
therapeutic listening (reminiscence therapy) 204
*This Is Going to Hurt* TV drama 177
Thompson, Paul 6
Todd, John 54, 195–6, 208
tombstone legislation 26
Trades Union Congress (TUC) 23, 26–7, 133, 135, 147, 160, 174, 182, 186–7, 191, 194, 198, 200, 208
trade unions 3, 12–13, 17–18, 21, 23, 28–30, 32, 34, 39–40, 51, 53, 55, 78, 84–5, 88, 101–3, 113, 121–2, 129, 133–4, 144, 147, 152, 160, 162, 165, 191–5, 215, 220–1
    activism 179–203
        victims' groups and community activism 204–15
    negative views on 181–4, 190, 195–6, 199
    neglect of (female-related) OHS 23, 181, 184–5

shop steward 130, 178, 194, 198–200
    work stress audits 133
tranquilizers 137–8
transgression 65, 75, 127, 165
Transport and General Workers' Union (TGWU) 49, 192–3, 195–6, 202, 205
transport workers 70, 166, 173, 176
Tressell, Robert (Noonan), *Ragged Trousered Philanthropists* 11
Trico Equal Pay (1976) 70
trinitrotoluene (TNT) poisoning 13, 64–5, 67
Tsui, E. K. 6
tuberculosis (TB) 13, 23–4, 44, 60, 79, 83, 106, 157, 161–2, 166–7, 176, 186–8, 194
Turner and Newall Asbestos Company (T&N), Clydebank 20, 26, 43, 47, 60–1, 66, 96, 98–9, 182–3
Tweedale, Geoff 24, 61, 85, 182, 186, 213–14
    *Defending the Indefensible* 32, 53

UK Data Archive 4
UK Data Service (Qualidata) Archive 131, 150
under-employment 79, 102
unemployment 2, 10–11, 13, 32, 47, 79, 81, 101, 120, 127, 133, 137, 167, 189, 214, 216
    adaptation and escape narratives 123–6
    downsizing and rundowns 120–3
    ill-health impacts of job loss 102–7
    scrap heap stories 108–19
Union Carbide company 32
UNISON (public sector workers) 130, 133, 147, 200
United States, The 14, 30, 32, 143, 160–1, 182–3, 186, 188, 202–3, 206, 214
Universities and Colleges Union (UCU) 144, 147, 200
unpaid household work 1, 3, 7, 22, 38, 62, 73, 131–3, 138, 148–50, 152, 156–7, 185, 220

vaccination 163–4
van Horssen, Jessica, *A Town Called Asbestos: Environmental Contamination, Health, and Resilience in a Resource Community* 61
Vernon, Horace Middleton 134
    *Health in Relation to Occupation* 129–30
victim-blaming of workers 24–7, 39, 220
violence 75, 100, 118–19, 135, 162
    domestic 118–19, 177
    economic 7, 9, 37, 42–56, 74, 85, 99, 115, 126, 212–13, 215, 218
    slow 46
viruses 3, 57, 157, 164–8, 170, 172, 174–5 (*See also* Covid-19; influenza)
voluntary social movement organizations 204–15

# Index

wage payment systems 19, 25, 40–1, 50–1, 80, 106, 121, 126, 167, 182, 184–5, 188
Wainwright, David 134–5
waitress 63, 161, 166
Wales 18, 38, 105, 116, 190
Walker, David 17, 27, 32, 39, 45, 52–3, 199
warehouses 143–4
Warrenby steel plate mill 71
Warr, Peter 105
Webbs (Beatrice and Sidney) 186–7, 191
Weindling, Paul 181
Welfare State 13, 188, 216
welfarist company 25, 188, 218
West Midlands, the 2
white-collar workers 27, 132
White's chemical factory, Rutherglen 52
Wikeley, Nick 182, 213
wildcat strikes 188, 197–8
Williams, Claire 21, 184
Williams, John L., *Accidents and Ill-Health at Work* 26, 33, 181, 227 n.96
Williams, Mari 67
Williams, Raymond, structures of feeling 56, 75
Wilson, Graham 181
Wilson, Nicky 55, 116, 120, 182, 204
Winslow, Michelle 4
Wolkowitz, Carol 131, 133, 135
women
    ban from working in heavy industries 61
    bullying, workplace 12, 134, 144–5, 147, 150–2, 154, 196, 200
    as carers/guardians of health (for sick and injured) 7, 78, 91–6
    double burden of paid work 148–55, 219
    in firefighting 21, 75
    in heavy industries 19
    inadequate toilet facilities/personal protection for 21, 66–7, 70–2
    job loss narratives 117–18
    in labour market 21
    miscarriage 64
    nursery for working mothers' children 41
    in public-facing sectors 131
    as railway worker
        first female railway freight guards 69–70
        first female train drivers (British Rail) 10
        on personal protection 198–9
    seamstress without PPE 22
    sexual harassment/verbal abuse in workplace 72–3, 131

as textile workers 46
and unpaid work ( *See* unpaid household work)
woman operator in Atlas Glass Works (Lancashire) 8
work narratives by wartime workers 61–74, 78, 219
work-related stress 137–41
Women's Trade Union League 186
woolsorters 159–60
work cultures 12, 19–20, 34, 40, 50–1, 57–60, 70, 75, 111, 121, 135, 192, 213, 220
workers' agency 3, 9, 25
workers' bodies 3–4, 13–21, 31, 33–4, 37, 55–6, 68, 101–4, 127, 143, 157, 163, 179–81, 185–6, 193, 198, 217–18, 220–1
work ethic 2, 20–1, 38, 40, 58, 111, 142–3
work-health cultures 1, 4, 6–7, 9, 12, 18–19, 27–8, 33, 35, 38, 42, 61–2, 67, 69, 74–5, 189, 192, 198, 201, 217, 220
working-class 1–2, 6–7, 9, 17, 19, 21, 32, 38–9, 49–50, 53, 69, 74, 77–9, 86, 89, 99, 101, 106, 111, 113–14, 117, 127, 136, 184, 214, 219, 221
working hours 2, 12–13, 57, 120–1, 138, 150, 154, 186, 191 (*See also* overwork)
work intensification 12, 26, 32, 103, 122, 134–5, 186
work-life stories 10, 35, 38–9 (*See also* oral testimonies)
    eye-witnesses (social injustice narratives) 39, 42–56, 72, 78, 111
    graft and sacrifice narratives 39, 56–60
    health-enhancing work narratives 38–41, 61–74
    risk denial accounts 39, 60–1
Workmen's Compensation Act (WCA) 13, 16, 160, 162, 185, 187, 192, 194
workplace(s) 3–6, 10–11, 18, 29, 33–4, 37, 78, 116
    competitive environment 21, 34, 67, 115
    dangerous 19–23, 34, 40, 42, 45, 49, 51–2, 54, 61–74, 77–8, 89, 101, 121, 125–6, 184, 187–8, 191–3, 197
    health and safety in (*See* occupational health and safety (OHS))
    occupational medicine services at 18, 25, 60–1, 259 n.161
    stress (*See* stress and burn-out at work)
    structural/regulatory flaws in post-war British 12, 26
Wright, Henry, 'The Next to Go' 95

x-ray techniques 13, 27, 68, 91, 94, 187, 212